Make Prayers to the Raven

A Koyukon View of the Northern Forest

Richard K. Nelson

The University of Chicago Press
Chicago and London

The University of Chicago Press, Chicago 60637
The University of Chicago Press, Ltd., London

Library of Congress Cataloging in Publication Data

Nelson, Richard K.
   Make prayers to the raven.

   Bibliography p.
   Includes index.
   1. Koyukon Indians.   2. Human ecology—Alaska.
3. Natural history—Alaska   I. Title.
E99.K79N44   1983   304.2'09798   82-8441
ISBN 0-226-57162-9 (cloth)   AACR2
ISBN 0-226-57163-7 (paper)

This book is dedicated
to the people of Huslia and Hughes, Alaska;
to my teachers, Steven and Catherine Attla;
and to those who will find wisdom
in a world Raven made.

Contents

Acknowledgments

This portrayal of the Koyukon people and their natural surroundings is based on sixteen months of living in the villages of Huslia and Hughes, Alaska. Most of the formal ethnographic work was done from September 1976 to July 1977, but I have also drawn information and experiences from several extended "vacations" spent in these villages (1968, 1970, 1971, 1972).

An ethnographer never works alone, and whatever merit his (or her) work may have derives largely from the interest and astuteness of his instructors. In Huslia and Hughes I have been fortunate enough to know people who not only were excellent teachers but also showed me a special kind of friendship and hospitality. My greatest wish is that every page of this book should reflect my admiration for them, should accurately record their teachings, and should have value and significance in their lives during these difficult times of change.

Members of virtually all families in Huslia and Hughes have contributed in some way to the work underlying this book, and I want to express my sincere thanks to them. I am particularly indebted to a number of people who have helped in special ways. Steven and Catherine Attla, my principal instructors, have become much more than teachers and friends to me. Their teaching is the basis for this study, and their words are quoted or paraphrased throughout the following chapters. Steven and Catherine remain much a part of my life today, and I cannot fully express my feelings of warmth toward them.

Other Huslia people I wish to thank include Fred and Edith Bifelt, Cue and Madeline Bifelt, the late Edwin Simon and his wife Lydia, Tony and Emily Sam, Herbie and Shirley Vent, Richard and Angeline Derendoff, Bobbie and Mary Vent, Marie Yaska, and the late Chief Henry and his wife Bessie. In Hughes, my special appreciation to Lavine and Suzie Williams, Henry and Sophie Beatus, Bill and Madeline Williams, Alfred and Helen Attla, Joe and Celia Beetus, and the late Abraham Oldman. To each of these people, my thanks for being such fine friends and teachers.

This book's final form was greatly influenced by critiques and comments generously offered by several readers. I am especially indebted to Eliza Jones, of the Alaska Native Language Center, University of Alaska, who read and edited the entire manuscript for accuracy. A native Koyukon speaker and linguist, Eliza provided invaluable help with Koyukon terminology and place names, and she made important contributions from her own knowledge of Koyukon culture. I also received thoughtful critiques from two anthropologists—my longtime friend Roger L. Poppe and an anonymous reviewer. Both offered extensive suggestions that altered the book's general content and its sentence-by-sentence details. I thank them for saving me from innumerable misjudgments and absolve them from responsibility for views I have stubbornly retained.

My work in Huslia and Hughes was part of a collaborative study of subsistence activities in and around the Gates of the Arctic National Monument. It was generously supported by the National Park Service and administered through the Cooperative Park Studies Unit, University of Alaska. I am grateful to the Park Service and the university for initiating this research and for providing excellent cooperation and assistance throughout its undertaking.

Zorro A. Bradley, of the Cooperative Park Studies Unit, University of Alaska, conceived and guided the research. Zorro and his wife Nattalie have become my family in Fairbanks and have shared the good and difficult times as only dear friends can. I also express my appreciation for the assistance and companionship of Kathleen Mautner. Her observations and reflections are very much a part of this narrative, and I am deeply grateful to her.

A special note of appreciation, admittedly cross-referenced, to Wendy Arundale, University of Alaska, whose help and encouragement in other contexts greatly lightened the burden of this writing. Much of this book was written during my appointment as a visiting scholar in the Anthropology Department, University of Washington. I wish to thank my friends and colleagues there for the support and kindness they gave so generously.

Nita Esterline typed and copyedited the manuscript and brought about the contented atmosphere that is so essential for a seemingly endless struggle with words. My parents, Robert and Florence Nelson, have been the source of strength, confidence, and encouragement behind all that I have done. My gratitude and love for them is unbounded.

Orthography

The spelling of Koyukon words used here follows a system developed by the Alaska Native Language Center, University of Alaska. Approximate sound values are as follows:

a　　As in English *another* or *sofa*.

aa　 As in English *bat* when next to consonants other than back velars, otherwise as in English *father*.

b　　As in English *bib*.

d　　As in English *did*.

dl　 As in English *paddling*.

dz　 As in English *adze*.

ee　 As in English *see*.

g　　As in English *giggle*.

gg　 Like English *g* but pronounced farther back in back velar position (voiceless unaspirated uvular stop).

gh　 Voiced back velar fricative, like the French *r*.

h　　A voiceless back velar fricative, as in German *buch*, or a voiceless pharyngeal continuant as in English *hill*.

i　　As in English *tip*.

k　　As in English *kick*.

kk　 Similar to English *k* but pronounced farther back in back velar position.

k'　 Pronounced like English *k*, but with a slight popping sound (a glottalized back velar stop).

kk'   Pronounced like Koyukon *kk,* but with a slight popping sound; a glottalized back velar stop.

l   Voiced *l,* similar to English *lid.*

ł   Voiceless *l,* pronounced with air released off the sides of the tongue.

m   As in English *milk.*

n   As in English *nice* or *bun.*

nh   Voiceless *n,* pronounced like English *n* but with air released through the nose (voiceless apical nasal)

o   As in English *cough* or *called.*

oo   As in English *boot.*

s   As in English *side.*

t   As in English *tip.*

t'   Pronounced as *t* but with a slight popping sound of releasing the vocal chords (a glottalized apical stop).

tl   Similar to English *butler,* but with air released off the sides of the tongue.

tl'   Pronounced like *tl,* but with the slight popping sound of releasing the vocal chords.

ts   As in English *shuts.*

ts'   Pronounced like *ts,* but with the slight popping sound of releasing the vocal chords (glottalized sibilant affricate).

u   As in English *put.*

y   As in English *yes.*

yh   Similar to the *ch* in German *ich* (voiceless palatal fricative).

z   As in English *zebra* or *jazz.*

'   Glottal stop, as the *t* is often pronounced in English *mountain.*

-   A hyphen is used to separate two letters that would otherwise be read as a single sound.

(Source: Alaska Native Language Center, University of Alaska)

Introduction

I was traveling alone with my dog team one bitter cold morning, on the trail that crossed Moosehorn Lake and led toward a distant bend of the Koyukuk River. An hour earlier, I had set out from the village of Huslia, where I was living with the Koyukon people, studying their ways of understanding and interacting with the natural world. Halfway down the narrow lake, the perfect stillness was broken by a rush of wings overhead. Looking up, I saw a raven flap heavily to the top of a nearby spruce. It scrutinized me as I drew near, then flew on and landed in a tall tree farther along the trail.

I whistled softly to quicken the dogs' pace, as I watched the silhouetted bird cock its head one way and another. During the many months I had spent among the Koyukon, I had gradually begun to look quite differently at ravens, as I began not only to know about, but also to *feel* the further dimension in nature that was so preeminently important to my teachers. Ravens had become more than just beautiful and intelligent birds. I found myself watching them and feeling watched in return . . . watched by something more than the ravens' gleaming black eyes. I found myself listening to their calls, not just to enjoy their strange ventriloqual gurglings but also to hear what they might be saying.

A third time the raven flew as I passed its high vantage; then it lit clumsily in another spruce at the end of the lake, where the trail ran up the bank and entered a stretch of timber.

I glanced back along the trail and saw only a dense cloud of vapor from the dogs' breath, hanging there in the stillness. Having confirmed what I already knew—that I was entirely alone—I looked intently at the raven above me. After a long, self-conscious hesitation, I shouted *"Tseek'aal* [Old Grandfather], bring me luck!" Then I looked behind me again, as my words echoed into the surrounding forest.

About the Book

During my year of study among the Koyukon people, I learned a different perception not only of the raven, but of every living and nonliving thing in the northern forest. Although I must emphasize that I did not relinquish my agnosticism, I nevertheless acquired an entirely new way of seeing an environment I had experienced fairly intimately over the previous ten years and thought I knew well. Through the Koyukon, I became aware of a rich and eloquent natural history that extends into realms unknown or ignored in my own culture.

This book is a detailed exploration of that natural history through the teachings of Koyukon tradition. Aside from my own fascination with the subject matter, I have several purposes in writing it and a number of different audiences in mind. Potential readers include anthropologists, of course, but also persons interested in natural history, environmental studies and conservation, northern regions and peoples, native American religion and culture, human ecology, and hunting-gathering peoples. The following summary of purposes may help to further orient readers to the material.

The first and most basic purpose of this book is to present a detailed account of Koyukon knowledge, belief, and behavior concerned with the natural world. This is *an ethnographic study* in the strict sense of the word—a descriptive portrayal of Koyukon culture and custom. Anthropologists oriented toward theory will, I hope, find a useful body of data here, but I leave the ethnoscientific, structural, and other theoretical analyses to them. My personal goal, here as elsewhere, is to create an accurate, sensitive description of a human lifeway.

A second purpose is to compile a natural history, a systematic assemblage of descriptive information about a particular environment. It is intended as a "guidebook" to the boreal forest, derived from traditional knowledge of the Koyukon Indians. As *a native natural history,* it stands outside the established realm of Western science, though it has been organized and filtered through a Western mind. Biologists, naturalists, and environmental scientists will find here an alternative view on the nature of nature, together with a different concept of humanity's proper role in the environment.

Like many guidebooks and natural histories, this one attempts to be comprehensive, covering the full range of entities in the boreal forest community. These include elements of the earth, sky, and atmosphere, all significant plant species, and every animal considered worthy of note by the Koyukon. Certain of these topics are covered very briefly, others in great detail, reflecting the degree to which Koyukon knowledge is elaborated. For example, the chapter on birds is extensive, as it must be to encompass the highly developed Koyukon ornithology.

A third purpose of this book, the most elusive perhaps, is *to show how real and tangible the Koyukon belief in nature is.* Because this belief differs vastly from our own, we may have difficulty appreciating its power and substantiality for those who are its inheritors. It lies beyond our emotional grasp, so we are inclined to pass it off as quaint folklore or mere fantasy. I hope the chapters that follow will make this Koyukon view of nature more concrete for persons who have learned to see a different one.

Many ethnologists and native North Americans will find the Koyukon people's basic perspective on nature a familiar one, sharing much in common with other native ideologies on this continent. Although the perspective is not new in anthropological literature, few (if any) studies have integrated it into a comprehensive natural history. The book therefore presents both a body of information and an expression of its emotional force for the Koyukon people. This is significant from not only a cultural but also an environmental standpoint, because Koyukon teachings can add a compelling new dimension to our understanding of the boreal forest.

The book's final and most important purpose is to *serve the Koyukon people themselves* by educating others about the substance and value of their lifeway and by providing for them a new way to pass traditional knowledge along to their children. It is an effort to preserve a part of Koyukon heritage for present and future generations, recognizing that written words have less power but more permanence than spoken ones.

The underlying thrust of this research was to protect the interests of Koyukon people by recording subsistence activities and traditions associated with lands that eventually became the Gates of the Arctic National Monument. Its primary ethical and practical goal was to help ensure that Koyukon villagers could continue their traditional lifeway on ancestral lands. The project has already served this purpose in numerous ways, through direct input to state and federal agencies as well as to the United States Congress.

Perspectives for Reading

Our expectations about forthcoming events or experiences strongly affect our understanding of what we encounter, and so I offer some further comments as a mental road map through the chapters ahead.

This book, like anthropology itself, sits squarely on the fence between humanism—we could call it "art"—and science. In writing *Make Prayers to the Raven* I have joined a body of data about the Koyukon and their surroundings together with my own impressions of both. My purpose here is to present "hard" information in the context of a living world, to convey not only facts but also feeling. I have never understood why anthropological discourse should have the humanity drained from it; every particle of human life, after all, is a blend of empiricism and emotion. I have therefore tried to better represent the whole reality by including both.

Throughout the following chapters I use my own recollections and quotations from my journal to give an aesthetic sense of the world I am describing. I have tried to set these clearly apart from descriptions and quotations representing the Koyukon view, so that readers will not confuse the two perspectives. Every account of another culture necessarily projects something from the writer's mind; but in this case I have made myself visible and explicit to expand the reader's total experience of my subject and my own reactions to it.

I should make it clear that in taking this approach I do not wish to idealize the Koyukon people and their culture, any more than I would want to reduce them to lifelessness. Furthermore, I have made a personal choice against discussing the negative elements and the malefactors, which of course exist in every culture.

I also advise cautious readers against using this account to represent the relationship between all native Americans and their natural environments. My intention is to describe accurately the ways in which one specific group of native American people—the Koyukon villagers among whom I lived—approach their surroundings. It would be unwise to presume without factual support that any other people, even if closely related, regard or behave toward nature in the same way.

Last, I need to emphasize that in a year's time I acquired only an introductory and incomplete knowledge of the subjects discussed here. This weakness pertains not only to elements of the natural environment and proper human behavior toward them, but (most important) to the complex ideology that underlies the Koyukon perception of the world. I nonetheless offer this beginner's account in the hope that its shortcomings do not outweigh the value of preserving the knowledge it contains.

This, I suppose, is the burden of all anthropologists, who are seldom able to advance beyond the stage of apprentices. But as compensation for this inadequacy, they have the privilege of experiencing again a child's discovery of the world.

1

The People

The Koyukon Athapaskans

The Koyukon Indians inhabit a huge expanse of wild country in northwestern interior Alaska, extending well to the north and south of the Arctic Circle. Their name derives from the Yukon and Koyukuk rivers, along which their villages and camps are situated. In their own language they are called *Tl'eeyagga Hut'aaninh,* a general term that includes other Athapaskan peoples as well. But with characteristic politeness they are willing to accept a name that outsiders can pronounce.

The Koyukon language belongs to a widespread family called Athapaskan, spoken by native people scattered throughout northwestern North America and in pockets as far south as California and Arizona. The northern Athapaskans include groups whose names seem appropriate to the forested subarctic wildlands in which they live—the Chipewyan, Dogrib, Slave, Yellowknife, Hare, and others in Canada; the Koyukon, Ingalik, Holikachuk, Tanacross, upper Kuskokwim, upper Tanana, Tanana, Kutchin, Tanaina, Ahtna, and Han in Alaska.

To one who loves the north woods as I do, these names ring with mystery and fascination. Mystery, because northern Athapaskans are among North America's least-known contemporary native peoples. Only in recent years have these cultures attracted the attention of anthropologists, who have resurrected the works of some early predecessors and begun ethnographic studies of their own. But still today, much of the beauty and richness of the Athapaskan tradition remains known only within the confines of the forest, where it perpetuates itself in the semi-isolation of distant villages. Perhaps this is in keeping with the quiet nature of the Athapaskan people themselves.

Huslia, the Koyukon village where I did this study, can be reached by a 250 mile "bush flight" from Fairbanks. Travelers destined for Huslia board a small plane at the international airport, usually early in the morning, and take off on the same runway used by the airline jets. As the plane lifts away into the clear air, passengers can see in all directions beyond the flatland, beyond the mountains, and beyond the farther mountains. Some will pick out Mount McKinley in the distance, and if they are Koyukon they will know it as *Deenaalee,* the High One.

Now the vastness of Athapaskan country becomes somewhat comprehensible, though even from this vantage the eye can encompass but a small fragment. Two thousand miles it stretches, from western Alaska to near Hudson Bay, and a thousand miles from its northern extreme in the Northwest Territories southward into lower British Columbia. All the territory between is the traditional homeland of northern Athapaskan peoples (whom anthropologists also call the *Dené,* approximating the word for *human* in most Athapaskan languages).

On this terrain the Athapaskan past has been played out and the array of cultures have been shaped to their present form. But very little remains here as a tracing of this human passage, so slightly has the land been altered. There are no visible scars, no straight lines, no crumbled ruins. The early Athapaskans made nearly everything from wood and hides, which rotted quickly beneath the moss. Ancient settlements were probably ephemeral at best and often were situated beside rivers that later changed course and swept away whatever remained. Sites that were not destroyed—deeply buried hearths with scatterings of stone tools around them—have been notoriously hard to find in the vast northern wildlands.

As a result, the remote prehistory of Athapaskan people is not well known. Some archaeologists surmise that their earliest ancestors may have crossed the Bering Strait into Alaska by 10,000 years ago. As the great Pleistocene glaciers receded, these people spread east and south into Canada, eventually reaching Washington state by 7,000 years ago. The northern environment had probably become much like it is today by the time ancestral Athapaskans arrived in North America, so they have had a very long time to perfect their ecological adaptation.

Artifacts that can be positively identified as Athapaskan date only to about 1,500 years ago, and these closely resemble items in use at the time of European contact. The picture before this time is therefore largely speculative. Some of the gaps in Athapaskan prehistory have been filled by analysis of language patterns. This evidence suggests that a single closely related group of proto-Athapaskans occupied east-central Alaska and adjacent Canada about 2,000 to 2,500 years ago. During the next 1,000 to 1,500 years

DISTRIBUTION OF THE ATHAPASKAN PEOPLES

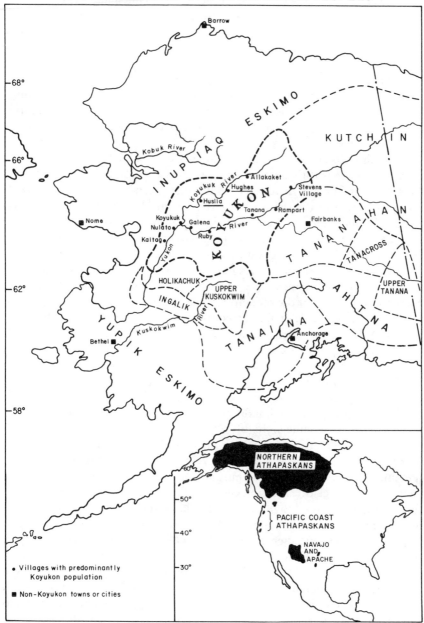

Based on Krause 1974

they spread across the western subarctic and diversified into the complex of modern groups. Others moved southward, establishing themselves in the Pacific Northwest (Pacific Coast subfamily) and the American Southwest (Apachean subfamily) about 1,000 years ago (VanStone 1974:5; Krause 1980:11–13).

Koyukon oral traditions give a different accounting of origins, one that links the people and their surrounding community of plants and animals through a common creation. Like the views of archaeologists and linguists, this connects the Athapaskans and their northern homeland since a time lost in the distant past.

If the flight to Huslia is made in winter, the deep cold and snow-covered landscape make it difficult to forget that this homeland is very far north. Most of it is beyond latitude 60° and some extends to about 68°, which means that many Athapaskans live farther north than the Eskimos of western Alaska and Labrador. Like the neighboring Eskimos, Athapaskans have adapted to one of earth's most difficult environments, and the size of the territory they inhabit is a good measure of their success.

After an hour or so, passengers bound for Huslia will see a great ribbon of water cutting broad meanders through the forested terrain below—the Yukon River. Eight of the modern Koyukon villages (there are eleven in all, with a total population of about two thousand) are situated along its banks: Stevens Village, Rampart, Tanana, Ruby, Galena, Koyukuk, Nulato, and Kaltag. Huslia people have relatives in each of them, but the intensity of their ties depends on how close and accessible they are. Planes bound for Huslia usually make a stop at Galena, the main trade and transportation center for the region. Here, people from the far-flung villages—some separated by as much as three hundred miles—can meet and maintain the personal contact they value so highly.

After taking off from Galena, the plane banks northward away from the Yukon, into the broad valley of its tributary, the Koyukuk. The three remaining Koyukon villages are ranged along this river. Huslia is situated in an immense stretch of flat country that surrounds the lower Koyukuk drainage. The other two—Hughes and Allakaket—are farther upstream, where mountains dominate the terrain and constrict the river's course. Set apart from the Yukon settlements, these Koyukuk villages are in some ways a society unto themselves.

People returning home to Huslia watch intently from the plane as the level expanse of land unfolds below. The irregular patchwork of forest and open muskeg, interlaced with lakes and streams, appears quite featureless to an outsider; but it is filled with names and associations for the Koyukon. The passengers also watch for animal tracks, which their practiced eyes can identify even from high above; and they check for conditions of land, ice, and snow that might affect their activities. And so, as they near home, the

travelers' minds shift from the modern world of the outside to the traditional world of village, land, and nature.

About half an hour after takeoff from Galena, the Koyukuk River bends
eastward and intersects the plane's more direct course. Huslia is not far off
now. If there is snow on the ground, dog-team or snow-machine trails can
be seen threading the timber and crossing the frozen waterways. Isolated in
the middle of a huge, monotonous flatland, the village is notoriously hard
for pilots and overland travelers to find, so the trails often are a necessary
guide for visitors. Only on clear, cold days is Huslia visible from afar,
because then steam and smoke from the chimneys create a bank of ice fog
like a white hill above the houses.

Huslia

The plane begins a gradual descent, and in a moment the village is directly
below. To a first-time visitor it looks miniscule and insignificant against the
magnitude of the surrounding country. There are perhaps forty houses
arranged in an irregular cluster, somewhat scattered at the edges, with
networks of paths and groves of birches between. The Koyukuk River
bends along the village's west edge, and because the bank is carved away
each spring the newer houses are built well back from it. A sharp-eyed
observer will notice that Huslia is situated on a low sand ridge, which runs
eastward for more than fifty miles across the flats. In Koyukon, the place is
called *Tsaatiyhdinaadakk'onh dinh,* "where the forest fire burned the hill to
the river." The people settled here in the 1940s, after they abandoned the old
village of Cutoff, which was a few miles upriver and a few feet lower in
elevation. They had grown tired of taking refuge in their elevated caches
during the regular spring floods, so they built their new settlement on the
safety of the ridge.

After circling the village to announce its arrival, the plane swings over the
nearby sloughs, makes its approach, and touches down on the long gravel
strip. By the time it has stopped, perhaps fifty people will have gathered,
with more on the way. This rush to meet arriving passengers is a good
reflection of the community's outgoing personality, a contrast to some
Alaskan villages where such arrivals attract less attention.

Passengers are greeted by rounds of handshakes with family members
and friends, while bags and boxes are loaded onto sleds (or a pickup truck in
summer). New visitors are usually invited to someone's home for tea or
coffee, and arrangements are made for a place to stay. Huslia elders emphasize the importance of hospitality toward outsiders, who in turn are expected
to explain their interests and to provide some service to the community.

A visitor walking through Huslia for the first time is sure to be struck by
a special beauty and character that set it apart from many northern set-

tlements. Elegant little log houses are set back from the trails, with small outbuildings and high caches beside them. Clusters and groves of birch trees have been nurtured, and the surrounding land is kept neat and clean. Some homes are well placed for a view of the sunset and the distant mountains to the north. Most of the homes have one story, divided into several rooms, although there are a few large ones with two stories. Huslia people take pride in the quality of their dwellings, which are extremely well built, snug, and comfortably furnished. Wood-burning stoves keep the houses pleasantly warm. Government-installed electricity and running water are fairly new conveniences here.

Elevated caches near most of the houses are used for storing meat, skins, and supplies. Usually there is a small shed for equipment like snow machines and sleds and a roofed smokehouse with slatted walls for drying meat, hides, and fish. For a newcomer the dog yard, with five to twenty "huskies" tethered among the trees, is likely to be of special interest. Sled dogs are an extremely important part of life here, and Koyukon villages (Huslia in particular) are famous throughout Alaska for their excellent teams and skilled mushers. Since the adoption of snow machines, many of the teams are used principally for racing; but they are work dogs as well.

Daily life here centers as much away from the settlement as within it—wood is cut and hauled from the surrounding forests, hunting and trapping excursions are undertaken, fishnets are set or checked, and trips are made to distant camps or neighboring villages. But there is much activity within the settlement as well: Women spend considerable time preparing skins, sewing cloth and hide garments, cutting and drying meat or fish, cooking meals, and tending their families. Men make and repair equipment, split firewood, skin fur animals, and do a variety of home-oriented jobs.

Amid these activities there is a strong undercurrent of social life, centered on visiting. Much of this is done at home in the evening and late into the night; but people are likely to have long conversations whenever and wherever they meet. Aside from the pleasure it provides, visiting perpetuates traditional cultural knowledge and allows exchange of information about subsistence activities. Koyukon is the primary language among the adults, but almost everyone is fluent in English as well. Most people under thirty speak only English.

Village social life also centers on several public gathering places. Most important of these is the cooperatively owned village store. Huslia's co-op is well stocked with hardware and groceries, although staples that can be supplied from the land are conspicuously scarce. Aside from the store the most important public place is the community hall, a capacious log building built in the late 1960s. Hardly a week passes when it is not filled with people for some reason—a village meeting, a movie, a dance (three kinds: traditional Koyukon, old-time American, and modern), a holiday gathering, or one of several kinds of potlatches (community feasts).

Christian churches are also important village gathering places. Most of the Huslia people are Episcopalian, except for the Catholics who originally came from Yukon River settlements. Services in Huslia's beautiful log church are fairly well attended, though the congregation is not a focal point of community social life. Ideologically, the Koyukon people have achieved a comfortable accommodation of both Christian and traditional beliefs, unlike most other native Alaskans.

This easy blending of cultural worlds has not carried over into education and socialization of the young, however. Each community has its own elementary school, and in recent years a small high school as well. Education in the white man's way has led to a tragic isolation of generations here; and it has created a conflict of values in the young (age thirty and under), resulting in considerable disorientation and psychological distress.

In recent years educators have brought cultural dimensions into the curriculum—for example, native language and survival skills—with some beneficial effects. But schools remain the primary source of social and cultural change in the Koyukon villages. Finding a satisfactory balance between modern and traditional lifeways will likely remain the Koyukon people's most difficult problem for some time to come.

History

Looking at a modern Koyukuk River village like Huslia, it is obvious that a process of change has been under way for many years. Even the oldest people, like Chief Henry, who died in his late nineties in 1977, have lived their entire lives in the presence of white men.

The first Europeans to enter Koyukon territory were Russians, who came up the Yukon River to Nulato in 1838. When they arrived they found that items such as iron pots, glass beads, cloth apparel, and tobacco had already reached the people through trade with coastal Eskimos. An epidemic of smallpox had preceded them as well, and in subsequent years European diseases would drastically reduce the Koyukon population.

The Russians established a trading station at Nulato in 1838 and remained there until the Alaska Purchase in 1867. Each summer they took business trips up the Yukon at least to Tanana village and explored the tributaries along the way. Lieutenant Zagoskin, who wrote the first ethnographic accounts of the Koyukon, traveled into the lower reaches of the Koyukuk River in 1842 (Michael 1967). But it was not until 1885 that Europeans pushed their explorations to the upper portion of the Koyukuk River (Allen 1887).

Relative isolation persisted along the Koyukuk until 1898, when the Gold Rush brought more than a thousand men to the river. They found little gold, and all but a hundred were gone by the following winter. Some remained, however, and after that time there were always a few whites living in or near the Koyukuk settlements. Koyukon people found work in the prospects, on steamers that now ran the rivers each year, and in the growing number of trading posts established to serve both Indians and gold-seekers. (For more complete histories of the region, see Clark 1974: 75–86 and Loyens 1966:99–199.)

Forces of change grew steadily and affected all aspects of the traditional culture and lifeway. The first Catholic mission was set up at Nulato in 1888, and the dogsledding Episcopal archdeacon Hudson Stuck founded a church called Saint John's-in-the-Wilderness at the site of Allakaket in 1906. Churches also served as schools and hospitals, with resident missionaries dedicated to introducing a broad spectrum of new ways.

During the first half of this century, Koyukon people gradually moved into a few settlements, usually near trading posts and missions. They abandoned their old pattern of scattered seminomadism in favor of a home base from which they traveled widely. Schools, stores, and missions grew, and government became a steadily increasing presence. People acquired more and more imported technology, while keeping traditional items that still served them best.

This process still goes on. The Koyukon people have blended their cultural life, maintaining a strong commitment to their Indian ways and identity while also accepting change. A casual visitor might easily conclude that much of their traditional culture has been lost, judging from what is immediately visible in a modern village. There is comfortable housing and a wide array of modern equipment; and the people adapt their conversation easily to the outsider's interests. But beneath the surface and beyond the confines of the village is the depth and power of a distinctly Koyukon world. We will explore a part of this world in the chapters to follow.

Previous Studies

The history of this region has included visits by people who took a special interest in recording traditional Koyukon culture. Although relatively few studies have been made, their overall quality has been exceptionally high. This is especially true of the work by Julius Jetté, a brilliant Jesuit priest who spent nearly thirty years among the Koyukon near the turn of the century. Jetté wrote a series of articles on religious beliefs, folklore, riddles, time concepts, and place names; and he compiled a monumental Koyukon dictionary. Leaving some ethnocentric indiscretions aside, the depth, insight, and magnitude of his work are unequaled in all of Alaskan anthropology.

Jetté worked mainly in the village of Nulato, and he was followed there by two other Jesuit researchers. In the late 1930s, Robert J. Sullivan studied the subsistence lifeway, and in the early 1960s, William J. Loyens did an ethnographic study focused on change. Also in the 1960s, Annette McFayden Clark carried out extensive ethnographic research in the Koyukuk River village of Allakaket. Excellent new material on Koyukon culture is being produced by Eliza Jones through the Alaska Native Language Center (ANLC). Most exciting is her collaborative work to refine, expand, and publish Jetté's Koyukon dictionary. Other regional work of interest includes the series of Koyukon biographies recently compiled by the Yukon-Koyukuk School District. Published work from all these sources is cited in the bibliography.

The Subsistence Cycle

Life in a modern Koyukon settlement is patterned around the changing seasons, the natural cycle that is preeminent over all environmental events. Every species of plant and animal in the subarctic forest leads several different lives, each according to the season. Such are the transformations of this world, from the warm, bright, and flowing to the cold, dark, and frozen. Perhaps no creatures are more affected by this cycle than humans, who must respond both to the physical changes and to the permutations of behavior in all other living things as well.

Spring

In a sense the subsistence year begins with spring—the living environment is renewed and the seemingly endless austerity of winter is swept away on a rush of warmth. (Incidentally, my dividing the year into four seasons is both a personal choice and a reflection of the modern Koyukon practice.) Spring begins with the long days of April, when snowshoe hares bask in the evening sun atop drifts at the thicket edge, where boys hunt them with light rifles. If the mountain snows have been deep, ptarmigan congregate in lowland thickets, another quarry for hunters seeking fresh meat. Caribou are also hunted in late winter and early spring, before they begin moving north out of the Koyukuk country. This is also the time for beaver trapping, when the cold is losing intensity but the ice remains thick and strong.

The Koyukon people are passionate travelers, and spring is the traditional season for long journeys. The uninterrupted daylight and relative warmth are ideal for wandering afar in search of game and taking trips to neighboring settlements. Occasionally someone chances upon a black bear, still fat after emerging from its den; or a moose may be taken if meat is needed for the breakup season. Prudent villagers also try to cut and haul a good supply of firewood before the snow softens to a quagmire.

As the season progresses, people begin watching for the earliest waterfowl, the white-fronted and Canada geese that land on newly thawed patches in the meadows. By early May the cold breaks, and flights of geese are joined by cranes, swans, ducks, and a host of smaller birds. Robin and blackbird songs drift over the melting snows, a counterpoint to the distant booming of waterfowl hunters' shotguns. Following an old tradition, some people establish spring camps at favored spots among the lakes and meadows, hunting birds, trapping muskrats, and absorbing the season's beauty.

The snow shrinks away quickly in the intense sunshine. Travel becomes difficult, then impossible. The river ice softens, lifts on the rising flood, and is carried away in chaotic floes during the early part of May. Breakup is an exciting and important event, perhaps the most dramatic seasonal transition in interior Alaska. Once the river and lakes are clear, people are again free to travel, this time with outboard-powered boats or small hunting canoes. They take a wide range of game, but waterfowl and muskrats are their primary objectives. Now, in the growing warmth, willow buds burst into new leaves, and summer is upon the land.

Summer

Some families celebrate the new season by establishing camps along tributary streams, where they set nets for pike and whitefish and occasionally hunt to provide a taste of fresh meat. Summer may begin with an expedition to a favored grove for house logs, if some family member plans to begin a new home or an addition. Cutting logs and rafting them to the village is a major undertaking, usually done by a fairly large work party.

June becomes warm, then hot. Mosquitoes rise in clouds along the grassy riverbanks. Some men leave the village for wage employment elsewhere in Alaska—to work in canneries, fight forest fires, crew on the river barges, or take construction jobs. The village becomes quiet, and idle sled dogs excavate long, cool burrows to escape the heat.

After mid-June people begin watching the river for signs of the first salmon, which usually arrive near the month's end. Nets are quickly mended and made ready. Boats loaded to the gunwales with gear and supplies pull slowly away from the village, heading for fish camps. The camps are managed principally by women, who do most of the fishing and related work. They are widely scattered along the river, near eddies known for rich catches of salmon.

By early July the drying racks are heavy with split, drying fish, and children jig for whitefish attracted by offal from the cutting tables. Salmon continue running through July, abundantly in some years and poorly in others. With luck the harvest will provide enough cured fish to feed people and sled dogs over the long months of winter.

In August the chum and king salmon runs quickly fade, and a smaller run of silver salmon passes the Koyukuk villages. Fish camps vanish one by one and the racks stand empty for another year. Ambitious people begin cutting firewood from woodlots near the river, hauling the logs home in their boats. Occasionally someone may shoot a few ducks or geese, perhaps even a moose if meat is in short supply; but late summer is mostly a time for waiting. By the end of August, blueberries are ripening in the muskegs, and

	APR MAY JUNE JULY AUG SEPT OCT NOV DEC JAN FEB MAR
caribou hunting	
moose hunting	
bear hunting	
fur animal trapping and hunting	
waterfowl hunting	
ptarmigan hunting	
snowshoe hare hunting and snaring	
river fishing	
lake fishing	
berry picking	
wood cutting	
wage labor	

cranberries will be ready soon afterward. People travel to the richest patches to gather them, always keeping watch for bears after the same delicacy.

Fall

Fall is the most important season for the wild harvest. By early September the sandbar willows are a blaze of brilliant yellow and hunters know that moose are entering the rut. Men, often accompanied by their wives, travel by boat to their favorite hunting areas searching for the largest and fattest bulls. They are easy to hunt at this time because they congregate near the water, and kills can be made where the meat is readily hauled to the boat. Black bears are in peak condition and are sometimes taken too. When the hunt is over, huge quarters of meat are hung in the smokehouses to age, and the freeze soon assures that they will not spoil.

Fishing continues past the end of summer and through the time of freeze-up (in early October). Gill nets remain in the river for sheefish and late salmon and at the mouths of sloughs for pike, whitefish, and burbot. Upper Koyukuk villagers seine prodigious quantities of whitefish just before the river begins to freeze. Afterward, gill nets are set beneath the ice in certain lakes where large, rich whitefish abound. As the lakes close, ducks congregate in the river and hunters in boats try to take a few before they fly away southward. Soon there is no open water anywhere and travel is impossible until the snow arrives. Night has come again to the northland, and winds whisper mysteriously in the new darkness.

Near the end of October the first serious snowfalls drive black bears into their dens. It is time for the most exciting, dangerous, and prestigious hunt. Men travel widely searching for occupied dens, sometimes going partway inside to shoot the animals. It is a feat of skill and bravery, and the hunters' reward is more than a rich repast of meat. The best parts of these bears are saved for winter potlatches, where the hunters receive praise and the meat is used for spiritual communion with the dead.

The last wage workers usually return home by late fall, anxious to prepare for winter. Once the supply of meat is in everyone waits for the early snows so they can start cutting wood and piling it beside their houses. As soon as the ground is whitened, snow machines and dog teams rush in and out of the village from twilight to twilight. The longest season is about to begin.

Winter

The door of winter closes suddenly with the deepening snows of early November and the onset of intense cold soon afterward. Thick hoarfrost comes as a warning; then the temperature sinks to $-30°$ or $-40°$, perhaps colder. Firewood cutters work to exhaustion in the shortening daylight, building large woodpiles that will free them for the trapping season just ahead. Periodically during the winter they will have to replenish their supply, and on any given day from now until April someone is sure to be at work in the woodyards.

Hunting falls off in winter, especially during the recurrent spells of deep cold. But snares are set for snowshoe hares, grouse are hunted as they feed atop the tall willows on winter evenings, and flocks of ptarmigan that appear late in the season are enthusiastically sought. From time to time families may run short of meat and remedy the problem by finding a moose. Some years, caribou move into the flats or nearby mountains, and hunters search widely for this favored quarry.

But the pervasive winter activity is trapping, which provides fur for personal or commercial uses as well as delicious meat from some species. As with many Koyukon subsistence activities, both men and women participate, although the men dominate those taking place in winter. Trapping gets under way after mid-November, the early season focused on mink, marten, and fox. Lynx, wolverine, otter, and wolf are also taken during the winter. Levels of activity depend on the abundance of each, the weather, and the species that are most common in a person's trapline. Trapping is not just an occupation for some Koyukon people, it is a passion, a reconnection with the freedom of life outdoors in the wild country where they were born.

As winter gradually slopes upward toward spring, trappers shift their efforts to beaver and muskrat. Days lengthen and the sun becomes perceptibly warm. Hunting intensifies as caches run out and people seek fresh meat—moose, caribou, ptarmigan, and other small game. The burden of long confinement is lifted; people visit distant villages and talk about where they will camp in the spring.

Old-timers listen as the distant tapping of hawk owls on tree trunks echoes into the forest. They are "measuring the winter," it is said: If they tap for a long time spring will come late, but if their tapping is short the winter will soon be over.

Readers who wish to familiarize themselves with the natural environment of the boreal forest before moving on should now turn to Appendix 2. This summary description of climate, landforms, flora, and fauna provides a general background for the detailed chapters below.

2

The Watchful World

There's always things in the air that watch us.

A Way of Seeing

This chapter describes the nature of nature, as it is understood by the Koyu-kon people. It is a general account of principles underlying Koyukon belief, a background for the more specific chapters to follow. As I said in the Introduction, I cannot be certain I comprehend these principles as a Koyu-kon person would; and so the discussion should be read as my interpretation of what I saw and was told. In spite of these shortcomings, I believe that the perspective it offers on the Koyukon view of nature is basically correct. Native American ideologies sharing a similar view are widely described in the literature and may be read for comparison.

Traditional Koyukon people live in a world that watches, in a forest of eyes. A person moving through nature—however wild, remote, even des-olate the place may be—is never truly alone. The surroundings are aware, sensate, personified. They feel. They can be offended. And they must, at every moment, be treated with proper respect. All things in nature have a special kind of life, something unknown to contemporary Euro-Americans, something powerful.

> I remember, when I was a boy, walking alone into a huge, beautiful, darkened cathedral. My entire body was alive with a sensation of being watched—by the walls and windows, the pews and pulpit, by the air itself. Now I have felt that again, but this time when I was traveling alone in the forest.
> Perhaps many of us have felt what the Koyukon people describe

from their experiences in nature. The surroundings are different, but the sensations may be alike. The ultimate source of these feelings is less important than the fact that they exist, for what each of us learns to be real is completely real, regardless. [Huslia journal, February 1977]

Over a span of millennia, the Koyukon people and their ancestors have sustained themselves directly from their surroundings. The intimacy of their relationship to nature is far beyond our experience—the physical dependence and the intense emotional interplay with a world that cannot be directly altered to serve the needs of humanity. This close daily interaction and dependence upon an omnipotent natural universe has profound importance to the Koyukon people and provides a theme upon which their cultural lives converge.

Koyukon perceptions of nature are aligned on two interconnected levels. The first of these is empirical knowledge. The practical challenges of survival by hunting, fishing, and gathering require a deep objective understanding of the environment and the methods for utilizing its resources. In short, the Koyukon people are sophisticated natural historians, especially well versed in animal behavior and ecology.

But their perception of the natural environment extends beyond what Westerners define as the empirical level, into the realm of the spiritual. The Koyukon inherit an elaborate system of supernatural concepts for explaining and manipulating the environment. From this perspective the natural and supernatural worlds are inseparable, and environmental events are often caused or influenced by spiritual forces. Detailed explanations are provided for the origin of natural entities and for the causation of natural events (which seldom, if ever, take place purely by chance). Furthermore, behavior toward nature is governed by an array of supernaturally based rules that ensure the well-being of both humans and the environment.

It is important to understand that Koyukon beliefs about nature are as logical and consistent as they are powerful, but that they differ substantially from those prevailing in modern Western societies. Our own tradition envisions the universe as a system whose functioning can be explained through rationalistic and scientific means. The natural and supernatural worlds are clearly separated. Environmental events are caused by ongoing evolutionary and ecological processes, or else they happen purely by chance. Finally, modern Western cultures regulate human behavior toward nature and its resources primarily on the basis of practical rather than religious considerations.

For the traditional Koyukon Athapaskans, ideology is a fundamental element of subsistence, as important as the more tangible practicalities of harvesting and utilizing natural resources. Most interactions with natural entities are governed in some way by a moral code that maintains a proper spiritual balance between the human and nonhuman worlds. This is not an esoteric abstraction, but a matter of direct, daily concern to the Koyukon people. Failure to behave according to the dictates of this code can have an immediate impact on the violator's health or success. And so, when Koyukon people carry out their subsistence activities they make many decisions on the basis of supernatural concerns. The world is ever aware.

From the Distant Time

As the Koyukon reckon it, all things human and natural go back to a time called *Kk'adonts'idnee,* which is so remote that no one can explain or understand how long ago it really was. But however ancient this time may be, its events are recounted accurately and in great detail through a prodigious number of stories. *Kk'adonts'idnee* (literally, "in Distant Time it is said") is the Koyukon word for these stories, but following from its conversational use I will translate it simply as Distant Time.

The stories constitute an oral history of the Koyukon people and their environment, beginning in an age before the present order of existence was established. During this age "the animals were human"—that is, they had human form, they lived in a human society, and they spoke human (Koyukon) language. At some point in the Distant Time certain humans died and were transformed into animal or plant beings, the species that inhabit Koyukon country today. These dreamlike metamorphoses left a residue of human qualities and personality traits in the north-woods creatures.

Taken together, the Distant Time stories describe a primordial world and its transfiguration into modern form. Some are so long that a single narration may require many evenings, even several weeks of evenings, for a complete telling. Stories of this kind—widely known as legends, myths, or folklore—are found throughout North America and elsewhere. It is common practice, however, to vastly underrate their significance in the lives of people like the Koyukon. They are not regarded as simple entertainment (though they are appreciated as such), and they are certainly not considered fictional. Stories of the Distant Time are, first of all, an accounting of origins. They are a Koyukon version of Genesis, or perhaps of Darwin. Woven into the plots of many stories are innumerable subplots or asides, which often describe the origins of natural entities.

The scope of Distant Time stories ranges from the minute to the cosmological. They explain the beginnings of entities that inhabit the sky—the sun, moon, and aurora. They account for certain weather phenomena, such as thunderstorms, which are the transformed embodiment of a formerly human spirit. For this reason thunderstorms have consciousness and can be turned away by people who know how to influence them. Features of the earth, such as prominent hills or mountains, are also given some accounting in these stories. For example, a hill near Huslia is called "Giant's Fire-makers" (*Yɨkuh tl'aala'*), because it was formed when a giant man lost his flints there.

A central figure in this ancient world was the Raven (it is unclear, perhaps irrelevant, whether there was one Raven or many), who was its creator and who engineered many of its metamorphoses. Raven, the contradiction—omnipotent clown, benevolent mischief-maker, buffoon, and deity. It was he, transformed into a spruce needle, who was swallowed by a woman so she would give birth to him as a boy. When the boy was old enough to play, he took from beneath a blanket in her house the missing sun and rolled it to the door. Once outside, he became Raven again and flew up to return the sun to the sky, making the earth light again.

And it was he who manipulated the natural design to suit his whim or fancy. When he first created the earth, for example, the rivers ran both ways, upstream on one side and downstream on the other. But this made life too easy for humans, he decided, because their boats could drift along in either direction without paddling. So Raven altered his creation and made the rivers flow only one way, which is how they remain today.

There are hundreds of stories explaining the behavior and appearance of living things. Most of these are about animals and a few are about plants. No species is too insignificant to be mentioned, but importance in the Koyukon economy does not assure a prominent place in the stories. Many of the stories about animal origins are like this one:

> When the burbot [ling cod] *was human, he decided to leave the land and become a water animal. So he started down the bank, taking a piece of bear fat with him. But the other animal people wanted him to stay and tried to hold him back, stretching him all out of shape in the process. This is why the burbot has such a long, stretched-out body, and why its liver is rich and oily like the bear fat its ancestor carried to the water long ago.*

At the end of Distant Time there was a great catastrophe. The entire earth was covered by a flood, and under the Raven's supervision a pair of each species went aboard a raft. These plants and animals survived, but when the flood ended they could no longer behave like people. All the Distant Time humans had been killed, and so Raven recreated people in their present form. My Koyukon teachers were well aware of the biblical parallel in this story, and they took it as added evidence of the story's accuracy. None suggested that it might be a reinterpretation of Christian teaching.

Distant Time stories were usually told by older people who had memorized the lengthy epics and could best interpret them. But children were also taught stories, simpler ones that they were encouraged to tell, especially as they began to catch game. Doing this after setting out their traps or snares would please the animals and make them willing to be caught.

Today's elders can recall the long evenings of their youth, when Distant Time stories made the hours of darkness pass easily. In those days houses were lit by burning bear grease in a shallow bowl with a wick, or by burning long wands of split wood, one after another. Bear grease was scarce, and the hand-held wands were inconvenient, so in midwinter the dwellings were often dark after twilight faded. Faced with long wakeful hours in the blackness, people crawled into their warm beds and listened to the recounting of stories.

The narratives were reserved for late fall and the first half of winter, because they were tabooed after the days began lengthening. Not surprisingly, the teller finished each story by commenting that he or she had shortened the winter: "I thought that winter had just begun, but now I have chewed off part of it." Or, more optimistically, "When I woke up in the morning, my cabin was just dripping with water!" In this case the narrator implies that the spring thaw has suddenly begun.

Distant Time stories also provide the Koyukon with a foundation for understanding the natural world and humanity's proper relationship to it. When people discuss the plants, animals, or physical environment they often refer to the stories. Here they find explanations for the full range of natural phenomena, down to the smallest details. In one story a snowshoe hare was attacked by the hawk owl, which was so small that it only managed to make a little wound in its victim's shoulder. Koyukon people point out a tiny notch in the hare's scapula as evidence that the Distant Time events really took place.

The narratives also provide an extensive code of proper behavior toward the environment and its resources. They contain many episodes showing that certain kinds of actions toward nature can have bad consequences, and these are taken as guidelines to follow today. Stories therefore serve as a medium for instructing young people in the traditional code and as an infallible standard of conduct for everyone.

> Nobody made it up, these things we're supposed to do. It came from the stories; it's just like our Bible. My grandfather said he told the stories because they would bring the people good luck, keep them healthy, and make a good life. When he came to songs in the stories, he sang them like they were hymns.

The most important parts of the code are taboos (*hutlaanee*), prohibitions against acting certain ways toward nature. For example, in one story a salmon-woman was scraping skins at night with her upper jaw, and while doing this she was killed. This is why it is taboo for women to scrape hides during the night. Hundreds of such taboos exist, and a person who violates them (or someone in the immediate family) may suffer bad luck in subsistence activities, clumsiness, illness, accident, or early death. In Koyukuk

River villages it is a rare day when someone is not heard saying, *"Hu-danee!"* ("It's taboo!").

Personalities in Nature

Stories of the Distant Time often portray the animal-people as having distinctive personalities, and this affects the way a species is regarded today. Often these personalities can be known only through the stories, because the animals do not visibly express them any longer. People sometimes have strong positive or negative feelings about particular species because of the way they are portrayed in the stories.

The sucker fish, for example, was a great thief in the Distant Time and so it is not well thought of. One man told me he could never bring himself to eat this fish, knowing what it had been and fearing that it would make a thief of him:

> *Even in springtime, sometimes we run short of food. But if we catch a sucker in the net, I just can't eat him.*

People will sometimes characterize someone by referring to an animal's personality. In fact, Jetté (n.d.*a*) writes that Yukon River Koyukon may inquire about a person by asking, "What animal is he?" Someone known as a thief may be described as "just like a sucker fish." When a person talks big, promises a lot but accomplishes little, or gets ahead by trickery, he or she is said to be "just like a raven." Although Raven is the creator, he is portrayed in the stories as a lazy trickster who usually finds a way to get ahead by the efforts of others. The Koyukon have a kind of jocular respect for ravens, mocking their personality but still awed by their spirit power.

When I asked about relatedness among animals, people usually answered with reference to their social behavior and personality. For example, a Distant Time story reveals that bears and porcupines are cousins, and people cite as proof their occasional sharing of a den. When relatedness is not mentioned in a story it may be revealed by a tendency to "get along." Muskrats and beavers often live close together and they eat the same kinds of plants, so they are considered relatives. Wolves may kill a loose dog, which shows that the two are not related.

Animal relationships are also shown by shared characteristics, but usually not those chosen by Western taxonomists. One story of the Distant Time says that all the smaller animals were related as sisters who lived together in an underground house. These included red squirrel, mink, fox, several owl species, short-tailed weasel, ptarmigan, and others. Another related group includes the four water mammals: otter, mink, beaver, and muskrat. Stories also reveal that the raven is mink's uncle. And in obviously paired species, the larger is considered the older brother to the smaller—brown bear to the black bear, for example, and flicker to the woodpecker.

The Koyukon people conceptualize a natural order, but its structure and foundation are quite different from our own. No one described to me a system of phylogeny or biological interrelatedness, but I did not probe this matter exhaustively and may have failed to ask the right questions. Such a system might exist, or perhaps the world's makeup is sufficiently explained in the stories.

The Place of Humans in a Natural Order

When Raven created humans, he first used rock for the raw materials, and people never died. But this was too easy so he recreated them, using dust instead. In this way humans became mortal, as they remain today.

How does humanity fit into the world of nature and the scheme of living things? For the Koyukon, humans and animals are clearly and qualitatively separated. Only the human possesses a soul (*nukk'ubidza,* "eye flutterer"), which people say is different from the animals' spirits. I never understood the differences, except that the human soul seems less vengeful and it alone enjoys immortality in a special place after death. The distinction between animals and people is less sharply drawn than in Western thought—the human organism, after all, was created by an animal's power.

The Koyukon seem to conceptualize humans and animals as very similar beings. This derives not so much from the animal nature of humans as from the human nature of animals. I noted earlier, for example, that today's animals once belonged to an essentially human society, and that transmutations between human and animal form were common. One of my Koyukon teachers said, however, that after the Distant Time people and animals became completely separate and unrelated.

Animals still possess qualities that Westerners consider exclusively human, though—they have a range of emotions, they have distinct personalities, they communicate among themselves, and they understand human behavior and language. They are constantly aware of what people say and do, and their presiding spirits are easily offended by disrespectful behavior. The interaction here is very intense, and the two orders of being coexist far more closely than in our own tradition. But animals do not use human language among themselves. They communicate with sounds which are considered their own form of language.

The closeness of animals to humans is reinforced by the fact that some animals are given funeral rituals following the basic form of those held for people, only on a smaller scale. Wolverines have a fairly elaborate rite, and bears are given a potlatchlike feast. In these cases, at least, animal spirits are placated much as human souls are after death.

Most interesting of all is animal behavior interpreted to be religious. "Even animals have their taboos," a woman once told me. From her grandfather, she learned that gestating female beavers will not eat bark from the fork of a branch, because it is apparently tabooed for them. The late Chief Henry had told her of seeing a brown bear kill a ground squirrel, then tear out its heart, lungs, and windpipe and leave them on a rock. Again, the organs must have been taboo (*hutłaanee*).

Once, on a fall hunt afoot in the *Kk'oonootna* (Kanuti on maps) headwaters, the late Chief Henry shot and wounded a young caribou. It fell and the rest of the herd ran away. But a short while later its mother returned:

> *She came back to it. And she started circling it the way the sun goes around . . . At the end of that she put her muzzle where the blood was leaking down. She kept her muzzle down there for awhile. I don't know what she was doing, maybe drinking its blood. And then she circled it the same direction again. And she put her muzzle on the other side where the blood was leaking down. And she kept her muzzle there for awhile. At the end she took her muzzle away. And all that time the calf was holding up its head. And it pushed out its muzzle and shook itself, like this. And then it took off and it looked like it was flying up river. And the late Linus said, "Look at that—she made medicine to her child."*
>
> *I guess that she made medicine to it and there was nothing wrong with it.* [Jones, n.d.:4–5]

The distinction between humans and animals is further blurred by recognition of a human creature that occupies the wildlands and remains almost totally alien from society. This is *nik'inla'eena*, "the sneaker," called "woodsman" in English. Woodsmen are as real as any other inhabitant of the Koyukon environment, but they are extremely shy and quick to vanish when people come near. They are said to be humans who became wild either after committing murder or engaging in cannibalism. Occasionally they harass people or steal from them, but they are not a great danger. People tell countless stories about encounters with woodsmen (see chap. 10) and regard them as regular inhabitants of the environment. They are especially interesting as a bridge across the narrow gap between humans and animals, or between the worlds of humanity and nature.

Nature Spirits and Their Treatment

From the Distant Time stories, Koyukon people learn rules for proper conduct toward nature. But punishment for offenses against these rules is given by powerful spirits that are part of the living, present-day world. All animals, some plants, and some inanimate things have spirits, vaguely conceptualized essences that protect the welfare of their material counterparts. They are especially watchful for irreverent, insulting, or wasteful behavior toward living things. The spirits are not offended when people kill animals and use them, but they insist that these beings (or their remains) be treated with the deference owed to the sources of human life.

Not all spirits are possessed of equal power. Some animal species have very potent spirits called *biyeega hoolaanh,* which are easily provoked and highly vindictive. These dangerous spirits can bring serious harm to anyone who offends them, taking away luck in hunting or trapping and sometimes causing illness, disability, or even death. Animals possessed of such spirits include the brown bear, black bear, wolverine, lynx, wolf, and otter. The beaver and marmot have similarly powerful spirits but are not so vengeful.

The remaining mammals, birds, fish, and some plants and inanimate things have less powerful spirits. Although these are very real and can inflict punishment (usually bad luck in taking the species), all my instructors agreed that no Koyukon word exists for this kind of spirit. In response to my perplexed questioning, one person explained:

> *The animal and its spirit are one in the same thing. When you name the animal you're also naming its spirit. That's why some animal names are* hutlaanee—*like the ones women shouldn't say—because calling the animal's name is like calling its spirit. Just like we don't say a person's name after they die . . . it would be calling their spirit and could be dangerous for whoever did it.*

While most Koyukon adults seem to concur on the basic premises of their ideology, they vary widely in their opinions about the specifics and apparently do not feel inclined toward a rigid, systematized theology. This often left me confused, no doubt because of my Judeo-Christian background; and if my account of certain concepts is amorphous or inconsistent it properly reflects my learning experience. Koyukon people must find us painfully compulsive and conformist about our systems of belief.

Perhaps this helps to explain some differences between my learning and that of Jetté (1911:101, 604, 605) and Loyens (1966:90). They found, for example, that whereas each human has a spirit of its own, animals have a collective spirit for each species. As the quotation shows, my teachers envisioned no such "keeper spirits" overseeing whole species. Individual animals, like individual humans, have their own spirits. Again, perhaps only an outsider would be troubled by this apparent inconsistency.

When an animal is mistreated, I was told, its individual spirit is affronted, but all members of its species may become aloof from the offender. In former times, shamans could manipulate spirits for the opposite effect. They made dream visits to "animal houses" that were filled with spirits of a particular animal, then attracted them to certain parts of the country to enrich the harvest there.

Many other supernatural beings inhabit the traditional Koyukon world (see Jetté 1911 for a full accounting), but these seem to have little importance today. Perhaps Christian teachings displaced or undermined these beliefs, unlike those concerned with spirits of natural entities. Devices used to catch and kill animals—such as nets, snares, and deadfalls—also have powerful spirits (*biyeega hoolaanh*) with many associated taboos. Like the spirits of natural entities, these are still considered important today. For example, if a person borrows someone else's snare, he or she may take sick or die from its spirit power. Similarly, stealing a snared animal exposes the thief to grave danger from the spirits of both the snare and its catch.

Proper treatment of natural spirits involves hundreds of rules or taboos (*hutlaanee*), some applying to just one species and others having much more general effects. The rules fall into three main categories—first, treatment of living organisms; second, treatment of organisms (or parts of organisms) that are no longer alive; and third, treatment of nonliving entities or objects. I will briefly summarize these rules, leaving the specific details for later chapters.

Treatment of Living Organisms

Koyukon people follow some general rules in their behavior toward living animals. They avoid pointing at them, for example, because it shows disrespect, "like pointing or staring at a stranger." They also speak carefully about animals, especially avoiding boastful talk about hunting or trapping exploits.

A man who said he would trap many beavers was suddenly unable to catch any; and someone who bragged about bear hunting was later attacked and seriously hurt. In fact, bears are so powerful that every word spoken about them is carefully chosen. Trapped animals are also treated respectfully, and powerful ones like the wolf or wolverine may be addressed in special ways before they are killed. One man said that he always asks trapped animals for luck: "My animal, I hope that more of you will come my way."

Keeping wild animals as pets is also prohibited, except for species whose personality traits are valued in humans. A child who keeps a red fox will become mischievous, but if a boy raises a hawk owl he will acquire its hunting skill and cleanliness. People seldom keep pets, because they are likely to suffer, offending their spirits and causing illness or bad luck for those involved in their captivity. A woman told me of losing her small child about a year after the death of a baby hawk owl her family had kept. The tragic connection was clear.

Taking individual animals away to zoos, even catching and releasing them alive as part of studies, is a spiritual affront that can cause a species to shun the area. For this reason Koyukon people are opposed to wildlife research in their country if it involves live capture of animals.

We have respect for the animals. We don't keep them in cages or torture them, because we know the background of animals from the Distant Time. We know that the animal has a spirit—it used to be human—and we know all the things it did. It's not just an animal; it's lots more than that.

Following from this, Koyukon people believe that animals must be treated humanely. The spirits are not offended because humans live by hunting, but people must try to kill without causing suffering and to avoid losing wounded animals. A starving moose, mired in deep snow near Huslia, was fed daily until it regained strength and could walk away. Once a man found a black bear with cubs, driven from their den by groundwater, hopelessly starving in the deep snow. He ended their suffering, then dismembered and covered their unusable carcasses, lest he offend their spirits by killing without at least symbolic utilization. "We'll come back for this later," he told his companion, a placating remark that he knew he would not abide by.

Treatment of Killed Game

The rules for showing respect to killed animals and harvested plants are myriad. I will give some general principles and a few illustrations here, leaving fuller details for the discussion of each species. There must be hundreds of taboos I never heard about, however, so this book contains only a sampling.

Today I was told about a man who had once jokingly stuffed debris into the opened jaws of a dried pike head nailed on a cabin door to ward off bad spirits. His companions were horrified that he would open himself to retaliation from the animal's spirit. "When you do something like that—when you don't show respect for animals—it's just like making fun of the Bible." [Huslia journal, March 1977]

The remains of animals and plants are treated with the deference owed to something sacred. For example, when fur animals (such as mink, beaver, or wolf) are brought inside the house for skinning, their names should not be mentioned, nothing should be burned lest the smell offend their spirits, metallic noises should be avoided, and even if it is unfrozen and skinned the carcass should be kept indoors overnight. One way to prevent difficulties is to plug the nostrils of smell-sensitive animals like mink by smearing lard on them. Cloth may also be wrapped around an animal's head to protect it from offensive noises.

I had bad luck with fox this year. Come to think of it, I was using noisy power tools while I had a fox in the house. Guess that's why . . . it's got really sensitive ears. When you get bad luck like this you just have to let it wear off. There's nothing else you can do.

There are also rules for proper butchering of game—for example, certain cuts that should be made or avoided for a particular species. There are rules for proper care of meat, such as keeping all meat covered when it is outside, protecting it from scavengers or from any insinuation that it is not respected. And a multitude of rules govern who eats an animal or parts of it. Young adults and especially women of childbearing age are subject to a wide array of these. Rules for each species will be detailed in the forthcoming chapters.

Finally, there are regulations to ensure that unusable parts of animals are respectfully disposed of. For example, bones of water animals such as beaver, muskrat, and mink should be cast into a lake or river. Bones of large land animals should be put in a dry place away from the village or completely burned in a remote spot. And the remains of small animals ought to be hung in bushes or burned (cf. Clark 1970:86). Adherence has declined today, but many people scrupulously avoid leaving animal remains to rot on the ground (especially where someone might walk over them) or mixing them with household trash.

Punishment for ignoring or violating these regulations depends on the power of the living thing and the gravity of the offense. Spirit vengeance can be as severe as death or decades of bad luck in catching a species. Disregarding the prohibitions against eating certain foods usually causes clumsiness or other physical problems. Only old people who no longer hunt can eat red-necked grebe, for instance, because this bird is awkward on land. A young person who ate it would become slow and clumsy or would have children with these shortcomings. I never understood whether animal spirits cause such "contagious" reactions, but the innumerable food taboos are generally respected as an important way of protecting health and well-being.

Many of the rules apply to everyone, regardless of age or sex. But a large number of special restrictions apply to women between puberty and menopause. Koyukon women are skilled and active providers—they hunt, fish, trap, and gather on their own or along with men. Although they are competent and productive, they are somewhat limited by their possession of special power that can easily alienate or offend natural spirits.

The menses (hutłaa) has its own spirit that contains the essence of femininity, and it can bring bad luck with animals, feminize men and alienate animals from them, or even cause sickness or death. To avoid these dangers, Koyukon women were traditionally secluded during menstruation (some pubescent girls are still briefly sequestered at the first menstruation), and they continue to follow a multitude of special taboos regulating their use of animals and their behavior toward them.

Spirits of the Physical World

Elements of the earth and sky are imbued with spirits and consciousness, much in the way of living things, and there are codes of proper behavior toward them. Certain landforms have special powers that must be placated or shown deference, for example. Even the weather is aware: if a man brags that storms or cold cannot stop him from doing something, "the weather will take care of him good!" It will humble him with its power, "because it knows."

> *In falltime you'll hear the lakes make loud cracking noises after they freeze. It means they're asking for snow to cover them up, to protect them from the cold. When my father told me this, he said* everything has life in it. *He always used to tell us that.*

The earth itself is the source of a preeminent spiritual power called *sinh taala'* in Koyukon. This is the foundation of medicine power once used by shamans, and because of it the earth must be shown utmost respect. One person who was cured by medicine power years ago, for example, still abides by the shaman's instructions to avoid digging in the earth. Berry plants have special power because they are nurtured directly from the earth. "People are careful about things that grow close to the ground," I was told, "because the earth is so great."

The Manifestations of Luck

Luck is the powerful force that binds humanity to the nature spirits and their moral imperatives. For the Koyukon people, luck is a nearly tangible essence, an aura or condition that is "with" someone in certain circumstances or for particular purposes. Luck can be held permanently or it can be fleeting and elusive. It is an essential qualification for success—regardless of a person's skill, in the absence of luck there is no destiny except failure.

The source of luck is not clearly explained, but most people are apparently born with a certain measure of it. The difficulty is not so much in getting it as in keeping it. Luck is sustained by strictly following the rules of conduct toward natural things. People who lose their luck have clearly been punished by an offended spirit; people who possess luck are the beneficiaries of some force that creates it. Koyukon people express luck in the hunt by saying *bik'uhnaatltonh*—literally, "he had been taken care of."

> *If a person has good luck, catches game, it is because something created the world, and that is helping him to get what he needs.*

Luck, or the absence of it, is specific to particular animals or even certain activities. A woman who violates tanning taboos may fail in preparing hides. Each person is possessed (or dispossessed) of luck for all the entities he or she interacts with. Thus a man told me that he had always been lucky hunting bears until he inadvertently treated one the wrong way. For many years afterward his luck was gone—he never took a single bear. Finally the effect wore off and since regaining his luck he has killed at least one bear each season.

Luck can be passed along to others, but it is a lot like money. The one who gives it up may be left with nothing. To illustrate, when beaver snaring was made legal years ago, it was very hard for young people to learn how to do it. The older men knew but were reluctant to reveal their ways, because telling someone how to make a trapping set also gives him your luck. Eventually people reach an age of inactivity, when their measure of luck becomes superfluous. Then they can confer their luck on others by simply wishing it so. This is why children often present their first-killed game to elders, and why young hunters give liberal shares of their catch to old men who no longer go out onto the land.

Possessions like sleds, fishnets, rifles, or snowshoes are also infused with luck. A man lamented to me that one of his high-caliber rifles had failed to kill a bear coming out of its den although it was at close range. He had to use another gun to finish the animal. This gun was "out of luck," he explained, and he suspected that a young woman had rendered it useless by stepping over it.

Putting on another person's mittens can either take away his luck or give him yours. Once I was traveling with a man whose hands became painfully cold, so I offered him my extra mittens. He finally took them, explaining that since I was leaving Huslia I could get along without luck in things like trapping. But a short while later he decided to take them off and endure the cold instead.

Luck is a finite entity, specific to each natural thing or even to certain activities. It can be lost, transferred, and recovered. Luck binds people to the code of proper behavior toward the natural world. And so success in living on the land involves far more than a mastery of technical skills. It requires that a sensitive balance be maintained between each person and the conscious forces of the environment.

Gifts from the Spirits of Nature

The Koyukon people live in a world full of signs, directed toward them by the omniscient spirits. The extraordinary power of nature spirits allows them to reveal or determine future events that will affect humans. This understanding is sometimes divulged to watchful human eyes through the behavior of animals or other natural entities.

Rare or unusual events in nature are generally interpreted as signs, often foretelling bad fortune. People say that events like this are taboo (*hutlaanee*), and they encounter them with fear. For example, a Huslia woman said that it is ominous to hear a raven calling in the night. She had heard it only once in her life, and two weeks later her brother-in-law suddenly died. It is also a bad sign to find an animal that has died in strange or bizarre circumstances. A woman found an owl dead in the entangling meshes of her fishnet, and later that year her daughter died. Another woman discovered a ptarmigan hanging dead by a single toe from a willow branch. Her grandfather, a shaman, warned that it was powerfully ominous; and death came to her newborn child the following spring.

Occurrences like these are both fascinating and frightening, and sometimes people talk as if they not only foretell but also cause the events that follow. Not all signs indicate bad luck, and not all come in strange ways. Some animals, like owls and ravens, give signs in their calls and flight patterns. These might lead a hunter to game, forecast the weather, or tell of good or bad hunting luck. And a few signs also come from the physical world, such as heavy hoarfrost, a powerful evil omen. These and others are described in later chapters.

> Very rarely, a beluga [a small arctic whale] swims far up the Yukon, and it is a sign of death. Years ago one was seen near a Koyukon village, whose people chased and shot it. The animal was lost, and later some people saw its remains downstream. After that the village began to decline and some of its people died badly—from freezing and drowning. [Huslia journal, December 1977]

Not all signs come directly from nature. Dreams are sometimes taken as forecasts of good or bad luck in hunting, although I was told little about it. In the Koyukon village of Nulato, Sullivan (1942:122–23) learned that people can receive dream signs about hunting or trapping from the spirits of animals. Bloody or murderous dreams reveal that an animal will be killed. Other foreshadowing events are more mundane—for example, if loops in the tie of a sled rope form the shape of ears, it is a sign of hunting luck. If such loops form when one lashes a pair of snowshoes, they will bring good luck to someone who uses them.

Although Koyukon people are helpless to change signs given them through natural spirits, they can sometimes use these powers to influence the course of events. Spirits can be propitiated, asked to benefit people or to contravene an evil sign. One way of doing this is to make "prayers" to certain animals, entreating them for good health or good luck. Such prayers are given especially to ravens, because their powerful spirits often show benevolence toward people. Appeals may be specific or general. For example, when people see certain birds migrating southward in the fall, they may speak to them: "I hope you will return again and that we will be here to see you." It is a request that birds and people may survive the uncertainties of winter.

Living things, or parts of them, can also be used as religious objects, again to tap the power of their abiding spirits. Hunters and travelers camp beneath large trees as much for spiritual as physical protection. Skins of certain animals (salmon, least weasel, flicker) are used as amulets, treasured possessions that bring good luck or avert the sudden malevolence of a harmful power.

There are also a few ways of using plant or animal spirits to affect physical things. For example, a fishnet can become "full of bad luck," especially if it is used by a woman who violates a taboo against eating freshly caught fish (which are not considered completely dead) while she is menstruating. This malevolence may be counteracted with an unidentified plant, possibly bluebell, which is called *łookk'a lodaaldloya* ("something that lies in the fish's mouth"). The net is hung up and this plant is burned under it so the smoke drifts up through the meshes.

By understanding the manifestations of spirit powers in nature, Koyukon people are able to foresee and sometimes change the course of events. They can help to create good fortune, they can avoid hardship or shortage, they can prepare themselves for preordained happenings that lie ahead, and they can sometimes directly influence the environment to their own benefit.

Harnessing the Powers of Nature

Modern Koyukon views of nature are strongly influenced by a cultural tradition that is probably not practiced today or that exists only as a remnant at best. This is the tradition of shamanism, the use of medicine power to control nature spirits directly. Although shamanism apparently is seldom, if ever, practiced today, most adult Koyukon have seen and experienced it many times in their lives. Medicine power has been used to cure many people of illnesses that they believe would otherwise have killed them. Today the old medicine people seem to have vanished without passing their skills along, but the concepts and beliefs surrounding them remain intact.

Koyukon shamans (*diyinyoo;* singular *diyininh*) did not have power themselves, but they knew how to use the spirit forces that surrounded them in nature. With this they could do good or evil, according to their personal inclinations. Each shaman—who might be either a man or a woman—had special associations with a number of familiar spirits. For example, one man "called for" Wood Frog, Birch Woman, Raven, Northern Lights, and others when he made medicine. Some spirit associations were begun in dreams (Sullivan 1942:120), but this man inherited his animal helpers from an uncle. Often he used the raven spirit to "scare away the sickness in someone," mimicking a raven's melodious cawing, spreading his arms like wings, and bouncing on both feet as a raven would. One of my Koyukon instructors who was sickly in his youth said that this man had cured him many times.

Aside from curing (or causing) sickness, shamans used spirit power to manipulate the environment for their own or someone else's benefit. Before caribou hunting, for example, they made medicine to bring animals to the hunters, to foretell their chances of success, or to show them where to find game. Spirit helpers assisted them by communicating with a protective spirit of the caribou (Sullivan 1942:79–80). As I mentioned earlier, shamans could also attract animal spirits to a given area of land, creating abundance there.

When shamans were active, they sometimes sent their spirit animals to the villages or dwellings of persons they wanted to harm. Unusual appearances of wild animals in settlements were presumed to be shaman's work. These animals were never killed because it would cause grave danger to the one who did it. It was always a bad sign to see a creature of the wildlands in a settlement, because it indicated danger from medicine power.

An old shaman, now dead, once said that "all of the medicine people in Alaska" worked their power together in the First World War, trying to help the United States toward victory. In so doing they shifted their source of power—the *sinh taala'* from the earth itself—far away from their homeland and onto the battlefields. But they lacked the power to bring it all back and it became somewhat diffused. After that the shamans' medicine powers began to wane.

Older people of the Koyukuk villages, who are ever watchful of their surroundings, say the loss of medicine people has disrupted the balance of natural things. Animals have nearly always avoided people, because since the end of the Distant Time they have lived apart from human society. Only as dangerous emissaries of the shamans did they lurk among village dwellings.

But today the older order is changing and animals have begun penetrating the human sector of the world. Moose wander near the villages, occasionally into them; fox tracks encroach on the limits of settlements; and mink sometimes come around houses in the night. Most distressing of all ravens have begun scavenging within villages. Huslia people say that ravens stayed away from their town until a few years ago, even though no one bothered or shot them. They just preferred to find their food out in the surrounding country.

A man once told me that a raven had walked fearlessly near him as he tended his dogs, looking for any scraps of food he might have dropped. He watched it and said, "Go ahead, eat by the dogs. But then please make them pull well." The bird flew away and did not come back again. He said it made him anxious and fearful, though he did not explain why.

A woman expressed her troubled thoughts about this as she described the ravens perching in low trees near her house and searching for food among her dogs. They are like orphans, she said, living as helpless tramps in a place where they do not belong, seeming to care little about their self-respect.

This is happening, she believes, because the shamans have gone and they no longer use the ravens' power. So now their spirits are adrift—helpless waifs without a purpose—somehow no longer able to watch over the well-being of their animal representations.

People should be using this power, she surmised, to keep the world in its ageless balance. The strange behavior of ravens, the most powerful among animals, surely indicates that this balance has gone awry. Medicine people were essential links in the pattern of nature—they helped keep the world in proper order. If ravens came near a settlement in times past, shamans told them to fly away and live out on the land where they belonged. But today no one has the power to maintain and reinforce this proper arrangement among living things.

> When I went to Fairbanks I saw a raven sitting on a streetlight pole. It looked all oily and messed up, just like it didn't take care of itself at all. I was upset about it, so I looked around to see if anybody could hear me. Then I just talked to it like my grandfather did. I said I wished it would go out where it could live off scraps from hunted animals; then it wouldn't be so poor and helpless.

The Koyukon View of Nature

For traditional Koyukon people, the environment is both a natural and a supernatural realm. All that exists in nature is imbued with awareness and power; all events in nature are potentially manifestations of this power; all actions toward nature are mediated by consideration of its consciousness and sensitivity. The interchange between humans and environment is based on an elaborate code of respect and morality, without which survival would be jeopardized. The Koyukon, while they are bound by the strictures of this system, can also manipulate its powers for their own benefit. Nature is a second society in which people live, a watchful and possessive one whose bounty is wrested as much by placation as by cleverness and craft.

Moving across the sprawl of wildland, through the forest and open muskeg, Koyukon people are ever conscious that they are among spirits. Each animal is far more than what can be seen; it is a personage and a personality, known from its legacy in stories of the Distant Time. It is a figure in the community of beings, once at least partially human, and even now possessed of attributes beyond outsiders' perception.

Not only the animals, but also the plants, the earth and landforms, the air, weather, and sky are spiritually invested. For each, the hunter knows an array of respectful gestures and deferential taboos that demand obedience. Violations against them will offend and alienate their spirits, bringing bad luck or illness, or worse if a powerful and vindictive being is treated irreverently.

Aware of these invisible forces and their manifestations, the Koyukon can protect and enhance their good fortune, can understand signs or warnings given them through natural events, and can sometimes influence the complexion of the environment to suit their desires. Everything in the Koyukon world lies partly in the realm beyond the senses, in the realm we would call supernatural.

3
Earth, Air, and Sky

The Physical Realm

The subarctic world of the Koyukon is dominated by physical forces that may be incomprehensible to an inexperienced outsider. If the spiritual powers of this environment seem ethereal, its physical powers are the opposite. The land itself is massive, both in its extent and in the amplitude of its upthrown mountains. Great rivers carve the terrain, running each spring with a chaos of fractured ice, periodically spilling over their banks to submerge the flats and make islands of the hills. The summer day lasts for months yet is too short against winter's darkness. And finally the weather—the omnipotent cold, the snow and storms, and the brief summer heat, when forests are set afire by passing thunderstorms. Weather is the hammer and the land is the anvil.

So it is to the outsider's eye; and, though less awed, even the Koyukon people see it as a hard and forceful world. Their lives must be patterned to the landscape, the cycles of light and darkness, and the inexorable turning of the seasons. Although at times the environment can be nurturing and easy, it is often difficult and indomitable indeed. And for the Koyukon, it is also sensitive to human behavior, because the natural and human communities originated together in the Distant Time and have never become completely separate.

The following pages will describe the nature of the physical world, focusing not on what can be seen and measured, but on what must be known through tradition. They will discuss the Koyukon way of perceiving and interacting with entities of the earth, air, and sky, and the aesthetic regard in which they are held. There will be some points about naming and categorization of phenomena, but most Koyukon terminology is left for Appendix 3.

Island of Earth

> the earth is conceived as an island completely surrounded by water; out of this each day the sun rises, makes its course across the sky, and then disappears into it when setting. [Sullivan 1942a:58]

This traditional conception of the earth has yielded to a different one as the Koyukon people have encountered Western ideas and traveled far beyond the former limits of their world. But in many ways their regard for the earth—more specifically the landscape—has not changed, just as the land itself has remained the same.

I was not told a great deal about the origins of landforms, but some of them, at least, are given an accounting in stories of the Distant Time. Near the upper reaches of the Nulitna (*Nolaaytna*) River, for example, there is an area covered with sand dunes. Scattered among the dunes are many depressions (perhaps twenty-five feet deep), said to be permanent despite constant shifting of the sands. These were made by two giant men who fought for possession of the dunes, making huge footprints in the sand as they wrestled.

The highest mountain in North America—Mount McKinley—was also formed in the Distant Time:

> *The Raven, incarnated as a young man, had paddled his canoe across a great body of water to ask a woman to marry him. She refused to be his wife, so he made her sink into the mud and disappear; and then he began paddling back home. The woman's mother kept two brown bears, and in her anger she told them to drown the young man. They dug furiously at the lake's edge, making huge waves everywhere on the water. But Raven calmed a narrow path before him and paddled on.*
>
> *Eventually he became exhausted, so he threw a harpoon that struck the crest of a wave. At that moment he fainted from the intensity of his concentration, and when he awoke a forested land had replaced the water. He saw that the first wave his harpoon struck had become a small mountain. Then it had glanced off, eventually striking a huge wave that solidified into another mountain—the one now called Deenaalee, or Mount McKinley. [Paraphrased from Jetté 1908:312–13]*

The landscape is also filled with other associations, many of them supernatural powers that lurk near certain places or emanate from them. Some of these are human spirits that haunt particular spots throughout Koyukon country, occasionally "bothering" people who camp near them. Many places like this are well known, so they are avoided whenever possible. If someone hears troublesome spirits moving nearby, they can be placated by cutting out tiny moosehide boot soles and burning them in the fire. This is a way of presenting them to the spirits, whose boots are worn thin by constant walking.

A nebulous but still threatening spirit power is associated with many places on the land, bodies of water, or stretches of waterways. This power, called *huyeega hoolaanh*, can be dangerous to people. Places imbued with it are avoided at night, though people usually do not fear them in daylight. This is true especially for places where spirits emerge to lurk after dark—old village sites, for instance. Besides avoiding them, the Koyukon may show deference toward such places in various ways. For example, they avoid talking about a mountain known by the questioning name *Dibaa Dlila'* ("whose mountain") because a shaman's spirit lives there, "inside, like a beaver house."

Stretches of water are often especially malevolent and may draw people in and drown them. These places may have been cursed by shamans, or they have acquired spiritual power some other way in a time beyond memory. Near the old village of Cutoff, the Koyukuk River is dangerous because of a shaman's grave and because two children drowned there some years ago. Two large lakes east of Huslia (*Hudo' Dinh* and *Hunoo' Dinh*) have a threatening power, and a person crossing them for the first time should carry the top of a spruce sapling. If this is done, the tree's spirit imparts lasting protection or nullifies the force of danger. (See chap. 12 for more detail on this subject.)

As I mentioned in the previous chapter, the earth's surface is filled with a generalized power called *sinh taala'*, which is essential for shamans' medicine. People can make use of the earth's surface, but because of *sinh taala'* they must treat it with respect. This is one way of recognizing the earth's awareness. Another, which may or may not relate to *sinh taala'*, is the short prayer made when an earthquake strikes. The elders advise that protection is given if people roll on the ground and say, "Let me roll away to safety. . . . Let me roll away to safety."

The Koyukon people's intimacy with the landscape is also expressed in a very different way—in a fondness or affection that transcends any dangers the earth may pose. This is often revealed in conversation, when they speak of the land's beauty or personal meanings, and it shines through in the simple poetry of riddles. These are often told in the brightening days of spring, and in themselves they are a statement about the Koyukon people's regard for nature. The teller introduces each riddle by saying, "Wait, I see something," then gives a simple statement:

Wait, I see something: The stars are rotting on my sides.
Answer: Deenaalee, or Mount McKinley.

In this example, from Jetté (1913:638), the "stars" are a metaphorical reference to birds, because both are inhabitants of the sky. Koyukon people explain that, in migration, birds such as cranes and waterfowl fly below the lofty heights of *Deenaalee*. On their way south in the blackness of fall nights, flocks of them sometimes collide with the unseen mountain wall, to die and decay on its slopes.

Of all the elements of physical terrain, none is more important for the Koyukon than water, none more constantly a part of their consciousness. Although they are an inland people, their lives are dominated by water and the habitats it creates. Water shapes and modifies the land, presents avenues or barricades for travel, supports a wide assortment of plant and animal communities, and both threatens and sustains human life.

Large rivers are by far the most significant bodies of water for the Koyukon, whose villages and camp are situated along them, and whose group identity derives from them. The entire Koyukon system of geographic orientation is based on rivers, not on the compass points used by Westerners. The four cardinal directions and modifiers for intermediate points are used mainly with reference to the wind.

Direction and distance on land are reckoned by a complex of terms meaning upriver, downriver, toward the river, away from the river, and across the river. Four prefixes measure distance for each term: *dodot* means nearby downriver, *aadot* and *nodot* move farther away downriver, and *yoodot* is a great distance downriver. Other features are also described by reference to the large rivers—for example, a lake has a shore toward the river, a shore away from the river, and upriver and downriver shores.

This is only a basic summary of a complex and sophisticated system for geographic location and mental mapping. The system combines locational terms, including the elemental ones above, with hundreds of specific place names known by Koyukon adults and elders. Besides these reference points, people develop their own mental maps of regional topography during their lifetimes. Jetté's unpublished study of Koyukon place names (n.d.*b*) is a classic, which includes native-drawn maps (see also Henry and Henry 1969 on Koyukon locationals and my own unpublished collection of place names).

I was often confused by the Koyukon people's way of orienting themselves by river current, because I was raised to think in terms of cardinal directions. Huslia people talk of going "up" to Fairbanks, for instance, because it is upstream from the mouth of the Koyukuk River. But Fairbanks is southeast of Huslia, so I considered it "over" or "down," certainly not "up." When Koyukon friends visited my home on a long, narrow inlet in southeast Alaska, they were constantly disoriented by the changing tidal current, which made "upstream" become "downstream" every six hours!

Although rivers are paramount features of the Koyukon landscape, they are not regarded as great sources of supernatural power. Nevertheless, they do have a consciousness that at one time of year must be supplicated. In spring, the rivers' benign quietude is dramatically interrupted. When the thaw comes, rising water and rushing current loosen the ice, break it up, and carry it downstream in a turmoil of churning floes. Great fractured chunks scour the banks and plow through flooded stands of brush. Sometimes huge jams suddenly form, blocking the river's flow and causing flash floods as the swollen river backs up and rushes out across the flatlands. If this happens downstream from a village the ice-filled water can destroy property and pose a serious threat to people's lives.

It is small wonder, then, that people make prayers to the river and to the ice as breakup begins, asking them to move along easily and do no harm. A very old man told me one of these prayers: "There is frog fat downstream; go down and it will be there for you." He offered no explanation for its content. Another man warned that people should show respect to the ice at this time, as he knew from his own experience. Once, when he was younger, he was shooting his rifle at the ice, wishing for the breakup to start. An older woman protested and began praying to the ice, but he sarcastically told it to ignore her. He thought his insulting behavior would make the ice move; but, he said, "That spring we had a terrible ice jam, and we had to run to save ourselves from the ice and water." The blame, he felt, was his.

Prayers are made to the ice in both traditional and Christian ways:

> This morning I went to church. After the service, everyone walked to the riverbank, where the fragmenting ice was slowly drifting by. Here they offered prayer, giving thanks to the ice that had been a safe and easy road to travel and asking that people be protected from the danger of floods and piling ice. [Huslia journal, May 1976]

Aside from its other meanings, water is also an essential "food." The Koyukon emphasize that it should be used sparingly, however, because the qualities of foods are contagious—and water is very heavy. If a young man drinks too much water he will be slow and clumsy, among people who prize quickness and lightfootedness. The late Chief Henry told me that when he was a boy his drinking cup was made from a squirrel's skull so that he could drink only a tiny amount at once. If he tried to refill it, someone was likely to bump his hand and spill it out. "Drink broth instead of water," I was advised; "otherwise you will be slow and heavy, like an old log in the river." An elderly man added his grandmother's admonition: "Water only runs downhill, never uphill." I occasionally saw young boys being scolded when they drank too much water.

> *Wait, I see something: It sounds like a lullaby is being sung to children in the other world.*
> *Answer: The sound of a swiftly moving current.*
> [Jones 1976]

Inhabitants of the Sky

> *The sun was once a beautiful young woman who persistently refused to marry. A lover came to her in the night and she slept with him, not knowing who he was. But after several nights she learned he was her brother, so she cut off her breasts and gave them to her brother on a dish of food, then flew off into the sky and became the sun. He followed her and became the moon.* [Paraphrased from Jetté, n.d.a]

Of all the sky's inhabitants, only the sun and moon strongly affect Koyukon people's lives. They are not given much importance in cosmology or religious practice, however. It is as if, being highly predictable—unlike nearly all other natural entities in the subarctic—they can be taken for granted. My Koyukon teachers said very little indeed about the sun. After relating the story above, Jetté quotes a Koyukon saying: "We do not look at the sun because it would shame a young woman." But I have no reason to believe that people also avoid speaking about her.

The moon is given a bit more notice in Koyukon ideology, but it is mostly significant as a source of light in the protracted darkness of winter. Unlike the sun, the moon goes through phases and frequent absences, altering its importance and creating a measure for the year's divisions. Traditionally, the moon was described as being "under water" when it did not rise above the island earth's horizon (Jetté 1909:7). When the new moon appeared, adolescent girls were sent out to offer prayers to it, asking that people be able to find enough food. Phases and conditions of the moon give weather signs, as I will describe later; and the moon's sudden disappearance in an eclipse is feared as a powerful foreboding of bad luck.

The brilliant beauty of moonlight is a special attribute of the Far North, and it does not escape poetic attention from the Koyukon:

> *Wait, I see something: I reach beyond the distant hills.*
> *Answer: The moon, or the sun.*

As Jetté explains (1913:637), people who have not experienced the shadow-casting brightness of a winter moon in the subarctic might not understand why moonlight is one of the riddle's answers. During the long nights, when a full moon circles high, the snow-covered mountains are often clearly visible at great distances, luminescent against the sky's blackness. And indeed, the light shines far beyond them.

Another bright dweller of the heavens is aurora borealis, which the

Koyukon name *yoyakkoyh,* "pulsing lights in the sky." The northern lights came from the spirit of a man who lived in the Distant Time. He broke his bow while shooting at caribou, and the stories say he eventually burned up in a fire. When the aurora runs in brilliant curtains across the night sky, trembling and flashing with a glow that illuminates the landscape, it is Northern Lights Man (*Yoyakkoyh Dinaa*) shooting his arrows into the heavens (Jetté 1911:649). If this happens in the fall, it is a sign that many caribou will come during winter. In times past shamans used the spirit power of the northern lights in making medicine.

On the clear, frigid nights of winter, the sky above Koyukon country is thick with sparkling stars. The long period of darkness and the clear skies present a matchless opportunity to watch and chart the heavens, but the Koyukon have little practical reason to do so. They navigate by landforms, and they devote their ideology to the more immediate living world, so they watch the stars just for pleasure or to mark the passage of time. Now, with the advent of clocks, there is no practical need for an indigenous astronomy. Only a sign remains important, a bright falling star that breaks up at the end of its flight, forewarning of bad luck. It has a special name of its own (*nokk'un dagheeghał*), and an ordinary meteor is called *tłoon' tsona,* "star's dung" (Jetté, n.d.*a*).

Before they could obtain or afford clocks, Koyukon people used the stars for telling time at night. Ursa Major, the Big Dipper, was by far the most important—even its name (*nosikghaltaala,* "it rotates its body") refers to the calculable circles it makes in the sky. In the Distant Time, *nosikghaltaala* was a man. After a violent quarrel with Raven, his spirit went up into the sky to become the measurer of time. As he appears now, the dipper's handle is his back, its last star is his head, and the two outer stars of its bowl are his buttocks (Jetté, n.d.*c*).

Older Koyukon people can tell the time of night by observing the Big Dipper's location in the sky and the handle's angle to the horizon. In midwinter *nosikghaltaala*'s head points toward the place of sunrise just before twilight begins. Jetté (n.d.*c*) heard people announce that it was time to get up by saying, "The Big Dipper has turned its head to the light." He also describes (n.d.*c*) marking time by the course of the moon when it is present and by watching several other stars or constellations, including Altair, Cassiopea, the Pleiades, and Orion's belt. Perhaps the oldest people today can recall these less-used astronomical measures, but my teachers had apparently never learned them.

Spirits on the Wind

Weather is the most immediate, temperamental, and tyrannical part of the physical world. Its seasonal cycles are of great practical importance to the

Koyukon, as the prime determinant of their subsistence round. Koyukon people are also affected emotionally by each season—by its comforts or difficulties, its pleasures or stresses. For example, spring seems to be a general favorite, beginning with the long, warming days of March and lasting through breakup. They love its moderating weather and its brightness, which bring freedom to travel widely, increasing game, and small rewards like the sound of birds singing. "Everybody is just smiling and talking like they're happy," an elder woman explained to me, contrasting the joys of spring to the seriousness of winter.

The same woman added that fall is her least favorite season—"It always seems like a sad time to me." Fall is chilly, dark, and gloomy, she said, a time of death among natural things. Her feelings interested me, given that fall is a rich season when food is plentiful and people enjoy the pleasures of hunting. Yet, though she had always been an active provider, her attitude grew from aesthetic feelings rather than practicality.

Considering its power over people's lives and emotions, it is not surprising that weather is the most fully personified element in the Koyukon physical world. The interchange between people and these conscious entities is fairly elaborate and intense. Oncoming weather is announced by signs, it is received as a communion of awareness, and it is sometimes manipulated by people who have learned its few points of vulnerability.

Formerly, at least among the Nulato Koyukon of Jetté's time, people recognized a benign spirit of heat and a malicious antagonist, the spirit of cold. The two struggled for supremacy at different seasons and the weather of the moment showed who had the upper hand (Jetté 1911:98). I asked unsuccessfully about them, but the precepts they entail are still maintained. The temperature is perceived as much more than a physical condition of inert air—it is a *thing,* an essence, as if a wild and moody animal controlled its own living heat.

But at least its moods can be anticipated. When deep cold approaches, the sun often has a bright spot, or "false sun," on either side. Koyukon people say, "The sun is building fires beside her ears," and if it is midwinter it may soon be −30° to −50°. This sign is caused, outsiders would say, by ice crystals precipitating from chilling air aloft—it is a very reliable one.

Other signs of cold or foul weather are discussed later, and a wise person will learn them well. In the Far North, cold can take people away with it—those who are caught outside with the wrong clothing or who become lost or venture onto bad ice. Cold comes with a dense and heavy calm that leans upon the land. If dogs are put in harness, they whine and lift their paws alternately; pulling the sled, they are hidden in fog from their own breath. Cold presses like liquid against clothing, pinches exposed flesh, and flows painfully into the vulnerable recesses of nose and throat. Thick ice fog lies over the village, and long curtains of vapor trail from the chimneys, drifting first one way and then another with the shifts of imperceptible air currents.

Because cold is confining and dangerous, Koyukon people avoid causing it. For example, boats are seldom moved during the winter because it brings the cold. Children used to be kept from throwing snowballs for the same reason. Burning a standing spruce tree can cause cold weather in the spring, but people sometimes do it to make a crust on the snow for easy traveling after the thaw begins. In fall this will bring stormy weather with snow or rain, so it is not done.

> *People used to be so very careful about causing bad weather, because if they couldn't go out they would get behind. So everything was just* hutłaanee, hutłaanee [taboo].

Koyukon country is often blessed with light winds or calm, but storms can sweep furiously across it, raising clouds of snow and piling drifts against cabin doors. Wind can be forecast in many ways, and travelers are ever watchful for the signs. Some people say their ears ring when a storm is coming; perhaps this is caused by changes in barometric pressure. When Koyukon people notice that the stars are twinkling intensely, they say, "Wind makes the stars sway," and they expect windy weather. Meteorologists would say the twinkling is caused by an increase in atmospheric moisture ahead of an approaching storm.

Wind, like heat and cold, is a personified atmospheric essence. Sometimes there is a short burst of flame in a campfire, as if a gust had struck it despite the calm. This is called a "wind spirit" (*ałts'eeyh doyeega*), and it warns of a strong wind. The Nulato Koyukon told Jetté (1911:8) that the spirit of wind creates breezes and storms, and it is blamed for the destruction caused by severe gales. In former times people influenced this spirit with songs and offerings, to create favorable winds for hunting or traveling. My teachers had not learned of this spirit, but they still knew ways of causing or preventing winds. For example, cleaning a bear skin by shaking it outside will bring on stormy winds with rain or snow. Dreaming about a bear, incidentally, means that foul weather is coming. Behaving disrespectfully toward certain birds, such as the gray jay, can also cause storms.

Wind often brings other weather along with it—clouds, chill, and rain or snow—so it usually causes more harm than good. There are ways of making a storm end, although they are not often used anymore. For instance, a member of the caribou clan (*bidziyhta hut'aana*) can take off his shirt and run around outside while other people throw snow at him (or moss in summer). People who have done this say it always works. Another way of stopping rain is to sing this short song:

Wolverine! Wolverine! Your child's parka is getting wet.
Sweep the sky with your tail!

Thunderstorms are another common weather phenomenon in Koyukon country. They brood darkly beneath towering cumulus formations on hot summer afternoons, moving slowly across the land. Koyukon people fear the sudden violence of lightning and the crashing noise, and they advise taking shelter and avoiding open water when thunderstorms threaten. When a tree is split or someone is knocked down, they say it is caused by the thunder striking.

Thunderstorms are transformations of a human spirit from the Distant Time, and because they have awareness they can be influenced. Pinching a female dog so that she yelps will sometimes frighten away an approaching storm. In years past people would paint a red circle on a canoe paddle and wave it toward the west as the dark clouds came near. At the same time they shouted: "Go out to the coast, where they will enjoy having you!" Apparently "they" refers to the Eskimos.

Thunderstorms outside their normal season are taken as a bad omen. Earlier in this century, several occurred on a day in early spring, and not long afterward a great epidemic swept through the region, killing "hundreds" of people. I was told this after some off-season thunderstorms happened in the vicinity of two Yukon River villages, and people expected ill fortune to follow this powerful sign. Another bad omen may come from the whirlwinds that sometimes spin high columns of dust in summer. If one of these hits a tent, canoe, or other belonging, bad luck will come to the owner. Here again is a manifestation of the awareness in everything.

For seven months each year, the subarctic environment is transformed by a gift (or perhaps some would say a curse) of the weather. This, of course, is snow. By midwinter the land is covered by soft powder lying two to six feet deep in the forest, hardened to dunelike drifts on the broad lakes and rivers, creating a nivean world of its own.

Deep snow can immobilize many animals, like the moose, belly deep and able only to follow its established trails. A man afoot without snowshoes might not survive; but with them his freedom is near complete. Packed down by a dogsled or snow machine, the snow becomes a slippery roadway, and travel is far easier than in summer. Snow can also provide drinking water, the material for shelter, a cache for burying meat, and a wonderful feast for the eye.

Wait, I see something: We have our heads in caps of mountain sheep
skin.
Answer: Snow-capped stumps.
[Jetté 1913:642]

The coming of snow is forecast by many signs, some of them mentioned earlier (and by some that I have described elsewhere: 1973:194–202). When the sky is bright orange at sunrise there will be snow, "usually two mornings later." Perhaps the best sign of snow is a moondog, a luminous circle around a bright winter moon. When the Koyukon speak of it, they say, "the moon pulls his [parka] ruff around his face," as if he is telling them that snow is coming soon.

If someone dies in the cold season, Koyukon people expect that a snowstorm or at least a strong wind will follow. This is especially true if the person was a member of the caribou clan, a group generally associated with bad weather. (The Koyukon have three clans, extended kin groups whose membership is inherited through the female line. The clan system no longer functions, though people know which groups they belong to.) Even though wind and storm are expected, people say it deepens their grief; and if good weather follows a death they are much cheered. In neither case is it interpreted as a sign; bad weather seems more an added emotional burden.

The Koyukon people regard snow as an elemental part of their world, much like the river, the air, or the sun. It can be a great inconvenience at times, but mostly it is a benefit. Without snow, the ease and freedom of winter travel would be lost, the movements of animals would not be faithfully recorded, the winter darkness would be far deeper, and the quintessential beauty of the world would be lessened. I never heard Koyukon people complain about snow, even when it stubbornly refused to melt away in late spring.

The culture of Athapaskan people like the Koyukon is highly adapted to the environment that snow creates. Their elegant and refined snowshoes are perhaps the most tangible expression of this, but there are others as well— more subtle but equally impressive. I have seen a man follow a bear's tracks made in frozen moss, then covered by two feet of undisturbed snow that showed faint but somehow perceptible irregularities in its surface. Knowledge of snow is also reflected in the elaboration of terms for its varieties and conditions. About twenty of these are listed in Appendix 3, but I am sure there are many more.

Certain kinds of snow are preferred for certain purposes. For example, beneath the top layer of powder the crystalline structure of snow becomes granular like sugar or rice. This snow, called *łiyh,* has a much higher water content than powder (*tseł koodla*) and so it is best for the teapot or the water barrel. But water melted from this heavy snow is tabooed for boys, who will become clumsy and slow if they drink it. They must use the soft, light surface snow instead. Even this used to be considered too heavy for a pregnant woman. To make her child quick and light—and therefore a good provider—she melted water from *duhnooyh,* the clumps of feathery snow that collect on tree branches or bent-down brush.

In the subarctic forest, snow rules the human senses for a good part of the year, and it is surely no wonder that Koyukon people see far more in it than outsiders can. The omnipresence of snow has not dulled their appreciation of its beauty and subtle qualities either. When he was describing a fall hunt to me, a man said, "There was hardly any snow on the ground; it was just like salt on meat."

> *Wait, I see something: We are sitting all puffed up across from each other,*
> *in coats of mountain sheep skin.*
> *Answer:* duhnooyh, *snow clumps on the tree branches.*
> [Jones 1976]

Not all beauties are without burden, however. Occasionally the winter sky clears after a warm, cloudy spell. If deep cold is coming, the air fills with a dense, glittering fall of ice crystals. After a night of this the world becomes—to the outsider's eye at least—a fantasy of frost. Every tree or bush, down to its smallest twigs, is thickly feathered with bright hoarfrost. But the gloomy fog of ice crystals (called *k'akk'utł dona,* "cold's food") is an ominous sign of powerful cold, and it may tell of death.

When frost crystals cover the snow and the temperature plunges, "nothing moves." Animals find refuge in snow hollows, beneath overhanging spruce boughs, or in underground dens. Sled runners stick on the superchilled frost, so that dogs pull laboriously and without their usual enthusiasm. In times past this condition was more than depressing—it was dangerous. If the confining cold persisted, people might run out of food; so they gave supplication. While the crystals fell, they scattered ashes around their houses, atop caches, and on trails leading from the settlement. At the same time "they prayed that the bad spirits would leave them alone," trying to negate this threatening sign.

When I was living in Huslia a very heavy fall of frost occurred, and two elders said it was a sign that "a body is out there someplace." About ten days later, a man from a neighboring village was discovered frozen to death on his trapline. And there was proof that he had died while the crystals of frost descended.

The Beautiful Island

> *Wait, I see something: My end sweeps this way and that way and this*
> *way around me.*
> *Answer: Grass tassles moving back and forth in the wind, making little*
> *curved trails on the snow.*

It may be clear already that Koyukon people see their environment not only as a source of life and spiritual power, but also as a world of beauty.

They perceive artistic elegance in the form of the land and living things, much the same as in our Western tradition. This sensitivity toward natural design is quite outside the pragmatism that might dominate the lives of people subsisting directly from wild resources.

Koyukon people often comment that a day or a scene is particularly beautiful, and they are attentive to fleeting moments—mountains outlined against the sky, reflections on still water, a bird's song in the quietness. In their language, words like *nizoonh* ("pretty") or *hutaadla'o* ("beautiful") communicate these feelings. This is not a new way of seeing, as the ancient riddles and the statements of elders indicate.

> A man spent several minutes describing a particular midwinter sunset, its color glowing on the frozen river and the snow-covered mountainside, snow on the trees reflecting amber, and long shadows cast by timber on the slopes. He said his wife had called him out so he could see it, and he stood a long time watching. Both he and his wife are old, and he says that the oldest people during his childhood had this same admiration for beauty. [Huslia journal, March 1977]

Expression of these emotions is sometimes tempered by the need to speak carefully about nature. In the past (if not still today), it was considered disrespectful to talk about the size or majesty of a mountain while looking at it. A child doing this would be told, "Don't talk; your mouth is small." In other words, this was "talking big," disregarding the need to be humble before something so large as a mountain. Once away from the scene, though, people could describe it in detail.

Animals and plants are appreciated in much the same way, especially certain species that are particularly elegant or lovely. Birds with striking plumage, for example, are sometimes stuffed so they can be admired at home. In fact, most living things are considered beautiful in some respect, just as they are by many people from Western culture. And similarly, each individual has different kinds or degrees of feeling for them.

I was deeply impressed by the genius of a man from Hughes village, whose knowledge was not only rich but eloquently verbalized. He showed much feeling for animals, especially the ones whose appearance or behavior struck him as beautiful, or whose personality somehow delighted him. He had strong negative emotions as well, toward animals associated with bad luck or unclean habits. When I asked about these he would sometimes shake his head and reply, "Oh, I know about that animal, but I don't want to talk about it." There weren't many like this, however. Usually when I mentioned an animal he would smile as if it were the name of an old friend. Much of what he had to say is found in the chapters that follow.

> *Wait, I see something: There is a trail of reflected light ahead and behind.*
> *Answer: The track of a sled—two lines of packed, icy snow, stretching*
> *across the whiteness, shining in the sunlight.*
> [Jetté 1911:640]

Koyukon people appreciate not only the beauty of the land, but also the pleasures of living close to it. Their prime avenue to satisfaction and prestige is providing a livelihood from nature. This is probably the most pervasive theme in their existence, manifested in an emphasis on practical proficiency in subsistence, on the complex ideological interplay with natural entities, and on certain ideal concepts of personality. Koyukon values emphasize the pleasures and rewards of hard work, foresight, striving toward security, and sharing.

> In praise of a man who had recently died, people said that his woodpile was the largest in the village and that his family never went short of meat. He was a good provider, and this, together with his kindness toward others, made him prominent among his people. [Huslia journal, June 1977]

Subsistence and the land are continually on people's minds. When hunters or trappers return to the village, they recount in animated detail what they have seen and experienced. This creates a steady dialogue on the turning of environmental events, both practical and esoteric. I once asked a man how he had enjoyed his airplane ride from Hughes to Huslia. He replied that it was good—no caribou tracks, but plenty of otter sign in certain areas, and many lakes with frozen overflow that would make travel easy.

For the Koyukon people, subsistence is a way of life, not just a way to make a living. Men and women speak with fondness and excitement about their past travels, their years on the trapline, their hunting or fishing exploits. Once, in early winter, a man explained to me that he could not feel good during that season if he was not out running his trapline. "I trap because I was raised with it," he added. "It's all I know to do this time of year."

People often express their love of being outdoors, living in remote camps, traveling over the broad expanses of land, setting out their traplines, and experiencing the abundant years for each kind of animal. They speak of these things with much feeling, yet without overlooking the hardships. They regard theirs as a most pleasurable way to live. Nearing death, the revered old man Chief Henry said:

> *I know that my time is near, though I cannot tell exactly when it will come. But I have had a good life. I have camped many times beneath spruce trees, roasting grouse over my campfire. So there is no reason to pray that I might live on much longer.*

4

The Plants

The Sheltering Forest

Newcomers to the north country are sometimes amazed to find that forests exist here, for they expect endless barren lands of rock, ice, and snow. This feeling may not diminish with time—after experiencing the intensity and duration of winter, the existence of a fairly dense, diversified forest becomes even more impressive.

> I have often thought this while traveling with my dogs through the silent, snow-laden trees: All the plants are dormant here for more than seven months each year. It is only the four or five months of warmth—that quick flourish of growth—that allows them to live at all. And because the animals could not exist without plants, they are equally beholden to summer. So whatever inhabits the subarctic winter lives on borrowed time, or more accurately borrowed energy, that carries it across the abyss of winter. [Huslia journal, February 1977]

Not surprisingly, plants that live in the north are a hardy and stubborn sort, more adventuresome than artistic, plants born with a Protestant ethic. The animals who depend on them share much of this tough determination, and so too do the people. In the Koyukon language, plants are called *midinolyaal,* roughly, "something that grows," and to that I might add an exclamation point. Even after they die, the trees decay very slowly in the arid cold, as if they refuse to give up.

Wait, I see something: We stand there and just stay and stay.
Answer: Old tree stumps.

The subarctic forests do not have the lushness found in temperate or tropical places, but they still create a sheltering haven within the overarching domain of cold and storm. Although the surrounding wildlands are mottled with tundra and open muskegs, the Koyukon are a people of the forest. They spend most of their lives among trees, in the timber or tall scrub, or moving across the openings between forest glades. Certainly they find many important resources in the open country; but they also feel vulnerable and exposed where the wind may strike unimpeded, away from the refuge of trees and the warmth of campfires. Home is in the forest.

To the cold eye of statistics, plants may seem to have little direct importance in the economies of subarctic people like the Koyukon. It is reasonable to estimate that plant foods have never composed over 10 percent of the overall diet (see Lee 1968:46, 48) though this could vary sharply from time to time. By this measure, few people in the world are less "dependent" on plants for food. But vegetation provides the Koyukon with the essential materials for housing, heating, and manufacture of equipment. When these uses are considered, few people anywhere depend more completely on plants for their survival, especially since the absolute imperative for heat can be met here only by burning wood.

In spite of their preeminence in creating the living subarctic environment and providing essentials for human survival, plants have only a minor position in the Koyukon spiritual world. Perhaps it is their stoic dependability, as opposed to the more temperamental and often far scarcer animals. There are notable exceptions, however: plants with powerful, though often benevolent, spirits. In contrast to the animals, the spiritually powerful plants are also the most important economically.

In this chapter I will touch on virtually all plant species directly significant to the Koyukon people. For some of these I will make only a brief mention of uses, because nothing was told me about any special meanings they might have. I will give more attention to the plants whose origins, spirit powers, and ecological or economic importance make them special inhabitants of the Koyukon world. As a matter of preference, I will begin with the large trees and work toward the ground; the categories I follow (conifers, deciduous trees, small plants) are my own, not reflecting any Koyukon systematics.

Green Spires: The Spruce Trees

The boreal forest is a mosaic of plant communities. Many of these communities have no trees or are dominated by deciduous trees and shrubs. But the particular character of this ecosystem, its strongest impact on the eye and the other senses, derives from two coniferous trees—the white spruce(*Picea glauca*) and its smaller, less elegant counterpart the black spruce (*Picea mariana*). These are the tall and narrow spires so often silhouetted against the horizon, enhancing the slow transfiguration of sunset or piercing the clear depths of moonlit sky. Along the river meanders, they lean gracefully from undercut banks, sometimes bending down to touch their own reflections on the water. Eventually their roots will wash free and they will be reduced to gray skeletons, stranded on sandbars after the spring floods.

White spruce grows mainly in the deep soils of river valleys and dry slopes, while its smaller sibling is relegated to wetlands, north slopes, and high country. Sometimes the two species look nearly identical, but equally often black spruce are stunted, sparsely branched, and crooked, like muskeg gnomes. White spruce is called *ts'ibaa* and black spruce is *ts'ibaa t'aał;* a rare case in which generic relationship is indicated by Koyukon names (neither of which has a translation).

The black spruce is a relatively small tree (fifteen to thirty feet high) and is only moderately important to the Koyukon. People sometimes cut it for firewood, especially in places like the old burn near Huslia, with its dense stands of dry trees. Black spruce are as tough as they look, and their narrow trunks make excellent poles for tent frames, drying racks, and miscellaneous purposes.

White spruce is everything that black spruce is not, at least from the Koyukon perspective. It is by far the most important plant the people utilize, and probably the most important single species in their economy and lifeway. The white spruce is invested with a potent spirit (*biyeega hoolaanh*), like that of the most powerful animals; but it differs in having mostly benign effects on humans. There are few special gestures of respect for it, though I was told that a white spruce must never be cut down without a reason. Once I heard a woman speak with real indignation about a boy who senselessly stripped the branches from a small spruce in her village.

People can use the spirit power of white spruce trees in several beneficial ways. The great old trees, with thick trunks and outstretched boughs, protect those who sleep beneath them. When they hunt or travel, people try to camp under such trees, and certain strategically located ones have become well known for this over a span of decades. People say that the tree "will take care of you," especially if malevolent spirits come near.

Power from the spruce is apparently concentrated (or at least accessible) in its boughs and top. In years past, shamans would brush people with a spruce top (*ts'ibaa łee',* "spruce head") so that the tree's spirit would take away sickness. Pubescent girls would put a spruce top into a moose or caribou track before stepping over it, to avoid alienating the animals from hunters. Spruce needles were formerly boiled to make an infusion, used as a rub or bath to cure dry skin or sores and as a drink for kidney problems or to promote general good health. Shamans prescribed such treatments, which tapped the tree's spirit power.

The white spruce often can nullify dangerous spiritual forces. Another manifestation of its beneficence is a very rare variety or condition of the tree that produces gold-colored needles. It is called *al doyonh* in Koyukon, "rich tree," or literally "rich boughs." I have never seen one, though I have always been watchful. Trees like this can confer good luck on those who find them, if they do the right things. First, they should walk once around the tree, going in the direction that the sun circles the sky. Then they should go back along their trail for a short distance, and afterward they can simply continue on their way. People also cut small boughs from golden spruce trees, take them home, and keep them safe as talismans.

I was also told about a peculiar kind of knot, called "stick brain" (*dikinh yee huyo'*), that comes from a spruce tree. It can be split into concentric rings, and in earlier years children sometimes wore one of these rings on a string around their necks to make them skilled with their hands.

White spruce has a sticky amber pitch that sometimes exudes from its trunk. The uninformed woodcutter whose clothing becomes caked with it might wish it did not exist, but the Koyukon regard it differently. Pitch is mentioned in several stories of the Distant Time, when Raven used it to make things. Pieces with the right consistency are chewed like gum, although the stories teach that people who chew pitch while trapping beaver or fishing will have no luck. Put on sores or cuts, pitch heals and disinfects, as I have seen several times myself. It is also excellent for caulking boat seams. One powerful old shaman used to burn spruce pitch (as well as swan feathers and tops from slender grass) when he made medicine for a sick person.

Spruce trees have an amazing number of uses for the Koyukon, their importance ranging from minor to indispensable. Almost every part has special uses and significance. The thick bases of roots, for example, are ideal for carving spoons and bowls. Long, supple roots, dug by hand and snaked from beneath the forest moss, are skinned and then used to lash birchbark baskets. Good basket roots are found only in specific places—along certain lakeshores, for example.

> In the Distant Time, Raven killed a whale in a lake and strung its innards around the shores. Since then, spruce trees growing along lakesides often have long, skinny roots.

The importance of spruce is reflected in the Koyukon language, which contains at least forty terms for describing parts of trees and kinds of wood, terms used mainly or exclusively for this species. White spruce is large (fifty to one hundred feet tall) and straight and grows in dense stands, which makes it ideal for cutting. Its wood is the principal heating fuel for most Koyukon households. For much of the subarctic year, heat is more immediately important for survival than food; in Koyukon culture prestige is accorded those who maintain large woodpiles and keep their homes well warmed.

Spruce logs are used for building the beautiful log houses most Koyukon people live in. Lumber from split or ripsawed logs is also used in house construction and for making boats, sleds, canoes, caches, tent frames, and hundreds of other items. Rotten or punky spruce wood, of which there are several varieties, is pulverized and mixed with rotten willow for smoking hides.

> I rest below the outstretched arms of a giant spruce. Beneath me, fresh-cut tips from the boughs make a springy bed, promising a comfortable sleep. Before me, dry spruce logs burn in a bright campfire, radiating heat against my face and sending sparks into the still air. Behind me is the tree's great trunk on which I lean, solid security for my body and for my mind. Above me, luminescence from the full moon scatters through a maze of needles. Small wonder that Koyukon people find such benevolence in the spirit of the spruce tree. [Huslia journal, March 1977]

Leaf-Bearers: The Deciduous Trees

However much white spruce may dominate the forest from a human perspective, it is certainly not the only useful or important tree. The deciduous trees and tall shrubs create their own environments, which are often far richer in wildlife than are spruce forests; and they have a wide variety of uses. Spruce is the all-purpose tree, to be sure, but for many special needs other species must be used.

The deciduous trees and shrubs include poplar, aspen, alder, an array of willows, resin birch (?), and paper birch. I should make clear that the category deciduous is European, and I learned of no Koyukon classification or term that groups them. Only paper birch comes anywhere near the significance of white spruce for the Koyukon, and only this species has comparable spirit power (*biyeega hoolaanh*).

Apparently, trees other than spruce are not prominent in the Distant Time stories, but each was transformed from a human. In one story, mink-man went to several tree-women and told them that their husband (Raven) had been killed:

> *When one woman heard the story, she cried and pinched her skin.*
> *Then she was changed into the spruce tree, with its rough and pinched bark.*

> *When another heard it, she cried and slit her skin with a knife. She became a poplar, with its deeply cut bark.*
>
> *When a third woman was told the story, she cried and pinched herself until she bled. She turned into the alder, whose bark is used to make red dye.*

Poplar, Aspen, Alder, and Willow

I have grouped these species for brief mention, because they seem to have minimal significance in the Koyukon spiritual world. I learned no special ways of treating or using these plants, other than their purely practical roles in the Koyukon economy. In this regard, all have some significance—as secondary sources of firewood and as raw materials for a wide assortment of purposes. Their brief consideration here reflects only their position in the Koyukon belief system (I have detailed their practical uses elsewhere, for the Koyukon 1978:277–79 and Kutchin 1973:38–39). Koyukon names for these species are listed in Appendix 3.

The Evil Shrub

My Koyukon teachers told me, almost reluctantly, about one plant that is truly evil—a common bush, about three feet tall, crooked and wiry, with dark and somewhat papery bark. I was never able to identify this shrub, which is probably either Greene mountain ash (*Sorbus scopulina*), or resin birch (*Betula glandulosa*). In Koyukon it is known as "mean stick," "ugly stick" (*kk'aan dikina*), or "the one not used" (*baahaa neeliniyyee*). As the name implies, it should never be used, lest something terrible happen. For example, anyone who skewers meat on a branch from this bush may starve later. The plant must have a fairly potent spirit, but no one mentioned this to me; nor did anyone explain why it is so malevolent.

Jetté (1911:614) describes what must be the same plant and says that if a young man touches it he will become useless in "manly pursuits." A young woman who handles it will bring bad luck and scarcity of game to her family. Only an old woman can obtain it, after she makes placating gifts and prayers. Then she breaks the shoots into pieces, boils them, and gives the infusion to sick children (as a rub or drink) to help cure them.

Paper Birch

Among boreal forest trees, paper birch (*Betula papyrifera*) is the ornate and beautiful one, whose white bark reflects the color of sunrise and whose fine twigs create intricate lacework against the sky. It grows nearly everywhere in Koyukon country, decorating the lowlands and slopes, but is not found in profusion or in pure stands. Birch mingles with the others, enhancing them all by its presence.

Wait, I see something: We whistle along the hillside.
Answer: Loose, half-peeled bits of birchbark, hissing in the wind.

Paper birch (*kk'eeyh*) is as useful as it is elegant. People consider it the best firewood because it burns slowly and makes a hot flame. It is also a fairly large tree (to about sixty feet), but unfortunately it is far less prolific than spruce. The only indigenous hardwood, birch is ideal for making sleds, snowshoe frames, and canoe ribs. Birchbark is one of the handiest materials the forest provides. It is stripped from the trees in spring and early summer (which does not kill them), then folded to make baskets and food storage containers. It also contains a highly flammable substance, so people often use it for starting campfires or lighting the stove at home.

The useful and delicately beautiful birch tree has a powerful spirit (*biyeega hoolaanh*), and there are ways of showing it respect. Birchbark is not peeled from a living tree in the winter, because this leaves the tree naked to the cold and will bring on frigid weather. If someone does remove bark, the stripped place should be smeared with black ashes to negate the bad effects. It is more proper to bring a birch log inside, thaw it, strip the bark, and then bury the log under the snow to protect it from exposure to the cold air.

This kind of treatment recognizes that living things do not die immediately when they are "killed" or cut down. Final death may not come for days, months, or years, depending on the organism. For example, an old shaman used the birch spirit to heal sick people, and for many years afterward they could not cut down birches. I knew a man who had been restricted in this way, so his wife had to cut the trees he pointed out to her. After a tree was completely dead, in about a week, he could safely work with it. Later his wife was given the same cure and could not cut birches either; but when the shaman died they both felt safe cutting live trees again.

An elderly woman was showing me how to split wood for snowshoes and fish traps, and I tried to help out by throwing bits of wood and shavings into the fire. She quickly stopped me, saying it is tabooed to burn scraps from wood being used to make things for hunting, trapping, or fishing. People who follow tradition will gather up their snowshoe shavings and deposit them out in the woods, well away from trails. This applies not only to birch, but to spruce and perhaps other trees as well.

People who violate these rules of respect will have bad luck in finding or working with birch trees, just as they can lose their luck with the animals:

> *Sometimes you just can't walk up to a good birch tree. Can't find*
> *it. . . . Lot of people told me about that long ago when I started making*
> *snowshoes. Don't leave the shaving on the trail they told me. Sometimes*
> *I can't find good birch or it will be hard to find. When I'm lucky, I could*

spot a good birch from way out by the shape of the tree. But if I'm bad luck, if I don't treat 'em right, I wouldn't find it that way, see.
[Yukon-Koyukuk School District 1979:26]

Earth Plants

I turn now to plants that grow mostly along the ground—the berries, small green plants, mosses, and fungi. These plants have an assortment of uses, although only the berries are of much importance today for Koyukon villagers. And as previous discussions would lead us to predict, the only small plants associated with strong spiritual forces are the economically significant ones—the berries.

Berries
One of the nicest surprises in the northern forest is the variety and abundance of berries, a delicious embellishment on an otherwise rather staid plant world. There are other edible plants, but not many, and certainly none with the juicy sweetness of the berries. Thirteen species of edible fruits are found in Koyukon country, most of them inhabitants of the river lowlands and muskegs, but some favoring dry hillsides or even mountain tundra. All of them are gathered, the quantities depending on availability and taste.

The less common berries are often eaten on the spot, and if any are brought home they quickly disappear. A few kinds, like bog blueberries, lowbush cranberries, and highbush cranberries, are often abundant enough so that large containers of them are frozen and used through the winter. These are not only a favorite treat, but also a valuable source of vitamin C and other nutrients.

In Koyukon tradition, berry plants are considered to have special power because they grow close to the earth and are nurtured directly from it. As I discussed earlier, the most fundamental of all spiritual powers (*sinh taala'*) emanates from the earth's surface. Low-growing plants like the berry bushes acquire some of this power, and so they are potentially dangerous. This is especially true in the evening and at night, so people must not gather berries (nor should they pick flowers or harvest any kind of plant) in dusk or darkness. Ignoring this danger could cause sickness or even death. In the old days, people who were being treated by a shaman did not eat berries, because it would neutralize or "chase away" the medicine.

Of all the plant fruits, bog blueberry (*Vaccinium uliginosum*) is most important to the Koyukon. In fact, its name (*geega*) is also the general term for berries. Blueberries grow in wonderful profusion, especially in certain muskegs and during certain years when conditions are ideal. Villagers gather them in great quantities when fall comes, and blue tongues abound among the children.

In addition to the general taboo on picking berries in the evening, blueberries are not gathered by men hunting bears. Doing this would cause bad luck in finding their quarry, and it would make the hunters sick. A woman told me of several men who violated the taboo, "and when they got sick they just laid on their backs kicking their feet around like a bear." Bog blueberry is said to be the only small plant that was human in the Distant Time. It was a giant man then, so big that after he was killed the people camped on him and ate his (blueberry?) flesh.

Next in importance to blueberries are the cranberries—two species plus a third that borrows the name because of its bright red fruits. The lowbush cranberry (*Vaccinium vitis*) is called *dinaałkk'aza* in Koyukon, "something red." It grows abundantly in the deep timber, while the equally common bog cranberry (*Oxycoccus microcarpus*) creeps on threadlike stems in the wetland moss. Bog cranberry is named *daałnodoodla'*, "some bird's eye," because in the Distant Time a bird lost his eyes and used these as a replacement. Highbush cranberry (*Viburnum edule*) is a fairly tall shrub, unlike the others, but it too has tasty berries and is gathered in fair amounts. Its slender, supple stems are also used to reinforce birchbark basket rims. In Koyukon this forest plant is called *donaaldloya*, "something hanging."

Alpine bearberry (*Arctostaphylos alpina*), called *geez nogha*, and kinnikinnik (*A. uva-ursi*), called *diniyh*, are two uncommon species that older people sometimes gather, store in grease or oil, and eat with fish or meat. The juicy, bland crowberry (*Empetrum nigrum*) hugs the mountain tundra, and hunters in the waterless high country gather it to quench their thirst. Its well-chosen name (*deenaałt'aas*) means "scattered charcoal." Another seldom-used fruit is the black currant (*Ribes hudsonianum*), named "raven berries" (*dotson' geega*) and somewhat avoided because of its association with this powerful bird. American red currant (*R. triste*), called *nots'ah-tl'oona*, is also uncommon and not often gathered.

Koyukon people love to pick the sweet, succulent, but sadly uncommon nagoonberry (*Rubus arcticus*). Gray jays also consider this berry of the damp forest a treat and often find it before anyone else does. It is called, somewhat mysteriously, *noghuy tl'aakk*, "frog sinew." The American red raspberry (*R. idaeus*) is similarly named—*dits'in tl'aakk*, "goose sinew"—and it is also both delicious and uncommon.

The lovely orange cloudberry (*Rubus chamaemorus*) hides among the prostrate plants of wet tundra, where older Koyukon people search for it. Young boys and girls, and women who may bear children, should not eat this tasty berry because it rots so quickly after ripening. Violators will grow old quickly and be poor at making a living. Its name (*kkotl*) has no translation.

Along the rivers and dry hillsides, the forest is often armed with thick stands of prickly rose (*Rosa acicularis*). This well-named plant bristles with thorns that penetrate the thickest trousers and punish the absent-minded one who sits in the wrong place. The plant (*hus dikina'*, "thornstick") is differentiated from its fruit (*kooyh*), which is bland tasting but rich in vitamin C.

Although it is common, Koyukon people do not gather it much today. To make the rain stop falling, Nulato Koyukon of Jetté's time would throw some rose leaves into the fire, saying, "The tresses [of the rose bush] begin to sweep the sky" (1911:257).

> Wait, I see something: Under the trees we have grown downwards, long and round.
> Answer: Fruits of the prickly rose.
> [Jetté 1913:199]

Miscellaneous Small Plants

The Koyukon people have uses for a few other flowering plants, but their significance in the diet is very slight. I was interested to see, for example, that the neighboring inland Eskimos of the Kobuk River are much more enthusiastic about edible plants, including the less abundant kinds of berries. I cannot say whether this has always been true or whether recent changes have created this difference.

Only two plants are occasionally gathered and cooked for eating in Koyukuk villages—these are sour dock (*Rumex arcticus*) and wild rhubarb (*Polygonum alaskanum*). Wild chives (*Allium schoenoprasum*) are occasionally gathered and eaten raw, alone or with fish. Grasses and sedges (*k'itsaan'*) are used for a few minor purposes, such as dog bedding and to produce smoke in smudge fires. The feathery goosegrass (*Equisetum*) found along river-banks is also used this way. Other useful plants include mosses from the forest floor (*tl'otl*), which make good chinking and roof covering for log houses. "Lake bottom moss" (*taah naana'*) served a vital purpose as baby diapers in earlier times, when people collected it from snags along the river where it hung and dried after the spring runoff.

The Koyukon apparently have never used mushrooms as food. General terms for them are *deeltsaa' baaba*, "mouse food," or the wonderfully descriptive *nin' dzagha'*, which means "earth ears." Similar creativity names the shaggy mane "raven's spear" (*dotson' kkuskkoya'*) and the puffball "raven's snuff" (*dotson' k'idiltsina'*) or "raven's sack" (*dotson' notkitl'a*).

The only fungus regularly used today is *kk'eyh anee'ona* ("lump on a birch"), a bracket fungus that grows on the trunks of dead birch trees. People often gather these and burn them as "punk" to repel mosquitoes, gnats, and flies. They also say the acrid smoke will keep bears away, something I have not had a chance to see. And this fungus can be mixed with tobacco to make an intoxicating snuff.

> The punk fungus was created in the Distant Time, when Raven made the world over again. At first it was just chunks of fat. He put them everyplace, on the trees, so people could eat whenever they want. But

Raven figured that was too easy for people; they could just eat without working. So he made his urine go on it, and after that it became birch fungus.

Before moving to the animals, I want to emphasize again that, although plants make up a small part of the Koyukon diet, they are vital to the people's survival. Beyond this, plants greatly affect the physical and sensory world in which the Koyukon live. Even the unnamed plants are appreciated and given notice. The abundant wild flowers, for example, are valued as objects of beauty. People bring them into their homes or transplant them to the village. And women often pick flowers that they find especially beautiful, study their form and color, then recreate their loveliness in the intricate and flowing beadwork designs on moccasins or mittens.

5

Earth Animals

The Invertebrates

This chapter is a short collection of notes on the few invertebrate animals that are directly significant to the Koyukon. I have included a single vertebrate species—the wood frog—but not because one amphibian scarcely warrants a whole chapter, and not because frogs eat insects. The reason will be apparent at the chapter's end. Aside from this, virtually all the invertebrate animals discussed here are insects.

By some measures the boreal regions are a poor place to look for insects. Far fewer species exist here than are found in the temperate and tropical lands—the chill climate, of course, is a deterrent to cold-blooded invertebrates. But anyone who took this principle literally and expected to see only an occasional insect would be surprised and sorry when summer came to the subarctic. What the north country lacks in diversity of insect species, it more than compensates in the abundance of those that are found. I suppose there are very few places in the world where a handful of species can affect human comfort so drastically without causing disease. Were it not for these species, insects would have scarcely any direct influence on the Koyukon people.

Some insects other than the noxious ones are significant to the Koyukon, and I will briefly discuss what little I was told about them. I must apologize beforehand for the lack of precise identifications. And I should note that the organization of species (or other taxa) throughout this book is my own, not a reflection of Koyukon systematics.

The Biting and Stinging Insects

Mosquitoes

The coming of insect swarms in the northern summer is a misery for nearly all animals except the swallows, flycatchers, and other birds that gorge themselves on that limitless repast. For the others, the rich warmth is a mixed blessing. Among humans, even the most dedicated and aescetic nature lovers must sometimes cringe and wonder why. The Koyukon are spared this, for although they suffer no less they at least have an explanation.

> In the Distant Time, Raven had six wives, and their constant bickering drove him to distraction. Finally he could take it no longer, so he ran them all off into the woods. But when he wanted them to come back, they refused and hid where he could not find them. So he created mosquitoes, and it was not long before the besieged women rushed back to the shelter of his house.
> Now Raven found himself tormented by hordes of mosquitoes. But he had a solution. He made punk, the birch fungus that repels insects, and people have used it ever since.

I heard another version of this, one that reveals more about the Koyukon people's attitude toward mosquitoes:

> After the Raven had created humans, a man came and stole his wife away. So Raven went out and gathered rotten willow wood, pulverized it to a powdery dust, then scattered it into the air. The particles became mosquitoes, which ever afterward would cause suffering for humankind.

Mosquitoes (tl'eeyh) are not the only biting insects that frequent the Alaskan boreal forest, but they are usually the most prolific. Sometimes a dry year curtails them and fosters the gnats instead; but mosquitoes normally prevail over all others. The first to appear in spring, often before the snow is gone, are the large, clumsy ones (genus Culiseta) that hibernate through winter. These have a special name in Koyukon: ts'aa tleelghant'ugha. They rarely manage to bite anyone, but they do serve notice that others will be along soon. By mid-June the smaller, quicker, hungrier Aedes mosquitoes have hatched. These will reach a peak from late June through July, then slowly diminish through August. In September they mercifully vanish.

Mosquitoes ordinarily feed on plant juices and nectar; but the females need one blood meal, which gives them the energy for developing eggs (Pruitt 1978:38). To my knowledge, northern mosquitoes do not transmit human diseases and are usually no serious threat to health. But when clouds of them descend on anyone who moves outdoors, or when they buzz ceaselessly against the tent walls, they certainly cause discomfort and psychological distress.

Fortunately, the Koyukon have ways to avoid mosquitoes, even during the bad years. Most important, people stay away from wetlands and shady forest during the mosquito season. Open areas are usually free of them during the midday sun, and at evening it is best to retreat indoors. Nowadays people also use commercial repellents and occasionally wear head nets. Houses and tents are protected with screens. But in the old days people had to depend entirely on smudges, burned continuously inside their houses and around their camps and carried with them as they walked or paddled their boats. Pulverized dry wood or birch fungus smoldered wherever there were people.

I often wondered what it would be like to confront mosquitoes without the modern protections. How did the elders tolerate it? Then I had a chance to see when I took a trip with an old woman and we brought no repellent. Our first landing was on a riverbank with deep grass and hordes of mosquitoes:

> The mosquitoes simply mobbed our exposed flesh, landing and clinging until we madly brushed them away, dozens at a time. As the minutes passed I became more and more desperate, then nearly panicked when my face and eyes were so covered with buzzing, pulsing insects that I could scarcely see. Each time I swept them away, others replaced them within seconds. I cannot express how unbearable it was—no way to avoid being bitten again and again.
>
> Finally, all I could do was dash for the boat, wait for my intrepid companion, then frantically start the engine and brush off the clingers as we sped away. I now can see how mosquitoes have incapacitated and killed people who did not know how to deal with them. And it might not take very long. [Huslia journal, June 1977]

After this experience, the woman showed me how to make a smudge in a tin can with a long wire handle, and for the rest of the trip we carried them with us everywhere. Each time we rested we built a smoldering fire and were protected by our little clouds of smoke. I came away convinced that the traditional Koyukon must have cared very little for midsummer. The only comment I heard was that people were miserable when they had to spend much of their time sitting inside smoke-filled houses.

Wait, I see something: It flies up, ringing the bell.
Answer: A mosquito, buzzing up into the air.
[Jetté 1913:189]

Gnats

My experiences with mosquitoes made it difficult to believe the Huslia people when they said, "After you see the gnats, you'll wish you had the mosquitoes back again." But, in the heat and dryness of August, they were certainly proved right.

The gnats appear as mosquitoes begin to diminish, and they prefer the opposite conditions—open places in the sun's full warmth. There are at least two kinds, the tiny "no-see-um" and a more abundant and voracious larger variety. All gnats are called *k'inodaguyhdla'*, which Jetté (n.d.*a*) translates "it gnaws." Indeed, they often leave a tiny pock and a speck of blood, where later a persistent itchy swelling will appear. Because they are so small, gnats are much harder to detect than mosquitoes, and they often crawl under your clothing, into your ears, or around your eyes before they bite.

In some years these nasty little creatures are incredibly prolific, but even then they last only a few weeks and can be avoided by staying in the cool forest. They love the sandy ridges at Huslia, and in a bad year I have seen the village come to a standstill because of them—during midday not a person was to be seen, as if the town had been abandoned. Not even at −60°, in the dead of winter, are the people so reluctant to go outdoors.

Flies

I turn now to the lesser nuisances. Several kinds of flies are common everywhere in Koyukon country, especially around villages and camps. They are mostly attracted to drying meat and fish, which must be protected by keeping smudges beneath them. But people still have to check regularly for fly eggs and scrape off any they find. Maggots (*gheeno'u*, "it comes to life") still manage to hatch and spoil some meat. Two kinds of flies are distinguished, the "dung fly" (*tson' dibiyh*) and the bluebottle fly (*dun'*). When I asked one of my Koyukon teachers about flies, he had only one short comment: "Now there's something that was made for nothing."

In addition to the common flies, large horseflies (*k'inot'odla*) often buzz around people (and animals) and occasionally manage a painful bite. The warble fly (*bidziyh ggoo'*, "caribou insect") follows and torments caribou in the summer, laying its eggs under their skin, where its larvae develop in large cysts. By late winter, caribou hides are perforated and almost useless because of these. There was some compensation in the old days when people ate the larvae (said to be sweet tasting), but this custom has long vanished.

Lice

The elder Koyukon people can remember when body lice (*yo'*) were a common affliction, but modern conditions have done away with them. When lice were still available they could be used to bring clear weather—one was put on a leaf and set into the river current with the request, "Clear the sky over me."

Although lice are gone now, Koyukon adults remember them only too well. I would like to credit the teller of the following story, but I think it best to preserve his anonymity:

> You know, years ago we used to have lice. Everybody had them. Up at old Cutoff once, I was really full of them. I must have had thousands! It's OK when I'm doing something—I never feel them—but when I sat still they started moving around all over me.
>
> Well, I decided I'll have to get rid of them. They had long underwear, union suits, at the store, so I got me one and went home. Everybody was outside playing the football game we used to play with a ball that had caribou hair stuffed inside. Even old people played it at that time. So I went in there while it was a good chance to change.
>
> Grandpa didn't like anybody to burn stuff like rags inside the house— it's hutɬaanee [taboo]—but nobody's in there to see me. So I got out of my old underwear and put it in the stove. It really took off, burning right up. I put on the new underwear and went out; and there they were, all smelling that smoke. A little breeze blew it to them. Well, somebody said the earth must be on fire, and Old Happy walked out to the riverbank to smell there. "Yup. . . ," he shook his head, "the earth is burning."
>
> Boy, I was scared about Grandpa, if he found out, so I didn't say nothing. It was two years before I told anybody—Jimmy—and boy, he sure laughed. Anyhow, after I put on that new underwear I was just full of lice again by evening. I don't know, they must fly on you from other people.

Ants and Bees

Black ants that live in the boreal forest are called noɬdiyhtɬ. They are not very common, nor are they attracted to people or their food; but occasionally somebody is nipped by one. Ants are segmented, the Distant Time stories tell, because a young girl who camped with an ant family cut them in half when they walked on her.

Bumblebees are native to Koyukon country, and although they rarely sting people do not like them. There are three kinds: the all-black one (k'inodzeedza, "stubby animal"), the large yellow-and-black one (k'inodzeedza kuh; kuh, "big"), and the smaller yellow-and-black one (k'inodzeedza yoza; yoza, "small"). No honeybees are found here.

All of these are associated with bad luck, though not strongly so. Encounters with dangerous spiritual powers are sometimes accompanied by a buzzing sound like that of a bumblebee. When an old shaman dreamed of bumblebees, he said it meant his enemies were near. People took an unusual abundance of bumblebees one summer as a bad sign. And, according to stories of the Distant Time, there are many bumblebees in the "bad place" where some people go after death. Needless to say, the Koyukon are not pleased when these insects buzz around them.

The Innocuous Invertebrates

This very short section covers the few other arachnids and insects I was told about. I should note that a more concerted effort on my part would have expanded this, perhaps considerably; but it does correctly indicate that Koyukon people devote much more attention to the larger creatures that have greater practical significance.

Spiders

Considering the importance given to spiders in Western culture, the Koyukon seem relatively unconcerned with them, even though they are common in the boreal wildlands. There is a familiar ring to their advice that stepping on spiders will cause rainy weather. They are called *taahoodzoya*, "scratches into the water," perhaps because they can walk on the surface. Spiderwebs, Jetté learned (n.d.*a*) are sometimes named "our face becomes tangled in it," and anyone who has walked through the spring woods will understand why. These gossamer threads were also described to him as snares set for migratory birds. One of my Koyukon instructors often said that the names of things and places are sometimes "riddles," and these are clearly examples.

Snow Flea

This creature, called *yił kkutłiga*, is a most improbable one indeed. At the end of my first winter in the northern forest, my trapping partner (a Kutchin Athapaskan) called me to look at a deep drift that was melting in bright sun beneath a riverbank. I was amazed to see the surface alive with miniscule creatures, crawling and twitching about on the glistening granules of snow. In certain places, like open grassy meadows, they can be "thick as dust." Good weather seems to bring them to the surface, and Koyukon people say that after their third appearance warm weather has arrived to stay.

Beetles

The very large (about two inches) and spectacular staghorn beetle is a common sight around Koyukon villages. It almost seems friendly, or perhaps it is just drawn to woodpiles and log houses. Not only is it large, but it has two very long and graceful antennae, like a creature from the rain forest. Its Koyukon name, *bidziyh yeega'*, means "image of caribou," comparing its antennae to antlers. The riddler calls these antennae "ears," however:

> *Wait, I see something: In a small hole in the ground, it drags its ears*
> *across each other.*
> *Answer: The "image-of-caribou" beetle.*
> [Jetté 1913:118]

The oldest living Koyukon people have heard, but not seen, that the large (up to an inch long) water beetle called *taak'idzee'an* was eaten before whites came here. They were said to have a sweet taste, but Jetté (n.d.*a*) writes that their taste is said to resemble boiled oysters. He refers to this insect (under the name *taah tso'*) as a "large gyrinus or hydrophilus, common in small lakes, of a dark brown color with a border of cream-yellow around the margin of the elytra and body. It was used as a food in the old times, when other foodstuffs were not available. The insect was stripped of its head, legs, and elytra and then boiled."

Butterflies and Moths

The Koyukon name these lovely insects collectively *nidinlibidza,* "it flutters here and there." Several species are also distinguished, such as the yellow swallowtail (*naggaałk'idinlibidza,* "king salmon's butterfly"), the clothing moth (*k'ik'il ahona,* "eats clothing"), and an unidentified moth called "with which it won't freeze again" (*biyił nohułteegiyee*). When this species appears in spring, people know there will be no more crust on the snow, because freezing weather is over.

One caterpillar, a black fuzzy kind (*diyoodza*), is associated with bad fortune, apparently because it comes from under the spiritually powerful earth. Seeing one out of season forebodes sickness or death, and if one drops on a person it is a sign of bad luck. A woman told me she had seen one of these on the fall snow years ago, and shortly afterward her baby died.

Two Stages of the Frog

The frog is a true anomaly among animals of the boreal forest, the only cold-blooded land vertebrate. The wood frog (*Rana sylvatica*) is, in fact, one of the northernmost amphibians in the world. I have found these little creatures at the forest's end, beyond the Arctic Circle in the Kobuk River valley. They are relatively short-legged and small, with slightly mottled gray skin. The Koyukon say their bodies have scar marks because in the Distant Time a frog-woman was killed by two boys who threw her back and forth. Afterward, another boy put her back together again and buried her in feathers. The frog-woman later came back as an old lady and brought good luck to her rescuer.

Wood frogs (*noghuya*) are heard calling in meltwater ponds in May, before all the snow is gone. After they lay their eggs they scatter to the wetlands and forest, and because they are camouflaged and secretive people rarely see them. In September or early October they dig down into little holes in mossy meadows or dry lake beds, beginning a hibernation that spans seven frigid months.

Koyukon people have a warm benevolent feeling toward frogs. They never harm or bother them, because the two boys who injured frog-woman in the Distant Time were made to suffer for it. When someone has a head-ache, a frog placed on the head will bring relief. "It makes medicine for you. When its throat moves, they say it is drinking your blood." Once I was traveling with an elderly woman who complained all day of a headache. As luck would have it we found a frog, and she let it sit atop her head for several minutes. It cooperated perfectly, keeping quite still except for the pumping of its little throat. Then she gently released it. In the busy activities that followed, I completely forgot to ask her if the headache went away.

I said at the beginning that there is a good reason for including frogs with the invertebrates. Some lakes in the Koyukon wildlands are said to have freshwater clams (*hułtl'ołga'*), apparently in some abundance. I cannot re-member ever seeing any, despite visiting many lakes; so they must be fairly rare. In any case, Koyukon people are forbidden to eat them, because eating *frogs* is strictly tabooed. Clams, they explain, are the first stage of the frog—their shells are even named *noghuy lootl'ok,* "where frogs came from." One is literally the other, an appropriate status for two anomalous creatures of the boreal forest.

6

The Fishes

Abundant Swimmers

It is midsummer. The pale blue sky is scattered with tall clouds that rise on thermals from the sun-warmed land. Distant stands of willows shimmer in distorted light above the sandbars. At their edge, the river runs swift and silent, reflecting tall timber atop undercut banks. Swallows weave figures of eight above the cool brown water, tinkling the air with calls.

At scattered places along the river, peculiar indentations in the bank create slow current eddies, natural resting spots for fish. In the best of these, long rows of net floats extend from the bank outward to the main current's edge. And not far from each net site, a tent is nestled beside the timber and a streamer of smoke diffuses into the calm heat. Near the water's edge, a latticework of drying racks hangs heavy with cut fish, bright red flesh against the dark backdrop of forest.

The interior wildlands of Alaska are strewn with an infinite assortment of rivers and lakes, many of them connected by long water ribbons that coalesce and extend clear to the sea. All of these waterways, except the smallest and most landlocked, are inhabited by fish, some of them residents and others seasonal migrants from the remote ocean. A fair number of fish species occur here, and in some years they provide a rich harvest for the Koyukon people. Equally impressive is the quality of these fish—most belong to the salmon-trout family (*Salmonidae*), perhaps the most esteemed eating fish in the world. The Koyukon are indeed blessed by their waters.

This does not mean they are a fishing society, in the sense that their economy is so focused. In certain years fish may be more abundant than all other resources; but in others they are relatively scarce. During Sullivan's stay at Nulato (1936–37), for example, fishing was more important to the economy than hunting. In later years, however, this was not the case at all. In the following chapters this same pattern will emerge for many kinds of resources. Nevertheless, fish are a very important part of the Koyukon economy, and their pursuit strongly affects the design of Koyukon culture and lifeways.

Salmon are the most spectacular of the fish resources. From midsummer through fall they run in great schools up the Yukon and Koyukuk, into the tributaries and the headwater creeks—here, spent and dying, they end their life cycle where it began several years earlier. But many of them end their journey farther downstream, intercepted by Koyukon fishnets.

Next in importance to salmon are the whitefish, whose abundance often equals or exceeds that of their larger kindred. These rich and delicious fish never enter the sea, but they do migrate seasonally between the rivers and lakes. The other salmonids—Dolly Varden and grayling—are taken in far smaller numbers. Northern pike, burbot, longnose sucker, and Alaska blackfish complete the list of species found in Koyukon country. Because the people make use of every species, one or another is usually available at every season; and should any fail there will probably be an alternative to replace it. This means that fishing is fairly reliable and can be done almost year-round (except for midwinter).

The Koyukon and other Athapaskan people have a special genius for devising ways to make animals trap, entangle, or ensnare themselves while the hunter is elsewhere. Their traditional fishing methods, focused on a variety of specialized and extremely clever traps, also show this genius. These ranged from complex weir systems in the major rivers to small basket traps set in creeks and lakes. All fish species were caught with traps in the old days, but since the advent of new fishnet materials traps have mostly been given up (see Osgood 1940:226–36 for detailed descriptions of Athapaskan fish traps). Koyukon people still make traps occasionally, such as large river weirs for burbot, which are usable long after thick ice forces them to remove any nets.

Cotton and nylon nets have replaced the traditional ones, which were made from far less durable and less effective willow bark. Once this happened, the Koyukon turned their intricate knowledge of fish behavior to this new technology. Now they use gill nets for almost every kind of fish, at nearly all seasons, under any water conditions, and at each specific location in a given waterway system. Just as Koyukon fishing was once based primarily on traps, today most of it is done with gill nets.

Fish are also caught with hook and line, especially pike, burbot, sheefish, grayling, and some whitefish. People still use the old-style handlines with lures, especially for ice fishing in the spring and fall; but when they fish in open water they prefer the modern rod and reel. Compared with nets, hook and line fishing is not very productive; but in certain situations it is the best and most convenient way to catch fish, and it is always the most fun. I also wonder if enjoyment might have been the prime motive behind an improbable old method of fishing: At certain clear-water eddies beneath steep banks, Koyukon people used to catch whitefish by slipping a snare around the narrow part of their tails and jerking them from the water!

Fishing dominates the lives of Koyukon villages through the summer months. Often they live in riverside camps near the best fishing places, where they wait at the behest of the fish. It is for the fish to decide whether to appear in abundance or scarcity, to pass the nets in midstream or move into the eddies where they can be caught. Waiting passively, the people can only hope that their nets are set well and that the fish will come to them.

In the face of such uncertainty, the Koyukon bring favor upon themselves by respecting the spiritual power of fish. The people I worked with in Huslia and Hughes did not outline elaborate rules for treating fish properly (as they did for some animals), but they followed the general premise that fish must not be disrespected, defiled, or wasted. Fish have a fairly powerful spirit, though it is the unnamed kind (see chap. 2) and not the potent *biyeega hoolaanh*. Interestingly, the nets possess this very strong spirit, which can punish anyone who steals fish from them or uses them without permission.

The Nulato Koyukon, who harvest the richer fish resources of the Yukon River, have (or at least had) some elaborate ritual observances for fish. In former times, shamans undertook seances to summon the fish upstream; and when the first king salmon was caught a short ceremony was given for it (Sullivan 1942:20–22). The Nulato people emphasized that all fish should be handled carefully—moved gently, kept clean, protected from scavengers, and stored securely. Fish must also not be eaten at the same meal with porcupine, Sullivan notes (p. 113), because their spirits would be offended by contact with this animal and the violator would suffer poor fishing as a result.

> A man has to be careful . . . not to throw fish bones where people will walk on them. "It don't look right, it isn't good—it's just like we don't care. When we are hard up, all this could come back to us, and we know we are being punished. . . ."
> Children are taught all this at an early age, and are warned against "fooling" with the fish, or stepping on it when it lies about before being used. The adults immediately scold the youngsters if they see them wasting fish or acting in a disrespectful way, and generally speaking, they themselves set a good example in this matter. [Sullivan 1942:19]

The spirit power of fish is not entirely dangerous to people—it can also protect them from supernatural harm. Pieces of dried fish skin or bone help to ward off malevolent forces or prevent a person from losing his or her spirit when suddenly confronted by a harmful power. A small bit of dried fish nailed inside a house will safeguard its occupants. Children may be protected from the lingering spirit of someone who has recently died by carrying a piece of dried or fresh fish, or especially dried vertebrae from the tail end of a fish. In the old days they even wore little vests made from dried fish skin, purely for spiritual protection. I have also seen men weave a strip of fish skin into their snowshoes to protect themselves from supernatural encounters in the remote forests.

My Koyukon teachers did not explain why fish have the kind of spirits and power they do. Nor did they explain why *any* particular class or species of animal manifests certain kinds of spirit powers—why some are strong and others weak, some are malevolent and others benign. There is little apparent order that an outsider could use to predict the way a given animal's spirit would manifest itself. This can be known only through the teachings of the elders, who usually take the Distant Time stories as their authority. This is my understanding, at least, though others may find a pattern I have failed to see.

The Salmon

In the fullness of midsummer, when bits of fuzz from willow catkins begin to drift on the breeze, elders turn their eyes to the river. Those whose vision is still acute may see a slight disruption on the glassy water, a nearly imperceptible V-shaped wave, as if a stick or rock is just beneath the surface. But it moves slowly, silently upstream.

> *Wait, I see something: We come upstream in red canoes.*
> *Answer: The migrating salmon.*
> [Jetté 1913:196]

In their traditional metaphors, the Koyukon people often spoke of salmon traveling in canoes, and here the red is an allusion to their breeding colors. When the first king salmon was caught, the Nulato Koyukon laid it on the beach, and people sprinkled water on it with willow twigs dipped into the river. While doing this, they said "Pull up your canoe here," asking that many fish would come to their camps (Jetté 1911:251).

My Koyukon teachers said that male and female salmon usually swim up the river in pairs, males on the shoreward side and females toward the center. The male fish are "lining up the river," helping the females, the way people used to pull their boats upstream with long lines from the shore. Fishnets prove this, they say, because males tend to be caught toward the shoreward end; and if the mesh size is right for catching both sexes, pairs are often entangled side-by-side. For some reason, I never thought to check this for myself during the many times I helped to pull the bulky, wiggling fish from the nets.

Three species of salmon run in the Koyukuk River. Of these, the dog or chum salmon (*Onchorhynchus keta*) is by far the most prolific. Individual daily catches of this fish vary between ten and two hundred, depending on the year and the phase of the run; and seasonal catches range from a few hundred to about two thousand. The dog salmon (*noolaagha*, which may translate as "island swimmer") is fair sized—about seven to twenty pounds—but unfortunately is not very rich. As the English name implies, it is principally used for dog food. Only the best ones, the small percentage with iridescent scales and bright red flesh, are saved for human use. But in many villages there are as many dogs as people, so the yearly need for fish is very great indeed.

The king or Chinook salmon (*O. tshawytscha;* called *ggaał* in Koyukon) is far less common than the dog salmon, but it is a prized delicacy because of its rich and tasty meat. Kings are not only the best salmon, but also the largest, ranging from ten to about fifty pounds. They are fairly rare in the Koyukuk River, so people sometimes visit their friends' or relatives' fish camps on the Yukon, where they catch plenty to bring home.

They also go there for silver or coho salmon (*O. kisutch*), which are second in quality to the kings. These fish are smaller (about ten to twenty pounds), but rich and fat, and they only have a small run in the Koyukuk. Summer silvers are called *saan laagha,* "summer swimmer," one of the few fish names with a clear translation. Fall silvers, which have become red and have hooked jaws, are called *nołdlaagha* in Koyukon. These fish are uncommon and not much preferred as food because they are lean like the dog salmon.

Since most salmon are caught in the warmth of July and August, there must be a way to preserve them. Some are eaten fresh, and nowadays some are stored in freezers, but most of the catch is dried. This slow and laborious task is done primarily by women, who are also the main net-tenders. Men, children, and elders of both sexes help out, but fishing is really the women's business. The work required to preserve fish allows people to stretch an ephemeral resource into one they can use all year long. Koyukon people have a wide selection of recipes for preparing salmon and other fish. Nearly all of them, in my experience, bring forth a delicious result.

Salmon not only are useful, they are powerful, probably more so than any other fish. The spiritual treatment and protective uses of fish that I mentioned earlier are most strongly associated with salmon. For example, children may be sheltered from the danger of "bad spirits" (*nik'itsaałdaagha, dinaaghaneedee*) by wearing dried salmon tails around their necks or carrying them in their pockets.

But all is not so serious, either. After eating dried salmon, people like to roast the skin over a fire until grease sputters on it, then eat it as a crispy treat. Children especially enjoy this, and as the skin heats up they recite a little formula: "Now the salmon is coming up the Yukon," they begin; and a few minutes later, "Now it is coming up the Koyukuk." Depending on where they are, they might say, "And now it is coming up the Dulbi." Finally they trace the salmon's journey to the fire they are standing over. I saw people do this but was never told whether the formula was for power or for fun.

Salmon are influenced by other spoken words, however. If people in a fish camp see a tree drifting downstream, half-sunken so it is vertical in the water, they may shout to it: "Let the fish pass on this side of you!" This done, the fish are said to swim near shore, where the gill nets wait to entangle them.

> *Wait, I see something: It is spreading softly on the surface of the water.*
> *Answer: Blood from the king salmon, clubbed in the water so it will not*
>   *upset the canoe when it is pulled inside.*
> [Jetté 1913:196]

Whitefish and Trout

Five species of whitefish and two species of trout inhabit the waterways of Koyukon country. Some are uncommon, others are at least periodically abundant, and all are fat and delicious. They range in size from the sheefish, which can weigh up to sixty pounds, to the least cisco and grayling, usually weighing only a pound or so. Some of these fish are very difficult to tell apart, but they are separated in both English and Koyukon taxonomies:

broad whitefish (*Coregonus nasus*)	taasiza'
least cisco (*C. sardinella*)	tsaabaaya
Alaska whitefish (*C. nelsonii*)	holahga
round whitefish (*Prosopium cylandraceum*)	hultin'
sheefish (*Stenodus leucichthys*)	nidlaagha
grayling (*Thymallus arcticus*)	tłaghalbaaya
Dolly Varden (*Salvelinus malma*)	ggaał yeega' (?) or siłyee lookk'a

The first five are grouped as whitefish in the Western taxonomy. The list of Koyukon terms above is minimal, and I learned of at least one more. This is a small fish (about six inches) with bluish scales, called *biłtibidza,* which may be a young broad whitefish.

The whitefish seem to be almost constantly on the move. Sheefish make long seasonal migrations up and down the major rivers, and the other whitefish move not only within the rivers but also in and out of the lake systems. In spring, schools of them enter the tributary streams and eventually congregate in certain lakes for the summer; in fall the movement is reversed. But there are also permanent river and lake populations. Old-timers say that large whitefish (probably broad whitefish) wintering in the lakes spend long periods hanging vertically in the water, snouts pointed toward the bottom, barely moving.

Whitefish are caught with nets or hooks in spots where schools mill and pass by at certain times of year. Watching such events for many generations, the Koyukon have learned their precise timing and location, their predictable variants, and the best ways to harvest them. This is well illustrated by whitefish seining, done along certain gravel bars near the villages of Hughes and Allakaket. It can succeed only in dusky light during the last days before freeze-up, and when the water is not running high. When this is done correctly and timed well, masses of fish can be taken and then simply allowed to freeze for winter storage. I have seen the long riverboats almost gunwale-deep in the water, loaded with a single evening's catch.

Trout and whitefish are given the same respect that should be accorded all fish, but they are not treated in other special ways. Formerly, Koyukon people had a small ceremony when the first whitefish was taken in spring. They had survived another winter—cause enough for a celebration—and now the secure abundance of summer was just ahead.

The whitefish ceremony had its frivolity, as everyone in the settlement joined in a footrace. But it was also serious: The first-caught fish was cooked, and people had to eat it without disarticulating any of its bones. It was especially important to keep the ribs and backbone intact by flaking the meat off with great care. If any bones fell out of place it foretold bad luck in the season ahead. Signs like this not only forecast the future but seem to actually cause or compel the events they predict. In some cases (discussed later) the sign and its effect can be negated by doing the right thing immediately; but most omens seem fairly binding.

Northern Pike

Looking into the water at the lake's edge, I noticed a pike waiting in ambush, its mottled body almost perfectly camouflaged amid a tangle of weeds. It was still except for the pulsing of its gills and occasional twitching of its fins and tail. Suddenly it exploded toward the open depths, leaving a swirl of water in its wake. In the wavering shadows I saw its jaws open wide and snap down on a smaller pike, whose panic flight came an instant too late. The fish hovered a moment, then dashed off to swallow its luckless prey. After devouring its still-struggling catch, the fish returned to the sun-warmed shallows, where its meal would digest more quickly. [Huslia journal, July 1977]

Northern pike (*Esox luscius*) may be the most voracious predators in the boreal forest. They are large fish, from five to fifty pounds and up to four feet long, with torpedo bodies and jaws armed with hundreds of sharp, recurved teeth. Shallow lakes abound with pike, as do many streams and sloughs; and the largest ones live in the river itself. In the right places, twenty or more can be caught on hook and line in an hour, having turned their appetite on the flashing lure. Koyukon people take large numbers in fishnets through the open-water season. They fight in the meshes like no other fish, and removing them is not only tedious but also dangerous because of their teeth. Describing a habit of his son, a man once told me, "That boy twists all up in his blankets at night, just like a pike in a net."

The Koyukon say that during one time of year, just when the ice is melting from the lakes, pike do little or no feeding. But when the water starts to warm they become ravenous. They will grab almost anything that moves in or on the water—mice, baby muskrats, weasels, birds, any fish—and they have been known to bite a hand carelessly dangled in the water.

I will risk my credibility with a fish story: Once, as I reeled in a pike I had caught, another charged up and grabbed the lure, tearing it from the first fish's mouth and catching itself. Then, as I pulled my new fish toward shore, a third, much larger pike suddenly lunged right into its body with jaws agape and refused to let go despite the great struggle that ensued. Only when I pulled the two ashore was the dispute settled in my favor. Small wonder that pike are named *k'oolkkoya,* "that which darts, or is thrown, at something," and that someone with a nasty disposition may be called "mean as a pike."

> *In the Distant Time, the pike ate a little baby that had just been fed from its mother's breast. The baby became its liver, and this is why a white fluid comes from pike liver when it is being cooked.*

Pike are not a prized food, but they are eaten for variety or when other fresh fish are unavailable. Large ones have the most fat, especially after the heavy feeding of early summer. The smaller, leaner pike are usually fed to the dogs. Koyukon people eat many parts of fish besides the meat; for example, the pike's stomach, intestines, air bladder, liver, and head are all considered edible. People are somewhat reluctant to eat pike head, though, because it is said to cause headaches, especially on hot days.

Given their extraordinary character and their uniqueness as the one fish that can be watched regularly in the water (making them more a part of the human world), it is not surprising that pike are invested with strong spiritual powers. These are often turned to the benefit of people, because they frighten or ward off various kinds of evil. An old shaman is remembered for using the pike spirit to cure people, who then avoided eating the fish for some time afterward.

In years past, children wore bracelets made from a pair of toothy lower jawbones, fastened together to form a circle and wrapped in a protective sheath of moose hide. One person told me that it guarded against spiritual danger, and another said that young boys who wore it would become skilled hunters like the pike itself. Also, a dried pike's head with jaws opened to show its teeth was sometimes nailed on a cabin door to ward off bad spirits. This was done especially at the lonely trapline cabins.

The only special treatment I learned for pike, aside from the usual gestures of respect, is that they must never be shot. Pike sometimes congregate in clear shallows where they could be taken this way. A recurrent theme in Koyukon morality toward nature emphasizes the alienating effects of metal. In the early days following contact, fish were never supposed to be brought into contact with metallic things. Today people are still restricted from using certain metal objects or machinery near specified animals or in particular circumstances. And, of course, using a rifle to catch fish is in itself a peculiar event, in a world where peculiarities and inappropriate juxtapositions are taken as ill warnings.

Koyukon people also tell of a giant pike, called *taahdlitona*, "stays still in the water." A fair number of them have actually seen such fish, which are known to favor certain places. One of these is the mouth of the Huslia River (*Hu\yakk'atna*) not far from Huslia, a dangerous place because the great fish inhabits it. A shaman who used the creature's spirit power for making medicine saw a giant pike at this spot, swimming with many normal pike.

An old Huslia man told me he once saw a giant pike while he was ice fishing on the Yukon. He described the eerie sensation of watching its great, broad back pass slowly, almost interminably, beneath the hole. Two other elders from the village had encountered one and shot it. It was so large that they cut it into three sections and carried away only the middle part. These men were still living when I was in Huslia.

Blackfish

I turn now from the giant to the midget, the tiny blackfish (*Dallia pectoralis*), which seldom grows more than six inches long. What these fish lack in size they make up in peculiarities. They live in lakes throughout Koyukon country, and in certain ones they must be incredibly prolific. By late winter the frozen lakes sometimes become critically short of oxygen, and blackfish begin swarming at natural openings—muskrat pushups, beaver runways, and current holes. The sluggish little fish constantly swirl to the surface gasping air, and over the days and weeks they gradually enlarge the hole.

Thousands of fish school around some openings, where they become prey for ravens, otters, and other predators that happen along. I have seen holes like this, strewn with half-eaten fish, the snow tramped hard all around by animals that return time and again to feed. People can fish in these places too, and in the old days blackfish swarms saved many from hardship, even from starvation. Using traps or dip nets, they might catch bushels of fish if they found a good swarm. This is still done occasionally, but people do not put much effort into catching blackfish nowadays.

The greatest curiosity about blackfish is their ability to forestall death. When people make a big catch they sometimes pile the fish beside the hole and cover them with a mound of snow. Those on the outside of the pile will freeze and die, but if the inside ones do not freeze solid they can live out of water for about two weeks.

Blackfish are called *oonyeeyh* (roughly translated, "sustenance"), and the Koyukon also distinguish several varieties—a brownish one (*dzonhyee*, "murky back"), a flat, slender one (*dagheets'eelee*, "slender one"), mentioned in Jetté's dictionary (n.d.*a*), and a large black one (*gidzeełbaanh*). This last kind is tabooed for young boys, who would acquire its slow clumsiness if they ate it. Otherwise, Koyukon people regard blackfish as a rich and fairly desirable food.

Another small fish, possibly the slimy sculpin (*Cottus cognatus*), lives in the swift, clear headwaters. It is only two or three inches long and has a big head that may account for its Koyukon name—*nitsootlee'*, "your grand-mother's head." It is food for animals like the otter, but not for people. Jetté (n.d.*a*) says that children are warned not to kill it, because doing so will bring rain.

Burbot

The burbot or louche (*Lota lota*) is a freshwater cod that inhabits lakes, streams, and major rivers. It moves slowly along the bottom, preying on anything its oversized mouth can catch. Its Koyukon name (*tl'aghas*) means roughly "something fat," or perhaps the appropriate "lump head" suggested by Jetté (n.d.*a*). Its peculiar stretched-out shape is explained in a story from the Distant Time, when the burbot-man decided to enter the water and was held back by his friends (see chap. 3 for a fuller recounting).

These strange-looking fish are usually between five and twenty pounds, but they can reach fifty pounds or more. Many are caught in Koyukon fishnets, and they are also taken with hook and line, especially through the ice in fall. Burbot liver is considered excellent, and the meat, head, and eggs are also eaten. Young people are not allowed to eat the eggs, however, because they are stout and bulky, which would cause the violator to have children with big, clumsy legs.

Longnose Sucker

The longnose sucker (*Catostomus catostomus*) is a singularly unattractive fish, a bottom feeder that prefers sluggish, muck-bottomed places. Suckers are caught in fishnets, especially at the mouths of sloughs, but people make no great effort to catch them except when food is short in the early spring.

Suckers have little meat except around the head, which is their best part. The liver is also cooked, and the air bladder and visceral fat are eaten raw. Koyukon people do not eat the eggs, testes, and other viscera.

In the Distant Time the sucker was a thief, which accounts for its name—*toonts'oda,* "bad person from the water." Sucker-man went around stealing things, and when he became a fish these things became a strange collection of bones in his head. Occasionally, when people are eating boiled sucker, an elder will carefully pick the skull apart and find each of the items that sucker-man stole. While this is done the story is told. For example, there is a bone shaped like a pair of moose antlers; there are two duck's feet, two little combs, and even a stump with a splayed-out base. After cramming these things (and more) into his head, the sucker had no room left for a bunch of needles he also took—these became the fine bones in his tail.

As I mentioned in an earlier chapter, Koyukon people do not think well of the sucker because of its transgressions in the Distant Time, and some even avoid eating it lest they acquire its thieving personality. Here again the Koyukon know a kind of interchange with the natural world that is quite beyond a Westerner's conception. Humans and animals share a communality of being, a mutual sphere of influence, a spiritually bound moral unity. To the outsider's detached eye it is another universe indeed, where the ethics of fish and humans are not separated.

7

The Birds

Birds are abundant and conspicuous inhabitants of the boreal forest, and the Koyukon people consider them prominent members in the community of natural beings. Traditional Koyukon knowledge of birds is voluminous and detailed, reflecting their cultural importance. In this chapter I have aimed toward a fairly thorough recording of this knowledge, though it does not approach completeness. It is intended as a *native ornithology,* an introductory account of this rich element in Koyukon natural history. Surprisingly little information of this kind has been recorded in the ethnographic or ornithological literature for native people anywhere in the world. With this in mind, I have included what some may find an overabundance of detail, knowing that others will see the need for more.

Heralds of the Summer

The boreal winter is a time of stillness and of silence that can be near absolute. The world becomes inert, and often the wind alone brings motion or sound. Of course there are animals, but they move at the edge of human vision, hidden by dusk or dark, earth or snow. The few birds that remain north through the winter tend to pursue the business of life quietly, seriously, saving their more exuberant activity and song for another time. Those of us who delight in being among crowds of living things often find the cold season a lonely one. We await the summer.

> The long trail to *Tsotlyeet* cabin had been clear and cold, with five inches of new snow slowing the dogs. The temperature was

near zero that night (April 28) when I went to sleep, and later I heard wind in the timber outside. The thought of more cold and storm depressed me.

Crawling from my sleeping bag the next morning, I was amazed to find the cabin warm inside. And then I heard it, above the sighing wind—a chorus of birdsongs! I hurried out the door to see the newly wet snow, the water dripping from the porch roof, and to hear the long-awaited sounds. There were robin songs and the creaking notes of blackbirds; and from the nearby flats I could hear geese and sandhill cranes calling. Through the binoculars, I saw long flocks of geese flying northward on the stiff tailwind.

The next day, when I hunted with Steven and Catherine at *Hudaałggaat Dinh,* a profusion of birds filled the land and sky. I saw and heard thousands of geese, hundreds of cranes, rusty blackbirds, robins, juncos, snipes, Bonaparte's and herring gulls, Arctic terns, Lapland longspurs, whistling swans, short-eared owls, some unidentified hawks, and many other birds whose calls I did not know. All this in country that was nearly lifeless two days before. Coming on a tide of warmth, the birds had vanquished winter at last. [Huslia journal, April 1977]

The Koyukon people share this excitement in the birds' return, and for many of the same reasons. Birds bring life back to the boreal wildlands, not only life that can be hunted and eaten, but life serving no other human "purpose" than to be seen and heard. They are the conspicuous animals, whose motion, color, song, and simple living presence transforms the northern world. In the Koyukon language, birds are collectively named *saanh ggaagga*—"summer animals"—each being almost inseparable from the others.

The day the first flights of migratory birds appear is one of the year's most noteworthy for the traditional Koyukon, along with the summer and winter solstices, the beginning of freeze-up, the first day of breakup, and the arrival of the salmon (Jetté 1909:5–6). Probably no event is awaited with more enthusiasm or greeted with greater pleasure. The reasons are not purely aesthetic, of course—the birds' arrival ends the season when food most often becomes short, and when in former times starvation most often occurred. Waterfowl are a particularly important resource during this period; in the past they provided a secure food supply at a critical time, and they are still the first source of fresh meat after the long winter's passage.

Wait, I see something: Little dots are far away in the distance.
Answer: The migratory birds returning.
[Jetté 1913:191]

However crucial they might be at particular times, birds do not approach the importance of fish and mammals in the overall Koyukon economy.

They are a "secondary" resource, but nevertheless one given extremely high cultural value as a native delicacy (I am thinking particularly of the waterfowl, but also of birds like grouse and ptarmigan). Measures of economic importance too often overlook these more subtle considerations, focusing instead on kilograms and calories. People everywhere make strong emotional and psychological investments in the food they eat, and the Koyukon regard for certain birds reflects this. So while I call this a secondary resource, I doubt they would ever conceive of such a judgment.

In addition, the cultural value of birds goes far beyond their esteem as food or their importance as an economic resource. Koyukon people are deeply involved in other ways with these animals—emotionally, aesthetically, and spiritually. Most of the following discussions will focus on these dimensions, the ways Koyukon people perceive and interact with birds.

I have included in this chapter some information on every species I could learn about from the modern Koyukon. Certain species are dealt with at length, but others are given little more than a name, perhaps only an uncertain identification. In all, the chapter covers about ninety birds, of which fewer than half (about thirty-seven) are utilized. I have chosen to group or organize species mainly according to Linnean taxonomy, and these categories should not be taken to represent a Koyukon system. In general, the economically important species are covered first, and those whose significance is largely cultural come later.

But I will begin—as did the Koyukon world—with the raven.

Raven

Here is the greatest character in the boreal forest, a judgment that may well transcend all cultural predispositions. The raven is almost universally familiar, a large ebony bird, the size of a hawk but utterly lacking the hawk's dignity, fierceness, and strength. What the raven has is a gift of cleverness and a potent ego, combined with audacious wit. In some ways the raven is a clown, but only if the humans it is said to have created are clowns as well. Both have genius, both love play, and both are perhaps too much inclined toward guile.

Ravens are a part of most days in the boreal wildlands, flapping determinedly toward some unknown destination, performing aerobatic follies in pairs or trios, croaking loudly somewhere in the distance. They remain in the north summer and winter, going about their dubious affairs regardless of heat or bitter cold. And they are everywhere, from dense river forests to broad muskegs and meadows, even to the tundra mountains, where they play and circle on the rushing updrafts. Whatever else ravens may be, they are indeed successful. But then, who should know better how to live on the land than its own designer?

It began with *Dotson'sa,* the Great Raven, who created and then recreated the world. He is the preeminent figure in stories of the Distant Time, appearing in many forms or disguises, manipulating and conjuring, and engineering the metamorphoses of nature to its present form (as described in chap. 2). But for those of us accustomed to remote and hallowed deities the Great Raven seems a most unlikely personage indeed.

> *It was during the run of the salmon.* Dotson'sa, *the Great Raven, was living in a camp with his two wives. He slept between them, covered with a dog skin blanket. One day he went out hunting with his nephews, who killed a caribou, butchered it, then decided to camp nearby for the night. While they were sleeping, Raven sneaked to the cached meat and gobbled up every bit.*
>
> *When he finished, he suddenly shouted, "Ha! A brown bear has been here." Of course, he had stolen it all himself, but when the nephews came, he lamented, "The bear came from over there. And my poor nephews who depend on me alone! I was so drowsy for want of sleep that I finally dozed. Oh, what have I done!" But even as he spoke, he thought, "I was watching during their sleep, for I am a thief."*

This story, paraphrased from Jetté (1908:363–67), is one of many that portrays Raven as greedy, mannerless, and thoroughly undignified. He even sleeps beneath a dog skin, an almost unthinkably tasteless proposition for the Koyukon people. From stories of the Distant Time, Raven emerges as a liar, a thief, a glutton, and a trickster of the highest order. His power and his personality are terribly mismatched from an outsider's perspective. But this presents no difficulty for the Koyukon, who do not share the compulsion to invest such a being with an idealized, exemplary personality. The Raven is a magical clown, whose great spiritual power is mediated through an affable scoundrel. He is both king and court jester. It is no surprise that he first created a world of flawless order and ease, then later transformed it to the imperfect one we know today.

The Great Raven's descendants, who inhabit the forest today, still manifest some of the power and personality of their singular forefather. Koyukon people see ravens as prepotent, perhaps even omniscient, beings who often turn their spirituality and insight to the benefit of humankind. Ravens are also capable of bringing ill fortune, though it is not really their nature to do so, and people protect their own welfare by showing them certain kinds of respect.

There is a paradox here, however, one that mirrors the paradox of the Raven himself. While the Koyukon give deference to ravens, they also use them as the measure of impudence and trickery. When someone gets ahead by deceiving others, or promises a lot but produces little, people will say, "He's just like *dotson'*, just like a raven." I have heard them describe politicians this way, for example. Jetté (n.d.*a*) writes that people sometimes imitate a raven's call (*ggaakk!*) as an expression of scorn toward someone, especially to say, "I am a good hunter, but you are not." Or they may describe an article as "raven food" to indicate that it is good for nothing.

Anyone who watches ravens will easily understand these attitudes. They are not much given to working for an honest living. As one old man explained:

> *You know, raven don't hunt anything for himself. He gets his food the lazy way, just watches for whatever he can find already dead. Like in the old story, he always fools everybody so he gets by easy. Only thing raven ever kills is blackfish at a hole in the ice; otherwise I never heard of it kill something for itself.*

But what ravens lack in industriousness or predatory instinct, they make up for with ingenuity. They are ever watchful from high vantage, and sometimes it seems that only the invisible escapes them. If they find wolves feeding on a kill, they will land almost among them, flap around the meat and foul it with excrement. The wolves seem to pay little attention to them, but eventually, it is said, "the ravens somehow make them walk away." (I noticed that my sled dogs acted the same way, as if the ravens hopping around near them did not exist.) This leaves the food for the interlopers. People say that even the feisty and often ill-tempered wolverine will do nothing to drive off ravens that land beside it to steal food.

An elder man from Hughes told me about seeing otters fishing at an open spot in the ice. He noticed a raven circling high above, also watching them. An otter surfaced with a big louche (burbot) in its mouth, then climbed onto the ice to feed. Immediately the raven swooped down beside it and started flapping around, trying to peck at the fish. The otter did nothing to stop the harassment and finally just went away, leaving the fish for the raven.

Of course ravens watch people as well. When they hear shooting in the waterfowl season, for example, they fly toward the hunter and keep watch from someplace nearby. If a wounded bird drops and the hunter cannot find it, the sharp-eyed raven certainly will. Anyone who sets snares for snow-shoe hare or ptarmigan had better keep the raven in mind, either by checking the snares at dawn (before the raven does) or by placing them in heavy brush where the sneak thief might not spot a catch.

Koyukon people know at least one way to beat the raven at its own game. Sometimes meat or fish must be left in the open for a while, where the birds are sure to see it. They say that a knife or ax left beside the cached food will often frighten ravens away, especially if the blade points upward. Or hunters may put fake snares (*nohtibaatl*) over and around the meat—open loops made from willow withes. These seem to fool the trickster himself and keep him off the catch.

*In the Distant Time, Raven was living with his nephew, the mink.
Raven liked this arrangement, because he could eat the fish that mink had
cached around the lakes. But after a while he grew tired of fish and
suggested that mink should catch a bear. So they made a plan. Raven
split a fish wide open, and mink hid himself inside it; then they put the
fish next to a bear trail. When a bear came along, it swallowed the fish,
and mink crawled out of it and cut the bear's insides with his knife,
killing it.*

*The next time it was Raven's turn to hide in the fish. Although he
didn't like the idea at all, he finally consented. But when the bear came
along and was about to grab the fish, Raven suddenly jumped out, and
with a loud, frightened* Kwaawk! *he flew away. That's how ravens
are, always afraid.*

Ravens are treated with exactly the mixture of deference and contempt
that we might expect. First of all, their spirit is mostly benevolent toward
humans, and Koyukon people are not strictly bound in their behavior toward such creatures. The animals most capable of producing bad luck or
evil are treated with the greatest care. But people who spoke to me about
ravens always seemed a bit cautious and awed—they may be amiable
scoundrels, but they are powerful nonetheless. Still, they are sometimes
subjects of ridicule or good-natured insults, and they can be tricked.

Killing ravens is the greatest trickery of all. My Koyukon instructors
agreed that it is tabooed (*hutlaanee*) but were not sure that a violator would
be punished: "We just don't do it." A Huslia man once told me that ravens
are supposed to have very short intestines, "But we never kill them, so we
don't get to see it for ourselves. A guy here always says he's going to shoot
one and look, but he never does it."

Despite these feelings, people say that ravens can be killed as a form of
trickery, an ironic means of acquiring good luck in the best tradition of the
Great Raven himself. Sometimes, for example, a gun becomes "full of bad
luck" and cannot hit game as it should. One man whose shotgun was
afflicted is said to have gone out and shot a raven; when it fell, he spoke to it:
"I thought you were a different kind of bird. Now wish your bad luck on the
other birds." After he did this, ducks and geese became easy prey for his
shotgun, stricken as they were with the raven's bad fortune. The man who
told me this hastened to add that he would never kill a raven himself.

The same thing can be done when a raven gets caught in a trap set for fur
animals. It must be let go alive, but the trapper may tell it to wish its own
bad luck onto other animals so they too will be caught there. When one man
released a raven this way, he told it again and again that the trap was not set
for it, that it should have stayed away from the place. The bird flew away,
and afterward he caught many animals there. Once, however, three of his
dogs grabbed a trapped raven and tore it apart. Some time later all of them
froze to death.

Ravens can also benefit or forewarn people by giving signs. If a raven sees people hunting it will occasionally help them find game. It flies overhead, then toward an animal that is visible from above, calling *"ggaagga... ggaagga"* ("animal... animal"). This is no philanthropic gesture however: "He does that so he'll get his share from what the hunter leaves behind." Also, hunters who see a raven tuck its wing and roll over in the sky will have good luck that day. Sometimes they keep watching afterward, and the bird begins to circle and frolic in one place. This may show where a bear or moose is standing, so it is wise to look there.

> *We were hunting along the river in falltime, me and a couple of young boys. A raven flew over us real low, and I told those boys to watch closely where it went, so it might lead us to something. It went across to the far bank and flew right along above the edge. We followed it with the boat and, sure enough, we came onto a bear standing on top of the bank. We shot it right there.*

Not all signs from the raven are welcome. It is a powerful omen, fortunately also a very rare one, to hear a raven call in the night. One of my teachers had a single experience like this, when she went out of her house into the darkness and a raven called nearby. As she stood watching, adjusting her eyes to the dim moonlight, she saw it flutter down onto the ground, still calling. Knowing it was a strong sign of bad luck, she ran to her grandfather's house and told a group of men there what had happened. The old shaman said that something bad would occur, and one of the men joked that he would probably die. A year afterward his own prophecy, and the raven's, came true.

The power of this enigmatic bird is most directly manifested in its ability to grant human wishes, to answer brief prayers that are made to it. When this is done, the raven is addressed as *Tseek'aal,* "Old Grandfather." If a raven flies over or roosts nearby, people may call out to it, *"Tseek'aal,* bring us good luck!" Or "I wish everything would come our way easy!" A hunter will sometimes shout, *"Tseek'aal,* drop a pack down to me!" If the raven rolls partway over in flight, as if it is dropping a loaded pack from its back, the hunter will find game. If it just keeps flying normally, the contents of raven's metaphorical pack are not forthcoming—it will be a poor hunt.

> *It's just like talking to God, that's why we talk to the raven. He created the world.*

Ravens even have the power to influence life-and-death situations. A Huslia woman said that she once became very sick in a remote camp and was being taken home in a sled. A raven appeared, and flew along overhead for several miles. This was more than a coincidence, and so the woman made prayers, asking the bird to help her and her family. "If somebody gets very sick and then comes out of it, another person in their family might die instead. So I asked the raven to help them if I didn't die." She survived her illness, and no one in her family was afflicted afterward.

The unpredictable raven may not only give but also take away. After returning from a moose hunt, a man described the bird's elaborate trickery. As he and several others prepared to leave for the hunt, a raven flew over them and one of the hunters' wives shouted to it, asking for luck. On their first day out they shot a moose, which they butchered and left behind to pick up later. Expecting to be gone only a short time, they made no effort to cover the meat. But as things turned out they were gone overnight, and the next morning they found their catch partly eaten and fouled by ravens. When the hunters came home, the man told his wife that he would never talk to ravens again, after what they had done. But she only laughed at the bird's clever deception—it had given them luck, then used its power to make them neglectful. The trickster had again manipulated his pawns to assure himself a rich repast.

And so Raven plays his game of wits, his unending frolic through the carnival world of his own creation. The humans in his menagerie—for whom he devised mortality, rivers that flow only downstream, mosquitoes, and an assortment of other difficulties—can only look on and shake their heads, return a trick or two, and perhaps sing his mourning song (which I paraphrase from Jetté, n.d.*a*):

> *Old man, where is that for which your beak is searching?*
> *Oh! Alas! Old man, old man, old man.*

The Awkward Waterfowl

The Koyukon divide waterfowl into two classes, each of them regarded and used differently. The first of these is the *too ggaagga,* "animals that live in the water" (literally, "water animals"), and it includes the heavy-bodied water birds that cannot walk easily on land. The core members of this class are loons, grebes, and the red-breasted merganser; and it somewhat marginally includes scoters and the old-squaw duck.

The principal reason for setting these birds apart is their awkwardness on land, which makes them forbidden foods for adolescents and young adults, especially boys. This applies to certain species (not all of them) whose slow, clumsy walk would be acquired either by the young person who ate them or by children born to the violator. Older people are exempt from the taboo, especially after childbearing age. All these birds, incidentally, dive for their food rather than "dabbling" it on the surface, and they are very agile in the water (note, though, that the other class of waterfowl also includes many divers).

There is a story from long ago (but not the Distant Time), about some men who were traveling afoot on the winter snow. One of them was constantly breaking through the snow and stumbling, so the others left him far behind. Later on he told his mother about his difficulties, and she confessed that she knew the reason: Before he was born she had thought her childbearing days were over, so she began sleeping on a pillow stuffed with feathers from a too ggaagga *bird, a heavy-bodied and clumsy one. Her son was born afterward, and now she could see that her mistake had made him heavy and awkward on his feet.*

The Loons

I will begin with the common loon (*Gavia immer*), a bird whose English name is somewhat inappropriate for interior Alaska, where it certainly is not abundant; nor by anyone's standards could it be judged ordinary. Common loons are very large birds, strikingly marked with a geometric design in black and white. According to stories of the Distant Time, the man who became *dodzina,* the common loon, used his medicine to restore another man's sight. In return he was given a cape with elaborate dentalium-shell decorations (dentalium shells formerly reached interior Alaska through trade networks), and its pattern remains on the loon's back and neck.

Koyukon people so admire and appreciate this bird that they sometimes keep its stuffed skin as an object of beauty. The entire skin, with head and beak intact, is filled with dried grass, and often it is hung inside the house where people can always see it. Other birds and animals are also kept this way, either for aesthetic reasons or for good luck. One family in Huslia had a red-throated loon, snow bunting, harlequin duck, bufflehead, flicker, and least and short-tailed weasels hung in the main room of their house. The flicker and weasels were also elaborately decorated with jewelry trinkets.

The common loon is even more remarkable for its voice—a completely indescribable arrangement of high-pitched falsetto cries, long wailing laments, and eerie laughter. Heard at evening in the silent wildlands, from the shore of a lake surrounded by deep timber, it is the essence and beauty of the north country itself. The Koyukon people express great appreciation for the loon's call, not only because of its resplendent sound but also because it manifests the animal's considerable spirit powers.

Traditionally the elders have listened to the loon as a source of inspiration in composing their own songs. An old man from Hughes once tried to explain to me just how important and powerful this inspiration is. He told me a Koyukon saying, then gave a figurative translation to impart its full meaning and substance in English:

When a loon calls on a lake, it is the greatest voice that a human can hear. [Ots'aa dodzin tongheedo beeznee eenee'λon; literally, "The loon's call is the one against which all others are judged."]

This man showed a remarkable gift for seeing nature in special ways, and no animal seemed to impress him more deeply than the loon. Its compelling personality fascinated him and inspired his respect. Once he told me, at great length and with powerful words that came much faster than I could write exactly, about the loon's first arrival in spring:

> *Loons always come in after good weather turns cloudy and rainy, around breakup time. If you happen to be in the right place, at just the right time, you might hear a rushing sound coming from way up high above. Then if you look quickly and can see well, you might see a loon diving right down, headlong from the sky, with its wings folded back, coming straight toward that lake. At the very last moment, the loon will swoop up and fly level at great speed just over the water. Then it will make a long skim on the surface, finally stop, and dive down underneath.*
>
> *A minute later you'll see it bob up; and listen, you'll hear it make a short cry, soft . . . it's letting everything know, it's announcing: "Here I am!" That's the loon when it gets here for the first time in spring.*

Stories of the Distant Time say that Koyukon songs originated partly from the loon's crying and partly from the human imagination. Perhaps this too is why loon calls are especially meaningful. After the late elder, Chief Henry, passed away, I was sitting near his house with an old man from Allakaket. "It would be good to hear *dodzina* [the loon] right now," he said quietly. "We really like to hear that music." He had tears in his eyes as he talked about that beautiful wild voice, about hunters listening to it as they paddle their canoes from lake to lake in the spring. And he seemed to wish for it now as a good sign or a gift from the natural world to the spirit of a great hunter. I could scarcely have troubled him to explain further.

A few days earlier, while Chief Henry lay near death, an old woman from a Yukon village walked to the nearby shore of *Binkookk'a* Lake. She stood at the water's edge and sang Koyukon "spring songs" to a pair of loons that had been in the lake for several weeks. Shortly, the loons swam toward her until they rested in the water some fifty yards away, and there they answered her, filling the air with eerie and wonderful voices. When I spoke with her later, she said that loons will often answer spring songs this way. For several days people talked of how beautiful the exchange of songs had been that morning.

Loons can give signs in several different ways. If someone walks up to a lakeshore and a loon in the water dives immediately with an abrupt, alarmed note, it is a very bad sign. Done repeatedly, it foretells serious illness or death for the person or a close relative. A certain long, wailing cry, on the other hand, means that an animal is nearby, often a bear. A loon flying upstream low over the water, giving short wavering calls, is foretelling rainy weather. And a person can expect good luck if he sees a pair of loons running toward him across the water, bodies erect and wings cocked peculiarly behind them.

Common loons are rarely eaten, and then only by elders who need not fear becoming awkward and slow. In times of food shortage, however, people would hunt birds like this, preferring to risk clumsiness rather than starvation. The loon's eggs are never eaten, because disturbing its nest will cause a heavy wind.

> *Sometimes people will hunt the loon, but me, I don't like to kill it. I like to listen to it all I can and pick up the words it knows.*

The yellow-billed loon (*Gavia adamsii*) is nearly identical to the common loon in size, voice, and behavior. It also looks the same, except that its bill is creamy rather than black and is slightly different in shape. According to one very knowledgeable man, these two loons are actually varieties of one form in the Koyukon conception. But the yellow-billed loon (*dodibeeya*) is more powerful. It makes the same signs, but they are more significant. And "it says the same words, but its voice is just a little different." A person who kills one and keeps its skin will have a lifetime of good luck afterward; but they are extremely rare, so taking one is nearly unheard of. An elder from Hughes told me that he knew of only three people who had ever succeeded.

The Arctic loon (*Gavia arctica*) is a similar-looking but smaller bird, with a frost of white on its head. Its Koyukon name, *tl'idlibaa,* was translated by one person (perhaps rather imaginatively) as "active in the water." It is said to be very quick, "almost like an otter," so it is difficult to shoot. Only old people are permitted to eat it, and like the other loons its skin is sometimes stuffed and kept for its beauty.

The red-throated loon (*Gavia stellata*), like the Arctic loon, is not accorded special power or significance in Koyukon culture. It is called *tokootsaagha,* "cries into the water," and people rarely hunt or eat it. Only the meat of loons or grebes is used for food, not the head, feet, or viscera. People occasionally also use feathered skins to make covered cushions, taking advantage of their natural designs.

The Grebes

Of all the awkward waterfowl, the red-necked grebe (*Podiceps grisegena*) is the clumsiest—it is scarcely capable of walking on land. In Koyukon it is named *tokkaa'a,* "its feet work only in water." I heard people talking about a man who tried to take his boat somewhere in poor water conditions, when he should have walked instead. "He must be just like *tokkaa'a,*" someone said in explanation. If a grebe flies very low over people, they may shout or make loud noises, which can frighten the bird so it loses its equilibrium and falls. If it lands on the ground it can be caught by hand, because it cannot take off without making a long run on water.

This bird is strongly tabooed for any but the oldest people, so it is rarely eaten. When a pair of grebes is seen running across the water side-by-side, it forewarns of a strong wind. According to Jetté (n.d.*a*), these birds are also associated with wet snow—when it falls in spring, people say, "the grebe has come back," and in autumn they say, "the grebe has flown away."

The horned grebe (*Podiceps auritus*) is a smaller, less conspicuous, rather uncommon bird in Koyukon country, and very little is said of it. Some people feel it is strictly tabooed for all but the elders, but one man believed anyone could use it as food. In the Distant Time, he explained, the horned grebe (*dzeeyaakk*) was renowned as a runner, and so eating it will not cause clumsiness. Differences of belief like this one are fairly common among the Koyukon.

Red-breasted Merganser

Linnaean taxonomy classifies this bird (*Mergus serrator*) as a duck, though its streamlined appearance and narrow, saw-toothed beak make it seem quite different. It is certainly an exquisite bird, geometrically marked on its body, with sharp feather crests on its brightly colored head. Mergansers (called *tsaghul*) are occasionally hunted by the Koyukon, and some people enjoy their tender meat, especially taken in the fall and roasted. Others say they care very little for the taste. Anyone can eat them, however, because they are not burdened with clumsiness like most of the other *too ggaagga*.

Koyukon people greatly admire the gaudy plumage of male mergansers, and so they are sometimes stuffed for people to admire at home. A Hughes elder once told me:

> *That's one of the fanciest birds there is. In* Kk'adonts'idnee *[Distant Time] his wife was one of the best needleworkers; she made him beautiful clothes and that's why he's so pretty today. I've tried to get one for so many years, just for the looks of the color. I want to look at it. But I never did get any. Somebody that gets one, he'll be a lucky hunter, but his money will always go fast.*

The Scoters

These are good-sized, but rather plain, black diving ducks. Two species frequent the larger lakes in Koyukon country, especially during the spring migration. Scoters are not given any special importance in the spiritual world of the Koyukon, but they are generally considered good eating and are regularly hunted. Outsiders might find their meat a bit tough and odd tasting, but the Koyukon appreciate that they are fatter than most ducks. Hunters know that these heavy birds must take a long run across the water before they can become airborne. This makes them especially vulnerable if they are cornered against the shore of a timbered lake, so they have to run toward the boat to take off.

White-winged scoters (*Melanitta deglandi*) are often called *yoolyeesga,* "whistling," a name said to describe their voice. They are hunted from spring into early summer (June), somewhat later than the other ducks because they wait longer to nest. The Koyukon avoid taking birds once nesting has begun, to foster their reproduction. People consider the white-winged scoter excellent eating, but unfortunately it is not found in very large numbers here.

This is the only scoter tabooed for young people because of its clumsiness, and not everyone accepts the prohibition. It has a second name in Koyukon—*ts'inh daadlagguya*—which means "wings are gray." Perhaps this is because when it flies the white speculum in its wings is so prominent. Like the surf scoter, this bird inhabits gravel-bottomed lakes; but it is far more common near the Yukon than along the Koyukuk.

The surf scoter (*Melanitta perspicillata*) is probably more abundant, but its tough meat detracts from people's enthusiasm for hunting it. These birds are taken along with other ducks in migration, and like the surf scoter they are hunted in early summer because they nest late. Their Koyukon name, *dotson'alaayh,* refers vaguely to their looking like the raven.

Old-squaw

This little duck (*Clangula hyemalis*) is fairly common in Koyukon country through the warm months, preferring especially the largest lakes (like the scoters, it is far more abundant on the Alaska coast). Their numbers are greatest during spring migration, the only time when much effort goes toward hunting them. In some years they are unusually abundant just after breakup, which is taken as a sign that many fish will come with summer.

The Koyukon identify two varieties of old-squaw. The first is called by the general name for the species (*aahaaga* or *aanhaaga*), which mimics its singular call. This variety is dark-headed, common, and stays along the Koyukuk all summer. It is also smaller, leaner, and considerably less tasty than the second type (*nodabaaghayee,* "coast bird"), which has a white head and only migrates through. This one is much preferred as food, but it is not at all common (bird guide books identify the two varieties as summer and winter plumages; e.g., Armstrong 1980:68). Old-squaws are tabooed for young people, who would acquire clumsiness or pass it to their children if they ate this bird.

The Agile Waterfowl

The second major class of waterfowl is called *nuggu ggaagga,* "animals that go out on land" (literally, "land animals"). This includes all geese and most of the ducks, birds that can walk easily and are light bodied. Young people who eat these birds are likely to become agile and light-footed, therefore well suited as providers; and their children may be similarly endowed.

It is good fortune, to say the least, that agile waterfowl can be eaten by everyone—they are generally far more abundant and available than the awkward ones, and they are rich, delicious eating. As I mentioned before, the Koyukon regard these birds as delicacies, and they prepare them in ways that would convince any skeptic. Most often, waterfowl are cooked in "soups" with noodles, rice, and vegetables; they are also roasted or broiled (a special treat when done over a campfire). In former years, when summer freezing was not possible, ducks and geese could be stored only by drying them. This is not often done today.

Besides waterfowl meat, Koyukon people eat the gizzard, stomach, intestines, liver, head, and feet, as well as the eggs (which are rarely gathered today). Eggs found inside female ducks are tabooed for young people, because they would cause clumsiness. The feathers are used for stuffing quilts, mattresses, pillows, parkas, and socks. Dried goose wings are also very efficient brooms if the user is willing to bend low enough.

The agile waterfowl are invested with spirits that must be respected to avoid alienating them or bringing bad luck to the gun that killed them. Ideally, their unused parts should be returned to the water as a reverential gesture, not thrown in a fire or left on the ground to rot. People vary in their adherence to this, but I saw little carelessness with these birds. Burning waterfowl feathers will cause bad luck for the hunter by making his or her shotgun ineffectual. Following a lesson from a Distant Time story, Koyukon people should avoid plucking waterfowl so their feathers fly out onto the water, lest they cause a heavy wind.

Whistling Swan

The great and beautiful swans (*Olor columbianus*) arrive with the thaw in early May and are the last waterfowl to leave in early October. When long ribbons of swans pass noisily high in the cold fall air, Koyukon people say that freeze-up will come very soon afterward. Swans are most common here in the spring migration, but some are always around through the summer, mated pairs widely scattered among the lakes. By early June they have built nests on floating moss along the shore, and soon the dark little ones can be seen swimming with their elegant parents.

The whistling swan (*tobaa* in Koyukon) is perhaps more spiritually empowered than any other waterfowl. An elder told me that it is one of the smartest birds and has been since the Distant Time: "It knows everything." To support this, he said that swans frequent only certain lakes, ones rich in food, that they always remember. Some of these are too small for a swan to take off from, but they land there nonetheless. After feeding they walk to another lake nearby so they can take flight again. Although it is hard for them to get airborne, he added, they are among the strongest fliers once aloft.

Swans were a traditional Koyukon food, but they are perhaps not used today. In any case they are tabooed for young people and for women of childbearing age, because they are slow and heavy. When people pray to the spirits of the deceased (which they still do regularly), they often burn offerings of food and other items. Wing feathers from the swan are among these customary offerings, because they are a source of good luck, a kind of amulet. In years past, swansdown was thrown into the air by shamans, then children scrambled for the feathers and put them inside their mittens. Boys who did this would become good hunters and trappers. The only special use of swans was for sewing—lengths of black skin from their legs made fancy stripping in clothing seams.

A man told me that twice in his life he saw groups of nine swans flying upstream just above the river. The first time it was in late fall, after freeze-up, and two people in his family died that winter. The second time it occurred earlier in the season, but something bad happened in a neighboring village afterward. So for him at least, and perhaps for others who hear his story, this event is tabooed, a sign of bad luck whenever it is seen.

The Geese

There are four species of geese (collectively named *dits'ina*) in the Koyukuk wildlands, but only two are common enough to be important in village economies. White-fronted geese (*Anser albifrons*) are the most abundant, although their numbers vary noticeably each year; and, as good luck would have it, they are also the best tasting. When they arrive in spring they are in prime condition (with some year-to-year variability), much better than the somewhat less common Canada geese. Their name in Koyukon is *k'idot'aa-gga'*, "bare beak." They have a fairly nondescript gray plumage, and their only flourish is orange feet and a pink bill, which Jetté's riddler (1913:191) has noticed:

> *Wait, I see something: It has taken the color of cloudberries.*
> *Answer: The bill of the white-fronted goose.*

Both white-fronted and Canada geese nest and raise their young in the Koyukuk valley. Flocks of young goslings congregate along particular stretches of tributary streams in late summer. Years ago, people would travel there to catch the delicious birds by hand just before they were able to fly. After mid-August they begin migrating gradually southward, stopping frequently at lakes along the way. Canada geese leave much later but rarely pause once they have begun. When the white-fronted geese have departed, and especially during the winter months, it is tabooed to imitate their call.

The Canada goose (*Branta canadensis*) is familiar to almost everyone—the "honker" of spring and fall skies, sometimes the incongruous inhabitant of city parks and riversides. This incongruity is most obvious to those who know it as the clever and wary bird of wilder places, the sharp-eyed one who sees the slightest movement and sweeps away beyond a hunter's range. Koyukon men and women hunt them especially in spring—the only time geese can be taken effectively—by concealing themselves in blinds at strategic places. The first ones shot are set on the ground as decoys, their heads propped up with forked sticks.

Canada geese (*bileelzina*) and white-fronted geese are perceived by the Koyukon as extremely good-natured and easygoing birds, like people who get along with everyone. Parents sometimes have their children raise a gosling so they will acquire the same personality. They point out that the little goose becomes attached to its adopted family. Describing the character of the Canada goose, a man said to me, "Even if it had the power to knock you over, I don't think it would do it."

The only special taboo for Canada (and white-fronted) geese is a prohibition against eating meat from the end of the wing (beyond the humerus) by anyone except an elder person. The restriction was never explained to me. These birds can also give signs: When a Canada goose flies over someone, making a series of short, light calls, an animal (such as a wolf) is somewhere nearby. When geese of any kind call very noisily as they fly north in spring, the weather will turn warm; and when they make little or no sound it will soon become cold. If a shot goose bursts open when it hits the ground, which rarely happens, it is a sign that someone is going to die.

The snow goose (*Chen hyperboreus*) was once pure white, but in the Distant Time she married Raven, and their children had black wingtips. This is how the bird came to look as it does today. These birds (*hugguh* in Koyukon, a vague reference to white color) migrate through the Alaskan interior only in the spring, usually flying so high that they are safe from hunters. None are seen in the summer or fall. They do fly very slowly, and at certain places they tend to be low enough for an occasional shot. People say that snow geese used to be seen in far greater numbers than today; and because they are excellent eating (especially when half-dried), they are missed by the elders who have tasted them.

The black brant (*Branta nigricans*) is extremely rare in Koyukon country, because it seldom wanders inland from its normal habitat on the coast. Very few Koyukon people have ever seen or taken this bird, which is named *k'ideelgho nodaala,* "goes the opposite way." Following from this, it is no compliment when someone is described as being "just like *k'ideelgho nodaala,*" implying a different or contrary approach to everything.

The Koyukon observe some special rules for the proper treatment of geese, regardless of species. Most important, geese should not be plucked until one or two days after they are killed—I presume this is because living things do not "die" completely for some time. This delay in complete death is often mentioned for various animals, and though I do not fully understand the idea, it seems to recognize the spirit's lingering presence. The spirit and the essence of life are so conjoined that each apparently encompasses the other.

People used to wait two full days before plucking geese, but now they often shorten it to a day or just overnight. This is done, in any case, "to show respect" and to avoid the bad luck in goose hunting that would follow a violation. For the same reason, goose wings used to be discarded by tying them together into bundles that were hung in a tree to decay slowly without lying on the ground.

According to a tradition not kept well today, the first few geese taken each spring should be cut apart in a special, respectful way. The terminal part of the wings is removed without severing the sinews that run to the shoulder and breast muscles. These are cut free at the shoulder, sometimes along with a little breast muscle, and left attached to the distal portions of the wing (which may be eaten only by old people). This is done because the sinews connect the wing to the area of the bird's heart, and severing this bond can bring bad luck.

The Ducks

Eleven duck species, known collectively as *nindaala,* belong to the agile waterfowl. All are hunted by the Koyukon, though their roles in the economy vary a great deal. Like geese, they are sought most intensively in the spring, their season of greatest abundance and accessibility, and the time when fresh meat is often in short supply. Ducks are also available in lesser numbers during the late fall, and people take as many as possible to freeze for a winter supply of this special food.

> A sure sign of the oncoming cold this evening: ducks flying from the lakes to feed in secluded places beneath the riverbanks. I saw them arcing like arrows over the tall willows, silhouetted against a blaze of sunset, then dropping onto the calm river. In the glow and stillness, I thought of my frail Athapaskan hunting canoe, of long silent waits as the dusk deepened, of hearing the sudden rush of wings and seeing the quick shadows overhead. Earlier, I had heard shotguns booming from far upriver, the sound rolling through the clear, cold air above the flats. Now I knew why. There will be no more silent evenings for a while— not with boats coursing up and down the river, and shotguns signaling the last harvest of waterfowl. Quiet will come when ice seals the river from the boats and sends the ducks away southward. [Huslia journal, September 1976]

The mallard (*Anas platyrhynchos*) is one of the largest and most common north country ducks, and one of the most beautiful as well. In the Distant Time, mallard-woman was expert at making fancy clothing, and the finery she sewed for her husband became the male's colorful plumage. When the animal-people lost anything of great value, such as a medicine object, mallard would retrieve it by using his curled tail feathers as hooks. Because of this association, one old shaman used to hang the hooked feathers inside his house, and he ornamented his medicine pouch with them each spring, apparently as a token of good luck. Ordinary people sometimes use these feathers for decoration as well, on their hats, for example. These ducks (or any others) can give one weather sign—when they suddenly sweep down from high above, making a load roar with their wings, it forewarns of a strong wind. Mallards (*ditłkkughuyh*) are otherwise important only for their meat, which Koyukon people savor highly and eat (as is the case for all ducks) without restriction by taboos.

The pintail (*Anas acuta*) is another large, tasty duck, and one of the most abundant as well. In the Koyukon language it is called *k'idzonula,* a cryptic reference to the black on its strikingly marked neck. Pintails are said to lay their eggs easily, and young girls are encouraged to eat their ovaries to bring easy childbirth.

Green-winged teal (*Anas carolinensis*) are much smaller ducks, difficult to hunt but avidly sought because they are so delicious. They are a bit lean in spring and summer, but by September they become very fat and especially flavorful. Koyukon hunters know the fat cycles of many animals, large and small, and this strongly affects their harvesting. I have been with expert hunters who could distinguish fat and lean ducks as they sped past us overhead; and of course they aimed for the best ones. There are two Koyukon names for the green-winged teal: the first and most common is *k'itsutł* ("whips around"), and the second is *tobaa ha'ałghalee,* "knocked the swan down." This rarely used name commemorates a Distant Time event when the petite duck defeated a swan in a wrestling match.

Other ducks that Koyukon people regularly hunt and eat include the greater scaup (*Aythya marila*) and lesser scaup (*A. affinis*), called by the single name *tontseedla,* "stays in the water." Only the most meticulous bird-watchers can distinguish these nearly identical species, and it is no surprise that Koyukon taxonomy lumps them. The relatively abundant American widgeon (*Mareca americana*), called *siseeya* in Koyukon, one of the most important ducks in the Koyukon economy. By contrast, the shoveler (*Spatula clypeata*) is among the least sought after, because it is not considered very tasty. Its Koyukon name is *dilolagga,* one of the many animal names that apparently has no translation.

The plump little buffleheads (*Bucephala albeola*) are a tasty catch for Koyukon duck hunters, but they fly so fast that very few are taken. They are called *toodakk'ona.* One man told me that when a bufflehead is chased by a falcon it folds its wings and rockets down over the water, then skips along the surface and suddenly dives to escape its pursuer.

The common goldeneye (*Bucephala clangula*) and Barrow's goldeneye (*B. islandica*) are very similar birds, grouped as *dikeenoya* ("nests in a tree") by the Koyukon. They are small and quick like the bufflehead, and they are eaten whenever someone manages to get one. Hunters are reluctant to use expensive shotgun shells on birds like this, knowing that they often miss the darting little targets and that even success brings only a pint-sized reward. But they always appreciate the goldeneye for its striking plumage, especially the sharply patterned black and white on its back. Occasionally one is stuffed and kept to look at, or given to a child for a "doll."

The lovely little harlequin duck (*Histrionicus histrionicus*) is also stuffed and hung inside the house, both for decoration and for luck. According to a Distant Time story, this bird was once a rich man, and so the person who keeps one as an amulet may have similar good fortune. But harlequins, called *taasa hut'aana* ("lives in whitefish lakes," or literally "whitefish person") are rarely seen. This is partly because they prefer the swift headwater streams where hunters seldom travel in summer, and partly because they are uncommon in the Alaskan interior.

Grouse and Ptarmigan

Aside from waterfowl, the only other birds of considerable importance in the Koyukon economy are grouse and ptarmigan. They are the "chickens" of northern wildlands, delicious, fat little birds whose populations cycle between abundance and scarcity. Elder Koyukon people can remember times when they lived, or survived, on a steady diet of grouse or ptarmigan, and they speak about these birds with real fondness. They are especially important because they are winter birds, most available when the fickle waterfowl have vanished to distant, unknown places.

> *Wait, I see something: It scatters little wood crumbs from the trees.*
> *Answer: The ruffed grouse, feeding in its high roosting places.*
> [Jetté 1913:192]

The ruffed grouse (*Bonasa umbellus*) is a bird of the forest and the tall willow and alder thickets. Koyukon men and women of all ages love to walk quietly through the sandbar willows in the still evenings, hunting for grouse that feed among the high branches. I have done this many times, half-frozen in the bitter cold of midwinter, stalking birds whose puffed feathers silhouette them roundly against the twilight sky. The rewards are well worth the trouble, because ruffed grouse is a real northland delicacy. They are considered best in the fall, when they have been feeding on berries, and as winter progresses their meat becomes less tasty.

In Koyukon, ruffed grouse are named *tsongguda,* which Jetté (n.d.*a*) translates "rock pounder." This refers, I suppose, to the birds' spring ritual of strutting back and forth on logs in the deep forest, drumming their wings to make a strange muffled, directionless noise that ends in a whir. This is called *k'itlida* ("that which pounds") in Koyukon, the same word used to describe the sound of crushing bones to render grease. I once shared a camp with Steven and Catherine Attla, and in the woods just a few yards behind our tents a grouse had its drumming log. Eventually we were able to approach very closely as it performed. My Koyukon teachers were no less interested than I was in the esoteric pleasure of watching it, with no thought of committing the bird to the stewpot.

On very cold winter nights, grouse fly down into the snow and sleep beneath the insulating powder. Traveling through the forest at dusk or dawn with a dog team, I have several times been startled by a grouse suddenly bursting from the snow beside the narrow trail. Once my Kutchin trapping partner made an incredibly adept grab for a grouse that flew out beside the snow machine he was driving at night. To my amazement, he caught the bird, and we ate it for supper.

In the Distant Time, a ruffed-grouse-woman had a tragic encounter with Raven:

> In a village long ago, some women wanted to cross the river to go berry picking. Of course Raven was there, and he offered to take them over in his canoe. They were happy to do this, and one-by-one they stepped into the boat. But when a young girl tried to get in, he said, "Oh, no. Don't you get in yet. You might step across my bow and cause it to have bad luck. I'll take you later."
>
> He made several trips, but each time he told the girl to wait. Finally, on the last trip, he said she should get in. She was the only one left, and she knew Raven must have something in mind. Sure enough, when they reached midstream he started acting tired. "I just can't paddle anymore," he complained. "I made too many trips already." Despite the girl's pleading, they drifted downstream, Raven paddling very slowly toward shore.
>
> The girl had been clever enough to fetch her needle bag when she saw she would be the last to cross. Now she kept urging him to hurry, but at the same time she sewed the tail of his dirty old caribou-skin shirt onto the crosspiece of his canoe. When they finally approached the far shore, the girl said she had to get out and relieve herself. "Do it in my hand," he said, reaching his palm behind his back. When she loudly refused, he ordered her, "Just do it in the canoe!" She refused again and insisted on getting out for a moment. So Raven gave in and paddled to shore.
>
> She walked into the brush, following Raven's instructions to hold onto the canoe rope, so he would know she had not run off. But she cleverly tied the line onto a tall, swaying willow to make it move; then she ran toward the village. In a moment, Raven called to her, and when there

was no reply he tried to jump from the canoe. But his shirt was sewed onto the boat and he fell down inside. In a rage, he jerked the crosspiece out and ran into the woods after her. He soon went between two trees, caught the crosspiece on them, and was thrown onto the ground. Now he was even more angry, but the girl had escaped.

When she reached the village she told her family what had happened, and they hid her in their elevated cache. Soon the Raven stormed in and demanded her—no one could ever kill him, so they could only watch as he searched everywhere for her. Finally he went under the cache and began poking up through its floor with a sharp stick. He poked and poked, until he saw blood running down through the logs. Now he kept on jabbing as more blood flowed onto the ground. But suddenly the girl was transformed into a ruffed grouse, and she flew from the cache and away to safety.

Ever since then, ruffed grouse have had whitish meat, because the girl lost her blood before she turned into a bird.

The spruce grouse (*Canachites canadensis*) is a fairly common but rather solitary bird of the timberlands. Unlike the ruffed grouse, it has very little fear of people and will often sit quietly on a spruce bough watching a hunter walk up beneath it. This is why old white trappers and prospectors called the bird "fool hen," an insulting name that would have little appeal for the Koyukon. In their language it is named *diyh* (no translation) or *ał ahona,* "spruce-bough eater." According to stories of the Distant Time, this handsome bird (as well as the ruffed grouse) was a woman noted for her fleet-footedness. She outraced the other animal-people for a bunch of raven feathers, and this is why the two grouse species have black feathers on their necks today.

Koyukon people hunt the spruce grouse especially in fall, and less in midwinter when they "taste like pitch." A bear hunter may get a double reward when he shoots one—if it falls dead on its back it is a powerful sign that he or his companions will get a bear. The meat, head, heart, gizzard, and intestines are all eaten, as with ruffed grouse. The crop from any grouse or ptarmigan is sometimes inflated, dried with its contents of seeds inside, then hung up in the house. I was never told a reason for this.

A third species, the sharp-tailed grouse (*Pedioecetes phasianellus*), also occurs in the Koyukuk country but is rare indeed. One man in his seventies told me he had killed only two during his lifetime. It is called *k'iłtułga,* "tail feathers twisted to a point."

Although several species of ptarmigan occur in Alaska, only the willow ptarmigan (*Lagopus lagopus*) frequent the Koyukon region. This is a northern bird in the purest sense, a denizen of Arctic and alpine tundra during summer, moving south to the forest only for the winter. People expect ptarmigan to appear after the deep snows of December drive them down from the mountains. Sometimes, especially in late winter and early spring, they are abundant in the Koyukuk lowlands, roosting in flocks everywhere among the willows and open scrub. In their pure white winter plumage (they are brown in summer), ptarmigan stand out sharply on bare branches and against deep blue sky; and their low croaking (from which their ono-matopoetic Koyukon name, *dilbagga*, derives) also helps to give them away. But when they land on the snow, they mysteriously vanish:

> I took the dogs for a little trip this afternoon and managed to shoot a ptarmigan to vary the moose-meat diet. The dogs saw them first, and I picked them out only after they knocked snow from some low-hanging willow branches. On the fresh snow, they were almost perfectly invisible. When I walked up to them, I could see only the ones in the bushes well enough to shoot; but I missed, they flew, and I followed them. As I approached again I managed to see one sitting on the snow (from perhaps twenty yards), but only by picking out its black eye and bill. That one I shot, and the others flew away. [Huslia journal, February 1977]

When flocks of ptarmigan gather in the tall shrubs they are easily seen, and men, women, and young boys hunt them with light rifles, returning to the village carrying packs bulging with the delicious birds. In past times they were also snared along the sandbar thickets, where they could be caught as they walked among the low bushes feeding on buds. When supplies of other foods have become short, ptarmigan have been a staple for the winter months; but this rarely happens today. Of course these birds are not always abundant, and in some years scarcely any appear. Koyukon people do not use ptarmigan feathers, though they would make excellent stuffing for pillows, blankets, or clothes. This is because the feathers' conta-gious whiteness would cause prematurely gray hair. Ptarmigan feet may be used as amulets—if one is tied around a boy's ankle it can help him become a fast runner.

> *Wait, I see something: Tiny bits of charcoal scattered in the snow.*
> *Answer: The bills of ptarmigan.*
> [Jetté 1913:195]

Birds of Lake and Shore

During summer the north country glitters everywhere with lakes, streams, ponds, puddles, rivers, swamps, and creeks. It is a paradise for birds of the shoreline and wetland, for the gangling sandhill crane that stalks the meadows, the gulls and terns that wheel and flutter wherever there is water, and the array of little shorebirds that twitter nervously on muddy river-banks. Although these birds have only minor significance as resources for the Koyukon, they are conspicuous inhabitants of the surrounding natural world, personages and personalities that people know well and sometimes treat in special ways.

The Gulls

I am including here not only the two kinds of gulls that regularly occur in the Koyukuk valley, but also the long-tailed jaeger and the Arctic tern. Most important of these birds for the Koyukon is *baats,* which refers to the large and common herring gull (*Larus argentatus*) and the very similar mew gull (*L. canus*). Neither the Koyukon nor most of us who are casual bird-watchers discriminate between them. The Bonaparte's gull (*L. philadelphia*) is an easily distinguished smaller bird, descriptively named *tleelzina,* "black head."

Koyukon people seem to regard gulls with compassionate disdain, if that emotional mix is possible. They are friendly birds, after all, not sinister or evil in any detectable way. But gulls are twice flawed—they are clumsy, slow animals, and they are scavengers who eat rotten things. Awkwardness is contagious; and uncleanliness is another bad trait that Koyukon people strongly avoid. Not only this, but the *baats* gulls are seen as gluttons who gobble down their food in big chunks—unkempt, clumsy gluttons. People who overindulge at a meal are sometimes unfavorably described as "just like a gull." Only the Bonaparte's gull is less harshly regarded; it has all these traits but not to such a degree.

Predictably, *baats* gulls are not considered fit to eat, because anyone who did so would acquire their objectionable traits or would pass them to future children. The eggs are also tabooed, except for old people or those who ignore such prohibitions: "Like that woman, she ate them, but her health didn't last long either." Both the eggs and the meat of Bonaparte's gulls can be eaten by old people, but again not by the young.

Long-tailed jaegers (*Stercorarius longicaudus*) are as inconspicuous as the gulls are obtrusive. They are very rare in Koyukon country—only occasionally seen fluttering above the open flats in spring or summer—and the people never use them in any way. Their Koyukon name is *dzonh,* which probably has no translation, although one man translated it "faded black." Eskimos strongly dislike jaegers because they harass other birds and steal food from them; but Koyukon people did not mention this to me.

The Arctic tern (*Sterna paradisaea*) is among the loveliest of northern birds, often seen flying effortlessly along the river or over the larger lakes. It is called *k'idaggaas,* in imitation of its rasping call. Terns are considered good eating but are tabooed for young people—one woman explained that they are "too close to a seagull," and another time she just said they are too clumsy. The same restriction applies to tern eggs, which can be gathered at nesting grounds along the river. When people used to gather eggs they were somewhat afraid of the angry, defensive birds, so they carried paddles to fend off their screeching dives. The Koyukon very rarely (if ever) use terns or their eggs today.

The Shorebirds

Although shorebirds are fairly common, they do not receive much notice from the Koyukon. This is partly because they are small, wary, and difficult to identify, and partly because they have only a slight role in the economy. In some cases I could make no better than highly tentative identifications, if even that. But there are some notable exceptions, and I begin with these.

The lesser yellowlegs (*Totanus flavipes*) is a large, common, and conspicuous shorebird, made more noticeable by its incessant piercing calls. It pipes repeatedly as it flies along the water's edge, or it flies straight up, then flutters down from high above, calling as it descends: *"Siyeets, siyeets, siyeets."* The word means "my breath." Occasionally someone will shout back to it, *"Siyeets!"* If it keeps on calling afterward, the person will have a long life; but if it stops, the person's life will be short. "I don't know why they do that," one of my Koyukon teachers said. "I don't want to know, myself."

In the Yukon River villages, Jetté learned that the yellowlegs' call means, "Get up! Get up!" It is crying out to the dead, but the voice worries them because they do not know who it is and they have no way to answer. And so the yellowlegs is sometimes called "the one who disturbs the dead by his voice" (Jetté, n.d.*a*).

Yellowlegs (ordinarily called *dzolnołga*, "long legs") are sometimes hunted today, though much less often than in the past. They are good tasting, especially roasted on a stick over a campfire or boiled with waterfowl. People consider the yellowlegs a very clean animal, and so they like to have their children eat it to help them acquire that trait.

These noisy little birds are also appreciated simply as a part of the natural surroundings, because their voice is such a strong presence during the fine days of spring and summer. Once I spent a warm day traveling the river with two elderly women, helping them with fishnets and other jobs. Several times they paused to say how much they enjoyed being out in the country this way, describing the sensations that especially pleased them. When we heard a yellowlegs' protracted call, one of them said, "Oh, I love to hear *dzolnołga* calling in early morning! So many times I've heard that when I used to live out in camps."

Another frequently seen bird, the common snipe (*Capella gallinago*), is hardly as well regarded. It is a secretive bird, rarely seen except in spring and early summer, when it constantly flies in high circles, winnowing its wings over the quiet land. Koyukon people avoid watching these flights because it can make them nearsighted (like the bird itself) or, far worse, can cause their spirits to leave them.

Stories of the Distant Time associate the snipe (called *yoleeł*) with unclean and evil things, because it was created—along with the rusty blackbird—from a monsterlike being (*K'its'a ło hul'aana*, "cannibal"). One person also explained the snipe's malevolence by saying that its ear holes run through its head, so light can be seen by looking into them. People never eat or use this bird, of course. A man even told me that if someone finds a snipe's nest, that person's family will die off in the next ten or twenty years. It is a bird to be avoided.

There is much less to say about the remaining shorebirds. Only a few of them are (or were) ever eaten. One of these is the semipalmated plover (*Charadrius semipalmatus*), descriptively named *bilaanh nok'idaalk'idee*, "scarf-like thing around its neck." An elder from Hughes said of these birds, "I like them. They're so good-natured. When you come upon their nest, they just try to baby you away. They get down low to the ground, real close to you, and run away from the nest."

The spotted sandpiper (*Actitus macularia*) is another of the few shorebirds that is eaten, though rarely. It is called *dilbeedza*, "flutters around the shore." The only other edible shorebird that I learned about is *bidilts'idla'*, which could be the whimbrel (*Numenius phaeopus*) or the bristle-thighed curlew (*N. tahitiensis*). It is good eating, one man told me, and he added that it likes to fly around in the fog calling repeatedly.

I was told of another bird, called *tl'eeyh ts'ineega'* (the name refers vaguely to mosquitoes), which also might be the long-billed dowicher (*Limnodromus scolopaceus*) or one of the two above. It is not eaten and is said to have a bad taste. The American golden plover (*Pluvialis dominica*) is significant only because it is called *bibidisis*. The word translates "bear belly," and because it contains the name for black bear (*sis*), young women are not allowed to say it. Finally there is the tame little northern phalarope (*Lobipes lobatus*), often seen paddling and bobbing on the placid lakes. I learned two names for it—the commonly used *tolyidla*, and *tiyee*, which is said to resemble its call.

Sandhill Crane

The sandhill crane (*Grus canadensis*) is far more important to the Koyukon than any of the gulls or shorebirds. It stands several feet tall and has a wingspread of six to seven feet. Cranes are occasionally taken by duck hunters in the spring (also sometimes in the fall), and their meat is excellent eating. For anyone used to chickens, or even turkeys, a crane drumstick or wing is indeed remarkable to behold as it emerges like a monolith from the stewpot. Not only the meat is eaten, but the viscera, head, and feet; and the rarely discovered eggs may also be used.

The crane is called *dildoola*, a word for the sound *brrrr*, which resembles the bird's truly incredible call. It has to be heard, clacking loudly above the timberlands, to be comprehended. Koyukon people fully appreciate this sound, regarding it as a curiosity and a delight. One man said that adult cranes teach it to their young in the fall, when they take them on short training flights. "People do eat cranes," he said, "but I don't believe in killing it myself. I'd rather listen to it."

Cranes are said to have excellent vision, and it is extremely hard to stalk them undetected. Anyone who tries to find young cranes will not succeed, I was advised, because somehow the lanky adults conceal themselves and their nests. When no one is around they make loud calls in their open meadow haunts, but they become silent and hide when someone is nearby. Nevertheless, people sometimes sing to them if they can get close enough, and when they hear the song "they'll do a dance for you." I have never seen this, but I was told of it by people who had done it themselves.

Cranes are large and obtrusive, but not really numerous. They vary considerably from year to year, and people recall that in the spring of 1943 there were so many that hunters went out specifically for them. Ordinarily they are taken coincident to other activities. (Readers may want to know that neither the endangered whooping crane nor the trumpeter swan frequents this region.) When they are wounded, their long, sharp beaks (formerly used to make arrow points, according to Jetté, n.d.*a*) are treated as dangerous weapons. Jetté was told that pairs of cranes sleep standing side-by-side. If one is wounded by a hunter, it is said to blame the other and to kill it with a thrust of its beak (Jetté, n.d.*a*).

In spite of this, Koyukon people regard the sandhill crane as a good-natured animal, largely because of the way it is portrayed by Distant Time stories. In one of these the crane-person saved many people by using its long legs as a bridge so they could get across the water. Another time, many arrows were being shot at the crane, so he deflected them with his forehead—this is how cranes acquired their featherless red crown.

The Hawks and Eagles

Hawks and eagles are the remote and solitary ones, nearly always seen from afar. They soar and tilt high above the flats or against the distant mountain faces, shunning the closeness of humanity. They nest on the cliffs and in tall trees surrounded by deep timber. As a bird-watcher, I have always found the hawks difficult to identify; as an anthropologist, I have found them nearly impossible. I rarely saw them when I was with my Koyukon instructors, and they found it very difficult to pick out familiar species in a bird book, where they could not use flight patterns, behavior, and calls to help with identifications. I was finally rescued by the kind assistance of Eliza Jones and James Kari (of the Alaska Native Language Center), who have carefully and systematically studied Koyukon bird names.

Koyukon people generally admire hawks as fellow hunters, and excellent ones at that. In former times they gave hawk feet to young boys, who wore them as amulets so they would acquire the hawks' predatory skill. A sense of communality between the Koyukon and predatory animals is also manifested in the expression of rights to each other's prey. If someone sees a hawk, eagle, owl, or other predator kill an animal, or just finds its prey, that person is free to take it. A woman told me that she once watched an owl fly into a flock of ptarmigan and kill one. So she ran there on snowshoes and frightened the owl away, then took the ptarmigan home and cooked it for her family. However, it is considered bad luck to see a hawk (at least the goshawk, and possibly any species) chase and kill a bird in flight.

I was told very little about each species of hawk, and these elusive birds seem to have a minor position in the Koyukon world. They are listed below under their Koyukon names, with probable identifications and comments following:

Yoda, Nik'eedoya

This is the goshawk (*Accipiter gentilis*), a quick and agile predator that sometimes catches other birds in flight. It also takes small ground-living animals such as snowshoe hares. One of my Koyukon teachers translated *yoda* as "flies high." An elderly Huslia man told me that, because his mother had raised a goshawk, he and others in his family should hunt alone to have good luck. If someone goes hunting with him, he has difficulty getting anything at all.

Hukeenoya

Another streamlined aerial predator, this bird is identified as the kestrel (*Accipiter sparverius*). A Huslia elder said of *hukeenoya:* "They're tough animals. They hang around bluffs when they nest, and they kill lots of other birds."

Ts'ibaak'itłaa

This is a large, soaring hawk, perhaps the Swainson's hawk (*Buteo swainsoni*) or red-tailed hawk (*B. jamaicensis*). Its name translates "spruce princess," and it apparently favors timbered country. Catherine Attla said that, if this bird sees something at night, it dives and climbs repeatedly, making a strange screeching sound. One elder told me that he does not think well of *ts'ibaak'itłaa* because it is messy; it sometimes catches fish and then leaves them lying around to rot. The Koyukon moral system—which sanctifies food and prohibits waste—applies to the entire community of living things, animals and humans alike. Here again is the overarching unity that links Koyukon people to the natural world of which they are a part.

Kk'olkk'eya

This name means "glide around" or, according to Jetté (n.d.*a*), "swoops," or "hovers." It is probably the rough-legged hawk (*Buteo lagopus*). The Koyukon word for the month of March takes its name from this bird.

Bakkant'ogga'

Most likely this is the marsh hawk (*Circus cyaneus*), a bird that floats elegantly just above the meadows and muskegs, then suddenly drops to catch its scurrying prey. Its name vaguely refers to whiteness, or to the top of its foot.

Taagidzee'aana

This is the osprey (*Pandion haliaetus*), a large hawklike bird that feeds mainly on fish. Its name translates "stares into the water" or, according to Jetté (n.d.*a*) "catches fish in the water." According to Jetté it is considered a miser because it can hold slippery fish as it flies, clutching its possessions and refusing to part with them. Koyukon people regard this as a highly disagreeable characteristic; here again is the moral order applied to all inhabitants of the boreal community.

The eagles are rare indeed in Koyukon country, if my own experience serves as judgment. Only occasionally is one sighted in the distance, making broad, easy sweeps and circles on its great wings. Like the hawks, these birds receive little attention from the Koyukon, an interesting contrast to their strong emotional and symbolic meanings in our own and many native American cultures. The golden eagle (*Aquila chrysaëtos*) and bald eagle (*Haliaeetus leucocephalus*) are both named *tilila,* and old individuals of either species are called *k'iyona'.*

Eagles are not eaten or used, but there is no taboo on killing them should someone have a reason. For example, an old shaman had killed one and skinned it, then stretched the skin and kept it on a wall of his house. Perhaps he did this because the eagle is known as a great animal through its exploits in stories of the Distant Time, when it performed feats of extraordinary strength.

Eagles are also considered dangerous if they are molested. I once told a Huslia man that I had crawled to an eagle's nest on a cliff in the Aleutian Islands, and the adults had flown frighteningly close to me. "They didn't hurt you because you didn't know any better," he said. "If you knew how dangerous that was, they would really come after you." Then he told me about some men who had raided an eagle's nest, back when bounty was offered by the government. Because these men "knew the danger," the eagles dove at them, and finally they had to shoot them in self-defense.

This illustrates an important concept in dealing with the Koyukon rules for treatment of nature—ignorance removes responsibility. Persons who are unaware of the rules are not bound by them and are forgiven their transgressions. This holds especially for outsiders and young Koyukon who have not learned the traditions; but older Koyukon people who know the rules but reject or disobey them will be punished in some way for their violations.

The Owls

For the Koyukon, owls are the predatory birds that demand most attention from humankind—owls that sit darkly among the high branches, blinking their huge golden eyes, hooting and cooing in the shadowed hush. Owls have a special power of foreknowledge and prophecy, an often frightening gift manifested in their ability to foretell or influence future events. After I had lived among the Koyukon, I appreciated owls more than ever before, but I lost some of the easy frivolity with which I had admired them. The night song had now become the night voice.

> *Wait, I see something: They are like bushes bending in the wind.*
> *Answer: The "ears" of the great horned owl.*

The preeminent sage among these birds is the great horned owl (*Bubo virginianus*), which the Koyukon name *nigoodzagha* ("small ears") or *nod-neeya* ("tells you things"). It is a very large bird with conspicuous tufts on its head, as the riddler has noted. Horned owls remain in the north year-round, but they keep to the forest in daytime, so people rarely see them. They are here, though, and in the frigid void of midwinter nights, when the moon casts long timber shadows across the snow-covered sloughs, their voices can be heard. Koyukon tradition says that sensation is curiously reversed for the horned owls, and when it is bitter cold they feel the way people do in uncomfortable heat.

Flying on silent wings, using their special nighttime senses, horned owls prey on all kinds of small animals; and occasionally they steal fish from the riverside drying racks. Koyukon people sometimes hunt them, not for revenge but to savor their excellent-tasting meat. Only the older people are allowed to eat them, however, because their slowness would affect the young (or their future children). Only the meat can be eaten, and it is usually baked; but owls are rarely taken nowadays.

When great horned owls speak to people, they utter only what is certain. Because most of their prophecies bode ill, Koyukon people do not like to hear them calling at all. However, Jetté (n.d.*a*) says that questions may be given to owls, and the answer is usually, "hoo...hoo," which is interpreted to be the word for yes (*oho'*). The nonpareil Jesuit Jetté then suggests that people may engineer their own predictions by asking questions with a yes answer in mind. The owl is a fearful being nonetheless, and Jetté continues that it is "the bugbear with which children are threatened to make them comply with the wishes of their elders; and to keep them away from a tent or house, it is enough to tell them that it is the abode of the [owl], ready to seize them if they enter it." In Jetté's time, children played a game similar to tag, in which the pursuer impersonated an owl, arms outstretched like wings, hooting and chasing the others.

Nowadays, people in the Koyukuk villages concern themselves mostly with the owl's augury. When it is about to speak prophetically, the bird first makes a muffled squawking sound—then it hoots in tones and patterns that can be interpreted. The most terrifying words it can say are "Soon you will cry" (*Adakk'ut daa'tohtsah*), meaning that someone close to you will die. It may even seal the forecast tightly with a name, and not long afterward its omen will be fulfilled.

Once, years ago, people heard an owl clearly intone (as always, in Koyukon words), "Black bears will cry." For the two following seasons, berry crops failed and bears had a difficult time surviving. But not all of the owl's words bring sinister messages. It may call repeatedly, "You will eat the belly of something" (*k'itoh hon'*, or *nik'itsaah bida' tohlggoot*), foretelling the hunter's good luck just ahead. And horned owls sometimes predict an oncoming storm:

> *When the owl makes a kind of grunting sound, like this,*
> Mmmmm . . . Mmmmm, *it means stormy weather is coming. Owl's*
> *call, that's the only weather report we used to have!*

The great gray owl (*Strix nebulosa*) is a rare and reclusive bird found only in the boreal forests—when it can be found at all. I have seen only one, despite years of careful watching. It was hardly the mysterious deep woods encounter I had always envisioned—the huge owl (there are none larger on this continent) sat conspicuously in a dead tree alongside *Noongga* Slough, watching us pass in a boat. The old woman I was with looked and said *"nol-dul,"* a name I knew well already. She was interested but nonchalant; I was ecstatic, in a way only a bird-watcher could understand.

Koyukon people say that great gray owls live year-round in their forests, that they are uncommon now but used to be seen more often. All owls, they explain, have become less numerous because hares and ptarmigan have not been abundant for many years. In former times people ate gray owls, but they were tabooed for all except elders, because they are slow and clumsy. Even their name reflects this—it means "clumsily dressed." A woman told me that her mother was once very ill and looked as if she would soon die. Her father saved her life, however, by giving her meat from a great gray owl. After that she became dull-witted and always moved around slowly.

> women are very much afraid of it, especially at dusk. If they happen to see one flying around, whilst they are enjoying a social gossip near a campfire, they immediately hush their voices, and suppress any laughter, as this is supposed to attract the bird. The reason of this fear is probably to be found in the story of the man-owl, who in times of yore, seduced a woman, and was the cause of her ruin and death. [Jetté 1911:612]

The hawk owl (*Surnia ulula*) is a common little bird of the forest, unusual for its daytime activity and its hawklike posture. Because hawk owls are fairly tame and often perch conspicuously in the open, people see them more often than any of the others. They remain in the north throughout the year; in April they tap loudly on the tree trunks, for a long time if a protracted spring is coming and a short time if the spring will be brief.

Hawk owls are called *k'itleedzodza* in Koyukon, "small head." They are considered good eating, prepared by boiling or roasting, but I doubt that people often use them today. Elders say that if a hunter kills one the bird will be reincarnated and return to the same person to be killed another time. For this reason they are sometimes called *noo ghanonodint'ugha,* "it comes back when killed." This happens only twice with each owl, though. In the Distant Time, Jetté (n.d.*a*) writes, the hawk owl was a shaman, so after it is eaten its bones must be burned. Then its spirit will go up the Yukon to be reincarnated, and afterward it will return to its original haunts.

> *Once we were going out hunting and a* k'itleedzodza *flew over us. We shot it for food. After that we killed one each day for fifteen days, but we didn't get a single other animal that whole time.*

The man who told me this also explained that hawk owls often give signs to hunters by the direction they fly overhead. If one catches up to a hunter on the trail and flies on past, it indicates good luck. But if it flies across the hunter's trail, or toward him, it forecasts a poor hunt.

> *I really hate to see one of those things do that. When it does I still go out, thinking I can beat him! But I never did yet; he's always right. If you see that, you might as well go right back home. You won't get any game anyhow.*

The Koyukon face a little paradox if they kill a hawk owl, because it will later return to the one who took it. This means it will fly toward the person, usually a sign of bad luck (and, remember, signs often compel the events that they forecast). Fortunately, there is a way out. If one is shot for eating, it should be cut up in a special way prescribed by a Distant Time story (sliced from each end toward the middle), and this will prevent its return.

Hawk owls are very well regarded by the Koyukon, because they are clean and because they kill things easily. If one is raised around children, they will acquire its virtues. The bird is a kind of living amulet. Sometimes a group of people will walk through an area where a hawk owl is nesting, trying to find young ones to use this way. I knew a little boy whose mother had raised a hawk owl years before he was born. His grandmother told me that he always looked carefully, deliberately, at his food before eating it, to be sure that it was desirable and clean. "He got that from the owl," she asserted. There are risks in keeping an owl, however, as the sad tale a woman told me will attest:

> Several years ago, she and her husband took a little hawk owl to raise with their small daughter. After a while, though, its leg was broken and its health began to fail. Finally they released it, hoping that it would recover. That winter her husband caught a hawk owl in one of his traps, killing it, and he felt that it was the one they had let go. The thought plagued him, troubled him profoundly. Not long afterward, the little girl broke her leg—the same one the owl had broken—and less than a year later she became sick and died. They would never keep any wild animal again, the woman said, because it might be made to suffer as the owl had, and as they had in consequence. [Huslia journal, March 1977]

The short-eared owl (*Asio flammeus*) is another daytime bird, most often seen as it flaps and wavers low above the open meadows in late spring. It is migratory, arriving just before the geese and leaving at summer's end. The Koyukon know it by two names: The first is *kk'oondzaah*, the word for a food made from fish eggs and cranberries. And the second is *hunlik*, "falls repeatedly like fainting," surely a reference to the owl's habit of making repeated dives as it flies. In the Distant Time, the short-eared owl once dropped a birchbark basket filled with fish and had to dive again and again to retrieve it; and so people may recite the little adage "His basket is falling" when they spot one of these birds. The Koyukon do not kill or use short-eared owls.

The snowy owl (*Nyctea scandiaca*) is another migrant, but the other way around. These beautiful white birds move south from their tundra domain only for the late winter or early spring, sometimes in fairly large numbers. Koyukon people consider them delicious, the best-tasting owls, but only old people can eat them because they are clumsy birds. Like the short-eared owl, they have two names—*yiłbaa* ("snow color") and *nokinbaa* (a vague reference to their vision).

Finally, there is the boreal owl (*Aegolius funereus*), a secretive little bird found only in the northern forests. These owls are called *ałkeeh doldoya*, "it perches in the lower part of spruce trees," a name that describes their daytime habits. Koyukon people never kill them, "because they move slowly and mind their own business—it wouldn't be fair to kill an animal like that." Jetté (1908:470) says that the bird has supernatural powers, and anyone who kills it might also die.

In any case, boreal owls are not given the wisdom of their larger brethren. In a Distant Time story, Raven assigned the boreal owl to guard his canoe, but the owl fell asleep. Later Raven was chased by a bear and ran for his life, only to find the owl-man asleep under his boat. He was so angry that he nearly left the owl behind, but in the end he took him along to safety. Because of this reputation, people describe someone who is slow and dull as "just like *ałkeeh doldoya.*"

In daylight the boreal owl is "blind," so people can walk right up to it. If one is found, they may catch it by twisting a stick into its soft feathers and pulling it from the tree. Then they tie a bit of dried fish onto its back and let it go. The woman who told me this said it is "probably" done for good luck and added that the owl is never let go without first giving it food.

The Songbirds

I come now to the array of "songbirds," the small ones who flit and hide in the forest thickets, usually too small and quick and clever to be hunted. Only a few are ever taken by the Koyukon, principally when food is dangerously scarce. Children occasionally raid their nests for eggs, which they boil and eat, perhaps imitating their elders. Even these uses are very rare today; but the little birds are far from irrelevant to Koyukon people, who have recognized and named all but the rarest and most elusive. Many are important beings in the forest world, their history known from the Distant Time, their powers respected and beseeched, their colorful beauty admired as living natural art, and their songs esteemed as the very breath of spring and summer.

Aside from their spiritual significance, perhaps the voices of the little birds mean most to the Koyukon people. Indeed, these provide inspiration for their own spring and summer songs (*too k'ileek,* literally "water songs," because water is the warm-season metaphor). Many bird calls are interpreted as Koyukon words, their meanings derived from events in the Distant Time, events recalled in stories that make the birds' phrases clear. What is striking about these song words is how perfectly they mirror the call's pattern, so that someone who knows birdsongs can readily identify the species when the words are spoken in Koyukon. Not only the rhythm comes through, but also some of the tone, the "feel" that goes with it. Unfortunately, written words lose this feeling almost completely.

I will begin this section with the gray jay, one of the most important of the songbirds. The species following it are ordered, for want of another system, approximately as they appear in a field guide. This mingles the important species with the unimportant ones, the "winter birds" (a Koyukon category including all nonmigratory songbirds) with the "summer birds," but it will perhaps be a comfortable sequence for those already accustomed to it.

Gray Jay

This is another of the boreal forest's strong and engaging personalities. The gray jay (*Perisoreus canadensis*) is a ubiquitous character, a year-round stalwart in the north country, made conspicuous by its compulsion to follow people around. It does this not as entertainment, but in the hope of finding—or stealing—a scrap of food or a share of kills. The early prospectors and trappers named the bird "camp robber," an English name still used by the Koyukon, who call it *zuhga* in their own language.

I have always had a special fondness for gray jays, because they are the most visible winter bird. They give life to the inert solitude of that season. When they spot a dog team coming they often fly to a tree beside the trail and wait there, chirruping and mewing, until it passes beneath them. If they see a hawk owl perched in a tree, however, they are not contented until they have harassed it into leaving. "They just keep flying around him," a Hughes elder told me, "laughing and laughing at him until he finally goes someplace else. They don't like him at all." Hunters have to be careful to cover their catch well if they leave it unattended, because the jays are always watching. If they have a chance, they peck away at the meat and fat, carrying it off to their own secret caches for later use. And, like ravens, they foul the catch with their excrement.

Koyukon people seem to like gray jays in spite of these habits, and they treat them with considerable respect. They apparently have a fairly strong spirit, and they are associated in special ways with cold weather. For example, they nest very early, before the snow melts, and children are warned against bothering the nest in the rare event that they find one. Not only should they avoid touching the eggs, they should not even look at them (the same is true, perhaps to a lesser degree, of the other winter birds like chickadees and redpolls). Violating this will disturb the bird's rest after a long, frigid winter and will cause unseasonably cold and nasty weather. "I did it once when I was young," a man confessed, "and a bad cold spell came after. I never told anyone about it though—no use to get in trouble!"

Gray jays are not eaten, but there is no strict taboo against killing them. If one gets caught in a trap, it should be killed quickly before it cries out, "telling its grandpa." Otherwise a period of severe cold or storminess will follow, and the violator is likely to suffer much discomfort (the identity of "grandpa" was not explained to me). After a jay is killed this way, it should be burned with some discarded material from camp or home, never burned alone or left to decay in the woods.

A killed jay must also never be plucked, again because cold and stormy weather would result. A woman once indignantly told me of finding that some young man had recently plucked a jay: "Oh my, when I saw those feathers, I just picked them all up and took them away. I made fire with birchbark and spruce boughs, and burned them all up. But next day it really snowed. I told Grandma Bessie about it and she said, 'No wonder this bad weather came!' " An elder from Hughes told of a foolish and irresponsible man who became angry at the jays for getting in his marten traps, so he plucked a trapped jay and left it alive. He was later discovered in his tent, frozen to death, the price for causing a jay to suffer.

Gray jays also bring signs to people, especially to hunters. If one persistently flies near someone, making soft squealing noises or "kissing" sounds, the person will have hunting luck soon. Sometimes the bird calls, *"k'i-tliyhtl...k'itliyhtl"* (I also heard it described as "chuk-chuk-chuk-chuk"). This is the sound of skins being cleaned, and a woman who hears it should say "I hope it is soon." This may happen from midwinter on, and it means that the woman will clean a big-game hide before long; in other words, it signals (perhaps compels) good hunting luck.

Once, years ago, my principal Koyukon instructor and her grandfather heard a gray jay speak in a human voice. Rain was falling, and the bird sat on a branch overhead, looking soggy and disheveled. Suddenly it spoke in clear words, "My brother...my brother, what is going to happen?" The old man, a shaman, was startled by the voice and worried by its message. Afterward the rain poured down for nine days, flooding bears from their dens and creating general havoc. And then people knew what the bird had meant.

Belted Kingfisher, "Fish Mother," and Northern Shrike

The kingfisher (*Megaceryle alcyon*) is a common summer bird in Koyukon country, often seen darting above its reflection along the rivers and tributary streams, making its harsh, raspy calls. In Koyukon it is named *dikiltl'aasga*. I was told little about this bird except that people never eat or use it. An elder from Hughes said it is careless and unclean, often leaving fish around to rot and go to waste. Once a kingfisher let its droppings fall into a creek as he was about to dip water from it for tea. He decided to go without tea rather than drink water that had been polluted by this animal.

I heard from several people about a bird called *łookk'a baanh,* "fish mother" or "mother of fish," but was never able to identify it. Elders from Koyukuk villages describe it as the size of a jay, uniform gray in color, and perhaps (according to one person) with red on its breast. People who had seen it many times could mimic its voice expertly, but I never heard the calls myself. It is said to frequent Koyukon country only in the early fall (September), and it stays along the rivers.

If one of these birds hangs around a fish camp, people will have good luck with their catches. It makes calls that sound like a person scaling fish, sometimes a small fish and sometimes a large one. "If you hear it, you better get right to work with your nets, because you're going to catch plenty, right away."

I had much difficulty identifying another bird called *ts'inok'itlk'oodla,* which is named for the screeching noise it makes (*"ts'iyeekk!"*). One man said, "It's a little hawk that flies like a bullet," but others said it was a little owl. Apparently, however, it is the northern shrike (*Lanius excubitor*), a jay-sized predatory bird not related (in Linnaean taxonomy) to hawks or owls. It is said to frequent river bluffs and mountains during the summer.

The Woodpeckers

The four species of woodpeckers found in the Koyukuk wildlands are grouped under two names in Koyukon. The first of these is *tsinil*, the yellow-shafted flicker (*Colaptes auratus*). The second is a group including three species, all called *dikiltlaala* ("chops wood"). These are the downy woodpecker (*Dendrocopos pubescens*), the very similar hairy woodpecker (*D. villosus*), and the somewhat distinct northern three-toed woodpecker (*Picoides tridactylus*).

Among the *dikiltlaala* group, Koyukon people most often recognize and speak of the three-toed woodpecker. In the Distant Time, this bird was an extremely jealous man who tried to starve his wife to death after finding a trinket given to her by a lover. He allowed her no food except broth from cooked beaver and ate all the meat himself. The yellow patch on this bird's crown appeared after a drop of the beaver broth froze atop his head. According to Jetté's teachers, the jealous woodpecker-man caught beavers by chopping their houses open. After every swing with his ax he would turn his head to make sure his wife was not eating furtively. This is why the three-toed woodpecker always turns and looks behind as it pecks on trees (n.d.*a*).

Aside from his extreme jealousy, the three-toed woodpecker did many good things and helped other people during the Distant Time. Perhaps this is why taboo prohibits killing the bird today. It can give people an ominous sign, however: If one lands on the side of a cabin and pecks at it, bad luck will come to the family who lives there.

Yellow-shafted flickers are seldom seen in Koyukuk River country, though they are very common in more southerly latitudes. According to one man, they favor the heavy timber, especially along hillsides and dead-end sloughs; and they are said to breed here, producing seven young in each nest. I heard flickers several times while I was living in Huslia, always in thickly forested places; but despite many careful stalks toward the calls I never actually managed to see the bird.

The flicker may seem ordinary to outsiders, yet for the Koyukon it is anything but—it is a source of great power, capable of protecting people and bringing them a lifetime of good luck. Only one other animal, the least weasel, has a similar power to help people. Someone who hears flickers more often than normal, for example, should have consistently good fortune; and Jetté (n.d.*a*) says that a person who sees one should ask it for luck.

But the best way to tap the bird's power is to kill one and keep its skin. They are wary, quick, and have excellent vision, so this is an extremely rare event. One elder told me, for instance, that he saw flickers only twice in his life, in 1926 and 1958, and only once did he manage to shoot one. As we spoke, he pointed to its dried skin, hanging on the wall beside his bed where he has always kept it. "It's a real protector animal," he added.

Anyone who kills a flicker keeps the skin someplace nearby where it is safe and secure. Occasionally, however, a few feathers might be pulled from it and burned for spirits of the dead. This is done to placate and propitiate them, because they valued the "lucky bird" so much in life. The woman who explained this to me had a most unusual experience when she was young. She had stepped out of her house and seen a flicker asleep on the low roof, and, using a stick she found nearby, she killed the bird. It was a strong sign, long since borne out, that her life would be well blessed with good fortune.

The Flycatchers and Swallows

Of several different flycatchers that frequent the Koyukuk valley (some fairly common), I could learn about only one—the olive-sided flycatcher (*Nuttalornis borealis*). This bird is not common, but people sometimes hear its singular, buzzing call from atop a tall tree far out in the wildland. Its Koyukon name is *duhtseeneeya,* "it says *duhtsee,*" and anyone who has heard it will agree. The flycatcher has the power to cause illness, and so people prefer not to hear it near their camps. Its call is easy to mimic, almost compelling, in fact, but doing so is strictly tabooed. Violation will cause a lingering death from an illness such as tuberculosis or cancer.

The swallows are certainly more benign, but their identity is confusing. They are abundant in the northern summer, with its lavish repast of insects; but they are so quick and tiny that eyes can scarcely tell one kind from another. I learned three names for the swallows:

> *biłʼon hooldloyee* ("nests under the bank")—bank swallow
>   (*Riparia riparia*)
> *kaałnooya* (no translation)—bank swallow
> *łaats anogha* ("digs sand")—violet-green swallow
>   (*Tachycineta thalassina*)

Western taxonomy identifies five species that should occur here. One step toward closing this gap is the terms for cliff swallow (*Petrochelidon pyrrhonota*)—*tłaaʼakʼitługha* and *kaaltsaaʼa*—listed in Jones's Koyukon dictionary (1978:22). Another may be the assertion by one of my instructors that certain brown-backed swallows are males and green-backed swallows females of the same species.

Irrespective of these technicalities, Koyukon people regard swallows as excellent food, "delicious as geese," although they are seldom used today. In the past they were taken especially when fresh meat was scarce in summer, to vary the diet of fish. Swallows can be easily caught by hand in their burrows, and then they are roasted on a stick over an open fire. Pubescent girls are encouraged to eat bank swallows so that their children will be pretty.

Certain of the swallows arrive precisely on the same days each summer. They also tend to leave fairly early in the fall. During their long migratory flights, especially in the fall, they are said to rest by hitching rides on sandhill cranes, holding on beneath their great wings.

The Chickadees

Although several species are found in the Koyukuk forests, the chickadees are all lumped as *k'its'ahultoona,* a name that refers to their loud voice in the Distant Time stories. Black-capped and boreal chickadees (*Parus atricapillus, P. hudsonicus*) are both commonly seen here throughout the year, busily twittering through the branches, hanging acrobatically as they pick out tidbits of food. They are often rather fearless, flitting around near people, either curious about them or oblivious to their presence.

In the Distant Time stories, chickadee sang a medicine song (*"Sikitseeyaa yeehoolaa eetoon . . ."*) that people remember though the bird no longer sings it. Chickadee had a "different" personality then, not a good one, and so no one should keep it for a pet today—I suppose to avoid becoming like the bird-person was. During the spring these little birds sing a plaintive little two-note song, familiar to anyone who listens closely in the forest. Koyukon people say they are "crying for winter," lamenting the season's passage. Some believe the call is an omen, a sign that they will soon cry over a death; but not everyone accepts this. Chickadees are never used in any way, and since they are winter birds their nests are left strictly alone (presumably because bothering them would cause cold weather).

The Thrushes

The long, dusky twilight of spring and summer in the boreal forest is given special enchantment by thrush songs, spilling out from hidden places in the deep thickets. They are among the loveliest, most compelling of all birdsongs, a whirring orchestration of flutelike phrases, ethereal as mist yet powerful as wind. Koyukon people share this feeling about the thrush song; they love to hear it as they sit quietly at sunset in their camps. And they give the song words, *sook'eeyis deeyo,* "it is a fine evening."

The beautiful singers are of three species—the gray-cheeked thrush (*Hylocichla minima*), Swainson's thrush (*H. ustulata*), and hermit thrush (*H. guttata*). In Koyukon they are given a single name, *gguzaakk,* a word the thrush says in one of its short calls. Although its twilight songs are considered exquisite, the thrush is also somewhat frightening because it often senses things that lurk nearby. If many thrushes sing, for example, it can mean that a woodsman (*nik'inla'eena*) is somewhere around. They also make a call, saying *nahutl-eeyh*, literally "a sign of a spirit is perceived," which means an unknown presence has frightened them. In the Distant Time, thrush called out this way when he sensed a ghost close by, and it can still be a warning to those who hear and understand it.

Another dusk singer is the varied thrush (*Ixoreus naevius*), a large and wary bird of the riverside underbrush. It is called *diltl'eeza* in Koyukon, a word that means "ringing sound." This describes its long, wheezy notes, often heard at dusk, mingling with the more elaborate songs of the other thrushes. Koyukon people appreciate this bird both for its calls and for its reputation as a "clean" animal. Like the other thrushes, its eggs and meat are traditional foods, but they are rarely eaten today.

Last among the thrushes is the familiar robin (*Turdus migratorius*), named *dilk'ahoo* by the Koyukon. Robins are common early migrants in the northern forest, and during times past they were one of the few foods available if starvation came just before spring breakup. Snares were set for them on the snowless patches beneath spruce trees, or they were simply collected after they froze to death in extreme spring weather. Other small birds were also taken, and the day's meager catch was boiled together in a pot.

Koyukon people think well of the robin: "It is a really wise bird," one man told me. "It gets to know someone who doesn't bother it, and then it can get real tame around that person." When robins sing their warbling phrases, they are making a little speech—*Dodo silinh k'oolkkoy ts'eega, tilzoot tilzoot silnee silnee,* "Down there, my brother-in-law tells me to eat pike entrails." When they say this, a man told me, they are singing happily about the food they have eaten.

As I will discuss in chapter 11, the Koyukon live in an ever-changing natural environment. Being astute and watchful people, they are always aware of this, and they speak of it in many contexts. Describing the robin's song, one of my Huslia instructors said, "Even the birds are changing. The robins don't say their song plainly any more—they only say it halfway, like a kid would when it's learning." Ornithologists recognize regional "dialects" in birdsong, and it is not surprising that songs may also change over time, as the Koyukon have observed.

Other Large "Songbirds"

This catchall section will discuss five birds that do not fit into the other categories. First of these is the wheatear (*Oenanthe oenanthe*), which the Koyukuk people rarely see. I have encountered it only once, when a flock spent several days around my cabin in Huslia after a late spring snowstorm apparently drove them down from the mountains. An old man who visited me recognized them but could not recall their Koyukon name. He said that they sing a sad song, *"Sooghayoo . . . sooghayoo,"* "My older brother . . . my older brother," crying over his death.

A far more common bird is the Bohemian waxwing (*Bombycilla garrula*), often seen in small flocks that hurry from one tree to the next, constantly pattering in wispy trills. This impeccable gray brown bird is called *diltsooga,* "he squeaks," by the Koyukon. According to a Distant Time story, the waxwing had a very jealous wife who once dragged him around by the hair, giving him the crest that now adorns his crown and making him cry out until his voice became nothing but a squeak. Koyukon people do not kill or use this bird.

The rusty blackbird (*Euphagus carolinus*) is often seen here, strutting in open places, blurting out its creaking "rusty hinge" call. Its Koyukon name, *ts'uhutlts'eegga,* resembles this sound, and it has another singularly uncomplimentary name, *bikeehu̱lgit* ("rotten anus"). All the implications of this sobriquet are accurate, for the blackbird originated from the anus of a cannibal being in the Distant Time (along with its relative, the common snipe). It is an unclean bird, messy, not interested in taking care of itself. If a blackbird is caught in a trap set for muskrats along a lakeshore, the trap will catch nothing for the rest of the season.

One elder told me that blackbirds are usually abundant around the lakes but keep well away from villages. In recent years, however, he has noticed that they congregate in a certain nearby community, and during the same time many tragic events have taken place there. The unclean bird, in his eyes at least, is a sign or a curse, which both tells and creates its evil portent.

The horned lark (*Eremophila alpestris*) was identified by one elder from Hughes as a bird that lives in the mountains, where it may be abundant in summer. Occasionally it is also seen along the river during bad weather, he said. Its name, *dli̱l tleekk'a bahoolaanee,* refers to its habit of living in the mountains.

The dipper (*Cinclus mexicanus*) is apparently found here during summer and is said to winter in the swift streams of Dakli Pass, which are kept open by hot springs. This bird is remarkable for its habit of walking on the bottom of streams, where it feeds on underwater creatures. Its appropriate Koyukon name, *nitsoo taaneelot,* means "your grandmother sank."

Warblers and Kinglets

Those who expect confusion here will not be disappointed. Only a few of these pretty little birds could be identified by my Koyukon instructors, and none have much significance except as lovely singers and flashes of summer color.

The yellow warbler (*Dendroica petechia*) is one of the most common and conspicuous of these birds. It is called *di̱ltsits* in Koyukon, "something yellow going around." No use is made of this warbler, or any others. One elder woman did say, however, that she had always wanted to catch a yellow-rumped warbler (*D. coronata*) to stuff and hang inside her house to admire.

This bird's Koyukon name is *łatsontłida*, "breaks up rocks." If a myrtle warbler stays near somebody's house or camp, it is a sign of "good luck with money" for whoever lives there. "We never use them," one man told me, "but they should be good to eat—they're clean birds."

Two other warblers could not be identified. First of these is *tsotł ghu doghon' neeł'oya*, "has its chest stuck through something made from belly skins." This is a noisy yellow bird, I was told, once common but now seldom seen. Someone who habitually tells on others is said to be just like this talkative bird, which could be the orange-crowned warbler (*Vermivora celata*) or Wilson's warbler (*Wilsonia pusilla*). The second unidentified warbler is a grayish bird also seen infrequently nowadays. Its name (*k'oot'anh*) is said to resemble its call. This may be the blackpoll warbler (*Dendroica striata*), an impression strengthened by one man's comment, "You hear it but probably can't see it," an apt description if my guess is correct.

The same comment would certainly apply to the tiny ruby-crowned kinglet (*Regulus calendula*). This bird holds forth at length from the high treetops in early spring, where only its miniscule silhouette can be seen. For two springs I chased this voice around, trying to identify its maker. I knew its Koyukon names, *tahoodzee neeyee* ("it says *tahoodzee*") or *taahoodzoya*, and I had been told that when it calls it is asking for breakup to hurry and come. Finally I recited the Koyukon words for its call to a more experienced bird-watcher—*chee chee chee chee tahoodzee tahoodzee tahoodzee*—and he immediately told me what it was.

The Seedeaters

This group of bird species is for some reason more important to the Koyukon than many of the other small birds. Most are very well regarded, as appealing personages who are essentially benevolent toward humans. Perhaps it is because they tend to be conspicuous birds, not much afraid of people or their settlements. And they are known well by their songs, which often enunciate a clear phrase in Koyukon, bringing to mind Distant Time stories that explain their words.

The pine grosbeak (*Pinicola enucleator*) is a large reddish bird that remains in the north year-round. It is usually called *kaayooda*, which Jetté (n.d.*a*) says is onomatopoetic. He adds that grosbeaks are said to imitate the calls of other birds, such as robins or thrushes, during the early spring. They do this so the others will answer if they have arrived, or so they will hurry if they are still on the way northward. Another name for the grosbeak is *kk'oghol-daala*, which one person translated "poor traveler," referring to the bird's Distant Time journeys, when he always depended on others for food. There is also an old name for this bird—*t'aghał daloggudla' ahonee*, "eats poplar cones."

Pine grosbeaks are not often seen, but if any are noticed around a fishing camp in early summer it is a sign that catches will be bad. These birds were hunted in times past, and people who have eaten them say they are very tasty.

> *In the Distant Time, grosbeak-man made a long trip, walking all winter and paddling all summer, and he had many experiences on this journey. Once he met a giant woman and decided he wanted to make love to her. She made him prove his strength first by knocking down a big tree, and then she consented. But when they made love he fell down inside her. Then he became a bird and escaped from her body, but ever afterward the grosbeak was colored red from her blood.*

The white-winged crossbill (*Loxia leucoptera*) is a very rare bird, almost never seen by Koyukuk River people. An old shaman who saw a crossbill only once in his life took it as a bad omen because the bird "doesn't belong here." People know of it, probably because of its extraordinary crossed mandibles, which are well designed for prying open spruce cones. A Hughes man said that if one is seen around a camp in early summer, there will be few fish that year. The crossbill is called *saak'idaatłggatł* or *saadok'i-daatłggadla*, "it has its bills crossed."

The nearly identical hoary and common redpolls (*Acanthus hornemanni;* and *A. flammea*) are known collectively by two terms—*k'ilodabeeza*, "flutters around," and *dilogha hutaadilghuzee*, "makes noise among the treetops." Because these are winter birds, their nests are strictly avoided and should not even be looked at.

Slate-colored juncos (*Junco hyemalis*) are early spring migrants, called *k'it'otłt'ahga*, a word that describes or resembles their call. These birds are not used or given special importance, but while I was living in Huslia somebody caught one and decided to keep it as a pet for a while. I asked if this was not tabooed (*hutłaanee*), as it is for most animals, and was told that an old man in another village had kept one for six months without any ill effects. This indicated that there was probably no danger from keeping this bird, so long as it was treated well. Here is a good example of the flexibility in Koyukon taboos, which can be relaxed if people break them without detecting later harm to themselves (and are strengthened if the opposite occurs). There are few absolutes in the Koyukon world.

Throughout the north country, one bird is celebrated as the harbinger of spring, the certain proof that winter is vanquished at last. This is the snow bunting (*Plectrophenax nivalis*), a plump white bird that twitters over the drifts in April and vanishes to places farther north a few weeks after it appears. Koyukon people take pleasure in attracting flocks of buntings by scattering meal around their cabin windows. Unlike the neighboring Eskimos, they do not eat these birds. They are given two names in Koyukon: *hugguh yoza*, "little snow geese," and *k'akk'utł ggaagga*, "cold weather animal."

Three kinds of sparrows are recognized by the Koyukon. One is the fox sparrow (*Passerella iliaca*), a fairly common summer bird, often heard as it sings loudly from the trees and thickets. Oddly enough, I could never learn a name for this conspicuous and well-known bird, and people seem to speak of it by a long reference to its song—"It says . . . ," reciting the words it sings. An elder woman from a Yukon River village called it *tsook'aał*, "grandmother." The fox sparrow's call is a sad lament, whose meaning is known from a Distant Time story. I was told the story several times, but I paraphrase Jetté's (n.d.*a*) more complete version of it here:

> In the Distant Time there was a beautiful woman who lived with her husband and grandmother. Once, when her husband was away, the old woman pretended to search through her granddaughter's hair for lice, but instead she thrust a bone awl into her ear and broke it off, killing her. Then she took her scalp and put it on her own head, disguising herself as the wife. She also put a bone needle into her navel and twisted it to tighten the loose, flabby skin on her belly. Finally she put on the younger woman's clothes; and disguised this way she fooled the husband into thinking she was his wife.
>
> But when she carried game from his canoe she could not move nimbly, so she had to excuse herself by saying that work had made her feel stiff. After they went to bed, however, the husband recognized who she was. He remained quiet until the next morning, and then he killed the old woman and dragged her body into the woods, where he also found his wife lying dead.
>
> Then the young woman's body became a little bird that flew into the air, singing: Sitsoo sidziy hułdaghudla gheeyits, "Grandmother poked a bone awl into my ear." Nowadays the fox sparrow still sings this way, telling of its death in the world of long ago.

Another sparrow found here is called *kitsaan' loy doldoya*, "sits on a stalk of grass." It is probably the savanna sparrow (*Passercula sandwichensis*). I heard very little about this bird, except that I was warned against ever looking at its nest, which could cause bad luck. Since it nests on the ground, I suspect this rule might relate to the earth's spiritual power. Neither this nor any of the other sparrows is eaten or otherwise used.

The white-crowned sparrow (*Zonotrichia leucophrys*) has a song and a story of its own. This common summer bird is called *k'itł'in ts'ahut'aana*, "dentalium shell person," its name derived from the markings on its crown. Like the fox sparrow, it is given a special accounting in a story from the Distant Time. Each spring, Koyukon people listen to its sad song—*Dzo do'o sik'its'eetee tł'ot*—and they remember what it means:

> Long ago, in the Distant Time, the man who became the white-crowned sparrow was walking across the Pah River portage toward a

spring camp called Ts'eetee tl'ot. He carried with him a band of the treasured dentalium shells. But he was weak and starving, and before he reached the camp he died on the soft snow.

At death he was transformed into the white-crowned sparrow, and he flew on to the spring camp. When he arrived, he could only sing, Dzo do'o sik'its'eetee tl'ot, "Here is Ts'eetee tl'ot, but it's too late." Today, the bird still sings these melancholy words, and the white marks on its head remain from the dentalium band he carried before his death long ago.

8

The Small Mammals

The Hidden Lives

I remember standing alone one midwinter morning on a frozen lake a few miles from Huslia. It was powerfully cold and still, so quiet that my own breathing and the beating of my heart were distracting to me. I felt encircled by a vacuum, as if I were alone in space.

But gazing along the shoreline I picked out the unmistakable hump of a beaver house, and beside it were twigs from a feed pile, barely protruding above the snow. And I remembered that in the fall I had seen muskrat pushups, little feeding houses, scattered across the lake's newly frozen surface—now they were hidden beneath the deep powder. Along the far shore, a lacework of hare trails wove among the willows, whose slender trunks were white with fresh gnawings. In the forest above the closest bank, a heap of scales from spruce cones marked the entrance to a squirrel's underground passageways.

There were animals all around me. They swam in dark waters under the thick snow and ice, possibly beneath my feet at that moment. They hunched safely in snowdrift hollows among the clustered willow trunks. Or they scurried invisibly through networks of tunnels, occasionally glimpsing dim gray light filtered through the deep overburden of snowflakes. I realized that the world that appeared so numb and inert was in fact a busy community of hidden lives.

Those of us who live differently from the Koyukon are likely to overlook the small animals, or at best to give them a minor role in the natural and human scheme. But what they lack in size they often make up in numbers, and so they are essential both as members of the boreal ecosystem and as resources in the human economy. Koyukon elders can recall times when hares, muskrats, or beavers were all they had to eat. But the small animals are not just survival foods—some are important supplements to the usual diet; and some are delicacies. Anyone who has not tried roasted muskrat or beaver meat would have a pleasant surprise in store if they could sidestep their cultural biases.

The animals to be discussed in this chapter are all gnawing herbivores (except for the shrews), and most are rodents. They include the "mice" (voles, lemmings, and shrews), snowshoe hare, squirrels (of which there are four species), porcupine, muskrat, and the relatively ponderous beaver. Nearly all of these animals are used by the Koyukon as a source of food and hides, and each has a special role in the people's cultural and spiritual world. Aside from this, the small mammals are vital to the overall health and ecological patterning of the boreal forest, because they are the principal food source for many larger predators.

Voles, Lemmings, and Shrews

Of all the mammals that regularly occur in the Koyukon wildlands (about twenty-three species), "mice" are the only ones not directly harvested and used. And there is a rare exception to this, when certain voles or lemmings are kept as amulets. Only the innocuous insect species are less directly important to human life and livelihood here. But the ecologically astute Koyukon realize that mice are indirectly vital as basic elements in the food chain. They may ignore or even avoid these animals, but they recognize them as essential co-inhabitants of the environment.

Voles

Voles are the abundant little stub-tailed "mice" whose networks of subnivean tunnels are so rudely exposed when snow vanishes from the meadows each spring. Several species occur in the Koyukuk valley, probably the boreal redback vole (*Clethrionomys gapperi*), tundra redback vole (*C. rutilus*), and meadow vole (*Microtus pennsylvanicus*). The Koyukon know them all as *deeltsa'a,* sensibly avoiding the taxonomic minutae required to tell these animalcules apart.

Voles are scarcely a favorite with Koyukon people, although they do not consider them evil. They have the bad habit of pulling patches of fur from animals killed in traps, to use as lining for their nests. Sometimes they damage hides even more by gnawing all the way inside the carcass. But even worse, for some people at least, is their occasional urge to nest in stored furs, clothing, mattresses, or other belongings. According to Koyukon tradition, finding a brood of voles among such possessions is a strong sign of bad luck for the owner or a relative. I was told about a woman who found a nest of voles in her mattress, and she died that winter: "But lately these things don't happen any more, maybe because most people don't believe in it now."

Those who still do believe are always careful to put clothes and fur in vole-proof places, such as high caches. One old man explained that he keeps the grass cut short around his house to discourage the little animals, so that they are less likely to get into things. They are dirty, he said, and they might nest in bad places or defile meat by eating from it.

Many people are less cautious about voles, but they are usually somewhat afraid of them (in a way that is familiar among outsiders as well). "In the old days," a woman told me, "we never used to be like that. Mice came inside our camp or our cabin all the time. It never bothered us." Another woman said that, when they lived in a tent, her uncle had taught her to hold a bit of food in her palm as she lay in her sleeping bag. If she felt a vole step onto it, she would try to grab it. Finally her uncle was bitten doing this, so they quit the game.

Very rarely, someone may find an albino vole (called *łoołtł'o deeltsa'a*), and if it can be caught it is a valuable amulet. One man showed me the little dried white skin (with the skull intact) of an albino vole he had killed many years before and has always kept among his special possessions. I heard no one mention albinos of any other species, so I cannot guess how they would be regarded.

Lemmings

Two species are probably found in Koyukon country, the northern bog lemming (*Synaptomys borealis*) and the brown lemming (*Lemmus sibiricus*). Both look like outsized voles, and their general life pattern is similar to that of their smaller compatriot groundlings. They are known by two Koyukon names (which apparently do not distinguish them)—*binobintł'ogga* (no translation) and *kk'uyhk'ideeltsa'a* ("willow vole").

If a lemming can be caught, which seldom happens, its skin is dried with the skull and kept as a charm or amulet for good luck. Explaining this, one man told me that the lemming (he specified *binobintł'ogga*) is a lucky animal, and unlike voles or shrews it will not gnaw on cached meat. It is very scarce here, but the person who gets one will have good luck in hunting and trapping. This man said he has managed to take only one lemming and has kept its skin for about thirty years.

Shrews

These are the tiniest animals, miniature predators that live on insects, carrion, or whatever they can catch. Three species probably live in this region—the masked shrew (*Sorex cinereus*), dusky shrew (*S. obscurus*), and tundra shrew (*S. tundrensis*). Most Koyukon people call them by the collective name *loodolts'iyhdla;* but one man said that this is the term for a small one (about an inch long), and that a larger one (about an inch and a half long) is called *toodohuggo.* Like the voles, shrews sometimes ruin trapped animals; they pull out the fur, and the meat helps sustain their high metabolism. Sometimes a trapper finds only the hollowed-out shell of his catch after shrews have worked on it. According to Jetté (n.d.*a*), an unusual abundance of shrews is considered an omen of epidemic or strange death.

Snowshoe Hare

> A rare event today: I saw a winter snowshoe hare. It was nearly as
> pure and perfect white as the snow itself, and had it remained still
> I never would have seen a thing. It hopped away through the
> willows, and when the dogs saw it they leaped ahead, lifting their
> noses as we rushed through the curtain of scent. In a month the
> snow will vanish and the hare will change its coat to match the
> brown earth—invisible once again. [Huslia journal, April 1977]

Snowshoe hares (*Lepus americanus*) are the quintessential denizens of the boreal forests, ideally adapted to the conditions it creates. Their feet splay out to float them atop soft snow, their color changes with the seasons, and they can sustain themselves on the ubiquitous, fast-growing willows. Winter is such a friend to them that they become fat during its passage, constantly elevated to new feed by the building snow. Despite their exquisite camouflage, they are caught by an assortment of predators, such as owls, foxes, and especially the lynx.

These boreal rabbits are notorious for their dramatic population cycles, with a usual period of seven to twelve years. At times the country is almost devoid of their tracks, then a few years later there may be literally crowds of them, trampling the snow hard among the willows. When their population grows or crashes, predators who live on them experience similar cycles. Hares have been relatively scarce in the Koyukuk valley for well over a decade, though they were increasing slowly when I lived in Huslia. During the past times, especially when other resources were scarce, the Koyukon virtually lived through the winter on hares. So they must be considered one of the most important animals in the overall subsistence economy.

> *Wait, I see something: We are wide open in the bushes.*
> *Answer: The snowshoe hare's eyes.*
> [Jetté 1913:195]

The best way to catch hares is to set little snares in their trails. This can be done year-round, by men and women of all ages, and it brings home much meat when hares are plentiful. People set out snare lines especially during the fall and tend them with diminishing enthusiasm until the spring thaw begins. Hares are also hunted with light rifles, particularly as they bask in the evening sun during late spring, and to a lesser extent during summer. They are fragile animals, easily killed by the bullet or snare, and people sometimes criticize a man by saying, "He doesn't have the strength of a rabbit." Hares should not be kept as pets, because the children of someone who keeps them will die easily.

In Koyukon the snowshoe hare is called *gguh,* an indefinite reference to white color. A special term may be used for it in summer—*saanh zooga',* which vaguely means "summer coat." Hares are invested with a fairly powerful spirit (*biyeega hoolaanh*), but it has little of the malevolence that characterizes some of the other animals so endowed. Hares are likely to avoid the snares of anyone who offends them—they will sit in the trails and look at them instead of entering them and being caught. When this happened in former times, people would rub ashes on the eyes of several dead hares while telling them, "Don't look at snares." A Distant Time story includes a song that the hare-man sang, and people can still sing it to bring themselves luck in catching these animals.

Stealing hares from someone else's sets invites spiritual retaliation, though not as severe as with animals like the wolverine. Bad luck or illness could befall the offender. It is also strictly tabooed to catch hares with a deadfall (traditionally used for trapping various fur animals), and if one is accidentally caught this way it is a sign that "somebody will become crippled." If a snared rabbit dies with a hind leg pointing up, either stretched in the air or braced against the snare or toggle (this occurrence is called *ditaatltona*), it is a sign of good hunting luck.

Someone who has a good snare line can bring home ten or twenty hares each day if conditions are ideal. Hares are skinned by peeling the hide off from the rear, turning it inside out the way some people do when they remove their socks. They have deep, warm fur, but their skin is very fragile and easily torn; so Koyukon people seldom use it today. In former times they cut the hide spirally to make long strips, which they wove into garments or blankets. The overgrown, furry feet served as washcloths and dishrags, and children also made toy dogs of them.

Hares are usually cooked in the stewpot—the meat, head, heart, liver, and intestines are all eaten. The *koleeyo',* a part of the viscera, is not eaten by women lest their children born afterward cry too much. Very rarely, someone will find dead, withered fetuses inside a winter-caught hare. This is a powerfully tabooed occurrence, a sign of ill fortune, possibly death in the finder's family.

When snowshoe hares are brought home for butchering, they should be treated respectfully to sustain a good relationship with their spirits. People used to break their hind legs when they were brought inside the house to thaw. This kept their spirits from "running around," which would be dangerous for anyone nearby. Once hares are brought indoors they should remain there until they are skinned; and they should not be taken back out the same day (this rule also applies to furbearers). I learned no special ways to dispose of hare remains, but Sullivan (1942:111) writes that the Nulato Koyukon put the bones in an out-of-the-way place and keep them away from the dogs. I suspect that the Koyukuk River people would agree, though they may not follow this very strictly today.

The Squirrels

Four different kinds of squirrels are known to the Koyukon people—the red squirrel, flying squirrel, Arctic ground squirrel, and hoary marmot. None has much significance in the modern subsistence economy, but they are important in other ways.

Red Squirrel
The red squirrel is another abundant boreal forest creature, like the snowshoe hare, but two more different characters can scarcely be imagined. The squirrel is as outgoing and obstreperous as the hare is timid and secretive. Every tree is its podium, and it always has plenty to say when anyone intrudes on its domain. It is an irascible, animated, and always delightful animal.

> I stood quietly beneath a huge spruce. Piles of fragmented cones mounded among burrows that led down into the moss left no doubt about who must be nearby. Then I heard an outburst of chucking and squeaking just above me—I made no move. Before long the scolding came nearer, and finally I saw a little red bundle nervously scurrying along a branch beside me. He was possessed with an improbable mix of hostility, fear, and curiosity; but curiosity was winning. In a moment he was fidgeting almost within my reach. I saw his little ribs puffing with each breath, saw where dark hairs stood against white along his side, saw a flake of bark stuck in the brush of his tail. And I saw the forest reflected in his eye.
> Then he blinked and vanished among a maze of branches.
> [Huslia journal, June 1977]

The red squirrel (*Tamiasciurus hudsonicus*) is strictly a forest animal, seldom seen far from a spruce tree. This midget among squirrels (it is scarcely larger than a chipmunk) divides its life between the high tree branches and the burrows it digs in the ground or beneath the snow. It is active all winter, but it comes to the surface and the trees only during warm spells. Squirrel populations seem to be fairly consistent and evenly distributed, and in the forest you always feel that at least one is close by. Listen for a while and your suspicion will probably be confirmed.

Although red squirrels are common, the Koyukon very rarely (if ever) eat them today. In times past they were hunted, especially in the fall when they were fattest. Sullivan (1942:112) wrote that the Nulato people occasionally hunted squirrels and professed "a strong liking for them." Koyukuk River people, on the other hand, seem to care little for eating them and regard them as a starvation food (nowadays at least).

A man from Hughes told me that, although some people used to eat squirrels, they are supposed to be tabooed, and violators may starve later on. It is also strictly tabooed to roast squirrels on a stick (many other animals are cooked this way), so they are always placed on hot coals or laid beside the fire until their meat is done. Red-squirrel pelts are extremely warm and durable, and people used to make parkas, pants, and mitten liners with them. Accumulating enough of these little skins for a parka must have been no easy accomplishment.

The red squirrel's spirit power manifests itself in several ways. Sullivan (1942:112) was told that, if a man wounds one of these animals and it escapes, it is a sign that his wife is unfaithful—and its spirit will cause her to die. A Hughes elder said that squirrel carcasses should not be burned, because this would cause storminess or extreme cold. They are best left out in the woods where scavengers will clean them up.

The Koyukon have several names for the red squirrel. It is usually called *tsaghaldaala*, "goes around in pitch darkness." Another name for it is *dliga*, which resembles its call (*dlik . . . dlik . . . dlik*). At night, however, the squirrel's ordinary names must never be spoken, and it should instead be called by the circumlocution *dikinh k'alyee*, "the one that is on the side of a tree." Doing otherwise would bring bad fortune to the violator.

It is also a powerful forewarning of bad luck (*hugho doldaalyeel* in Koyukon) to hear a red squirrel chattering or scolding in the night. Several people who told me about hearing this with someone else said the other person died within a year. Once a group of men in a remote camp heard a squirrel calling in the darkness outside the tent. "What are you guys worried about?" one of them asked. "That's for me." The next summer he drowned.

Flying Squirrel

This animal (*Glaucomys sabrinus*) is known to the Koyukuk River people, but it occurs only farther south, along the Yukon. It is called *nindibidza* ("it flutters here and there") or *ts'ikinleeda'* ("it glides down"). My only information on the animal comes from Jetté (n.d.a), whom I quote in full:

> To see a flying squirrel, or to catch one by accident, is an ill omen, foreboding the death of a near relative of the person to whom this happens. Children are earnestly cautioned against laying their hands on this dangerous beast, but it does turn out, every now and then, that they get hold of one and even bring it into the camp,

to the great vexation of the wiser ones. To avert the threatened misfortune, the animal is chopped in pieces, and these burnt to ashes.

Arctic Ground Squirrels

People who live along the river and spend most of their time in the lowlands seldom see the Arctic ground squirrel (*Spermophilus undulatus*), because it is principally a mountain and tundra animal. Only occasionally is a colony of burrows found along the riverbank, with its plump little inhabitants standing alert like boreal prairie dogs, chattering nervously or making forays into the surrounding vegetation. Serious hunters must look for ground squirrels in the uplands, where they are often abundant in the spring and summer. The other half of the year they devote to hibernation.

In Koyukon the ground squirrel is called *hundaggaza,* "it stands erect over an area." People relish its fat and tasty meat but do not get it very often. I was advised that the meat should be boiled, not roasted on a stick over an open fire. Apparently this is because the fat, dripping onto the fire, will attract brown bears. Ground squirrel hides were used for parkas, hats, and mittens, but this is rarely done today. When a man leaves to hunt ground squirrels or trap them at their burrow openings, he must always tell someone (particularly his wife) what he is going out after. If he neglects doing this, his wife or a family member will become sick and suffer a lingering death.

Hoary Marmot

Even more so than the ground squirrel, the hoary marmot (*Marmota marmota*) is a mountain animal, almost never seen away from the high tundra slopes. People from Hughes, which is near the mountains, encounter marmots far more often than those who live in flatland places like Huslia. These animals possess a very powerful spirit, similar to that of the beaver, which the Koyukon regard as a close relative (according to Jetté, n.d.*a*). Also, some of the taboos associated with marmots are the same as those for ground squirrel—they must not be cooked on a stick over the fire, and a hunter must tell someone before he goes after them.

The marmot is called *ṭaa ggaagga,* "boulder animal," a name well suited to its habitat. It is regarded as a very clean animal with extraordinary vision; no creature except the wolf can see as well. Perhaps this is why hunters listen for one of its calls—a long, loud whistle that ends with a "clapping sound"—as an indicator that a large animal like a fox, wolf, or bear is somewhere nearby. It also makes a long whistle that fades at the end, a sign that rain will come later in the day. Incidentally, if a marmot should ever appear near someone's house it is a "menace of death," according to Jetté (n.d.*a*), and the place should be abandoned. Given the animal's usual haunts, this would be one of those rare occurrences that are always taken as a bad sign.

Marmots must never be left to rot or go to waste, because their potent spirits would punish such neglect with bad luck or sickness. Sometimes a hunter wounds one, however, and it becomes wedged down among the rocks. Every effort should be made to retrieve it, so men sometimes carry a long stick with a hook on the end for this purpose. If it cannot be pulled out, wood should be pushed in around it and set afire, so that the carcass is at least partially (or symbolically) consumed. This way it has not just been left without doing anything to it.

Marmots have delicious meat, and their fat is so rich (especially in August) that people become sick if they eat more than a small amount. Sometimes the fat is rendered to make a clear oil that meat is dipped into, as people also do with seal oil obtained in trade from Kobuk Eskimos. When a marmot is butchered, people take care to remove two glands (*kkutl*) and discard them. These glands are considered "devil meat," which must never be eaten (other animals have them too, such as the beaver). Marmot hides were used in the past for making parkas, pants, socks, and hats, but I did not see anyone using them today.

Porcupine

Everyone is familiar with the porcupine (*Erethizon dorsatum*), a rotund, pincushion animal that plods methodically through the forest. Aside from buds and greens, the porcupine's usual diet is spruce bark. The hungry animal simply climbs to a suitable perch, or sits at the base of a tree, and gnaws off a patch of it. These bare, toothmarked spots slowly turn gray with age, but they remain for years as evidence of a porcupine's woody feast. When I lived in the Koyukuk villages, porcupines were not very common, but their population is subject to marked ups and downs. No one can predict when a porcupine will be found, because they wander everywhere; and so they usually turn up unexpectedly:

> I was walking through willows along a meadow near our camp this afternoon and was startled by a porcupine. It made no movement until I nearly stepped on it; and then, as suddenly as a porcupine can, it tried to waddle out of my way. It was a big one, perhaps fifteen pounds, and lighter colored than usual.
> The porcupine quickly gave up "running" and turned its well-bristled back toward me. I wanted some quills, so I poked a few off with a stick, then picked them up or pulled them from the wood, following the animal as it slowly moved away. Finally, harassed beyond patience, it crawled into a little space beneath a tangle of thick roots and stared out between them as I bent down

to look closely into its sad face and watery eyes. It is hard to
imagine a more humble expression than I saw there, and I walked
away feeling guilty. [Huslia journal, June 1977]

At the end of summer, porcupines become restless and begin moving
widely. People hunting moose along the river sometimes see them on the
sandbars, and they are rarely left alone at this season because they are fat and
delicious. During the first half of winter they still travel around a good deal,
leaving their distinctive tracks as a testament to their slow, rather aimless
explorations. They are also hunted at this time. But as the cold weather
wears on they usually "hole up" in old bear dens or other hollows, and
people seldom hunt them because they have become too lean.

When they find a porcupine during the right season (fall or early winter),
Koyukon hunters usually kill it with a club, then singe off the quills in a
large fire. This helps to flavor the meat (which is later boiled) and removes a
danger. Porcupine quills are barbed so that they slowly work inward, and
people say they can completely penetrate an animal. An elder from Huslia
told me he once found a fox with two quills protruding from its side, points
outward. It was noticeably stunted, and he found scars on its organs where
the quills had worked clear through its body. If a dog gets quills in it they
are very hard to pull out, but some Koyukon people say that snipping them
off at the skin will keep them from working deeper.

The porcupine is called *dikahona,* "stick eater," or *ligidza,* "that which is
crooked," referring to its humped back. Koyukon people enjoy the animal's
meat, which tastes to me like strong pork, as well as its rich, thick fat.
Neither the head nor the viscera are eaten, but in former times various body
parts had several other uses. The "intestine," with fecal pellets inside, was
dried and used for a baby's belt, to make it have hard feces. This was no
small advantage in the days when moss was the only diaper.

During their puberty sequestration, young women (at least in the Yukon
River villages) wore the same kind of belt, or one made from the heads of
porcupine femurs strung together. This was done so the girl would acquire
the animal's ease in giving birth (according to biologists, porcupines have
proportionately the largest young of any North American land mammal). If
an infant porcupine was caught, a pubescent girl would slip the prickly little
carcass (very carefully, I am sure) down through her parka to the ground,
again to promote easy childbirth. I presume this also explains why porcupine was the only fresh meat that girls in this transition period were
allowed to eat (Sullivan 1942:113).

Little boys used to play a game with a porcupine's pelvis: first they hid
their eyes while one of them tossed it away, then they all searched for it.
Whoever found it first would be lucky with bear hunting in the fall when he
grew up. The same thing was done with a bear's "knee bone." The person

who described this said it was just like hunting for a bear's den, a sort of childhood "practice." The only other useful part of the porcupine is its quills (k'uh), formerly flattened and dyed, then used like long beads to make beautiful trim for skin clothing. Older women still know how to do this, but it is scarcely ever seen today.

There are few special ways of dealing with the porcupine's spirit, aside from the usual basic gestures of respect for all living things. A taboo forbids setting steel traps for these animals. Once a woman caught a porcupine this way at its den opening and it escaped by breaking off its leg. Later one of her legs began to wither, and eventually it was lost, her punishment for treating the porcupine in a forbidden way. If one is inadvertently caught in a trap set for other animals, however, there is no need to fear retribution from its spirit.

Porcupines are great wanderers despite their labored gait, as anyone knows who has followed their tracks winding almost endlessly through the forest. They are given a special power to know the landscape, I was told, and this is why people should never set traps for them (no further explanation was given). Beyond this, their familiarity with the geography is described as a kind of "understanding," as if their comprehension of the terrain is really just a metaphor representing something much greater.

> Porcupines know all the country. Even though they're low to the ground they really know the land. They're powerful animals. My old man said, "The whole of Alaska is just like something inside the palm of a porcupine's hand."

For the Koyukon, no animal is just that and nothing more. Even the least imposing of creatures, those that seem insignificant from the lofty perspective of humanity, have dimensions of being that extend far beyond the realm and power of the senses. It is not a world where humans may become too proud, for nothing that lives is truly humble, regardless of how it may appear.

Muskrat

Muskrats (Ondatra zibethicus) are plump little rodents, usually just over a foot long, that inhabit the northland rivers, sloughs, and lakes. Webbed feet and a vertically flattened paddling tail equip them for their aquatic life, as does their dense coat of brownish fur. They are also fairly accomplished engineers, a lesser version of their close relative the beaver. For houses they pile up mounds of vegetation in the shallows and hollow them out above water level, or they excavate dens in lakeshores and riverbanks, with secure underwater entrances. They also make little winter feeding houses, called "pushups," by gnawing holes through the lake ice and building hollow mounds of vegetation over them. This gives them places to breathe or to sit and eat the water plants that make up their diet.

Muskrats are among the more common animal inhabitants of Koyukon country, though their numbers fluctuate between abundance and relative scarcity. They are important as a source of both food and pelts, and people sometimes put quite an effort into harvesting them during late winter and spring. There are two ways to catch muskrats—people shoot them on the ice before breakup or in open water later on, or they set traps for them inside their pushups or at feeding spots along the shore. Their fur becomes prime by late winter, the same season when they are fattest and most tasty. Later on, by mid-May, breeding-season fights make them lean, and bites damage their hides; so the harvest season ends.

Muskrats (bikinaala; in Koyukon, "long tail") are pugnacious creatures, and people use them as a standard for toughness—"He fought just like a little muskrat." Trappers and hunters are ever wary of their teeth and temperament.

> We got only one muskrat today. It was in a trap and had torn its pushup fairly well apart. When we walked up to it the little animal was all fight, coming straight after us ready for anything. Our size didn't seem to matter a bit. Muskrats must have some fine battles in the spring, and it's small wonder their hides end up full of holes. [Huslia journal, April 1977]

After they are brought home or into camp, muskrats are skinned and prepared for the stewpot. People who follow Koyukon tradition leave the "collarbones" and scapulas attached to the forelegs, because severing them will alienate the animal and make it difficult to catch more. In former times, they also left the forepaws on the legs when they butchered and cooked muskrats, but this is no longer done. Besides the meat, Koyukon people eat the liver, head, and feet. The tail is also cooked, but it is tabooed for the young because it wiggles so much when the animal swims that it would cause them to shoot poorly. Women (except those past menopause) must not eat meat from the muskrat's pelvis, lest they acquire the animal's difficulty with parturition.

Muskrat meat is tender and excellent tasting, not only for the Koyukon but for anyone who is willing to try it. Before they had access to freezers, the people preserved muskrats by drying them, then boiled the meat to prepare it for eating. The viscera are usually given to the dogs, as is the meat of animals whose skin is punctured by fighting. Fluid from the musk glands is used as an ointment to heal skin rashes. And the hide is used to make beautiful parkas, traditional summer pants, hats, and mitten linings. Pelts are also sold to commercial fur buyers, but only when people have more than they need for themselves.

The traditional way to dispose of a muskrat's bones is to throw them in the water with a request that they come back again, literally "be made again in the water" (tononlitseeyh). This is a way of asking that the animal be reincarnated, so it can be hunted again. People explain that this tradition is fading because they usually skin muskrats at home rather than in camps, so it is not convenient to return bones to the water.

The local population of muskrats may be affected by a giant form of the animal called "mother of muskrats" (bikinaal baanh). It is the size of a beaver, people say, and its fur is yellowish. These creatures are rarely found, and the only one in the Huslia region lives in a lake called Toneedza ts'ibaa la'onh dinh. Muskrats are always abundant there, even though many people hunt and trap in the area each spring. The mother of muskrats is "the boss of the muskrats . . . it's where all the muskrats come from."

The muskrat and beaver are siblings. They look alike, live similar lives, even eat some of the same foods. Sometimes muskrats live inside beaver houses; and they may even act as protective lookouts for their larger relatives:

> Back when it was legal to shoot beavers, we used to wait for them
> where they would come out through a hole in the ice in springtime.
> Sometimes we would see a muskrat come up and swim around in that hole,
> just looking around, and then it dove back down again. My old man
> never let me shoot that muskrat, and I never used to see it come back to
> the hole again. But in a while a beaver would show up—that muskrat
> told him that it's safe to come out. That's why we had to let the muskrat
> alone, because we would have a chance for the beaver if we just waited.

Beaver

I have often wondered if the beaver thinks in abstractions. In my own culture, one of the supposedly unique elaborations of humanity is the ability to conceptualize, make, and use tools to modify the environment. Here is an animal—a rodent at that—who makes elaborate and effective dams to create deep ponds or lakes, builds large, multiroom dwellings with underwater entrances, and stores an entire winter's supply of food where it is easily accessible but protected beneath water and ice. Small wonder it is among the more powerful animal spirits in the Koyukon world.

> Wait, I see something: I drag my shovel along the trail.
> Answer: A beaver, with its broad, bare tail.
> [Jetté 1913:188]

The beaver (Castor canadensis) is a widespread and very well known animal, valued for its rich and durable pelt, famous for its extraordinary paddle-shaped tail. And the Koyukon savor it as one of the best foods the northern forest provides. Almost everyone is acquainted in some way with the beaver, but few realize how large it is—three or four feet long and up to fifty pounds or more. I can well remember my astonishment the first time I saw a big adult swimming beneath the riverbank where I stood. It took a long moment's thought before I realized what animal it was.

Koyukon elders also speak of a giant beaver, an extraordinary creature many times the size of its smaller counterparts. A man from Huslia encountered one at a lake in wild country west of the village, and he said it was nearly the size of a bear. He shot at it ("I don't know if he should have done that," my instructor said), but the bullet ricocheted and the animal did not appear again.

Ordinary beavers (noya'a) center their lives on the lake or stretch of river where they build a lodge or excavate a den in a steep bank. Their principal food is tree bark and branches which they cut along the shore and drag down short trails into the water. These forays on land expose them to predation by wolves, wolverines, and bears; and occasionally they are killed when a tree they are cutting falls on them. Winter is a safer season, but a wolverine sometimes tears a lodge open to get at the beavers inside. And the indomitable otter may enter the lodge from under water at any season, with disastrous consequences for its occupants.

Beavers have a well-deserved reputation as hard workers. It is a high compliment, for example, when someone says of a woman, "She's just like a female beaver" (Loyens 1966:40). They fill the long twilight hours, from breakup to freeze-up, with constant labor preparing for winter, when their lives will depend on food they have stored away. They even become lean from their work, and this (as well as pelt condition) is why Koyukon trappers prefer to wait until spring to catch them. After many months of leisure and indulgence from the feed pile, they have become fat and prime.

Sometimes heavy rains in late fall cause high water that sweeps the feed piles away from river-dwelling beavers. If they can't gather enough again before freeze-up they will probably starve in the winter cold, because food plants do not grow in the rivers and streams (unlike the lakes). These animals gnaw holes in the ice and come out to gather food ashore, but they may freeze their feet and tails doing so. Trappers sometimes catch animals with their tails half gone, survivors of these winter hardships.

When all goes well, beavers are very active in February, their breeding season. Inhabitants of the lodge usually include a mated adult pair, some smaller adults, and yearlings from the spring before. Although beavers may have up to seven embryos inside them, Koyukon people say that only one to three young are born. From this they conclude that the animals are unable to care for more than three kits. Beavers of different ages are distinguished in Koyukon (Jones 1979:18):

noya'a or *ggaagga* ("animal")	beaver
ggaaggateeya'	male over three years old (biggest beaver)
neenol'aala	large beaver
k'iłnoya	female beaver
k'inohusloona	kit one year old
bikonh k'idaadlitłeeya	female beaver with young

The Koyukuk wildlands are well populated with beavers, especially in the flats where water dominates the terrain. Their numbers fluctuate, though, and in the past decade or so they seem to have declined. People explain that disease has reduced them and that the lakes are drying up so they have fewer places to live. When flying above the Koyukuk flats, it is not unusual to see lakes that have shrunk away from their shores, leaving beaver lodges high and dry. Here again is the process of natural dynamics that is so familiar in the Koyukon world.

Beavers are significant in Koyukuk village economies, although they are never more than a secondary resource. This contrasts with eastern subarctic peoples like the Cree, for whom they are a staple food. In any case, beaver meat is one of the very best foods the land provides—it is excellent tasting, rich, and nutritious (see Cooperative Extension Service 1974:11 for nutritional data on Alaskan game foods). The Koyukon not only value it for themselves, but also consider it the best food for keeping their dog teams fit and healthy.

In addition to the meat, Koyukon people eat the liver, kidneys, and tail (which is rich in fat and ranks as a delicacy). The hind feet are tabooed to all except elders, because they would cause young people or their children to become pigeon-toed. The head used to be cooked and eaten, but nowadays it is discarded (taboo forbids giving it to the dogs). Meat from the pelvis is tabooed for women who may bear children, because, like the muskrat, this animal is supposed to have difficult parturition.

Beaver meat is usually boiled, but sometimes it is roasted over an open fire or in the oven. It is also excellent when dried or smoked, then boiled for eating. Other parts of the animal that are used include the humerus and femur—if a man can break a humerus with his bare hands, he is considered strong; if he can break a femur he is very strong (cf. Loyens 1966:46). And the pelt, of course, is much sought by fur traders. Often, however, Koyukon women keep much of the catch for making parkas, mittens, boot trim, and hats.

As I mentioned earlier, beavers are regarded as perceptive and powerful members of the natural community. Koyukon people watch them closely to see just what sort of creature they are, perhaps to understand their special kind of intelligence. For example, two of my instructors who have both trapped the animal all their lives told me that beavers seem able to talk. Once both of them were watching a beaver cut down a tree beside the river, while several others swam nearby. The animal was frightened by a noise (beavers are said to have excellent hearing) and it began making a strange sound. The other beavers immediately vanished, apparently having heard a warning.

The beaver can also make a loud humming sound that varies in pitch and rhythm. Koyukon people say it resembles someone mumbling, or an old man singing Indian songs. One man said his father had explained it to him this way:

> You know, beavers work hard all fall and winter, so every spring they take a vacation. They drift down the river someplace or they wander around through the lakes. Then, later on in summer they start heading back home, and it really makes them feel happy. So that's when they like to sing the most, while they swim along toward home.

Koyukon people watch animals with fascination and with empathy based on their understanding that animals and humans are much the same order of being. When they are not hunting, they watch animals as an end in itself, born of curiosity and a desire to understand the community of natural things. Sometimes, as the story above shows, they explain the behavior of animals in terms of more complex emotions than an outsider would attribute to nonhuman beings.

As another example, one of my teachers said he had seen a beaver lose its temper. The animal had cut down a tree so it fell into a lake and then tried to push the tree off the bank. But it was stuck on the bottom and refused to budge. So the beaver crawled down, slipped into the lake, chewed off some branches, then climbed back up and pushed once more. But it still stuck tight. Down the animal went again, this time more quickly and impatiently, but with the same result. It went through this routine several more times, marching up and down faster, showing more irritation with each failure. Finally, in an apparent fit of frustration, the beaver fairly threw itself off the top of the bank, and the people watching laughed so loudly that it was frightened away.

Beavers not only are considered fascinating and intelligent, they are also given a powerful spirit that tempers the way people treat them. Although not among the most potent animal spirits, beaver (together with marmot) is just beneath them. Disrespectful behavior toward creatures with such spirits is dangerous indeed.

When a beaver is trapped, its meat should be left for about three days before any is eaten. This is the time it takes to become completely dead, as if the threatening emanations must die away, leaving it peaceful in death before it is further disturbed. The same waiting period (or longer, because full death may not come for a week) should be observed before feeding beaver to dogs. In the old days, when people were short of meat just after spring breakup, they often shot beavers for food. These animals, having been taken in a less spiritually significant way, could be eaten without waiting.

When a trapped beaver is brought into the house or trapline cabin, it should be skinned before anyone sleeps, because it is tabooed to keep the animal inside overnight with its skin on. And the skinned carcass should not be put outside until the next day. Care is taken not to slice the beaver's eyeballs, nor should its throat ever be cut. There is a special way to butcher it, so the head, trachea, lungs, and heart are all removed without severing them. The "collarbone" is also left attached to the shoulder, because catches will become poor if they are cut apart. And there are certain parts of the viscera (which I could not identify) that should not be cut away.

> My brother doesn't follow hutlaanee [taboos]. When he cut a
> beaver's throat in front of me, it just hurt me to see that happen.

As with the muskrat, beaver bones should be returned to the lake or river, with a request, "Be made again in the water." This customary means of ensuring the animal's reincarnation is seldom practiced today. Traditionally, anyone who discarded the bones carelessly or fed them to dogs would suffer bad luck in trapping beavers. If there was no water nearby, the bones were either hung in a tree or burned (Sullivan 1942:108; Loyens 1966:47).

The custom of tossing bones into the water originated in the Distant Time. A young man spent a winter living with the beaver-people, and he married a woman from among them. When spring came, he wanted to go back to his own people, but there was no food to sustain him on the way. His wife offered to be killed as provisions for his trip, and in return her parents said he should throw her bones into the water and ask for her reincarnation. After he did this, she returned to them alive (Sullivan 1942: 107–8).

Although they no longer dispose of beaver remains in this way, people are careful not to leave them lying around on the ground where someone might walk over them. The same basic respect shown to all animals, in other words, is shown to them. They do follow another special practice, however. Beavers and bears "don't get along," and so traditional people avoid eating bear meat during the beaver-trapping season. A man who violated this taboo said he caught no beavers until the next year. It is also bad luck to eat beaver (or bear) and then vomit it up. One woman said her brother did this with a beaver she had trapped, and she never caught another that spring.

When a man is trapping beaver his wife should work hard like the animal itself, and its spirit will help him make good catches (Loyens 1966:46). The man should avoid sleeping with his wife while he is trapping, however. Beavers used to be killed by underwater deadfalls that broke their backs, and violating the taboo will cause back trouble. The association between beavers and human spouses is also expressed in a sign—if a man sees a dying beaver evacuate its bowels or bladder, it is revealing his wife's unfaithfulness (Jetté 1911:606).

Menstruating women are prohibited from eating beaver meat and from trapping or hunting the animal. The menses has great power to alienate animals or make them aloof, through its own spiritual energies. So, for example, an elder woman tried unsuccessfully to take a beaver when another woman and I were along, then understood her failure when she learned that her young companion was menstruating.

As with the other animals, no one should ever brag about his or her ability to catch beavers, because doing so will almost assure bad luck with them. It is also powerfully tabooed to be bitten by this animal, which will cause death. Years ago, Koyukon people would chop beaver houses open, wait for the animals to return for air, then grab their forepaws and throw them out onto the snow. A woman who was bitten on the breast doing this is said to have died as a result.

If a beaver slaps the underside of the ice with its tail it is a powerful sign of bad luck. A woman told me that once she got angry at a beaver that was apparently too clever or wary to be caught in her traps. After finding that it had eluded her again, she blurted out, "I wish I would see you in the spring; then I would just shoot you!" A moment later the beaver slapped the ice beneath her with its tail. That spring she lost her baby, and she blames the tragedy on her disrespectful outburst.

Nature is filled with powers, sometimes benevolent, sometimes perilous, but ever watchful. The more potent these powers are, the more demanding they become of human deference and respect, and the more numerous are the ways of showing it. Beaver is the first of the powerful animals in this narrative; I will discuss others in the following chapter.

9

The Predatory Mammals

The Powerful Ones

They share with humanity the gift of cunning. They are quick and agile, inquisitive of mind, always restless. They move at the open edge and the precipice, rush suddenly upon errant prey, then vanish like shadows, leaving flecks of blood to soak into the snow.

They are the predators. Elsewhere on this continent the most elegant and powerful of them have disappeared, victims of habitat loss and competition with a human society that refused to tolerate them. Only in the northlands has the full community of these animals survived into the twentieth century, among people who are content to share the world with them rather than hunt them to extinction. In part this is because the people, whose lives emerged from the forest, recognize not only strength but also power. In the natural world of the Koyukon, predators include some of the most watchful and demanding of spirits.

Predatory animals that inhabit the Koyukon wildlands represent a wide assortment of lifeways and personalities. They include the lemming-sized least weasel, short-tailed weasel, mink, marten, otter, and wolverine—all members of the weasel family (Mustelidae) in Western taxonomy. There is a single wild cat, the lynx. And, finally, there are two from the dog family, the red fox and the wolf. I have left the bears and the domesticated dog for the next chapter, because they are not essentially predators, nor are they furbearers like the others discussed here.

The predatory furbearers have a special position in the Koyukon people's economic life. First of all, they are taken primarily for their pelts. This is not merely a result of the Euro-American fur trade; it is a long-standing Athapaskan tradition. In the centuries before contact, fur animals were sought for hides to be made into clothing and other essential products. This remains true today, though materials from outside have reduced the villagers' dependence on pelts, while commercial interests have created a new incentive for taking them. Fur is a source of cash. On the other hand, furbearers are of little importance as food. Some are fed to the dogs or occasionally eaten by people, others are not used this way at all.

In the modern context, these animals are also unique in the ways they are taken. Though all of them may be hunted, they are caught mainly with traps and snares. This creates an entirely different relationship between people and their prey, because the animal is not directly stalked and killed by a hunter. It must be lured and trapped while the person is far removed in time and distance. In the human mind at least, luck and chance play a greater role here than in hunting, even though the trap is a deadly hunter indeed. Furthermore, the quest for furbearing animals entails a life-style of its own, centered on lengthy journeys along far-flung traplines, where the nights are spent in isolated camps or cabins. And so the predators occupy their own niche in Koyukon subsistence and economy.

Before discussing each of the furbearers in detail, I want to make a few general comments about their position in the spiritual world of the Koyukon. I have mentioned that they include some of the most potent animal spirits; but not all of them are so possessed. In fact, some (like the short-tailed weasel and mink) seem to be no more powerful than animals like the snowshoe hare or muskrat. And predators have no monopoly on spiritual potency—bears and beavers, for example, are at least equal to most of them. The most spiritually powerful of the predators is the wolverine, and it is followed by the wolf, lynx, and otter. Taken collectively, these animals are a greater locus of power than any other group of animals.

There is a constant interplay between the spirits of predatory animals and the people who pursue them. A person's success in catching them depends primarily on his or her measure of luck, and luck derives in various ways from the supernatural. This is why some people can set their traps "any old way" and still make good catches—luck makes the animals come to them. A kind of spiritual volition preordains, bringing their destinies together. Of course, offenders against the animals experience the opposite effect, and even their most carefully and cleverly set traps will catch nothing. The most powerful predators are always more seriously affected by these things. Koyukon elders also say that some people have difficulty catching animals like the wolverine, wolf, or brown bear no matter how hard they try or how much they respect taboos. This is because these animals only "go to" certain people, for reasons they cannot explain.

Even the equipment used for trapping and hunting enters into this spiritual interchange. Behavior or events associated with a particular trap (or trapping place) may affect its luck for catching animals. Also, new sleds and snowshoes are treated in certain ways to make them lucky. The first time they are used, they should move in a downstream direction to bring them luck, never upstream, because that is the direction traveled by spirits of the dead. There are also formulas for luck that apply only to one person. For instance, a man told me that when he traps with someone else he can camp and travel with them, but he has to make sets on his own separate trails. If the two alternate sets along the same trail, the animals will go to the other person's traps.

Certain general rules apply to the treatment of predators after they have been caught. Traditionally, a piece of dried fish was always placed in the animal's mouth or fat was rubbed on its teeth, but nowadays this is done only with the most powerful species. Any fur animal brought inside the house or cabin must be put where no one (especially a woman) will step over it. People also avoid burning rags or trash, so the animal will not be offended by a bad smell. Loud noises, especially metallic sounds like hammering or sawing, are also insulting to its spirit.

There is also a rule that carcasses of furbearers must be kept inside the house overnight, even if they are skinned immediately; and they must never be taken back outside before their skins are removed. Sullivan (1942:123) writes that trappers keep silent until their animals are skinned, and they wait some time before telling anyone what they have caught. Some people avoid telling anyone how many animals they have caught until the season has ended, lest they sound boastful (this is not to avoid stimulating competition, since they own private rights to their traplines). At most, someone might say "Oh, I'm doing OK" or make some equally nebulous comment. If any of these rules are ignored, the offended animals may become aloof from the violator or cause sickness in his or her family. Improperly treated animals may also be reborn in another area (Clark 1970:86), making them scarcer where they have been treated badly.

The Weasels

I found a hare in one of my snares this morning—or I should say part of a hare. Most of the frozen animal's hind quarter had been dragged away by a weasel, who signed his work with a scribble of tracks. When I bent down for a close look I was startled by a barrage of little barks. There was the culprit, peering over a fallen willow just four feet away, laying claim to his prize.

When I refused to leave he became incensed, puffing and scolding. He twitched boldly forward along the willow log, then scrambled down under the snow, reappeared farther away, vanished again, and popped up beside the log once more. I backed off a little, and he immediately went for the hare and began tugging and gnawing at it, stopping every few seconds to glare nervously toward me. His tiny black eyes were quick and intense, his body a slink of pure white, punctuated with black at the tip of his tail. Finally, still barking angry protests, he reconsidered and left me with the remains of my catch. [Huslia journal, January 1977]

The short-tailed weasel (*Mustela erminea*) is fairly common in the Koyukuk valley lowlands, though people rarely see it. This is partly because it is secretive and small (about a foot long, including the tail), and partly because it changes camouflage with the seasons—brown in summer and white in winter. Outsiders know the winter phase as ermine, and they once paid high prices for its pelt. Today these animals are less valuable, so Koyukon trappers make little effort to catch them. Those taken in sets made for other furbearers are used locally or sold. Their meat is not eaten.

In Koyukon, short-tailed weasels are called *kaaghozina,* "black tip on its tail." Another variety, smaller than this but larger than a least weasel, is distinguished as *bit'o k'idaalee,* "that which is used to cook something on." I never saw this animal or heard anything else about it; and the fact that male and female short-tailed weasels differ greatly in size may account for this taxonomic distinction. The short-tailed weasel is not spiritually powerful. People should avoid letting one rot in a trap, however, lest their children be afflicted with ear trouble. If a weasel is caught in the last trap at the end of a trapline, it is a powerful sign of good luck.

After the early snows each winter, Koyukon boys go into the woods near the village and set a few traps. Most often, the first animal they catch this way is a short-tailed weasel, and it is an event of some importance. In one Huslia cabin I saw a stuffed weasel hanging from the ceiling, decorated with an assortment of bracelets and jewelry. The people explained that it was the first animal one of their boys had trapped.

> *Wait, I see something: It looks like a bit of charred wood waving around in the air.*
> *Answer: The short-tailed weasel's tail in winter.*

The dwarf among northland predators is the least weasel (*Mustela rixosa*), whose miniature tracks are seen on rare occasions in the winter snow. I have never seen the animal itself, but its dried skins are almost mouselike, with only a stub for a tail. What it lacks in size, however, it makes up in a special kind of power. *Kusga* (its Koyukon name) is one of the most potent sources of good luck, equaled only by the flicker.

Any kind of proximity to this animal is likely to bring some benefit. For example, if one appears from time to time near somebody's house, it is there to bring the occupants good luck. Catching the animal or finding a dead one portends a lucky life, especially for hunting and trapping. The skin is dried with the skull intact, then kept as a talisman. According to Jetté (1911:246), some people consider the skull, and especially the teeth, to be the source of its power. One elder told me not to kill a least weasel unless I was going to dry it and keep it for a long time. Another man showed me a beaded moosehide pouch containing seven least weasel skins, his lifetime catch. This was an unusually large number, and, as tradition assures, he has been a most fortunate and successful man.

Mink

Mink (*Mustela vison*) are creatures of the waterside, seldom found away from lakes, sloughs, creeks, or rivers. They reach about two feet in length, weigh between two and four pounds, and have a rich coat of short, dark brown fur. Their abundant energy is devoted to finding eggs and catching fish, birds, insects, and a variety of small mammals up to the size of muskrats. It is a measure of their toughness that they often dig their way into muskrat pushups, overpower and kill the pugnacious animals when they come to breathe, then drag them off to a den for later feasting. "Mink is an animal that never goes hungry," the people say, because it keeps caches of meat and fish for times when food is short.

> Today I followed a mink's trail along a lakeshore. It was a shared adventure, an insight into a nervous and nimble mind. The tracks went up and down the bank, out onto the ice and back again, sometimes with the apparent aimlessness of someone burning away an excess of energy. They alternated between a loping gait and short belly slides, sometimes even vanished beneath the snow for a stretch and popped up farther along. The animal seemed full of zeal mixed with curiosity; it passed nothing without turning off for a closer look. Every little thing deserved at least a sniff—tufts of grass, hollows and holes in the bank, and an endless assortment of other special places amid the lakeshore tangle. The mink must be exhausted when its day ends. [Huslia journal, November 1976]

During the early winter mink are very active with hunting and fishing. Koyukon trappers pursue them especially during this season, setting steel traps in their shoreline haunts and at the openings of their dens. When the cold really sets in, mink seem to "hole up," waiting for midwinter to pass. This is why the Koyukon will say of someone, "She stayed inside all winter, like a mink in its burrow." In their spring breeding season (March and April) they travel widely, following each other's tracks. Trapping lasts only until January, however, because their pelts lose quality after that time.

The Koyukon name for mink is *taahgoodza*, "bites things in the water." People say that its close animal relative is the otter, "because otters won't eat them." Both are also noticeably alike in being denizens of the water, and their behavior is similar in many ways (Linnaean taxonomy also considers them near relatives). Elders speak of a strange creature called "father of mink," snaky, headless and tailless, about four feet long. One is said to inhabit the expansive Dulbi Flat near Huslia, and its presence accounts for the abundance of mink there. "This is what the mink come from," they explain.

Mink are fairly well regarded by the Koyukon, although some consider them dirty (no one explained why). Aside from their toughness, people seem most impressed by their curiosity. They just cannot resist watching if they see a person nearby, and so they are one of the most commonly sighted predators. A Kutchin trapper I traveled with used to squeak his foot on the snow next to occupied mink dens, and sometimes the dark face and strange deep eyes would come poking up from below. If a child stares at people too much, Koyukon people will say, "You're just like a mink at its hole."

Nowadays mink are trapped exclusively for their pelts, which are either sold or made into mittens, trim for parkas or boots, or (formerly) hats worn only by widows. Musk from their scent glands is used as bait for trapping mink or weasels. In former times mink was eaten by men, but it was tabooed for women. Violation would make it difficult for the woman or her husband to catch the animal and could cause her children to cry a lot, like the mink. A man who had eaten mink said its taste reminded him of muskrat. To prepare it, the animal was boiled for a short while, then the water was poured off and it was rinsed with cold water and finally it was roasted. People also used to eat the grease from a drying mink skin.

I was told no special taboos or ways of treating mink, but Sullivan (1942:94) mentions that their bones must never be given to dogs or thrown carelessly on the ground. They should be thrown into the water, like those of beaver and muskrat, with a request for the animal's reincarnation. Mink heads, he says, are scattered around a person's trapline, where they will rot and attract fur animals to the area. Koyukuk elders today recommend burning mink carcasses to dispose of them respectfully.

Marten

My attention was caught by a strange growling and huffing noise partway up a large tree. I saw a dark form hunched on a branch next to the trunk, something the size of an overgrown housecat. I worked my way closer, and when it moved farther up the tree I recognized it—a dark-furred marten. It craned its neck at me, glowering and angry, growling almost constantly.

Then a red squirrel chattered loudly from another tree nearby, scrambling back and forth in animated apprehension. I realized what I had interrupted: The marten had been stalking its favorite prey, ready to begin a wild chase through the branches. Now it could only growl at me and stare intensely at the squirrel, torn between fear and predatory desire. I watched awhile, then left them to work out their own designs. [Huslia journal, April 1977]

The marten (*Martes americana*) looks like a slightly overgrown mink, usually with lighter-colored and somewhat longer fur. It is an animal of the forest, especially the open wooded slopes of hills and mountains. It is a quick and skillful predator like the mink, and it hunts mostly for small animals like squirrels, hares, mice, and birds. Marten are fairly common in Koyukon country, especially away from the flats. Their population is subject to marked changes (as is that of the mink, incidentally), and they are known as wanderers. For a while their tracks may be abundant in an area, then they abandon it and move on to another.

In Koyukon, the marten is called *sooga,* and there are several other words to designate sex and age classes:

diyidla'	male (also fox, wolf, mink, lynx, otter)
soodzidza	large female (also fox, mink)
soodzaaya	small female
k'aggoya, k'idin'aa'	young one (any animal)

The marten and the wolverine are related, "like brothers." People say they know this because wolverines will take marten from traps but will not eat them. Sometimes a trapper will follow the thief's tracks and find the marten abandoned, in perfect condition and suitable for sale to a fur trader. According to the Koyukon, a wolverine will eat any other fur animal (like a fox, mink, or otter) that it steals from a trap, but not its relative. Aside from this, marten seem rather similar to wolverines in appearance and behavior; they make a pair, as do mink and otter, though Koyukon people never described it to me this way.

Every active trapper probably catches a few marten each year, and those with traplines in the hills may take fairly large numbers (thirty or more). Their furs are either sold or used to make clothing. The marten-skin hat is an essential part of the Koyukon man's outfit—it is light, amazingly warm, and it does not restrict his peripheral vision as a parka hood does. In former times marten was eaten, and the late Chief Henry said it tasted good, "like rabbit." Sullivan (1942:94) writes that marten is eaten only when people are short of food; otherwise the carcasses are hung up in a tree. Modern Koyukuk people say the remains should be burned or else deposited out in the wilds, well away from any trails.

If a marten urinates on someone's trapline trail it is a sign that he or she will have no luck with this animal for the rest of the year, perhaps even longer. The Nulato Koyukon advise that when a marten walks around a man's trap and urinates on it, without getting caught, it means that his wife is unfaithful (Sullivan 1942:94). People must be careful to check their traps often, because if a marten is caught and left to spoil, the offender's children will develop ear problems. Marten are also more sensitive than other fur animals to burning smells, so people must put nothing offensive (like rags or garbage) in the stove while their carcasses are inside the house. Some take the extra precaution of plugging their nostrils with a bit of grease to avoid accidentally affronting them.

This animal is exceptionally susceptible to the vagaries of luck, which explains why people have such fluctuating success with it. As one man put it, "That's a tough animal to get bad luck with. If you run out of luck, you might as well forget it for a while. You won't catch any for maybe ten days, or a month, even all season. But if you're going to catch them—if you've got your luck for them—they're really easy."

> Wait, I see something: Near relatives, in their marten coats, stretch their
>   hands toward each other.
> Answer: The marten's ears.
> [Jetté 1913:193]

Otter

The otter (*Lutra canadensis*) is a much larger animal than the mink or marten, from three to five feet long and weighing fifteen to thirty-five pounds. Its streamlined body, webbed hind feet, muscular tail, and slick, dark fur make it incredibly adept in the water. And its intensity, quickness, and power make it a formidable predator. Koyukon people say that otters feed mostly on fish but also eat water insects, birds, and small mammals like muskrats and beavers. When they find an occupied beaver house, otters sometimes "clean it out" except for the largest ones, who can occasionally escape or defend themselves.

These sleek, beautiful animals are fairly common throughout the Koyukuk wildlands, although they are wary enough so that people do not often see them. Unlike most other wildlife here, they are said to maintain an almost constant population level over long periods. Otters live wherever there is water, and they take shelter in bank dens or hollows under the banks. They also occupy old beaver houses, sometimes after eating the former occupants. In winter they settle down where the current keeps holes open in the ice, so they can range overland to hunt or (as one of my instructors put it) "just come out to roll around in the snow and get some fresh air."

At the beginning of winter, on the other hand, otters are continuously on the go, wandering all over the country and never staying in one place for more than a few days. I have seen the lakes scribbled everywhere with such an abundance of tracks that the new snow was trampled hard in places.

There may also be signs of hunting amid this scramble—muskrat pushups dug open, smears of blood on the ice beside them. As they travel, otters alternate between running and sliding on the snow, and they always seem to be in a great hurry. Perhaps they really are, because out of the water they sometimes fall prey to wolverines, wolves, and bears.

Koyukon people characterize otters as incredibly tough and wily, which makes them hard to catch and hold in a trap. They are also very serious or intense, I was told, unlike animals such as the fox or lynx. In defense of their young (which are born in June, under driftwood piles or in old beaver houses) they can become really fierce, even swimming up to a boat and threatening the people inside. But the Koyukon are well aware of their lighter side, their devotion to play, set in motion by a seemingly hyperactive personality. One elder told me, "They never can sit still. On the land they don't ever seem to quit moving, and in water they just dive and come up, dive and come up. They don't just swim like beaver or muskrat."

> Steven and I were standing beside a deep little creek, not four feet wide, with undercut banks. He was explaining how to set blackfish traps there, when an explosive snort from right below interrupted him. "Otter!" he whispered. We saw only its ripples, but seconds later we heard it again upstream, and then another downstream. The quiet was suddenly gone, as strange snufflings seemed to erupt everywhere. "I think there's four of them," Steven exclaimed.
>
> After several minutes of hide-and-seek, an otter popped up near me, snaking its neck high, alternately staring at me and looking away. Its ears and eyes looked much too small for the size of its head, and water dripped from its long whiskers. Then it snorted once more and dived, leaving a wake on the surface as it torpedoed away. A few moments later we heard them far upstream, then quiet surrounded us again. [Huslia journal, October 1976]

When we were discussing communication among animals, a Huslia man explained that otters sometimes talk to each other. Once he saw a frightened female run up a bank and into the brush, leaving her pups behind in the water. In a moment, she reappeared atop the bank and made a series of clucking noises. The pups immediately swam toward the sound and ran up to her. Another time he saw nine otters "talking back and forth with each other" with clucking sounds. Again, they used their voices as a way of getting back together.

Koyukon trappers have several effective ways to catch otters during the open season, which extends through winter into spring. They are somewhat protective of their methods, however, because each has its own complement of luck. A man told me that he had once shown someone else how to make a particular otter set and the other person used it with great success, but he himself never got another otter that way. He had given away his luck along with his knowledge. "Beaver is even worse for that," he added.

The otter's pelt is rich and durable, usually worth a good price from fur traders. It is also used for men's mittens, boots, and clothing trim, but never for anything worn by women. Although women can trap the otter, they should not skin it or use anything from it until they have passed menopause. Violators would have bad trapping luck or their children would be unclean and high-strung like the animal. Women should also go outside when otter meat is boiling in the house, to avoid breathing the vapor. This is no longer a problem, however, because otters are not eaten nowadays. One man who had eaten the meat (the organs were never used) said that it tasted like muskrat.

Otters are among the most spiritually powerful animals, although they are not subject to the array of taboos affecting some of the others. Contact with women is especially alienating for them. In fact, women are forbidden even to say the animal's name, *bilaazona*. To avoid offending its spirit, they call it by the circumlocution *biziya*, "shiny black." Otter bones should never be given to dogs, though some people are careless about this: "If you do it, otters will be hard for you to catch—and they're hard enough to get anyhow." The traditional way to dispose of them is to throw them into a lake (rather than water with a current), asking that the animal be "made again."

Simply reciting the rules for proper treatment of a creature like the otter does little to communicate the *feeling* of power that is associated with it, the very real need for respect and deference that is evident not so much in what people say as in how they say it and how they act. The most important and meaningful essence of the otter is not something that can be understood just by looking at it or comprehended by reading an objectivized description of its spiritual dimensions. For the orthodox Koyukon the animal is surrounded by strong emotions of respect and fear, a need for strict, faultless adherence to the rules set down to avoid offending it.

In our culture we can easily enough understand the sanctity of physical symbols like the cross or the star of David; we venerate them or empathize with those who do. Here among the Koyukon, a kind of sacredness is an inseparable part of living things. They are not symbols, but rather living objects of veneration and physical manifestations of spiritual power. The reality is somewhat different, but the underlying emotions are similar. With this in mind, I turn now to an even greater power among the animal spirits.

Wolverine

"*Doyonh ghahol!*" A man who had caught a wolverine would announce loudly as he came into the village, "The great one, the chief of animals, arrives!" Inside his house, it was dressed in a special outfit of fine clothes, then sat upright in an honored place. While this was done, men began to enter, bringing food and placing it around the animal, grasping its paws as they made their presentation.

Then the men sat in front of the wolverine, partaking of the food and telling stories of *doyonh* and its exploits. Young women were not allowed to attend, and old women who came were prohibited from eating the food offerings. Aside from this, it was much like a person's funeral potlatch, only on a smaller scale. Afterward, the carcass was skinned, dismembered, and burned with food for its spirit. Honored this way, *doyonh* would bring good fortune to those who attended.

This ceremonial for the wolverine (described by Sullivan 1942:101–2 and by my Huslia teachers) has given way to a less elaborate ritual, which I will discuss farther on. But today, as always, the wolverine is considered the greatest of all animal spirits, most demanding of obeisance and respect. It is a dangerous power that must be treated in strict accordance with tradition, lest some tragic misfortune befall the violator. Men, who are less susceptible to these dangers, call the wolverine *niłtseeł* (no translation), or *doyonh*, from the Russian *toyon*—chief, great man, or rich man. Women must never affront the animal by speaking its real name but must call it instead *tl'onyee* or *hubaaghayee*, words for the wolverine trim on clothing. Violation can make their children rough and unmanageable.

Quite aside from its spiritual powers, the wolverine (*Gulo luscus*) seems to keep itself a mystery and a stranger. It lurks always somewhere beyond seeing, leaving only its tracks and having no physical embodiment. Only occasionally does someone catch a glimpse of it, usually far away or just vanishing into the timber's shadowy edge. It is the largest land-dwelling member of the weasel family, three or four feet long, twenty-five to thirty-five pounds, thickset and short-legged, built like a little hunching bear. Its fur is a bristle of dark brown, with two yellowish stripes curving outward along its back, and its brushy tail is stiff and disproportionately short. The face of *doyonh* broods darkly, with small black eyes, powerful short jaws, and a grizzle of gray on the crown.

Wolverines are recluses, much given to wandering. Koyukon people say they range around a broad circuit, and their tracks usually pass by the same places every ten days or so. In late winter (February to April) they follow in each other's trails, the break in solitude a sign of their mating season. During that time they are even greater nomads than usual, and they more readily fall prey to Koyukon trappers and hunters. Wolverines nearly always travel fast, with an exaggerated loping gait that leaves peculiar tracks in the snow. Their broad feet make a complex and unmistakable imprint, with the five toe marks characteristic of all weasels.

I have never seen these tracks without stopping to look closely, to think of the marvelous eccentric who made them, and to wonder if its eyes were on me at that moment. This animal is always scarce, but there are as many in Koyukon country as elsewhere in the north woods. It is normal during a long trip to see one or two sets of tracks, though not necessarily fresh ones. The elders say that wolverines were more common in the past than they are today, indicating that their population fluctuates, like that of most other animals here.

Although they might seem formidable predators, wolverines apparently get most of their food by scavenging. Their jaws and bodies have extraordinary strength, so they can gnaw away or carry off almost anything. Their habit of following traplines and stealing whatever has been caught wins them no favor with trappers. They are also great thieves of cached meat and will even enter cabins and leave them a shambles, liberally fouled with urine as a final gesture.

Koyukon people say that wolverines also do some hunting of their own. I mentioned earlier that they will kill and eat a beaver if they catch one out of water; and they sometimes dig their way into a lodge and wait there for the occupants. If a lodge is impenetrable, built with thick poles and sticks, the wolverine may dig a tunnel from the bank behind it, entering near its unobstructed base. In the upper Dulbi (*Dolbaatno'*) River, where beaver houses are often made of dirt and gravel, one man saw that a wolverine had lain on a place until it thawed, then dug, thawed, and dug again until it got through the frozen wall. Steven Attla and I once came across a lodge that a wolverine had tried unsuccessfully to dig open.

Wolverines will prey on an assortment of other animals. Small ones like the otter are not difficult for them to kill, but they apparently take larger ones as well. Some elders say they can kill a caribou by jumping onto its back and biting its neck. One man even described finding a dead moose with only wolverine tracks around it, as if the wolverine had killed it. When people find game killed by any predator, they feel free to take it for themselves, except when the predator is a wolverine. The animal fouls its catch so badly that it is inedible—apparently, one man suggested, to make sure nothing else will bother its food.

Carrion is an excellent place to set traps for the wolverine. They must be concealed impeccably, however, and be heavy enough to hold this sinewy creature. Even then a wolverine will often gnaw its foot off and escape, living afterward with three legs. Snares and traditional deadfalls are probably more effective ways to catch them, because they kill quickly. When someone finds a wolverine in his trap (which is likely to happen only once or twice, at best, each winter), the animal should be shot or pierced to kill it instantly. A man who killed one with a club, which is strictly tabooed because it is too slow, told me he has never gotten another since.

When they catch any furbearer, people are beholden not only to the animal's spirit, but also to the spirit of the trap, snare, or deadfall. It, too, is mindful of a person's behavior, especially when the wolverine is involved (the introduced steel trap, incidentally, has less spiritual power than the traditional snare or deadfall). If a man comes upon a wolverine (or a wolf) caught in another person's trap, he must kill it and then hang it up so it will not be lost or damaged. Before shooting it he should say, "You are not my animal, but I have to kill you. I am trying to help you." He does this to show respect and to bring luck upon himself. The owner of the trap must find out who killed the animal for him and make a small payment. Otherwise someone in his family will suffer from illness. Women are not allowed to intentionally trap a wolverine or to shoot or skin one.

During most winters, about seven or eight wolverines in all are caught by Huslia people. Most of these are used locally—for men's parkas or boot trim (prohibited for women) or for the ruff and trim on men's or women's parkas. Wolverine hides are prominent in the dances and presentations at Koyukon memorial potlatches; the presence of this preeminent creature symbolizes the importance of the deceased person. People·may fasten a wolverine's tail to a boy's belt to make him a fast runner. Trappers also sell wolverine pelts to other village people, but I doubt that many are sold to fur buyers. Wolverine meat is never eaten today, though it was apparently a starvation food in former times. According to Jetté (1911:611), parts of the head could be eaten only by the owner of the trap that caught the animal, and anyone else who ate them would quickly die.

Earlier, I described the traditional Koyukon ceremony given for each killed wolverine. Today this has been simplified, although people explain, "We're supposed to do all the other things, but we quit doing them." When a man brings a wolverine into his house, he first rubs some rich, fatty food on its mouth, then tosses the morsel into the stove to feed its spirit. While the animal remains inside, he makes several more offerings. Each time he says, "Here is some food for you," as he puts it in the fire (this is the traditional way of giving food to any spirit).

Jetté's teachers in the Yukon villages explained the ritual feast for the wolverine (also given for a wolf in that area) by telling a story of the Distant Time:

> Three men set out together for a hunting journey—two of them were rich and influential chiefs, and the other was poor but very smart. After they had wandered far and wide without success, the smart man returned home. But the other two kept on, becoming thin and ragged. Their skins tanned and their hair grew long; and finally they began to live like animals. Then they were transformed, one into a wolf and the other into a wolverine. This is why the wolverine's ceremony begins with an announcement that the chief has arrived, and why these animals are pre-

sented with a "banquet," remembering their hardships long ago. The smart man, who left the others and returned home, became the first sha-man. And since then, a shaman always officiated at the ritual. [Jetté 1911:157–58]

A Huslia man told me that his father once decided to skin a wolverine without burning food for it. But while he was working on it, he heard an uproar of barking from the dogs. He went outside to look and a wolverine was there, growling and full of anger. It was clearly a sign and a warning, so he immediately went to put food on the fire, and after that he knew that the custom must be followed.

As with other fur animals, the wolverine's carcass must be kept in the house overnight, but it should never be near a small child—its spirit is too powerful and could make the child seriously ill. One man told me he put a wolverine close to his infant child, and the baby refused to stop crying until he moved the animal farther away. A young girl is said to have become crippled after a wolverine carcass was left on top of the house where she lived. Even hanging the hide too close to a child can threaten the little one with bad luck or illness.

A wolverine's pelt has considerable power, and one elder told me that people used to wait a year before using it. Only after this time has it become completely dead and safe to handle. It is bad luck to sell, trade, or give a wolverine hide to another Koyukon person without first cutting off the snout. Some people advise that the nose should then be burned; others recommend hanging it on a tree in your trapline to bring good luck. Only when the hide is sold to an outside person, like the fur buyer, should it be left whole.

After skinning, a wolverine's carcass is cut into pieces, sometimes quarters and sometimes small bits, then (either immediately or after the trapping season) taken to a remote spot in the forest. There the man builds a large fire and cremates it, making certain it is completely consumed. He also burns a nice piece of fat as a final offering to its spirit. "You have to make sure you do this," a man told me, "It's a strong *hutlaanee.*" In this context the word I translate loosely as "taboo" means something that is required or that it is forbidden *not* to do. Actually, *hutlaanee* means anything caused by, done for, or avoided to show respect for spiritual powers.

A wolverine found dead out in the wilds is the one animal a person should not leave untouched. To nullify the danger of this encounter, the entire animal, hide and all, must be burned. An offering of food is also placed in the fire to appease its spirit. One man who neglected to do this had to make a two-day trip, find the carcass again, and burn it. If a wolverine dies in a trap and is then damaged by other animals, it must also be burned in that place together with an offering of food—doing otherwise could bring death to the offender (Sullivan 1942:104).

Clearly, the consequences of offending the spiritually potent wolverine can be extremely severe. Illness or death are the most real and frightening threats, but there is also the prospect of bad luck in trapping. One man who mistreated a wolverine said he has had no luck with the animal for twenty-five years. Wolverines will go near his traps but rarely into them, and if they are caught they get away. When wolverines become alienated from a man, he can set no trap large enough to hold them; and they may even play impertinently with his traps just to "show him." But someone given good luck with these animals catches them easily, and they will not escape even from a small trap. The lucky man is somewhat disadvantaged, however, because wolverines are drawn to his traps and often steal any animals caught in them.

When he was young, one of my teachers was repelled by the smell of a wolverine his father was skinning. "I hope I never even catch one of those," he blurted thoughtlessly. "They stink so bad." His father reprimanded him and lavishly praised the value of wolverine hide, but it was too late to counteract the insult. Throughout most of his life, this man had poor luck catching wolverines, and they even refused to steal from his traps. Once he cached a bear's carcass in a tree and a wolverine climbed up to it; but because it was his the animal went completely against its nature and ate nothing.

This man told me how his father had manipulated the wolverine's spirit in a really unusual way, turning the taboos to his advantage. He had great trouble with these animals stealing from his traps, so he intentionally bragged that if he caught a wolverine he would kill it with a club. He followed up on his word, and for four years afterward he never caught a wolverine, nor did any raid his traps. He said he was willing to go without taking this valuable animal to be free of its plundering. Then he finally caught one and decided to treat it properly, telling it, "I guess I'll give you another chance."

> In the gloom of dusk I saw a shadowy figure slip silently from the trees, not thirty yards from the tent. It stopped and pulled itself up tightly, becoming small, held its head low and faced toward me, making no profile. Very slowly I leaned over and picked up my binoculars, not knowing what this creature was. A wolverine.... It was curious and grave, reaching out with its nose, slowly wagging its head, trying for a scent. It lifted one foreleg tentatively, then loped a few steps my way. I looked directly into its eyes and knew that I understood nothing. Then it cringed back, turned its head away, and vanished again into the forest. [Huslia journal, June 1977]

Lynx

They are spectral creatures, gray phantoms of the northern wildlands. A person may spend years in the forest and never see one, though they are always there, hidden in the brush, looking down from high places with fierce cat eyes. Only their tracks make them tangible, reveal their travels along packed sled trails and through the open forest, usually walking slowly and deliberately. Their unconcern for cover may deceive the watcher, because tracks do not reveal the time of their making—the lynx is a dusk and nighttime wanderer. Only in summer must it hunt in daylight, but even then it avoids human eyes almost unerringly.

In the winter northlands, nothing, not even a lynx, moves over the snow-covered terrain without telling at least a part of its story:

> On a long oxbow lake just off the river, we encountered an extraordinary scramble of tracks made by a lynx and a snowshoe hare. They had burst from the willows and run in wild zigzags out onto the lake. Finally their tracks joined, there was turmoil in the snow, and blood stained a hollow where the broad paws found their mark.
>
> The hare's track emerged from the scuffle, but it was oddly shaped now, and flecked with blood. Alongside it was the lynx, frolicking back and forth, then pouncing on its hapless prey, batting or tossing it aside. The game continued, tracing its erratic path for a hundred yards or more. Here and there, little stained depressions marked places where the lynx held its victim for a moment. In the last of these there was a deep blotch of red, and only lynx tracks went on afterward.
>
> Looking back over the snow, I could see it all perfectly in my mind—like a house cat playing its innocent yet deadly game with a mouse. Then afterward, the lynx with its head high to keep its soft, limp catch above the snow, walking slowly to a hidden place above the bank. There it hunched in the gray moonlight, tearing and gnawing the hare's still-warm flesh. [Huslia journal, December 1976]

The lynx (*Lynx canadensis*) is the only wild cat commonly found in Alaska, and it occurs throughout Koyukon country. Its favorite habitat is lowland scrub and forest, where snowshoe hares are most abundant. In fact, lynx are so dependent on this animal for food that their population grows or declines along with that of their prey. This apparently accounts for the relative scarcity of lynx around Huslia for the past two decades. Aside from hares, lynx take a variety of other small animals, such as voles, grouse, and ptarmigan. Koyukon elders I asked had never seen evidence that they kill large animals like caribou, though they may scavenge from them.

In appearance and behavior, lynx closely resemble their more southerly relative, the bobcat. They are fairly large (fifteen to thirty-five pounds), with long legs and oversized paws for travel in deep, soft snow. Their beautiful long fur is dark gray, with a thick ruff around the neck and an elegant black tassle on each ear. In Koyukon, lynx are called *kaazina*, "black tail," a reference to the black tip on their stumpy appendage. But because they have great spirit power, women must speak of them indirectly, using the name *nodooya*, "something going around."

Lynx are not considered a relative of any other animal in the Koyukon world. Their distinctive appearance is explained in a story of the Distant Time, in which an errant husband left his wife to live with two other women. She eventually found their house, killed the women, and waited for his return. When he arrived and found what she had done, he tried to throw hot rocks from the fire at her. But when he grabbed them his hands shriveled up. So he tried to kick the rocks, and his feet also became shriveled. Then he tried to bite them, and his face became pugged. As these things happened he was transformed into a lynx, with its stubby paws and flat face. Finally, as he turned to leave, his wife picked coals from the fire and threw them at him, blackening the tip of his tail.

Koyukon people have ample respect for the fierceness and agility of this wild cat. A trapped lynx shows little fear of its captor, and anyone scythed by those long, curved claws would be terribly wounded. One man told me that lynx have jumped onto people from trees, though I never heard a story about its actually happening. Also, females will furiously defend their litters of spotted kittens, which are born in June, so people are advised to stay away from them.

Trappers consider lynx fairly easy to catch, either in steel snares or in traps. They have the curiosity of a cat, so they are drawn to scents or dangling things used as bait. In past times little wooden dolls were put on each side of a snare bait to represent the two women that lynx-man's wife killed in the Distant Time (Sullivan 1942:99). I do not know if this is why people from Koyukuk villages often draw a face on a blazed tree as bait for their lynx traps. Hunters using snow machines cannot chase and kill this animal as they can wolverines or wolves. The lynx is too smart, they say, always able to escape by dashing into deep brush and hiding, even diving under the powdery snow where it cannot be seen.

Lynx are taken for both their hides and their meat. In recent years their pelts have been extremely valuable on the commercial market, and so trappers have made much effort to catch them. Use of the pelt is limited by the animal's spiritual power, because only men are permitted to wear clothes (parkas, mittens, or caps) made from it. In the Distant Time, lynx suffered from stiff joints, and so boys are not allowed to wear boots made from its hide lest they become afflicted with arthritis later in life.

The Koyukon consider lynx meat an excellent food, but women are strictly forbidden to partake of it. If a woman violated this taboo she would probably lose one or more of her children, because the animal dies easily. And if she had a baby inside her the lynx would "eat out of her stomach" and take away its life. After a lynx is skinned, its leg joints should be partly severed, and whatever is left of its carcass (including the organs, which are not eaten) should be taken to a remote place in the forest to be burned. If a trapped lynx is unavoidably spoiled (by scavengers, for example) it should be burned on the spot.

As I mentioned earlier, the lynx is among the most powerful animals, given the kind of spirit called *biyeega hoolaanh*. It is not equal to the wolverine, bear, or wolf, but it is more potent than the other animals. People who do not treat it with utmost respect may be struck with illness or permanently lose their luck in catching this animal. For example, some trappers are said to have caught only one lynx in their lifetimes. This animal can afflict a person with a more complete and lasting alienation than any other, as the stories warn:

> In the Distant Time, the bear and lynx were talking. The bear said that when humans began hunting him they would have to treat him right. If he was mistreated by someone, that person would get no bears until he had gray hairs on his head. But the lynx said that people who mistreated him would never get a lynx again in their lives.

Red Fox

Perhaps no animal of the boreal forest is more widely familiar than Reynard, the red fox (*Vulpes fulva*). This small member of the dog family is found almost everywhere in North America, and it is common in the Koyukon homeland. Most often the fox is bright rust in color, with dark socks and a white-tipped tail. It has several varieties, however, notably a black or "silver" phase and a gray or "cross" phase. These are recognized in Koyukon terminology:

nohbaaya	a reference to poor vision	} general terms for fox
naaggadla	"twisted eyes"	
diltługha	"something brown or yellow," red phase	
daałt'ogga	cross phase	
dilzina	"something black," black phase	

These names must not be used when a fox is brought inside the house for skinning, however, because they would offend its spirit and the trapper would lose his or her luck with this species. So in its presence the fox is called *bakk'a hulonee*, "many tracks." Anyone who has followed its straight and stippled tracks will appreciate the accuracy of this little circumlocution. And it illustrates again what the Koyukon say of themselves, that they often speak in riddles.

The red fox is an artful predator, specializing in small animals. It is a great hunter of voles, and a careful watcher may see one prowl through the meadows, ears cocked forward, then suddenly pounce on its microtine victim. It also eats insects, catches birds and raids their nests, and takes hares, squirrels, and muskrats. Every fall the newly frozen lakes are criss-crossed with fox tracks, leading from one dug-open pushup to another. I have never seen a place where the fox actually caught a muskrat, but it must happen or their enthusiasm would surely wane. During the winter, red foxes even catch and eat blackfish when they swarm at holes in the ice. And they are scavengers:

> During the nights in camp, we had foxes coming around to gnaw on the caribou innards we left nearby. Eventually they appeared in broad daylight and became accustomed to us. One in particular grew very tame—it was a beautiful bright red but had lost part of the fur on its tail. Both Catherine and I got within a few yards of it as it gnawed on a frozen piece of neck. It crouched nervously beside its feast, looking first at us and then away, its bright eyes more clever than fearful.
>
> Catherine was filled with excitement, even though she has spent much of her life in the forest. She is a passionate animal watcher, with powerful empathy for wild creatures. Steven is less a watcher than a hunter, and the foxes were furs to him—he wanted so badly to hunt them. But Catherine, who is herself an accomplished trapper, prevailed. The foxes were still visiting when we finally pulled our beaver traps and headed back to Huslia. [Huslia journal, March 1977]

Koyukon people respect the fox as a clean and clever animal, but it is also mischievous. Although its young are easily taken from dens in the spring, they warn that children who raise (or are near) a pet fox will acquire its penchant for bad behavior. Trappers take advantage of the animal's aptitude as a scavenger by setting their traps and snares around kill sites or carrion. But the same nose that helps Reynard to find his way there will also warn him of the trap unless it is kept clean and is well concealed. The fox is not an easy animal to catch. Since the advent of snow machines, hunters sometimes chase and shoot foxes that they find in open country; but many are still taken with traps.

During the course of winter, Koyukon trappers or hunters may become acquainted with individual animals, knowing them largely through their tracks. For example, some foxes are so wary of humans that they will not even touch a sled trail—they will jump clear across it rather than just walking over. Such a fox jumped across a man's trail at the same spot several times one winter, and finally he decided to try outsmarting it. So he made a special kind of snare set, using a long pole so that no footprints were near it, and eventually he caught the wily fox. This familiarity, in which the hunter comes to recognize one animal as an individual apart from the rest, is another dimension of the intense interaction between Koyukon people and their natural environment.

Today foxes are trapped or hunted exclusively for their fur. The rich, thick pelt is often sold to fur traders, and women also use it for making parkas, clothing trim, or ruffs on children's parka hoods. Fox meat is edible, but even in the old days it was used only when other foods were scarce. After a fox has been skinned, people are supposed to put a bone in its mouth. "This is like giving it something to eat, so we'll have luck in catching fox. We do this because of what we learn from *Kk'adonts'idnee* [Distant Time] stories—it's not just something somebody made up." I was never told any special way to dispose of fox carcasses, but I presume they are best taken away from the village and burned, as with other fur animals.

This is not a spiritually powerful animal, but people follow the general rules of respect whenever they deal with it. So, for example, foxes are always kept indoors overnight after they are skinned, and loud noises or burning smells are avoided so that their spirits do not become offended. They are also given some special power to bring signs to people: if a fox urinates on someone's trapline trail, he or she will have no luck with this animal for some time to come.

When a fox is heard barking near a camp, it means a death will come soon. This is especially bad if it happens in the fall, because foxes are usually quiet then (they bark often in the spring). Killing the fox or chasing it away will negate the sign, especially if it is done by a shaman (Jetté, n.d.*a*). People told me that after hearing a fox bark a person should shout at it, "Go and die yourself!" This is wishing the warning of bad luck onto the fox itself, so that it might die instead of someone dear to the listener.

> *Wait, I see something: Far away yonder a fireflash comes down.*
> *Answer: A red fox, glimpsed as it dashes brightly through the brush.*
> [Jetté 1913:190]

Wolf

I had hiked far up onto one of Indian Mountain's ridges, and I sat down on the hard snow to look over the valley below. Caribou were scattered everywhere, pawing through the drifts for feed. Suddenly a herd of several hundred began to run, first coming together and then curving toward a spur of my ridge, like a flock of birds turning in unison. I looked behind them and saw what had caused the panic—a pair of wolves coming on at full speed.

But they were no match for the caribou, who easily outdistanced them and left no stragglers. The wolves read them quickly and veered away, knowing they had no chance for a kill. Before the herd passed me, their mouths agape from the heat of their climb, the two wolves had found an old carcass and were gnawing at it. I watched for a long time through binoculars as they pulled off bits of carrion, interrupting themselves for bouts of wrestling on the packed snow. Finally they sprawled beside one another, and while they slept I walked quietly away. [Huslia journal, April 1977]

The wolf (*Canis lupus*) is the master predator among animals of the north, possessing intelligence and strength, keen senses, and above all the ability to hunt cooperatively. Like the humans that they watch from afar, wolves multiply their muscle and mind by cooperating in pursuit of prey, then share the spoils. Indeed, for the Koyukon, the similarity between wolves and humans is no coincidence—in the Distant Time, a wolf-person lived among people and hunted with them. When they parted ways, they agreed that wolves would sometimes make kills for people or drive game to them, as a repayment for favors given when wolves were still human.

A strong sense of communality, a kind of shared identity, has held since that primordial time. Koyukon hunters still find wolf kills, left clean and unspoiled for them, and it is their right to take what is found. When hunters leave cached game behind they might place some fat apart from the rest of the meat, and if wolves happen along they are expected to take this rather than disturb what people want for themselves. One elder told me that he does not care for killing wolves, although he has done so a number of times. "They're too smart," he said, "too much like people."

This remarkable and elegant animal is also given great spiritual power in the Koyukon world, exceeded only by that of the wolverine and the bear. It is less malevolent, less threatening, but extremely dangerous nonetheless as a spiritual being. Elaborate rules govern people's behavior toward wolves, and severe punishment may come to those who fail to show them proper veneration.

The wolf (*teekkona* in Koyukon) looks like an outsized sled dog, weighing from about 75 to more than 150 pounds at adulthood, with a uniform gray, brown, or black coat. Some wolves have dark markings on their faces, a trait acquired in the Distant Time, when Raven tricked a wolf-person by throwing caribou innards in his face. Although wolves look and act like dogs, Koyukon people do not consider the two animals relatives because they get along poorly. When dogs encounter a trapped wolf (or wolverine) they will refuse to attack it; in fact, they even keep away from wolf hides. The whole business of wolf blood in Alaskan sled dogs is vastly overplayed, incidentally. Very few successful matings occur, and on the rare occasions when they do the offspring are usually too intractable and untrustworthy to function as anything but curiosities. Koyukon people seem little inclined to involve themselves with this peculiar fantasy of outsiders.

Wolves are fairly common in Koyukon country, although their overall population varies and their movements strongly affect local numbers. It would be unusual to make a long trip without seeing at least one wolf track, however. Although wolves generally avoid settlements, they are seen or heard fairly often around the village of Hughes, apparently because the river valley is so constricted there. This proximity can be upsetting, but not because Koyukon people share the outsiders' fear of wolf attacks—they fear signs. When wolves behave strangely it can foretell misfortune. Once some wolves howled in a strange way across the river from Hughes, and someone died fairly soon afterward. Another time wolves came right into the village, and one of them was later killed when they fought among themselves nearby. This was a bad sign, and again someone died in the village a short time later.

According to the Koyukon, wolves tend to follow the same circuits around an area during winter, passing a given spot every ten days or so. They wander farther afield in February and March because it is their mating season. Often a male and female will pair up and go off by themselves, moving away from the pack until mating is over. The pups are born in a shallow den during May, and for most of the summer the pack remains nearby. These dens are used year after year, and Koyukon people know where many of them are situated.

Wolves prey on a wide range of animals, from voles to moose and caribou. One animal they apparently leave alone is man—they are too smart for that, one old-timer told me. When they kill an animal they often eat only the best parts immediately, then leave it for a while. But people say the pack will return to it again and again, even over the full stretch of winter. This makes them susceptible to Koyukon trappers, who can predict where they will most likely appear.

Kill sites are less important in hunting wolves, which people can do very effectively now that they pursue them with the fast and tireless snow machine. Even at this, wolves are often too quick and clever to be caught. A small, lean female is fastest, the hunters agree, and most likely to elude its pursuer. If a man comes near a free or trapped wolf he should never shoot while it faces toward him, because the shot will miss. One man who tried this told me that his first bullet did not fire and his second missed. Then, having seen that the taboo was correct, he waited until the animal looked away and killed it with one shot. After a rifle has shot a wolf, it should be placed in the front left corner of the house and left there for four days (Clark 1970:85).

Wolf traps and snares are set in a variety of ways, either baited or placed near carrion. Fresh kills are especially good places to catch wolves, because they will probably return fairly soon. Traps must be well set and perfectly concealed if they are to catch this wary creature. But something more is needed, because only certain people have luck for the wolf, and those who do not are rarely successful. Luck is easily lost even by those who have it.

For example, a wolf should never be allowed to escape with a trap on its paw, though this sometimes cannot be avoided (this is true for wolverine and lynx as well). After this happens, the offended species may remain aloof from the trapper for years.

If someone kills a wolf that has another person's trap on its foot, the animal belongs to whoever owns the trap. In return, the trap owner should make a small payment to the one who killed it. "If he didn't, that animal would work against him. It would bring him bad luck." This also applies to the wolverine and the uncommon coyote (*Canis latrans*). I was told of one man who blatantly violated this rule, and his loss of several children over the following years was attributed to his severe breach of taboo.

Women are completely forbidden to hunt, trap, or skin wolves, a taboo that originates in a story of the Distant Time:

> There was a girl who met up with a wolf, back in Distant Time, when wolves were human. The wolf wanted her for his wife, even though he had two wolf wives already. When he took her home his two wives smelled her and knew she was human. After a while she had a child—a boy—and the wolf decided to kill his two other wives. He did that, but afterward the spirits of those two wolf wives killed his human wife and ate up her insides. Since then, women are never supposed to kill wolves, and they should not work with wolf hides until the animal has been dead for a while. They must follow these rules until they are too old to have children.

If a woman should catch a wolf (or wolverine, lynx, otter) in one of her traps, a man must skin it for her. Also, while the animal is being skinned, children should stay outside the house (Clark 1970:85), though I am not sure this is followed today. I once saw a small boy try to play with a wolf hide, pulling it over him and growling like a wolf, but his parents immediately said, *"Hutlaanee!"* ("It's tabooed") and made him stop.

Wolf pelts are extremely valuable today, for both commercial sale and local use. Koyukon women sew parkas, traditional boots, and mittens from this beautiful fur, but these can be worn only by men. Its most important use is for men's and women's parka ruffs—the long fur protects the wearer's face from chill winds and the hairs shed frost easily. The entire hide is used, even the head skin (for mittens) and the legs (for boots and mittens).

Wolf meat and organs are not used nowadays, but in the past the meat was eaten. The late Chief Henry told me he had eaten it, and Sullivan (1942:105) writes that the Nulato Koyukon used it in times of scarcity. I also heard of a man who eats a tiny piece of mesentary fat from each wolf he catches. Presumably there is a supernatural reason, although the person who told me about it was not certain.

After skinning a wolf, people used to sever all its leg joints, but nowadays they cut only the "knee" and "elbow" joints, either partially or completely. If they neglect this their children will become arthritic or crippled. Some people also cut the animal's brisket open and remove or expose its viscera, to avoid seeming to abandon the carcass without "using" it. Afterward the remains are placed somewhere out in the country along a trail, never burned like those of a wolverine. A man who burned a wolf carcass told me he had poor luck catching any more that year.

It is also important to put a piece of dried fish in the wolf's mouth, and to take a chunk of prized body fat from a moose or caribou, rub it on the snow, and "give it to the wolf" by burning it. While doing this a man should say, "You can go home to your father now." This ritual originated in the Distant Time, when Raven sent the wolf's son out to hunt for him. In exchange, the wolf asked that his son be given the best part of whatever he caught. And so people continue to give him special bits of food today.

On rare occasions someone comes across a dead wolf out in the wildland. When such an animal is found it is a locus of spiritual danger and must be left alone (one elder said it should be burned, but others said nothing at all should be done with it). A man told me he found a dead wolf years ago, freshly killed by another wolf, and the person with him wanted to take its hide for sale. But doing so would have caused grave danger, so he talked his companion out of the idea. Even touching such an animal may cause bad luck, illness, or some crippling malady, as people know from the tragic experience of a few who have ignored the elders' warnings. The death of this wild and powerful being without human intercession should be left completely within the omniscient domain of nature.

When we were about fifteen miles from Hughes, we saw a skinned wolf carcass alongside the trail. It was lying on pieces of wood and cardboard that kept it off the snow, probably so it wouldn't rot directly on the ground when the thaw comes. Its legs were all askew, their joints severed except for the tendons. The brisket was cut out so that we could see the animal's insides. And pushed between its teeth was a piece of dried fish.

A powerful spirit had been appeased. Yet those frozen, sightless eyes could still see; those severed, disfigured ears could hear. And so we left it to the stillness of the remote muskeg where it lay, hurrying away to the nether edge of its power. [Huslia journal, April 1977]

10

The Large Mammals

Deep Tracks

I walked alone across a broad sandbar that had only recently
emerged from beneath the spring flood. Dense quiet pressed the
solitude in around me. Then, halfway around the sandbar's curve,
I came upon a straight line of tracks punched far down into the
mud at the willows' edge. A bull moose had been there, feeding
on tender shoots.

Not far beyond them, another set of large tracks wandered out
onto the bar—the footprints of a black bear. Its hind feet were
only a bit shorter than the track I made beside them, and considerably deeper. The sign was so fresh that I wondered if the bear
was still nearby, listening as my footsteps hesitated beside his
own. His trail had revealed him, as mine now revealed our near-
meeting. It is a burden of size, leaving deep tracks to be seen by all
who pass later, a reminder that no one is ever alone in the wildland. [Huslia journal, June 1977]

This chapter brings together the remaining animals of the forest, an assortment I have grouped mainly because they are large, but also because
each has some very special importance to the Koyukon people. Apart from
this, they are a dissimilar collection indeed. Some are of great significance to
the village economies; others have little or no significance. Some are given
awesome and dangerous spiritual powers; others receive only the slightest
supernatural regard. Some are very common and conspicuous inhabitants of

the forest; others are almost never seen. And some are distinctly animal in every respect, while others resemble humanity or bridge the gap between the human and natural realms.

The discussion begins with moose and caribou, the only ungulates (hoofed animals) regularly hunted by people from the Koyukuk villages where I lived. Both figure prominently in the modern Koyukon economy; in fact, the moose is easily the most important resource among all animal species. Next the chapter will consider a very different pair of creatures— the black bear and brown bear. Although they are less significant economically, their extraordinary physical and spiritual power gives them a preeminent position in the natural world of the Koyukon.

With the bears, we have begun impinging upon something akin to humanity, some special behavior and consciousness that, in the Koyukon perception, moves beyond what is purely animal. And the next creature—the dog—has clearly entered the human domain. It is an animal, surely, but its spiritual makeup and its close association with people have given it human qualities in the eyes of the Koyukon. Last in this discussion of forest inhabitants is the enigmatic woodsman, the human turned wild, having crossed back into the natural domain and forsaken the company of its own kind. The woodsman is a final reminder that humans can never stand apart from their surroundings, that the illusion of separateness has no place in the world Raven made.

Moose

It is almost an axiom of human existence that what we desire most is scarce or difficult to obtain. And so it was with moose for the Koyukon people until a few decades past. This large animal, with its savory meat and treasured hide, was so rare that long journeys and persistent hunting were required to find it. But then the moose gradually increased to a point of real abundance in the Koyukuk wildlands, and it has remained common ever since. On a trip of any distance, summer or winter, it is quite normal to encounter several moose and see the tracks of many more. Sometimes, in fact, it can be more difficult to avoid them than to find them.

> I came across a cow and a calf moose this evening near the slough called *Nok'idaanee'o Hu*. The dogs smelled or heard them before I saw anything. Shungnak was prancing and jumping wildly at lead, looking into the brush to the left. I saw nothing but stopped the dogs to find out what they sensed. In a moment the cow lumbered up onto the trail and crossed into the woods on our right, followed by her first-year calf. If we had kept going we would have reached the spot just when they did, which could have been a real disaster. I am always cautious in that area, especially at dusk, because moose seem to favor it. [Huslia journal, January 1977]

1. Huslia is near the middle of a sprawling flatland, on the bank of the Koyukuk River. The clearing in the foreground is Huslia's airfield.

2. Snow is the medium on which natural events are recorded for the watchful eyes of Koyukon people. Here the raven landed and walked off to investigate a bit of carrion.

3. Trails used by dog teams and snow machines traverse the Koyukuk wildlands. This one passes through a broad muskeg dominated by stunted, gnomelike black spruce.

4. A small log house situated at the edge of Huslia. In the background, beyond the line of bare birch trees, is Binkookk'a Lake.

3

4

5. Moose are the most important source of food for Koyukuk people today. This summer bull with velvet on its antlers was briefly interrupted as it swam across the Koyukuk River.

6. Caribou on a mountain near the village of Hughes. In the old days caribou would "sing through" people, revealing their presence by songs that came to hunters on awakening.

7. Black bears are among the most spiritually powerful inhabitants of the northern forest. Women should not look at a live bear like this one, and they should call it *hulzinh* ("black place") to avoid offending it.

8. A short-tailed weasel in its white winter coat, stealing moose meat from a hunter's cache. This is often the first kind of animal trapped by young Koyukon boys.

6

7

8

9. People gather along the bank at Huslia during breakup, watching the ice move downstream in crushing floes. Prayers may be offered to thank the ice for a winter of safe travel and to ask that it move harmlessly away.

10. A porcupine in hiding. It appears humble but has power; it moves slowly but knows all the country in detail.

11

11. Lydia Simon with a young hawk owl, *k'itlee dzodza*. If the fledgling is raised by a young boy, he will become fastidious and a clever hunter.

12. Koyukon people regard the red fox as a clean, clever, but mischievous animal. Living up to its reputation, this one is stealing caribou meat outside a trapper's cabin.

12

13. Steven and Catherine Attla in summer camp with members of their family. Camps are important for subsistence activities like fishing and making birch-bark baskets, and for passing traditional knowledge along to the youngsters.

14. A fishing-hunting camp near Huslia in early summer, with cut pike and whitefish hanging to cure in the dry air. Newly leafed birches stand behind the tents.

13

14

15. One of Huslia's smaller log houses, photographed in early spring, when long days bring endless light and a welcome thaw.

16. Boats tethered along the Koyukuk River at Huslia. The bank is a hub of summer activity—people coming and going from fish camps, hunting trips, or visits to neighboring villages.

17. Steven Attla cutting dog (chum) salmon at a camp on the Koyukuk River. His son Benny carries fish to a nearby rack for open-air drying.

18. A trapped beaver just removed from beneath the ice. To show respect for its spirit, the trapper should skin it quickly, avoid cutting its throat, and carefully dispose of its unused remnants (pictured: Steven Attla).

19. Steven and Catherine Attla butchering a caribou shot near their trapping camp. Koyukon women take part in many subsistence activities, although taboos restrict them from involvement with some animals.

20

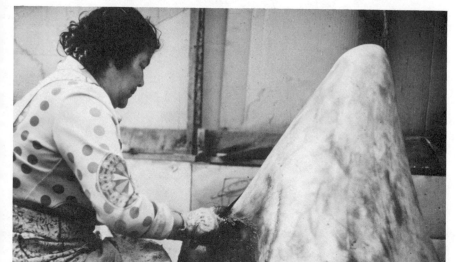

21

20. A wolf's powerful spirit is pacified by putting a piece of dried fish in its mouth, severing its leg joints, and placing its carcass out in the wildland away from human activity.

21. Scraping and tanning hides is an important women's activity. Here Catherine Attla does some initial cleaning on a large moose hide.

22. Boreal forest and mountains along a Koyukuk tributary near Huslia. Meandering rivers with associated sandbars, sloughs, and oxbows create a rich habitat for subsistence resources.

Moose (*Alces alces*) are denizens of the thicket, the ever-present brush that lines the waterways and wetlands, reaches up the high slopes, and covers the land after forest fires. Their favorite haunts are among the willows, which provide both rich browse and cover; but they also feed on birch, aspen, and a variety of ground and water plants. Relatively sedentary animals, they seldom wander more than a few dozen miles during the year's passage. A prime bull moose is an imposing creature indeed, weighing up to 1,500 pounds or more and standing over six feet tall at the shoulder. Cows are somewhat smaller but can weigh more than 1,000 pounds. The moose is often called ungainly, but in fact it moves with controlled, elegant power. Few animals are more impressive, especially when they are encountered deep within the wilds.

According to the oldest living Koyukon people there was a time, perhaps a hundred years ago, when moose were absent from the entire Koyukuk valley. Determined hunters found them by journeying upriver to present-day Bettles, then trekking eastward into the Ray Mountains and the Yukon drainage beyond. Sometime before 1900, moose began filtering into the eastern tributaries of the Koyukuk, westward down the Yukon, and up into the Melozitna River headwaters.

During the first quarter of this century, men from the Koyukuk settlements traveled to these remote areas for moose hunting. The animals were still fairly scarce, however, and so bulky that only the hide and a little meat could be brought back home (most of the meat was eaten on the trail). Men often tracked a moose for days on snowshoes before they managed to overtake and kill it.

By the 1920s moose were spreading down the Koyukuk valley and steadily increasing in numbers. They reached Hughes late in that decade (about 1927) and ten years later finally entered the great flats surrounding Huslia. Old-timers emphasize that not one track was seen before that time; but within a few years they had spread across the flats and were increasing toward a peak of population reached in the late 1960s. Their numbers have since declined somewhat, especially in the upriver areas (Allakaket, Hughes) and to a lesser degree around Huslia. The Koyukuk villagers, now heavily dependent on these animals, are much concerned with nurturing their population.

Hunters try to carefully select each moose they kill, so that only the most useful ones are taken. They know well the pattern of seasonal change in the quality of moose, and the variations because of sex, age, and other circumstances. Generally, moose are best in the fall, from about mid-August to mid-September (after this time the rutting bulls become poor). Luckily, this coincides fairly well with the legal hunting season. After this, and through winter, only cows without calves are in good condition. Spring moose tend to be lean, but during the summer they grow fat and prime again. Skilled hunters can pick out the best animals at a glance by their dark color, the curve of their backs, and their general fullness.

The various age and sex classes of moose are distinguished in a specialized Koyukon vocabulary. The basic terms (from Jones 1978:104–5) are as follows:

dineega	moose (general term)
k'iyeedza'	largest bull
didaayee gida'	four-year-old bull
didaayee yoza	two- to three-year-old bull
diyozee	cow
baggoy adinee	cow without calves
koltaaya	cow before having calves
ditseega	calf in first year
didaayee	calf over one year old

The Athapaskan people have perfected a wide array of techniques for hunting moose, methods far too complex to be described here. It is enough to say that the Koyukon are immensely skilled in pursuit of this favored animal, which they now take with rifles, often using a boat or snow machine in conjunction with the hunt (see Nelson 1973:8–111 for detailed descriptions of Athapaskan moose-hunting techniques). Both men and women regularly take moose—couples often hunt together by boat in the fall, but women sometimes hunt on their own. After one of these huge animals is shot it must be butchered and the bulky quarters must be carried, so a wise hunter prefers to have companions.

There is also safety in numbers when people are around moose, especially during certain seasons. As these animals have become common in the Koyukuk valley, they have also grown more aggressive. In fact, they are probably more dangerous than any other creature in the surrounding wildlands. During the fall rut, people are ever watchful for bull moose, especially on the river sandbars where they congregate for mating. When someone breaks sticks to make a fire, a bull may come hulking from the willows, answering what it interprets as the challenge of another bull raking its antlers in the brush. Prudence dictates a quick retreat to the boat, as the animal strides toward the noise, head lowered and antlers just above the ground, apparently certain that another moose awaits it.

In spite of their great bulk and spread of antlers, bull moose can move through the thickets with scarcely the slightest sound. This makes them all the more dangerous, because sometimes people find themselves closely confronted without time for a graceful escape. This leaves no alternative but to shoot, climb a nearby tree, or run. In open areas a moose is faster than a man, but if the trees are closely spaced a person can get away by weaving back and forth between them. Everyone in the Koyukuk villages has stories of close calls with bull moose, and uncomfortable meetings are common. They warn that a rutting bull with a cow is always most dangerous, but that none are to be trusted.

Deep or heavily crusted winter snow also brings out the worst in a moose. Frustrated by the difficulty of wading through a quagmire, they take over the packed trails and often refuse to move when a dog team or snow machine comes along. These animals are extremely dangerous, especially for the dog musher, who may be pulled into a fracas by his excited team. People tell many stories of moose being shot point-blank as they charged into a sled or snow machine, although I never heard of an injury's resulting. Judging from the tales, this is partly because of luck, partly because of quick and clever thinking, and partly because firearms are always kept ready during winter travel. Incidentally, the probability of such encounters is increased by the animals' habit of moving close to villages in winter to escape wolf harassment.

> Got a good scare this afternoon. Going through a portage, the dogs suddenly sniffed the air and grew excited. I looked around but saw nothing. Then I glanced to the right and saw a big moose charging straight toward the sled, full speed, head down and hackles up. No time to grab my rifle; I just shouted at the dogs, jumped off, and pushed for all I was worth. We managed to pass him before he reached the trail, where he stopped and glared angrily toward us. When we were safely away I braked the sled and looked back, my heart pounding hard. There were no tracks on the trail, so he had just gotten mad over nothing. People have told me time and again that this can happen, but somehow it means a lot more now that I have seen it for myself. [Huslia journal, March 1976]

In May and June, cow moose with newborn calves can also be extremely dangerous. For example, we once came upon a cow whose calf had been killed by predators, and for days she charged toward us each time we passed in the boat, sometimes even coming well out into the water. It is awesome to think of meeting such an animal when afoot in the woods. This danger would exist even if moose were rare, but the other dangers I have discussed seem related to high population. Koyukon elders emphasize that before moose were abundant they were extremely wary of humans, and they fled at the slightest sign of being approached.

Large as they are, moose do fall prey to other animals, especially wolves. People also say that brown bears are capable of killing even the great antlered bulls. Black bears apparently leave moose alone, although I once saw one feeding on a dead calf. Interestingly, moose seem to have an aversion to caribou and will leave an area when caribou move into it. A Koyukon elder explained that they dislike the noise caribou make, walking carelessly through the brush and running to and fro without reason. Moose are quiet animals, he said, and they cannot abide these clamorous intruders.

The position of moose in the Koyukon spiritual world seems a paradox. It is a vital animal for contemporary village economies, a physically powerful and dangerous creature, a prominent and conspicuous forest inhabitant—yet it is accorded very little supernatural significance. In fact, few animals seem to have a lesser role in the society of natural things. I was once told that moose is the "only animal" not mentioned in stories of the Distant Time. Perhaps this is because moose only recently entered the Koyukuk region. But I doubt that they were ever absent from all of Koyukon territory; and they might have inhabited the Koyukuk valley in times before recent memory.

Jetté (1911:609) describes a Nulato Koyukon belief that moose possess a spirit (*yeega,* in his translation), but only during the fall rutting season. People from the Koyukuk villages told me nothing of this, but their behavior toward moose shows the same deference given all spiritually endowed creatures. They carefully avoided wasting moose, they protect its meat from defiling influences (such as scavengers), and they treat the living animal with respect. If a moose is killed and found to be diseased, it is simply left where it fell. No symbolic butchering or covering is done, as would be for a spiritually powerful animal like the bear.

People who are going to hunt moose avoid talking directly about their plans, making cryptic references instead. For example, someone might say, "I will go out and try to see a moose track." Or, "I will go to such-and-such place to look for a moose track." This recognition of the animal's spiritual awareness is often neglected today, especially by younger hunters.

Like other animals, the moose can give warning signs by association with unusual events. For example, a Huslia man told of shooting a moose that, when it fell, uttered a strange sound, as if it wailed, *"Abaa!"* This is a Koyukon way of expressing pain. As he butchered the animal, his knife slipped and cut his hand so badly that he had to be flown to a hospital for treatment.

Taboos regulating the uses of moose also indicate some spiritual endowment and sensitivity. Eating moose feet, for example, is said to give a person rheumatism, a restriction that is nevertheless often ignored. The animal's lower jaw and lower lips are tabooed for all except old men; the neck bones are avoided by anyone of childbearing age because they can cause slowness or clumsiness; and glands from the head are strictly forbidden to anyone, as are most animal glands. Aside from this, parts of the moose are used freely, a contrast to the elaborate restrictions on spiritually potent creatures such as the bear.

Few animals, if any, are as thoroughly usable as this one. The meat is rich and delicious, as are many of the organs. (Appendix 4 details the thoroughness with which Koyukon people name and utilize the various parts of a moose.) A wide selection of traditional recipes are followed in preparing this animal, and almost without exception the dishes are delicious even to an uninitiated newcomer. Most preparations involve the meat, which is boiled, fried, roasted, or dried—a thin stew or soup is probably the most common daily use. There are also exotic-sounding dishes such as boiled moose nose or moosehead soup, the latter a tasty concoction of fat, muscle, lips, and assorted tissues. Besides its importance as food, the moose provides a large, extremely durable hide, which is still fashioned into an assortment of items from clothing to sled lashings.

Indeed, it must have seemed like a miracle to the elders when they saw this great animal slowly spreading into the Koyukuk tributaries and down the valley to the wildlands around their settlements. Few events could have been more fortuitous. But in a world where change is the rule, no one would assume that the moose could not disappear again.

> I made a short trip with the dogs late today to haul in a supply of wood. After the sled was loaded I loafed around the woodyard, not wanting to leave for home. It was a classic boreal midwinter evening—dead still, powerfully cold (about −40°), orange sky smothered to deep blue overhead and black toward the northeast horizon. The dogs sat attentively, lifting their noses to the scent of moose, turning their heads in unison when they heard sounds in the nearby willows, ears perked forward, whining and quivering with excitement.
>
> I went off along the low ridge, walking quietly, staring into the dark, dense brush, hoping I might glimpse a moose. Intermittent snapping sounds, quite loud now, disturbed the stillness surrounding me. I could hear the willows slowly crack as they were bent down to be browsed, and occasionally the sound of a heavy breath or a foot being pushed down into deep powder.
>
> Gloom descended heavily in a hush of cold. I turned for the sled, watching nervously all around lest one of those dark, hidden figures heave onto the trail and dispute my right to use it. [Huslia journal, December 1976]

Caribou

The caribou (*Rangifer tarandus*) is the smallest northland deer, and I suppose the most delicate and lovely one. Unlike the uniformly brown moose, the rich chocolate of the caribou's body is set against a striking white mane, shoulders, and flank stripe. From late summer until January the bulls are adorned with a graceful sweep of antlers, and cows and adolescents carry much smaller antlers that are not lost until winter's end. An adult caribou weighs from two hundred to four hundred pounds—a substantial animal, especially considering that many are often found together.

Caribou herds range in size from a few animals to several hundred, occasionally more. They summer on the Arctic tundra far north of Koyukuk country, but with the approach of fall they migrate southward into the

Brooks Range. Eventually they filter through the mountains and enter the Koyukuk valley in October or November. Here they move into areas above timberline or scatter across the open-forested flats, to remain in small herds through winter, feeding on lichens, mosses, and other ground plants. Then, by March or April, they begin their long trek from the timberlands northward to the tundra plains breeding grounds.

> Wait, I see something: It makes a noise like tutɬ-tutɬ in the gully.
> Answer: The clicking sound of caribou hooves as they walk over the ground.
> [Jetté 1911:189]

Unfortunately, this annual migratory cycle is anything but predictable, and wide variations in timing, route, destination, and numbers are the rule. Like most nomads, caribou are steadfastly independent. They are made even more unpredictable by a pattern of fluctuating population, which strongly affects the occurrence of caribou in marginal areas like the Koyukuk. These changes may elevate caribou to major importance as an economic resource or may totally remove them from the subsistence picture for periods ranging from a year to several decades.

Village elders say that caribou (called *bidziyh* in Koyukon) were common in the Koyukuk valley during the past century, and whites who visited the Nulato people (on the Yukon River) in the 1840s noted their importance in the subsistence economy (Loyens 1966:43). But by 1865 the explorer William Dall mentioned that all big game was very scarce around Nulato, the caribou having left this area. Perhaps somewhat later they also vanished from the Huslia region, as the entire western Arctic caribou population declined toward a low ebb reached about 1880 (Hemming 1971:5). No one knows why this change occurred, but similar fluctuations are widely known for this animal.

By the turn of the century the herd began a period of increase and gradual expansion into territory abandoned long before. By the late 1940s they returned to the Koyukuk country, and they continued to increase until the mid-1970s (estimates for the entire herd were 119,000 animals in 1948 and 242,000 in 1969, more than doubling in twenty-one years). This increase took place in the constant presence of subsistence hunting and animal predation (the Koyukon say that wolves and wolverines take caribou).

Then, between 1970 and 1976, the population crashed to fewer than 50,000 animals, and caribou were suddenly scarce once more in the Koyukuk valley. Regrowth has now begun, but it may be years before this valuable animal is again significant in the village economy.

Koyukuk River people hunt caribou with dog teams or snow machines, pursuing them across the tundra or open muskeg until they are near enough to shoot. In the forest, however, they often hunt afoot or on snowshoes. Small bunches tend to "yard up" among the trees, staying in one small area for weeks or even months. A careful hunter can sometimes find one of these groups and stalk them undetected. Among the trees, caribou are often wary and elusive, but in open terrain they can be foolishly unafraid or confused by approaching hunters. They are fleet-footed, however, and often whisk away over the tundra before anyone comes within shooting range. Sometimes they are not so clever:

> When I made the ridgetop, I looked out over a broad tundra flat, and near its center was a herd of about fifty caribou. They were several hundred yards away, feeding placidly through crusted snow in the blaze of sunlight; and from my low vantage they stood stark above the level plain. There was not even a large stone to give cover, so my only hope was to walk openly toward them, my arms upstretched like antlers. They saw me immediately but only stared in bewilderment, lifting and lowering their heads, unable to solve the puzzle I had caused.
> Then one leaped and ran, and the rest blindly followed along the ridge's far edge. I sprinted as if to cut them off, and their overestimate of my speed made them suddenly stop, mill, and turn back across the flat. By the same ploy I made them turn again, and again, each time drawing nearer, until less than fifty yards separated us. I had the entire herd corralled at one end of the expansive ridgetop, until finally they rushed around me in a thunder of flying snow, flanks rippling and heads held high. I watched in breathless exultation as they swept away over the distant edge. [Huslia journal, April 1977]

By the time caribou enter the Koyukuk valley in early winter, they have grown lean from the long journey, and the bulls' flesh tastes strong with the rut. Their hides are in fine condition, however, a thick new coat that is ideal for clothing or for warm camp mattresses. Caribou hide is unequaled for warmth, and today the people use it especially for making traditional winter boots soled with tanned moosehide. As winter progresses, and especially near spring, the animals fatten and become more desirable as food, so hunters search widely to find them before the migration. Koyukon people relish the excellent meat, which they use almost exactly as they would moose. And, as Appendix 4 shows, they have uses for almost every part of the animal.

In the Koyukon spiritual world, caribou seem to be regarded much like moose. They apparently have some spirit power, but less than most other creatures. In Nulato, Jetté learned that caribou have two spirits (*yeega*), including one for the forefeet (he writes forelegs, but uses the Koyukon word for feet). These must not be eaten lest they cause rheumatism

(1911:608). He also writes that anyone who stole a caribou from another's snare would suffer epileptic seizures or pass them on to offspring.

Modern villagers also accord the usual respect to caribou, such as deferential treatment of their meat. As with moose, there are no special rules for disposing of unusable remains, but the bones are usually burned or deposited away from the village. Both animals can be used as dog food, though people usually give dogs only the least preferred parts.

Caribou is the only creature for which there were hunting songs, which "came to" a hunter as he awakened (I say "he," because women rarely take this animal, though apparently no taboo restricts them). People say that caribou would "sing through" a person, either to let him know they were nearby or to reveal that a taboo concerning them had been broken. For example, if a menstruating woman ate fresh caribou meat in violation of taboo, someone would awaken with a song. The person given a song would sing it afterward to bring luck in finding and hunting caribou. Koyukuk elders still know many of them, but I am not sure whether they are much used today or whether caribou still give them to people. In any case, these songs are said to please the animals' spirits (Sullivan 1942:80). During earlier years, shamans could also approach the caribou's spirit and use its power to make caribou come to hunters.

Although the caribou and moose are not spiritually powerful, they are, like all living things, imbued with the essence of the supernatural. Everything here exists on two levels—the domain of the senses and the domain that lies beyond. But clearly, practical significance to humanity does not assure a position of great power among the spirits of nature.

Black Bear

> The late Chief Henry, when just a boy, was traveling on foot through the forest with a group of people. Somewhere along the way he heard a strange thing, an old man off in the timber, shouting to the others, "I found a place where a white man froze to death back here last fall!" Everyone understood what he meant—that he had killed a hibernating black bear in its den—and that he used cryptic language so he would not offend its spirit. Everyone except Chief Henry.
>
> Following custom, the men waited several days and then held a ceremonial feast in that place, to eat parts of the animal and to honor its spirit. Chief Henry's mother insisted he go; but when they offered him meat he refused it, horrified to think of what they were eating. Afterward the men made him take some meat home; and when his mother told him to eat it he refused again, finally admitting that he was not going to eat human flesh. She had to eat some of it herself before he would believe that it was bear meat, and that the old man was only talking in riddles when he called out in the forest.

The black bear takes us near the apex of power among spirits of the natural world. Its close relative the brown bear is given almost identical regard, though it is more potent and dangerous. And the wolverine, most powerful of all animal spirits, stands above them both. But wolverines are small and reclusive, while bears are conspicuous, imposing, sometimes even awesome personages. They move regularly within human sight; they are often hunted; and their remains, vibrant and electric with spiritual energy, are frequently brought near people. Wolverine is like a hermit king, more powerful, but less to be reckoned with than the prince who marches through the streets.

It is difficult to separate black and brown (or grizzly) bears here, because Koyukon people treat them so much alike. But they are also quite different. Although both have considerable spiritual and practical importance, the black bear is far more significant in the subsistence economy. It ranks high as a resource, esteemed as a food and as a ceremonial delicacy. And taking the animal is far more than just a way of getting food—it is a quest for prestige and a high expression of manhood.

Black bears (*Ursus americanus*) are creatures of the forest and thicket, found especially in the river valley lowlands. They are fairly common in the Koyukuk region, and their population seems to change little with the passage of years. Bears escape the rigorous northern winter by retiring to underground dens from late September until the end of April, emerging just before the snow vanishes. In spring they wander around scavenging for carrion and anything else they consider edible, quickly losing the fat left over from their long dormancy. When the plants appear, they feed on willow buds and shoots, rushes, and various grasses. Vegetarian fare sustains them through summer, occasionally varied with fish and small mammals.

During June bears gather in open areas such as lowlands or mud bars with abundant rushes (*Equisetum*). Because it is their mating season, the animals in these congregations can be aggressive and dangerous. Certainly they are fearless, as a trip along a Koyukuk tributary showed me:

> The abundance of black bears was astonishing—we saw one or two idling among the rushes on almost every bar. Most of them lifted their heads to gaze myopically toward the oncoming boat, then stood there either unconcerned or unwilling to move. Some eventually rambled back into the willows; others just watched or returned to their grazing; and a few chose the indiscretion (or gesture) of urinating copiously when we approached within a few yards. None of the dozens we saw made a hostile move toward us, but we were obviously beyond reach, and in the boat we posed no territorial threat. [Huslia journal, July 1977]

As fall approaches, black bears turn their attention to the ripening array of berries, which helps them accumulate the prodigious amount of fat they will need for dormancy. They move slowly through the berry patches, occasionally looking up or lifting their noses to sniff the breeze. An old man who had sneaked close enough to watch a feeding bear told me it grasped each branch in its mouth and pulled to one side, neatly stripping off the berries. This is why bears seem to be constantly shaking their heads among the berry bushes.

In September black bears find old dens or dig new ones, then gather moss and grass for a soft bed inside. After the first snows they enter, plug the entrance, and begin their long repose. Early warm spells may bring them out again; but otherwise the winter is uneventful until about February, when the young are born inside the den. One or two cubs are the rule in this area (never three, I was told), and hunters who have found newborns say they are about five inches long.

Koyukon people hunt bears in their dens every year, but they almost never find a female with unborn young inside her. Sullivan's Nulato teachers said that "when a pregnant female is killed she mysteriously causes the fetus to disappear, so that only the empty uterus is found in the body" (1942:88). There is a vague idea, he adds, that the bear's protective spirit causes this to happen. Only one Koyukuk man, the late Chief Henry, ever found embryos inside a bear. It happened twice, in fact, both times in January—and one of the animals carried three fetuses. Frightened by these unusual happenings, he consulted a shaman and was advised that they were not an ominous sign. He would sleep inordinately for some time (as the bear itself does), the shaman warned, and then all would be normal again. This counsel proved correct, Chief Henry later recalled.

In Koyukon the black bear is called *sis*. Women cannot use this name, however, and so they call the animal *hulzinh*, "black place," to avoid offending its spirit. Men often use this same circumlocution when they are hunting bears. Several other terms specify certain ages or types of bears (black or brown):

k'itl'intl'a "big"	largest male
diyodla	second largest, either sex
k'a'o taalyoyee "that which went away"	one- or two-year-old
k'aanee eenaatltaanee "it went to bed for something"	two- or three-year-old female, a a year before mating; the fattest kind of bear
k'aggoya	small cub

The Koyukon also recognize a "half-breed" bear, brown in color but the size of a black bear, which they call *sis tseega'* (outsiders would call this a color phase of the black bear). The animal has a reputation for meanness, because it is a brother to the brown bear. And there is a long-legged, long-bodied variety of black, brown, and "half-breed" bears called *bizik ninaalee* ("long body"). These slim animals are also considered especially mean and dangerous.

Koyukon people often comment on the physical similarity between bears and humans, although to them this does not imply kinship. The resemblance is striking, and somewhat frightening, when a skinned bear is laid out on its back. Adult black bears usually weigh under two hundred pounds and are about five feet long from nose to tail, not much different from a stocky man. Bears can also look like people in the forest, especially when they stand erect to get a better look at something. I was told that they occasionally stand to peer across an open area, shading their eyes with one paw just as a person would.

These human characteristics make Koyukon people a bit uneasy—the solitary figure standing mysteriously at the edge of timber at dusk, the skinned carcass lying like a corpse in deep grass. Stalking, killing, and dismembering such a creature seems to have a faintly murderous and cannibalistic feeling about it, something not consciously felt with any other animal.

These sensations notwithstanding, the Koyukon people are bear hunters without peer. Their knowledge of these animals is deep and detailed, their hunting methods sophisticated and complex far beyond what can be described here. Black-bear hunting starts before the ice is gone in spring, when the animals are still fat and delicious. They are also rather tame then, so it is easy to approach within shooting range. After breakup they have become lean and poor, and they remain so through most of the summer. In former times a few were killed for fresh meat during the warm months, but this is seldom done today.

Bears grow fat and tender on their fall berry feast, and hunters traveling the rivers for September moose always watch for them. Stout, short-legged ones are the fattest and are preferred over the slender, long-legged animals. By early to middle October, depending on cold and snow, the black bears have entered their dens—it is time for the *real* hunt to begin.

> *Wait, I see something: I am looking everywhere for a lost arrow.*
> *Answer: The search for a bear's den.*
> [Jetté 1913:647]

Koyukon men travel widely through the wildlands each fall, searching for occupied black-bear dens. They begin afoot before the snow, then continue with dog teams and snow machines at least through November. Each hunter checks many dens known from long experience, and he looks for new ones as well. Of course knowledge of preferred denning habitat aids the search, as does an eye for minute signs—bits of grass on the snow, incongruously broken twigs, old bear tracks subtly revealed by irregularities of the snow surface.

But while they allow that skill has a role in finding bears, Koyukon hunters say that luck is the essential factor. Only certain men are lucky with bears, either because they have shown scrupulous respect all their lives or simply because the bears favor them. And there are special reasons—for example, a man born with six toes on each foot will be very lucky in bear hunting.

Once a den is located there are dozens of ways to find out if a bear is inside, but even a seasoned expert may need to study it carefully before he knows for sure. Then, depending on many different circumstances, he might chop open the den roof, coax the animal out, or even crawl inside the den mouth to shoot the bear. Needless to say, the hunt is fraught with danger, but an ample reward of prestige compensates for the risk.

Koyukon men are thoroughly dedicated to den hunting—it is the truest test of their outdoor skills and a fundamental part of their masculine identity. The hunt is often undertaken by pairs or groups; and if it is successful a ceremonial feast or "bear party" is held afterward, so it also has important social value for men (women are excluded by strict taboo). Den hunting is a significant source of food for the village—for example, men from Huslia take ten to thirty bears this way each fall.

Hunting black bears in their dens requires many gestures of respect, beginning with the etiquette of speech. Sometimes, for instance, a man will decide against hunting an occupied den alone; but when he comes home he avoids any mention of his find, knowing that the animal's spirit is ever aware. Then, shortly before he begins his trip back to the den, he goes to another man and explains his discovery with indirect words, asking if he will come along for the hunt. Talking openly about it would assure that the bear would be gone when they reached the den.

Men often return home for help when they locate an inhabited den, unless it appears to have a young animal inside. Older bears are usually unaffected by hearing someone prowl around, but younger ones often abandon the den quickly afterward. How, then, does a man know the age of his quarry, hidden deep within its lair? If he puts his head into the entrance and listens carefully, he may hear the bear's heart pounding, growing steadily louder and faster. This is a young animal, its heart beating with fear. An older bear's heart does not pound or race, because it is unafraid. A man may hear it licking its chops, but that is all. Thus the master hunter can detect his prey's emotions, and from this he designs his plan.

Even in the flow of everyday conversation, Koyukon people choose their words carefully when they speak of den hunting. The late Chief Henry, though he was inactive and no longer needed to protect his hunting luck, still showed respect for the bear by using cryptic language:

I didn't want to go home yet, and while letting my traps go for two
*   nights.*
Why don't I just walk around up this way, I thought.

Even though later in my life
I was to come upon
You know what kind of place, that day
I spent the whole day fooling around good ground, and I found nothing.
[Jones 1979:10]

Here, "walk around up this way" means den hunting, and "you know what kind of place" refers to a den with a bear inside.

When men hunt together, the one who finds an occupied den shouts to his companions, telling them directly what he has found. Even a hunter alone should do this, following a lesson set forth in a Distant Time story. But if women are nearby he must use the disguise of circumlocution, as the story from Chief Henry's boyhood illustrated.

After he returns home, a successful den hunter must say nothing of where he went or what took place. He should even clean his ax if he used it to dig open the den, so that no one can tell what he was doing by looking at it. Later that evening he might remark, "I found something in a hole," making no mention of a bear. Or, if it is before trapping season, he might say, "I caught something for a parka ruff," and people would know that he could mean only one animal. Speaking more directly of the kill would offend its spirit and bring bad luck down upon the hunter.

If a female bear is taken in late winter, as occasionally happens, she may have very small cubs with her. Because they have revealed themselves to the hunter, he is obligated to kill them all. The infant cubs may be taken home, but they should be eaten only by old people. Some men prefer not to bring them back at all, but they must still be butchered in some way (for instance, removing the viscera and heads) to avoid the offense of killing a creature without "doing something to it." Much larger yearling cubs are also sometimes found with denning females, and these are fully used.

Finding a crippled or deformed bear in a den is a sign of bad luck for the man or his family. This holds true only if the malady is natural, however, not caused by something human like a rifle wound. It was considered ominous when Chief Henry found a bear with no ears, for example, but he was spared any ill fortune.

Occasionally a bear makes its den in a poor spot and overflow from a nearby stream floods the animal out. Then it has no choice but to wander around in the cold searching for a new den, while its fur gradually becomes coated with thick frost ("because it isn't made for being out in winter," someone explained). The Koyukon have no special fear or regard for such bears, unlike the neighboring Kutchin Athapaskans, who consider them extremely dangerous. A brown bear abroad in winter is more fearsome to the Koyukon, especially a long-legged kind that lives in the Old Man (*Kk'oonootna*) River country. As one elder explained:

> There's a good story I been meaning to tell you, about a guy named Big Moses that went out after a bear with his nephew. This was years ago. He had only a spear and ax, because he gave away the rifles he got when he went out to Nome. Well, the two of them happened to find a bear hole. A big black bear was inside, but instead of staying in there it charged right out after them. It was so fast, Big Moses's nephew had no chance to hit it with his ax; and Big Moses couldn't get it with his spear because it came straight at him. Somehow—I don't know why—he just grabbed it, and all of a sudden he was right on top of its neck, holding onto its ears.
>
> That bear charged away with Big Moses on it and the nephew running after them. And, you know, he found out that if he twisted its head to one side it would turn that way! So he turned it around so it ran back toward the den. His nephew saw it all happening, and I guess he figured if Big Moses was brave enough to ride the bear, he was brave enough to kill it with the ax. So when the bear got to him, he swung down at its head! His uncle shouted to watch out for his hands, and he pulled down hard on the ears to get out of the way. Well, that ax hit it perfect, right across the forehead, and the bear fell dead. I always say that guy was a crazy fool to give away his rifle, so he had to keep hunting with just his spear and ax.

People's behavior toward black bears is subject to an extraordinary number of taboos, a few of them already discussed. My Koyukon teachers often commented on this, especially the women, who are subject to far more restrictions than men. Most often they said, "Men must have made all those *hutlaanee* [tabooed] things so only they get the best parts of the animal." This was a half-serious reference to the many food taboos that I will detail later. One man said that bears are very hard to find in their dens and their meat is extremely valuable, so people must treat them with the greatest respect. In other words, they need all the luck they can get, and the way to have luck is to show deference to their powerful spirits.

Disregarding or violating bear taboos can be sharply punished. Ordinary offenses alienate the animal, make it elusive or invisible, usually for years. An offender who suffers bad luck for bear will pass right by the animal or its den without seeing it, while another will see it immediately or be drawn toward it. More serious offenses can bring illness to the person or a family member, or even death. Insulting comments or gestures toward the animal, whether it is dead or alive, rank among the most severe transgressions. Bear attacks, which are exceedingly rare, may be interpreted as retaliation for such insults.

Respect for the living animal is shown in other ways besides those mentioned above. For example, men should wear new boots each fall when they start den hunting, although recently this has been neglected. Great inhibition is always necessary whenever women and bears are involved—women not only are forbidden to hunt these animals (until after menopause), but they should even avoid looking at them. They are also advised not to pick pussy willows in the spring, because bears eat them. During the fall bear season, men should limit their contact with women, refrain from discussing bear hunting around them, and not talk about women while they hunt. Once a man told his den hunting companion that they should have a woman along to cook for them. Because of his comment, they hunted for many days and got nothing.

From the Nulato Koyukon, Sullivan (1942:86) learned that a hunter should never point at a bear he has seen, because it will feel this and run away. And when he is ready to shoot a bear he should talk to it, telling it where and how to move. For example, he might say, "I am your friend—be easy with me—go slow—put up your head." Hearing this, the bear will obey.

Black and brown bears are both considered very dangerous when met in the wild. Unexpected encounters are all the more likely because these animals can move silently through the forest or thicket. In the springtime, when bears are irritable and incautious, people often camp on islands, keep dogs in camp to warn them of interlopers, and make noise when they walk in the woods so they will not surprise a bear. But sudden meetings still happen. If an alarmed or angry bear acts threateningly toward a man, he should say, "I'm not bothering you, so you might as well go away now." He emphasizes that he intends no harm to it and that it should do no harm either. A woman approached by a hostile bear should expose her genitals to it and say, "My husband, it's me." This will shame the animal, quiet it down, and make it leave.

Koyukon elders seem to agree that black bears are more dangerous than brown bears when they are suddenly confronted or are wounded. If they start rushing angrily toward someone they are said to be less inclined to swerve off and run away. I was once charged by a wounded black bear that showed no intention of changing course; it died within a few yards of me. Brown bears may rush forward or act threateningly, but people say they are more likely to retreat when a person stands ground and speaks to them. In practice, however, the Koyukon are unafraid of black bears and extremely wary of brown bears.

Rules of behavior toward killing bears, or remains from them, are far more elaborate than those toward the living animals. When a bear is killed it should be skinned and butchered on the spot, never hauled or dragged somewhere else with a sled or boat. If one is shot inside its den, it should be pulled out the old way, by hand and with rope, no matter how great an effort it takes. Easing the job with a snow machine would deeply offend the animal's protective spirit. Pulling it out with chain instead of rope is also tabooed, even more so if the chain has been used to tether dogs—metal often alienates natural spirits, and dogs are highly polluting to bears. A man who violated several of these rules with one denning bear told me he did not take another for twenty years afterward. Mistreating a bear can also affect the area, making it difficult for the man to take any game there for many years.

Before he starts butchering a bear, the careful hunter will slit its eyes so that its spirit will not see if he should violate a taboo. And he may take off its feet to keep its spirit from moving around. The head is also removed, and in no circumstances must it ever be taken home. Meat and tissues from the head are eaten by men away from the village. They are considered delicacies, though they are used less today than in the past.

The bear's brain is never eaten, because it would cause a person to anger easily; but it should be removed "so it doesn't rot in there." Bear heads or skulls are either hung up in a small tree near the kill (the traditional way) or burned in a clean fire (containing no trash). The lower jaw should be disposed of with the skull, preferably tied onto it before it is put in a tree. Any part of a bear's head is strictly tabooed for women or children, lest they or their offspring be quick-tempered.

The hide is also treated very carefully to avoid any alienating contact with women. Bear skins retain their life, their extreme spiritual potency, for several years. Female contact during this time is strongly tabooed and will bring bad luck to the hunter. Even after the hide is fully dead, a woman should not use it for clothing, sleep on it, or step onto it.

One of my instructors described her great discomfort when she found herself sitting with a bearskin rug at her feet. Her non-Koyukon host finally noticed that something was wrong, so she explained and the rug was taken away, much to her relief. Many problems could have befallen her because of this, but I suspect her husband's luck in bear hunting was most in jeopardy. A white woman in Huslia once bought a hide to use for a rug, and the man who killed it got no more bears for ten years. "Oh, sometimes I just *think* of her stepping over that bear skin when she got out of bed every morning," a woman lamented.

The spiritual essence of a woman, which is strongly linked to her menses, manifests itself especially when she steps over something. This is why, for example, a hunter can lose his luck if a woman steps across his legs while he sits on the floor. Older women carefully avoid doing this, but men are always ready to move their legs quickly when young girls (past puberty) are around. These girls often do not know the taboos, and at this age they are at a peak of spiritual potency. Fear of careless violation by young women also explains why many Koyukon hunters no longer bring bear skins home, preferring to leave them where the kill was made. They have few uses for bear hides anyway, and selling them commercially would almost ensure later contact with women.

A very successful bear hunter told me that he always protects his luck by following the rules precisely. Nowadays he never brings a hide to the village—instead, he cuts it into fairly small pieces and leaves it "for the animals to clean up." Once again, cutting something apart is a symbolic use, a gesture of nonwaste. If a hide is brought home, it should be scraped and tanned only by a woman past menopause. I do not remember ever seeing a bear skin in a Koyukon household, although some men are said to keep them.

A few days after one or more black bears are killed, the men gather to honor their spirit with a ceremonial feast, called *k'itlee' alkk'aa* ("where you finish eating bear's head"), or "bear party" in English. Originating among the animal-humans of the Distant Time, this feast is always held in the woods, so that the most preferred and spiritually potent parts of the animal can be eaten in a "clean" place. Women have not been walking there; no female pollution will offend the sensitive bear. In former times the feast was held right where the animal was killed, but today it takes place near the village. Only men and boys can attend. One elder told me that the bear feast is a way of showing proper "manners" to the animal, that neglecting it would be like eating piggishly while you are a guest in someone's house. But more than this, it is a kind of funeral ritual, a final act of deference and respect.

In Allakaket, Clark (1970:83) learned that the "bear death ceremonial and ritual are second only to that of man." It is essentially a memorial potlatch held to honor the killed animal, much like the ones given for departed persons. She adds that a man should stay awake all night after killing a bear in its den, because its wandering spirit should not see him sleeping (p. 84). This is probably no longer done, but it mirrors the practice (still followed) of not sleeping after a person dies. Women sometimes complain that they should be allowed at the bear feast, in spite of the potent spiritual incompatibilities this entails, because they know that the best delicacies are eaten there. But the taboo remains inviolate, and the fresh, powerful, still-alive flesh is kept well away from feminine influences.

A streamer of smoke rose through the riverbank treetops and diffused into the clear, cold air. In the timber below, twenty men and boys sat on logs and spruce boughs, pressed close around a broad bed of coals and crackling flames. Clouds of steam rose from two great boiling pots, filled with choice pieces of bear— meat from the front quarter and neck in one pot, the whole head in another. At the fire's edge, skewered and sizzling on sticks that leaned over the glowing coals, were the four skinned paws.

"What we eat here," an old man explained, "is the main part of the bear's *life.*"

The fire lasted several hours, pulsing warmth against the cold that gradually numbed hands and feet. Throughout this time there was feasting on hot meat pulled from the frothing kettles, and a feast of stories from the old men as well. Much talk was about the bear, about hunts and encounters, about the great animal itself. But there was plenty of easy talk on all subjects—the same lack of solemnity that prevails at Koyukon death watches and wakes.

When evening approached, men began trekking slowly homeward on snowshoes. The last to leave fed the fire a bit, assuring that no fragments of bone would remain unburned. Behind in the quiet, the flames slowly began to fade, ebbing like the conciliated power of the killed one. [Huslia journal, September 1976]

After a bear feast is held, the leftover meat is brought home, and men or boys will eat it later. Other parts of the animal are prepared at various times, again subject to an array of special rules and considerations. After a few days or a week, the bear's ribs, hindquarters, pelvis, and lower backbone meat can be eaten at home. Usually the man who kills a bear gives much of it away, saving only small amounts for his own family.

The most valuable parts of bears are saved for potlatches, community feasts in which great tubs of excellent food are served. Choice meat from the ribs and pelvis, and especially the thick slabs of bear fat, are distributed to everyone who attends a potlatch. Apart from the bear feast, these memorials to the dead are the main time when meat from this animal is eaten. Bear meat for potlatches must be prepared in a bachelor's house, away from any women. People remember one such gathering at Huslia recently, for which the men provided twenty-one bears. The entire accumulation had to be cooked in one man's home, because it was the only place where no woman lived.

Various parts of the bear are protected by other taboos, regulating especially who is permitted to eat them. Women are allowed nothing from the head, for example, and only old men can eat the lower jaw meat or tongue. The hind feet are tabooed for women of any age and for young men, the front feet for women to the age of menopause. Men in their active years should never eat *dikadlo lodzeeda,* a fatty organ attached to the stomach, because it would make them clumsy when hunting. Bear heart is prohibited for young men or women because it would make them "jumpy," easily frightened.

Meat from the first neck joint is not eaten by anyone, because it would cause slowness (the bear moves its head so slowly). The rest of the neck and backbone meat are tabooed to women, but the tail meat is eaten only by postmenopausal women. The first three ribs are exclusively for men at bear feasts, and the rest, though ideally reserved for men, are eaten by anyone today. Only women should eat bear kidneys. Finally, two special parts are reserved for elders of either sex—the *bitaala'*, a foot-long organ between the stomach and liver, and a kind of sausage made by stuffing the stomach with mesentary fat and then roasting it.

This leaves only the hind legs and pelvis, as well as the rich back and body fat, without at least theoretical restrictions. Bear fat is rendered to make grease, esteemed as a kind of "butter" that is eaten with meat or other foods. It is also used to avert the powerful omen of a twitching lower eyelid, a sign that the person will soon cry over the death of someone close. Grease is smeared on the eyelid, then removed and burned. The man who described this to me added regretfully, "It never works, though," indicating that the sign is too strong to be reversed.

It is not hard to understand why Koyukon people regard black bear meat so highly—it is rich, fatty, and delicious. They make an assortment of tasty dishes with the animal's meat and organs, and very little goes unused (see Appendix 4 for details). Bear meat is strictly tabooed for dogs, because any who ate it would become so mean that they would have to be destroyed. Telling me about an exceptionally smart dog he once had, a man recalled having left it with the carcass of a bear he had shot. He loved that dog, but he warned it not to touch any of the meat while he was gone, lest he have no choice but to kill it. Luckily it obeyed.

After he finished this story, I told him about other Athapaskan people who believe that feeding (brown) bear meat to dogs will make them lazy rather than mean. His response showed the relativism that may help explain the continuance of traditional beliefs among the Koyukon, despite the influences of Christianity. He easily accepted the idea that other people's dogs became lazy. "But for us it's different," he explained. "If *we* feed bear meat to our dogs, they get mean."

For Koyukon people, other people's ways are not viewed as right or wrong, good or bad. Different belief systems can coexist because each is self-contained, independent of all others. If someone is raised to believe something, it works for that person whether or not it works for anyone else. And so the Koyukon are not troubled with the idea that everyone must follow the same ways, or that one way is accepted only at the expense of another. Diversity is a virtue; there are many truths.

Once a bear has been used, the final gesture of respect is proper disposal of its bones. Nowadays this requires burning them in a "clean" fire, making certain that nothing remains except ashes. This assures that no one will walk on the bones and that they will not be defiled by scavengers. Such an insult would offend the bear's spirit and bring bad luck to the hunter. In former times, Sullivan writes, the Nulato Koyukon either burned bear bones or put them in a birchbark basket and hung it from a tree (1942:85).

There is a story, told by the late Chief Henry, of two men who learned something about bears the hard way. They had found a den, killed the bear, and pulled it out onto the ground. This was long ago, before metal, and it grew late as they slowly cut up the animal with stone knives. So they decided to spend the night in the bear den.

The two crawled down inside, partially closed the entrance with grass and brush from the bear's nest, and then slept. When they awoke later it was dark outside, and assuming it must be the middle of the night they fell asleep again. They did not realize their mistake, that it was close to New Year's; and afterward they slept very deeply.

Finally one of the men woke up again, and this time it was light outside. When he moved to look out, he felt very stiff . . . and he saw that there was no snow. "It must have rained in the night," he said as he awoke his partner.

But when they opened the den's entrance and crawled out, the willows were green with new leaves. Then they looked for the bear they had killed, and they found only a scatter of bones. Mice and shrews had eaten everything else. "Gganaa' [my friend], we must have slept all winter!" said one of them in disbelief.

They ate some marrow from the bones and then headed for home. When they arrived, they heard singing and dancing—the sounds of a funeral potlatch. But when the people saw them, they suddenly became silent. The men they were honoring in their potlatch had appeared, alive. Then the two began to eat, because they were hungry after sleeping all winter.

So the Koyukon people know that a person should never sleep inside a den, because something from the bear will not let him awaken until spring.

Brown Bear

We come now upon an even greater power, one whose physical and spiritual presence moves menacingly through the Koyukon world, whose very name should be spoken with utmost caution, if at all. Nearly everything that is done to respect and placate the black bear is also done for the brown bear; but the acts and emotions are intensified, the danger and fear are greater, the consequences or error more grievous. I noticed that the tone of people's voices often became lower and softer when they talked of this animal. This, as much as the words they spoke, revealed the meaning of the bear in their lives. For nothing else that visibly or invisibly occupies the wildland did I hear this change of voice.

Not surprisingly, Sullivan writes that the Nulato Koyukon invest this animal with the strongest of all spirits (1942:85). But my instructors from the Koyukuk River villages held without exception that the wolverine has a more powerful spirit, though the animal is not physically threatening like the bear. Perhaps it is this difference—the bear is dangerous in two ways and the wolverine in only one—that accounts for the Koyukon people's seemingly unparalleled feeling of awe toward brown bears.

A creature of the open slopes and high mountain tundra, the brown bear is not often encountered in forested river valleys. In former times, older Koyukon people say, its tracks were never seen away from the mountains, but over the past forty years or so it has spread gradually down into the flats. "When I was a kid," a Huslia woman recalled, "we could walk anywhere without a gun. No brown bears or moose around here. But now it's not like that, and we've got to be more careful." Nevertheless, brown bears are not at all common anywhere, and it is unusual to see one.

Biologists have had difficulty with the taxonomy of these animals. Most recently they have preferred brown bear as the English name and *Ursus arctos* as its scientific designation. This lumps the inland and coastal populations together, though common usage in Alaska differentiates them as grizzly bears and brown bears. The coastal bears are larger and often darker. Interior bears range from five hundred to eight hundred pounds (for males); they are brownish, with noticeably humped shoulders and very long claws.

A carefully maintained code of etiquette governs naming of the brown bear in Koyukon. My teachers in Koyukuk villages gave it the basic name *ghonoy tlaaga,* which they translated "bad animal." This word is used only by men, and when women are within hearing they call it simply *ghonoya.* If a woman used these proper names the bear would be angered and offended, and bad luck would come as a result. Instead, she should refer to it obliquely as *dlil ta bahoolaanee,* "those who are in the mountains." In English the women usually call it "big animal," again to avoid the familiarity of its true name.

Jetté (n.d.*a*) mentions a variety of the brown bear reputed to be exceptionally fierce and of lighter color than usual. It is called *tsoltl'deenaalaaya,* a name that translates metaphorically as "that which doesn't have long belly moss." However, to avoid directly naming this animal, people may refer to it as "the one we call the shrew" (*loodolts'iyhdla dozeel'aana*).

I was told about two varieties of the brown bear. One is found in the Kanuti (*Kk'oonootna*) River country and is described as lean-bodied, long-legged, and especially aggressive toward people (I did not learn a special name for this variety). The other is oddly proportioned, with a small body but abnormally large head and feet. It is said to be quick, powerful, and extremely dangerous, and it is fittingly named *bik'ints'itldaadla,* "keep out of its way." In the early days men would never even try to kill one of these creatures, because it was too much for a spear. The late Edwin Simon and his companion once saw one of them in the mountains, and since they had powerful rifles they tried to intercept it. "But it moved so fast, just like a ptarmigan, and there was no way to catch it." This is the most dangerous kind of bear—"If he sees you, I don't think he'll back away from you."

Someone not familiar with its habits might expect the brown bear to be a rapacious predator, but generally it is not. Its omnivorous diet includes a wide assortment of plants and roots, carrion, small animals like ground squirrels, and occasionally large game. Koyukon elders say that a brown bear will sometimes stalk a moose while it is lying down, then jump onto its back and kill it. In October and November, black bears often become prey to their larger relative. Hunters occasionally find a brown bear's track wandering widely over the countryside, investigating every potential den from which a black bear might be pulled. In turn, both brown and black bears are sometimes attacked and killed by wolves, proving again the efficiency of the social predator.

Needless to say, Koyukon people have great respect for the unpredictability, aggressiveness, tenacity, and physical power of brown bears. Unnecessary encounters are strictly avoided, and any approach to them is made with utmost caution, very different from the confidence hunters show in pursuing the milder, more predictable black bear. When a man comes across brown bear tracks on the fall snow, he is likely to leave the area immediately. If he returns to hunt the bear he will probably bring along a group of men. Then if the bear is found it can be killed with a volley of bullets, insuring against anyone's being hurt. People emphasize that this is a very difficult animal to kill, that a man alone could shoot it many times and still be attacked. There are many stories about wounded bears charging hunters, though all of them end without harm being done.

I cannot overstress the caution Koyukon hunters exercise when these creatures are involved. They always carry heavy rifles for fall den hunting, largely in case they meet a brown bear. People apparently do not hunt brown bears in their dens, I suspect because it is considered too dangerous and because such a den is rarely discovered. If hunters find brown bear tracks they avoid moving upwind of them, lest the animal begin stalking their scent. And even a group of men, after locating a bear, will all shoot it at once from a good distance. One man who described several brown bear hunts to me ended each story by saying, "We got rid of that one." It underscored his feeling that these animals are not only a resource but also a menace.

Brown bears seem to keep away from people, but there are occasional exceptions. A few years ago, for example, two men were charged by an unprovoked bear, but the animal was stopped by a lane of open water in the otherwise frozen Koyukuk River. They hurried back to their camp, keeping a close watch for the animal. A short while later it came up the riverbank toward their camp and they killed it. The bear was in very poor condition and was obviously hunting them. The man who told me this story ended with a warning: "When you come across a mean grizzly, either you kill the bear or it kills you." And he added that "mean bears" are often ones that have been wounded earlier and are in poor condition because of it. For this reason a hunter should always do everything possible to track down and kill a bear he has wounded.

Most of the rules and gestures for proper treatment of living brown bears are the same as those I discussed for black bears, but doubly important. For example, if someone is confronted by a threatening brown bear, talking to it will usually soothe the animal and calm it down or else drive it away. People say a brown bear is more likely to respond to this than a black bear.

Men should generally avoid talking about the brown bear around women or children. When they discuss plans to hunt this animal, men are extremely circumspect. A man who has found brown bear tracks may go and ask others to help him hunt it, but he will make no mention of its name: "I came to talk to you, cousin. A big animal has been bothering my trail, and I want to find men to go after it. Be sure that no one talks about it." The man who told me this added, "One year I did this with another guy and we took our two boys along, but we didn't even tell them what we were going to hunt."

It would be especially bad, perhaps fatally so, to brag about hunting the brown bear—to say something like, "I'm going to go out and kill such-and-such animal." One man who did this was later attacked and seriously injured. Similarly, no one should ever lie or exaggerate about brown bears, for example, claiming to have seen one when he had only found tracks. "That animal might come back to you, let you know about it." If a man kills one of these bears he does not announce it immediately when he comes home, but will let people know by making obvious hints some hours afterward. At Huslia I went to see a movie called *Night of the Grizzly,* and in it a boy shouted triumphantly to his mother that he had killed a menacing bear. As we left the movie, a man shook his head and commented to me: "Gee, that was real *hutlaanee* [taboo] there, the way he just shouted that he killed the bear!"

Women should not speak much of brown bears, cannot hunt them, and must look away if one should come within their sight. When two of my Koyukon instructors visited my home in southeast Alaska, we chanced upon a brown bear:

> Catherine saw the animal before any of us, and even though it was far off she mumbled softly that "a dark thing" was on the far riverbank. When we did not understand, she finally said, "a big animal is over there," without pointing and while looking in the opposite direction. Our boat drifted toward the animal. It showed little fear, and as we approached Catherine remained silent, her eyes averted and her back partly toward it, her entire countenance almost morose. Everything about her expressed the danger of a woman coming so close to a creature of such spiritual power. I do not believe I ever saw her more serious than during those minutes before the great bear finally turned and ambled into the brush. [Journal, July 1978]

Men who do not precisely follow the rules for respect toward brown bears will have difficulty finding them. They might pass one right by and not see it, though they may notice its tracks after it is gone. The bear is simply not giving itself to them, though it may come easily to someone else. Sometimes a man tries to shoot a brown bear from good range, but nothing happens even though the bullets "couldn't miss." This means more than just bad luck with the animal—it is a sign that the hunter or someone in his family will encounter misfortune, perhaps illness or death.

When a brown bear has been killed, none of its meat should be brought into the village for some days or weeks; it is too fresh and potent with easily affronted spiritual energy. During earlier years, in fact, it was left in a cache at the kill site until the midwinter potlatch memorializing people who had died in the previous year. The meat was finally brought in just before it was cooked. Nowadays it is left "out there someplace" at least until it is frozen. Doing this ensures that the meat is fully dead before it comes near the dangerous presence of women. And it eliminates all chances of getting the animal's blood on the sled, canvas cover, or anything a woman might later touch or step over.

Each brown bear that is taken receives a ritual feast, just as is done for a black bear (I have not attended one, but I was not told of any differences). The meat is also used for village potlatches, after being cooked in a bachelor's house where no woman will come near it. Women must take care never to breathe the steam from the cooking brown bear meat, or even to smell it. And the meat or any part of this animal is strictly tabooed for women, except perhaps the very old. When it is present at a potlatch an older man sees that it is set well apart from everything else, and when it is passed out he makes sure that each recipient is told what it is—this way no woman will accidentally eat or handle it. Violating these taboos would make a woman mean, insane, or physically ill.

Aside from the complete taboo against women eating brown bear, I learned only one further restriction that applies to men. Nothing from the animal's head should be eaten by young men—in fact, it is best avoided by anyone—because it can cause meanness and quick temper. The brain should always be removed and burned; and one elder advised hanging the skull in a tree somewhere near a regularly used trail, where it can be seen but not approached too closely. "That way people can see that one of those bears has been killed."

Brown bears are less tasty than their smaller counterparts, and their quality is unpredictable. Even fat ones may not be very desirable: If the fat is white like a black bear's the meat will be good, but a brownish color indicates that it is poor. Incidentally, the Koyukon people always try to freeze or dry all bear meat immediately, because they say it spoils very fast. Once it has spoiled a bit they consider it inedible, unlike meat from other animals.

The brown bear's hide is rarely used today, and hunters prefer to leave it in the wilds to ensure that no woman comes near it. In earlier times the hide was stretched and dried, then kept in a secure place for several years before it could be used. It was mainly used as a door on the traditional winter house, perhaps also to cover things; but never was it placed where someone might step over it. Since the hide would be touched by women it had to be well aged to ensure that no more life remained in it. The spiritual potency of this animal's hide was perhaps greater, or at least more dangerous, than that of any other object a woman might regularly touch.

> Some old-timers—Chief John, Old Thomas, Big John—told me this a long time ago: Every hair on the brown bear's hide has a life of its own. Every hair moves, vibrates, by itself when something surprises the bear; so it can't keep still; it can't keep its temper. It takes a few years for all that life to be gone from a brown bear's hide. That's the kind of power it has.

Dog

Among animal inhabitants of the Koyukon world, the dog (*Canis familiaris*) stands clearly apart, unique in the society of living things. It is somehow like the other animals, somehow different; invisible spirit and visible behavior place it between the natural and human realms. And for the Koyukon people, dogs occupy a very special place in life, in many ways a dominant one. They know all the animals well, very well indeed, but they *understand* dogs. For them, dogs are a focus of interest and elaboration of knowledge—practical knowledge for the most part but elevated far beyond simple necessity or expediency.

In some measure, dogs (*leek*) are a way of life for the Koyukon. This was especially true before snow machines revolutionized travel here (beginning in the early 1960s), but it remains so in an altered form today. I am not certain when or why Koyukon people developed their fascination with dogs—probably it began generations ago when they were strictly involved with work teams but accorded prestige to those with the best, fastest, and most skillfully trained animals.

It was almost surely racing, however, that ultimately raised dogs and dog knowledge to the position of high importance they hold today. Since the 1940s, Koyukon teams and mushers have consistently ranked among the best in North America. From the Koyukuk villages alone, men like Jimmy Huntington, Bobby Vent, Cue Bifelt, Warner Vent, and Alfred Attla are prominent; and George Attla, from Huslia, is regarded as the all-time champion among dog-team racers of this continent. (*Spirit of the Wind*, a feature-length film depicting George Attla's life, was released nationally in 1980.)

Although many other Athapaskan and Eskimo groups are represented each year in Alaskan dog races, none even approaches the dominance and consistently excellent showings of Koyukon mushers. There are several reasons for this: Koyukon dogs have extraordinary physical stamina and speed, and they have apparently been bred with considerable astuteness. The animals used in major races are usually the best ones from several men's teams. And the men who drive them are dedicated, clever, and uncommonly expert in handling dogs.

> Dog racing talk again tonight—nothing seems to move around here during the big races; everybody is glued to the radio. Cue picked up a Fairbanks newspaper and studied a picture of one of the teams. He could tell just from the photo that the dogs were not correctly placed. "Good dogs," he thought aloud, "but they're all mixed up in that team. He's gotta switch them around to different places . . . that's his problem."
> Koyukon mushers are attentive not only to each dog's capabilities, but also to the way it matches the pace of the animal next to it and blends with the overall rhythm of the team. Dogs must pull evenly together, harmonically, if the team is to perform at its best. They can detect subtleties that completely escape my eyes. This kind of sophistication surely accounts for their great skill as dog mushers. [Huslia journal, March 1977]

Although snow machines are completely integrated into village subsistence activities today, working dog teams are still in use. In fact, the high cost of buying, maintaining, and fueling machines has created a resurgence of teams over the past five years. In the late 1960s dogs had nearly vanished, except the few used for racing. But today there are many teams in the villages, used both for work and for pleasure. Summer fish camps, the principal source of dog food, had once vanished from the riverbanks, but now they stand once more. Each winter the far-flung wildland trails are again silently trodden by teams, sinewy from long hauls with heavily loaded sleds. And howls echo once again in the forest surrounding remote cabins.

Aside from pulling sleds, Koyukon people formerly used dogs for packing loads on overland treks during the summer. Each animal carried a pack with pouches on both sides, stuffed full of supplies or meat from kills. Since dogs were very large in the past (one hundred pounds was not unusual, whereas today's swifter dogs are half that size), they could carry substantial loads.

Dogs are also used for protection, especially in camps where animals might create some danger. In the spring, for example, they will bark and alert people if a black bear approaches looking for food. The noise alone often drives the bear away, but if not the people can take action. The Koyukon say, however, that dogs often stand silently, tails lowered in fear, when a brown bear, wolf, or wolverine comes near. Or they might only make soft, breathy "woofs." This is very different indeed from the pandemonium of excited barks that erupts when they spot any of the other large animals.

When dogs have outlived their usefulness they are usually shot, because people cannot afford to feed animals that no longer work. But in no circumstances are they eaten or used in any way—this is beyond possibility for Koyukon people. Jetté records a Distant Time story in which Raven used a dog-skin robe, which he says "conveys an absolutely disgusting idea" to the Koyukon. In the first place, dog skin has a strong smell, especially when it is damp. Second, and more important, "the dog is a domestic animal, a part of the household, and its skin would be a reminder of lost affection, somewhat—though in a less degree—as the clothes of a deceased relation" (1908:365). Using dogs this way is perhaps akin to cannibalism, given their closeness to humans.

Koyukon people regard their dogs as far more than just work animals or beasts of burden. Dogs are given much affectionate attention, though not (traditionally, at least) in the same way outsiders treat their pets. There is a kind of double standard here, derived from the dog's spiritual position. In former times, people were tabooed from keeping them inside the house, because it would make the children behave like dogs. Presumably this means eating unclean things, acting wild and unruly, being half animal. At the same time, however, Koyukon people have always been deeply attached to their dogs, perhaps beyond what is emotionally comfortable for them.

The person who owns dogs is called their "grandfather" (bitsiya) or "grandmother" (bitsoo) in Koyukon, and the animals are referred to as "grandchildren." Interestingly, the dog is the only animal whose name is given the -kka plural form (ɬeekka) in Koyukon, which is otherwise reserved for humans. Feelings toward dogs are also revealed by something I was told about the Distant Time. In that ancient society the dogs could talk with humans, but Raven knew that if this continued people would become too fond of them. "When someone lost a dog it would be just like losing a person." So Raven took speech away from them. Until sometime in the fairly recent past, a taboo prohibited people from speaking to their dogs. The elder who told me this offered no explanation for it, saying only that people had to walk ahead of their teams because there were no leaders trained for verbal commands.

Nowadays this taboo is gone, as is the restriction on keeping dogs inside the house. Since the 1960s, Koyukuk people have begun acquiring "pet dogs," which are physically and conceptually different from sled dogs. For teams, they use fairly typical "huskies"—variously colored but generally large, with erect ears and curled tails. But pet dogs are other breeds, ranging from Labradors to terriers. Rarely is a sled dog brought inside, even when it is a puppy; but pets are treated much like their counterparts among outsiders.

The relationship between people and their team dogs is by nature intense. Each animal is a distinct personality; it must be handled, manipulated, or reinforced in its own way. I have often wondered if wild animals have as much individuality as dogs, whose peculiarities are thrown into strong relief when they work together and in such closeness with their handlers. Surely they do, if we only knew them well enough, but our distance from the forest inhabitants masks their distinctive personalities and emotions. (I mentioned earlier that Koyukon hunter-trappers sometimes become acquainted with the peculiarities of individual animals through repeated encounters.) In any case, a team of dogs is a mix of very different animals, and the skilled musher knows each one intimately.

> Village dogs have their own subsociety, a world apart from the larger community of humans with which they also interact. I puzzle over which is most important to them and feel certain it is their private dog world. Their daily lives center on barking at loose dogs or passing teams, posing antagonistically toward their enemies, whooping at approaching visitors, urinating on the brush around their tethers, anticipating the day's feeding, and howling.
>
> All that the dogs do fascinates me, but the howling absolutely captivates my senses. It is a wild shower of sound, as if voice were given to the quaver and pendulation of the aurora overhead. More than anything else, it epitomizes life here at the edge of the wildland, that separate world in nature that surrounds us but remains always beyond our grasp. [Huslia journal, February 1977]

In the Koyukon spiritual world, dogs occupy a position of power, though not actually ranked among the wild creatures. The dog's spirit is called *biyeega hoolaanh*, like that of the more potent animals. In this case, *biyeega hoolaanh* implies a kind of "sixth sense," possession of an extra power not available to normal people. Interestingly, Koyukon people say that human babies sometimes possess this same power. Its existence is revealed, for example, when dogs sense a human spirit that has begun to wander just before someone's death. Adult humans do not have this power, nor does any other animal. When a dog makes breathy, woofing barks at a frightening intrusion in the night, but nothing tangible is around, it is a sign of impending death. Someone's spirit is lurking among the darkened houses, having left the one who will die. The elders lie awake, wonder, and pray.

When a dog behaves like this, barking or howling in some strange way, someone may give it a piece of good food from inside the house, hoping to avert misfortune. This shows once again that a sign is somehow causative, and if it can be neutralized the event it foretells may not occur. Dogs can give death signs in other ways as well—for example, by walking into the house or tent of a sick person and then walking out again (Jetté 1911:247).

Also, if a dog howls in its sleep it is a warning of some accident or sickness. For this reason people usually wake up a dog that starts yipping as it dreams. In this case they try to prevent the sign from ever being given, another way to forestall the difficulty it would predict.

Two of my Koyukon teachers said they would not kill a dog if someone in the village was dying. This is partly because of the emotional strain in causing death to something so close spiritually to a human. When the specter of death is upon them, causing another death would seem out of place. It is also because a dog's spirit might "bother" the spirit of the person after he or she dies. The human spirit must begin a long journey away from its place among the living, and people should do all they can to ease and hasten its departure. A lingering spirit is dangerous enough without making matters worse.

When shamans were active they used the spirit power of dogs to assist them in making medicine, "just like any other animal." Some people who were cured through a dog's spirit were then forbidden to kill this animal. "If we did kill one," such a person told me, "it would be just like killing ourselves." So, although they had killed old or infirm dogs before their cure, they must never again do so.

Shamans could also transfer some of their spirit power to a dog, then use it as an agent for good or evil purposes. For example, one man (now deceased) had a dog named Dan that was given power by his grandmother. She never told him about the arrangement, but the dog acted as his protector. Then one night, as he traveled alone through a certain place, Dan suddenly fell dead. He put the dog on his sled but found he could not budge the runners. Realizing that something strange was happening, he cast the animal away, and instantly the sled was free. When he told his grandmother what had happened, she revealed the dog's protective power. And she scolded him for going through that place in the night, because it was known to be a "shaman's trap," where medicine people attempted to snare one another with power. The dog apparently died from absorbing that power, which otherwise would have taken his master.

While I was living in Huslia, people heard about a dog in another village that had been "laughing" like a person. This went on for only a short time, but it was long enough to alarm its owners, so they killed it. "Dogs never do that," people said, meaning that it was completely unnatural and therefore impossible without some supernatural influence. It was taken as a bad sign, smacking of shamanistic manipulation. One elder speculated to me that a spirit had been put into the dog, a strange and frightening thought because people had believed that shamanism was no longer being practiced.

Spiritually powerful animals of the wildland are easily alienated by the dog, much as they are by offensive human behavior. Apparently this is because dogs are unclean animals, whose proximity can offend the greater purity or potency of certain creatures. Contact between them is easily avoided, however, by keeping dogs away from their hides and carcasses and by never using any part of them for dog food. These animals include the black bear and brown bear, wolverine, wolf, lynx, otter, mink, marten, and parts of some other animals (mentioned elsewhere). Some people are careful to abide by these taboos, but others are less mindful of them today.

When a dog dies or is killed, it should be burned, not left along a trail where scavenging animals will eat it. The old man who told me this explained that dogs are considered unclean because they eat scraps and offal that are unfit for people. "If you put your dogs beside the trail, then catch the animals that eat them out there, it's just like you're eating your own dogs." Here is a concept that animals have "essences," and these can be passed to one another along what biologists would call a food chain. It hints at something I will discuss in the next chapter, the Koyukon people's concepts of ecological functioning.

> I took the dogs out this afternoon, but only for a short trip because it was −40° and falling. The sled pulled hard over fine crystalline frost that drifted in a glittering haze from the super-cooled air. It was like sand under the runners, so the dogs had a tough pull, but they were full of life and rushed exuberantly along the twisting forest trails.
>
> Such inordinate pleasure, riding behind the dogs through the timber and thicket, along the broad river, down the narrow sloughs. I love the quiet of dog travel, its intense immersion into the surroundings, not isolated from them by a wall of noise. I love to watch the rhythm of dog feet and flanks, and tails waving in the chill, and breaths puffing into the dense air. I love to feel the sled slipping along hard-packed trails, or tilting down a riverbank behind the galloping team. And I love to see the dogs curving out ahead as the trail bends, sensing that I know them, yet knowing that they are a part of this wildness. Still, for these moments we are one together—our tethers left behind, we share freedom. [Huslia journal, December 1976]

Woodsman

It is as real as any other creature in the vast Koyukon wildland, but far more mysterious. It is always there, somewhere, but almost never seen. It is an incongruous sound in the distance, a movement just beyond the thicket, a diabolical laugh in the darkness. It is something unaccountably thrown toward a lonely hunter, meat that vanishes in the night from drying racks, something stolen from an unattended camp, a child gone without a trace. It is called *nuhu'anh* (also *nik'inla'eena* or *nik'il'eena*), "it sneaks here and there." And in English it is named woodsman.

Long ago, before the security of modern times, Koyukon people occasionally ran perilously short of food in their remote camps. Sinking toward death from starvation, people would sometimes resort to the almost unthinkable desperation of cannibalism. But the price was very great indeed. Anyone driven to the point of surviving on human flesh (or sometimes a person who committed murder) would vanish into the forest. There the culprits became wild, suddenly lost fundamental aspects of their humanity, and never again returned to the society they had left. Although it has been many decades since anyone fled this way, woodsmen still stalk the wilds, hiding themselves almost completely from human contact, living more like animals than humans.

To some degree, in fact, they have become animals. Although they remain human in appearance, their bodies are covered with short fur. According to Jetté (1911:105), they have long arms and clawlike nails. They are both male and female, but they live a solitary existence. People speculate that they must get together sometimes to produce offspring, but this is not known from Koyukon tradition. Woodsmen are in many respects superhuman, in both physical and spiritual ways. Their life span must be very long, far beyond that of ordinary people—otherwise they would likely have died off by now. They run so swiftly that even in the open they are difficult to see. Three men who saw a woodsman run across a meadow said that only the dust settling behind it was visible. And they have other powers as well, because woodsmen can vanish at will. Their spirit is so potent that they seem almost to be spirits themselves.

In the winter woodsmen retire to dens much as bears do. This, and their power to leave no trace, explains why their tracks are so rarely found. The few people who have seen footprints say they are humanlike, but longer, quite narrow, and with the big toe set apart from the rest. Perhaps the most tangible contact people have with them is when someone stumbles across a den:

> In 1953 my brother and I were trapping beaver up there. My old man and other people used to say there's a hill up there called Nuhu'anh Kkuno. That means "woodsman's house." They always tell us, don't walk around on that hill, so we always kept off of it. But my brother didn't know. He was trapping beaver right in that area. He checked his set, and beaver had cleaned up the bait.
>
> So he started to climb that hill, and the higher he got it looks like it's better for bait up above; and finally he got right up on top. There's a big hump over there, like a bear den. So he forgot about his bait and he started to walk over there. He said you could just kneel down in the opening; it's kind of oblong. He cut a stick and he shoved it inside, to see if there's a bear inside it. But the stick he cut was too short. Pretty soon he cut one off that's twenty-some feet long, I think he said. He shoved it in there, but no end yet.
>
> Pretty soon he went back to his dogs and got his 30-30. Went back up

there and got birchbark, dry birchbark, and he burned it. He started to crawl back in there with it. He wanted to see what's back there, I guess. And he shoved that stick in, so it's going in ahead of him. And the farther back he got in there, he said it was so much stink. *Whatever was in there—probably woodsman breath or something—it was so much stink he said he had to get out. And he barely got out. Something like gas fumes. Boy, he said, it was just terrible! He just left it right there.*

He came home that evening. When he came in, boy was he sick! He started throwing up. Then he came out of it. I told him that's a woodsman's house, and first thing he started talking about is we should get people—capture it. I told him if you did that you'll always have tough luck and all that, so finally he gave up on it. Quite a few years later, when I worked on the river, I'd tell that story. They'd try to talk me into taking them there, but I wouldn't do it. Even if we did go there, you know, probably it wouldn't be there; probably nothing at all, not even a sign of the den. If you did catch one, your family would suffer for it.

Certain places scattered around the country are known as woodsman haunts, inhabited by these creatures for many years. People usually try to avoid these spots when they set up camps, although some are much less frightened than others. Woodsmen are mainly regarded as a nuisance rather than a serious threat. They often steal meat, fish, and other things from summer camps; and they harass people by whistling, throwing sticks, or making evil-sounding laughter nearby. I was also told that "a woodsman will play tricks on people too, if it's a playful one—like stretching somebody's fishnet out in the trees." Probably all adults in the Koyukuk villages have experienced these things many times, though to my knowledge none has ever had a clear look at the creature itself.

The sound of shots somewhere out in the wilds, when no one should be around, also reveals the presence of woodsmen. Over the years they have managed to steal rifles and ammunition from camps. A man said that once he heard shots and went to investigate. Alongside a beaver pond he found the moss tracked and pressed down, and so he concluded that a woodsman had been shooting at beavers.

The greatest threat from woodsmen is their desire to steal children and raise them as their own. This is one way, people speculate, that they keep from dying out. I heard stories of children vanishing without a trace, including some within the lifetime of today's adults, and each case was attributed to a woodsman. Once, for example, a woodsman took a baby from between its sleeping parents. The father, who was a medicine man, awoke and gave chase. Seeing that the creature was a female, he shouted that he would "make her his wife," so she finally slowed down and he managed to catch her. Then he hit her with a killing blow and got the child back. When the baby grew up, his eyes had a mongoloid shape, as people often say the woodsman's eyes do. And he was an incredibly fast runner, "so fast you could hardly see him."

Jetté (1911:105) learned at Nulato that if a woodsman pats a sleeping child's head, the child will grow up to become a shaman; and an adult who even sees one may become insane. To avoid this, a person must either be gentle toward the creature, stroking and caressing it, or must kill it and then eat its liver (to avoid retribution from its spirit). My Koyukon teachers advised leaving woodsmen alone, trying to avoid them as much as possible. They are not really threatening to adults, as long as people tolerate their malicious theft and prowling. They are only unfortunate recluses, after all, and it is best to pity them for the life they have led. The old-timers also advise that people who see a woodsman should refuse to be afraid; otherwise the fear will make them temporarily sick.

> South Fork people went bear hunting one fall, this was long ago. Pretty soon somebody hollered, thought he found a bear den. So they all gathered up there. But then they heard something crying in there, just like a person. Well, the old-timers found out right away when they heard that, so they talked to the woodsman. They told him, "We only made a mistake, that's all. We'll just walk away, and you just mind your own business too." They could capture it that time, but they didn't want to bother it.

A Huslia man told of an experience he had one spring while hunting muskrats with a young companion. When he suggested they camp for the night at a certain spot, his partner said no—his grandmother had warned him it was a woodsman's haunt. "I don't know what got into me," he said. "I told him there used to be woodsmen long ago, but they all got old and died. You know, that's really what some people say."

The two men finally bedded down; but sometime during the night the one who told the story began to hear something. It was coming toward him, but he was unable to wake up, as if he was "hypnotized." All at once his blanket was torn off him, landing about twenty feet away. He jumped to his feet but saw nothing except a wiggling branch that the woodsman had brushed as it fled. "That woodsman probably bothered me because I said those things, acted tough. He probably wanted to show what he could do to me. I never talked like that again afterward."

One of my Koyukon instructors said that when he was young he thought he would try to kill any woodsman he saw, but now he would leave it alone. Anyone who did manage to kill one of these creatures should tell no one, because doing so would bring illness and every kind of bad luck to that person's family. Traditionally, a Koyukon person nearing death would tell someone the bad things he or she had done. Killing a woodsman was among these. But only one person has ever made such a revelation; many years ago a man said he had killed three during his life. All of them were in the general region of Hughes and Huslia, all were females, and all harassed him beyond his tolerance before he killed them.

The first happened during fall, when he was hunting alone. He had killed too much game to carry in his canoe, so he made a little smokehouse and camped there while the meat dried. But each night some of the best meat would disappear, and he suspected that the thief was a woodsman. Then one night he saw the woodsman enter his smokehouse, check the meat in the moonlight to find the best pieces, and make off with an excellent fat goose. This was too much for his patience, and as the woodsman began slipping away he shot it with his rifle. "It yelled just like a dog . . . just like you whipped a dog. And he heard it fall down over there." He never moved and never slept for the rest of the night, and when daylight came he looked to see what he had killed. Not far from the smokehouse he found it, a young female covered with short fur. Strangely, it wore high-laced shoes and a small black hat and carried a fancy brass-handled knife. He took it to a nearby creek, where he cut its remains into pieces and put them in the water.

The other two he also encountered while hunting alone, and each time the woodsman followed him as he tried to get away from it. One stayed near him for several days, sometimes laughing diabolically; finally, as it came closer, he shot it. The other pursued him as he paddled across lakes and portaged between, gradually catching up to him. In the end it grabbed hold of him: "I don't know, probably it wanted to hug him, make love to him, I guess." He killed this one with his knife. Both of these he cut up and disposed of as he had the first.

Sometime after the last incident his wife had a child, and he gave it a name meaning "I got scared suddenly." Koyukon names often tell something as a "riddle," and from this people were able to surmise what had happened. So the stories he told before his death only confirmed what everyone already suspected. "I guess there's lots of other people that killed woodsmen too, but they never said anything about it."

Koyukon people often speculate on the ultimate fate of the woodsmen, whether these obscure and enigmatic creatures are disappearing forever from the wildlands. For a period of years there seemed to be fewer and fewer encounters. Perhaps, people thought, they were dying off because starvation was a thing of the past and no one withdrew into the forest any more. But recently, strange events have occurred again around the camps, and each summer there are reports of woodsmen heard near their old haunts.

Some elders suggest that they had retreated, for reasons unknown, to the region of the Alaska oil pipeline. Then, disturbed by the activity and intrusion there, they were driven back to their home country. But others feel that there are more encounters now simply because village people are spending the summer in camps again. For a while woodsmen had the forest to themselves; but now people have returned. And the night sounds of the sneaker are heard once more.

All spring this woodsman was bothering us. It even took our matches, or we missed rifle shells, you know. We knew there was nobody around, and yet we'd hear shooting, in different areas, about every night or every other night. We knew there was a woodsman around.

Every once in a while we'd hear somebody whistle at us. Another time it threw a stick at us too—that's when I really saw that stick. Not a stick you just picked up now; he carried that a long time, you could see it. It wore out. It landed right by us. My old man went over, picked it up, threw it back where it came from. He was not scared . . . no. Sometimes they tell a woodsman, "I'm going to cook your liver!" That's the way you scare him away. But my old man didn't. I figured any chance I get I'm going to kill him, not tell my old man about it.

One time I heard it real close. I was sitting down below the bank, watching beaver way out in the lake, and pretty soon I thought I heard my old man coming back. He came just above me, then he just let out a sharp whistle. I should have known right there, that's not my old man. So I whistled and I was coming out. Whatever it was, it just took into the brush right there! Then I knew. I knew right there, that's not the old man. I was scared. I was really scared.

Only place I felt safe was right there under the bank, so nothing could get me from behind my back. So I loaded up my 30-30, all ready to shoot. Pretty soon I hear something coming back. I figure before he gets any chance at me I'm going to shoot him. Then all of a sudden I saw it was my old man, carrying two big beaver! But he never saw I had my gun pointed at him. Right away I told him a woodsman was there, but he never said anything.

After we got home he told Mom he heard a woodsman real close; first time. He was packing those two beaver, and right there in the big trees a woodsman just let out a sharp whistle. But he knew better, not to face that way. He didn't even look . . . just kept on walking. That's what I always say about my father, you couldn't scare him. Old man used to tell us it's not going to bother you; it's only teasing you. So when you hear him, just don't mind him, just let him go. He'll mind his own business.

11

Ecological Patterns and Conservation Practices

I sat for many hours one midwinter night, listening to an older Koyukon couple. They spoke in vivid detail about their lives, especially about their many experiences hunting and trapping in a broad territory east of Huslia. At one point the man said, "My father trapped that country before me, and I trapped there all my life. But if you go there now it's still good ground—still lots of beaver in there, plenty of mink and otter, marten; good bear country. I took care of it, see. You have to do that; don't take too much out of it right now or you'll get nothing later on."

His wife listened and nodded agreement. She was the more philosophical of the two, and she had a habit of ending his stories with something general or instructive. This time she talked for a few minutes about periods of scarcity, then she concluded: "People never kill animals for no reason, because they know there's times when they'll really need to kill anything they can find."

This sums up an important element of Koyukon interactions with nature—the conservation ethic and its associated practices. Faced with an unstable and sometimes impoverished environment, the Koyukon people have attempted to alter the natural balance in their favor. Sometimes they do this by intensifying and expanding subsistence harvests, to compensate for immediate shortages. But during normal periods they often do the opposite, limiting or restricting their use of natural resources. In this case they are looking ahead, hoping to nurture resources for the future.

A great deal of popular interest has been devoted, especially in recent times, to the existence of a conservation ethic among native North American peoples. Much admiring attention has been given to their spiritual reverence for nature, their sophisticated understanding of natural processes, and their possible status as "natural conservationists." But despite this widespread interest, there is really very little on the subject in the ethnographic literature; and the chance to learn more has already been lost for many peoples. The exact nature, and even the existence, of traditional conservation practices can never be known for a large number of native groups on this continent. In this regard I must repeat a caution given in this book's Introduction: *The following account of traditional conservation ethics and practices pertains to the Koyukon alone, and it should not be generalized to any other native American people unless accurate, reliable information exists to support such conclusions.*

Several scholars have offered strong counterarguments to the ideal of the native conservationist, detailing cases where conservation practices have been either absent or violated. The best-known of these researchers is Calvin Martin, whose ethnohistorical work (1978) has shown that some native North Americans severely depleted furbearers in the early historical period. Most of his cases are from the eastern boreal forest, where he attributes overharvesting to the pathological results of European contact. Paradoxically, he chooses the Koyukon as an example of the same phenomenon in the western boreal region. As this chapter shows, my work with the Koyukon led me to far different conclusions.

The most full and detailed accounts of ideologically based conservation practices are those written about native peoples of the boreal forest. This is especially true for the Cree (Tanner 1973, 1979; Feit 1973; Rogers 1963), as well as the Naskapi (Speck 1935) and Ojibwa (Hallowell 1955), all of them Algonkian speakers living in eastern Canada. For Athapaskan peoples of the western subarctic there are many brief comments on the subject, and in this regard the Koyukon are the best described (Jetté 1907, 1911; Sullivan 1942; Loyens 1966; Clark 1974; Nelson 1982).

This chapter will describe Koyukon conservation practices against a backdrop of boreal forest ecology. It will begin by detailing two ecological patterns that strongly affect Koyukon subsistence: localization of subsistence resources, and variations in resource abundance over time. The Koyukon have explanations for each of these patterns, which I will summarize in turn.

Next the chapter will discuss what effect the chronic fluctuation between abundance and scarcity of resources has on Koyukon life and economy. Finally, it will describe the ways Koyukon people attempt to maintain environmental productivity. These include subsistence range and territoriality, attitudes toward competitors, avoidance of waste, and sustained-yield practices.

Localization of Resources

Anyone who travels in or over the boreal forest quickly recognizes that it is made up of many different natural communities—a sprawling puzzle of forest, muskeg, thicket, wetland, and waterway. But this is just the *visible* complexity, for there is another level beyond it, one known only to those who derive their livelihood directly from the wildland. Only through lifetimes of use and dependency is the hidden labyrinth of the northern forest revealed.

Most of the plants and animals that enter into Koyukon subsistence are distributed very unevenly over the terrain, but the inequities are subtle enough to escape the casual observer's notice. Each species tends to be localized, concentrated in specific places that are limited in size and scattered in a complex pattern. And so, for people like the Koyukon, the environment comprises myriad specialized resource places. These places cannot be predicted simply by knowing the distribution of plant communities and landforms, because they are apparently caused by subtle differences in microhabitat or by other forces that are not immediately evident. In any case, the Koyukon recognize that every area on the land's face presents a unique arrangement of resource potentials. Each hillside, valley, river bend, lake, creek, mountain slope, or stretch of flatland has characteristics and possibilities that are entirely its own.

For this reason, success in harvesting resources depends on thorough familiarity with the natural landscape. It is possible, of course, to look at a given place and predict what plants or animals *might* be especially common there. But only years of experience in each area, at all seasons, and under all possible conditions will show whether these potentials are realized. Koyukon subsistence activities are therefore based on knowing the profusion of potential harvest places at any point in time and under any set of conditions.

I have chosen the following examples to illustrate various kinds of specific resource places; but bear in mind that they are only a few out of the thousands that are scattered throughout the Koyukon wildland.

Physical Environment

Features of the earth and atmosphere create localized conditions that strongly affect living things. Most of these are fairly obvious, because they derive from landforms such as mountains, lakes, or rivers. Some are less evident—gentle slopes or soil conditions, for example. And a few are very subtle. This is especially so for weather conditions, which show much local variation and significantly affect the distribution of subsistence resources.

Localized wind patterns are the most striking and important of these weather characteristics. For example, in certain valleys or areas amid the flats, consistently strong winds blow, drifting and hardening the snow, affecting the growth of vegetation and occurrence of animals, and often influencing human activities. Other areas, even very close by, are predictably calm, creating pockets of intense winter cold and allowing deep accumulations of powder snow, again affecting the resources and activities that occur there. The pattern of windy and calm areas is complex, but however difficult it may be to understand, it is an important factor in determining resource distribution and the subsistence design.

Vegetation

An outsider might expect that one stand of birch or spruce timber would be essentially identical to all others, but the Koyukuk River people know this is far from true. In windy areas, for example, the trees often have a twisted grain, making them difficult to split for firewood. Certain patches of white spruce are especially tall, gently tapering, and straight-grained, ideal for cabin logs or lumber. Koyukuk people sometimes travel long distances to cut trees from these rare and widely scattered stands. Edible plants are also highly localized—some muskegs are rich in blueberries, for example, and others that look no different produce few.

Fish

Fishing sites are always highly localized according to water conditions, season, and species of fish being sought. Certain eddies along the Koyukuk River produce salmon, while others are rich in particular kinds of whitefish. Erosion of the mud banks along the middle Koyukuk often changes the configuration of eddies, but in the upper Koyukuk rocky banks in some areas give them greater permanence. Beach seining places are found only along certain gravel bars, where whitefish and sheefish congregate during a few weeks in late fall and where floodwaters do not deposit roots and logs that entangle the nets.

Fishing places are localized in other ways as well. Some lakes, or even specific parts of lakes, yield quality fish of a particular species at certain times of the year. Each Koyukon villager knows many possible sites for netting, trapping, or hooking fish, depending on circumstances at the time. There are a few excellent blackfish lakes, for instance, and one of these (*Hudo' Dinh*) has thin ice near a certain creek mouth in late winter, making it especially attractive for the oxygen-starved schools. Or fat pike can be hooked in the shallow place where a small creek (one of many) empties into the *Hulyakk'atna* River.

Huslia people say that most river fish taken near their village have less fat, and thus are poorer in quality, than those caught near upriver communities. The better fish must pass by Huslia in midstream, they explain, and so they avoid people's nets. One man told me he tried drifting his net down the middle of the Koyukuk to test this theory, but the net tangled and he caught no fish.

Birds

Ducks and geese have very specific gathering places, according to the season and other conditions. Around each Koyukon village, certain lakes, sloughs, meadows, and stretches of river are used as resting, feeding, or breeding areas or are frequented by migrating flocks. Some of these are used by mixed flocks, others by only one species. A slough near Huslia, for example, is favored by migrating Canada geese, but the preferred white-fronted geese are rarely found there. Snow geese congregate on one grassy lake in the spring, and at a certain time of day they fly to one sandbar out of the many along a nearby river.

Mammals

Similar patterns characterize both the land and the water mammals in Koyukon country, patterns that strongly affect the people's hunting and trapping activities. Certain lakes, or groups of lakes, have especially large populations of muskrat or beaver, while others not obviously different have far fewer. Some creek systems are unusually rich in mink or otter. Particular mountain areas have an abundance of marten. Some willow stands are especially rich habitat for snowshoe hare.

Among the larger mammals, moose favor specific lakes in late summer and particular willow stands in midwinter; and they predictably choose certain trails when they move from one area to another. Similarly, caribou follow specific routes for their seasonal migrations and may concentrate in localized wintering areas. Bear dens represent a somewhat different kind of localization, but a very important one for Koyukon hunters.

An actual listing of localized resource places for the Huslia region alone would probably fill a book this size, so I have only given very general examples. The essential point is that resource species are often concentrated in particular areas that tend to be circumscribed and unevenly scattered across the landscape. Koyukon providers base their harvesting activities on a detailed knowledge of these innumerable places, knowledge that they acquire through many years of learning and experience. Equally important, they have watched these places undergo their natural changes in productivity over a long span of time, a point I will return to later.

Explaining the Localization of Resources

Aside from the localization of individual species, there is a tendency for certain areas to be very rich in a variety of animal species, while others are comparatively poor. Some of these are areas of diversified terrain—hills, valleys, lakes, rivers—or they may be fairly uniform, such as a flat covered with lakes and muskegs. The Koyukon have an explanation for these regional variations.

In former times shamans could attract animals to certain areas, often for their own benefit but sometimes for others as well. A trapper might give small payments to a shaman, who would then make medicine to bring animals to his trapline. In this way local areas of abundance were created. Sometimes medicine power affected only one animal and lasted only a short time. For example, a shaman once had a dream about red fox, and afterward he made medicine to heighten the dream's power, hoping he would attract foxes to his trapline. His success is well remembered by people who say that they caught more foxes that year than in any before or since.

A tract of land just west of Huslia is known for its exceptional richness in fur animals. "It's a funny little place," one man told me, "especially because it's got so many fox, beaver, muskrat, and mink." This country, which looks in no way exceptional, is said to be rich by design. Years ago it was a medicine man's trapline, and he constantly worked his power to make his small territory productive enough to support him. In doing this he also affected the surrounding lands, enticing their furbearers away and making them poor. The old shaman died some twenty years ago, but the effects of his medicine have not yet worn off. Eventually, people say, the magnetism will fade and the animals will scatter more evenly again.

In this same way, shamans used to affect whole regions. For example, lands surrounding one of the Koyukuk villages are unusually rich in game and fur animals. Elders told me that the shamans created this abundance by attracting animal spirits and keeping them in spirit "houses" nearby. They worked for the good of everyone in their area, draining the wealth from other regions and bringing it to their own. Lethal battles of power raged between medicine people trying to overcome one another in this quest for natural abundance. In the aftermath of one such contest, the marten became scarce around Huslia, having been taken away to another part of Koyukon territory. People say the greatest medicine fights used to be waged over caribou, which was the most valued game animal before moose became common.

> Once a man without medicine power had a strong dream that he had discovered some animal spirit "houses" belonging to shamans. He listened beside one of them and heard what he thought were many many caribou antlers clacking inside. So in his dream he took this house to his own area and broke it open. That year he expected to see caribou everywhere, but instead there were millions and millions of mosquitoes. He had no medicine power, so I guess medicine people wanted to teach him a lesson. That year was the only time I saw dogs die from so many mosquitoes.

Temporal Variation of Resources

The second ecological pattern that powerfully affects boreal forest resources is instability of population. Almost every animal and edible plant species significant in the Koyukon economy is subject to marked fluctuation in numbers. In fact, probably no other natural community is so characterized by radical population changes as is the subarctic forest.

Several patterns of change affect plant and animal species here. First, there are drastic seasonal shifts in resource availability—plants bear fruit only during the summer, waterfowl migrate in and out, bears hibernate, animal furs are prime only during certain months. But aside from these predictable variations, there are irregular changes that can create short- or long-term scarcity, even absence, of important resource species. Some of these are markedly cyclic, following a roughly ten-year periodicity that is common to certain species throughout North America's boreal forests. Others are irregular or aperiodic, taking anywhere from a few years to many decades between high or low points. The livelihoods, and even the lives, of Koyukon people have been seriously endangered when several key resources fell to simultaneous population lows.

The dramatic instability of subarctic animal populations is widely known among biologists, who have worked for many decades to analyze and explain them (see Elton 1942; Keith 1963; Pruitt 1978). I will briefly list some examples that are important to the Koyukon, drawing not from the literature but from their own accounts and observations.

Vegetation

There are two ways plant dynamics affect Koyukon subsistence. First, berry crops fluctuate dramatically from year to year. Cranberries and blueberries, the most important plant foods used by Koyukon people, can produce rich harvests one year and virtually nothing the next. Sometimes only one species is affected, but cold weather or hail may damage all species for that year. I never heard people mention longer-term fluctuations in berry crops.

The second kind of change is caused by wildfires that may burn large areas during the summer. Fires have the immediate effect of destroying most vegetation and creating sterile deserts, valuable only as a source of dry trees for firewood. But in subsequent years dense thickets cover the burned land, making rich habitat for useful animals such as moose and snowshoe hare. The constant shifting of river courses has similar effects, as does vegetational filling of lakes. Koyukon elders also say the climate is becoming drier (their Kobuk Eskimo neighbors say the same thing), causing lower water levels and favoring the spread of thickets or forests in the lowlands.

Fish

The most important kinds of fish used by Koyukuk villagers—salmon and the various species of whitefish—experience pronounced changes in abundance or availability. Older Koyukuk people say that salmon (primarily chum salmon) undergo sharp changes in numbers from year to year.

Rich years, when individual catches can reach one thousand to two thousand fish, are offset by poor ones with catches as low as a hundred fish. The impact of such changes is strongly felt, because salmon are an important food for both people and sled dogs.

Catches of whitefish, sheefish, and pike in the rivers also fluctuate, because of population changes, movement patterns, or adverse water conditions for netting. High water before freeze-up, for instance, can seriously curtail or eliminate the usually bountiful whitefish seining by upper Koyukuk villagers. Even more dramatic changes affect fish populations in the lakes. For example, a lake called *Nidaaloda Kkokk'a,* near Huslia, once produced rich harvests of broad whitefish each fall—"sometimes more than people could handle." Originally the fish were very fat and abundant, but later they became lean and scarce. Finally the catch faded to nothing at all, and the resource was at least temporarily gone.

Birds

Koyukuk people have seen long-term changes in the numbers of many bird species, the economically important ones as well as those not used at all. For example, elders say there are far fewer songbirds nowadays than in the past, and they lament the quiet mornings, remembering daybreaks filled with a torrent of beautiful songs. They also mention that predatory birds like owls have declined, attributing this to the present scarcity of small prey like hares and grouse. Cyclic changes in grouse and ptarmigan, textbook cases in biology, are well known and profoundly important to the Koyukon. These birds can be a major element in the winter food supply for a period of years, then become too scarce to have any role in the economy.

Waterfowl are esteemed as food and hunted with great enthusiasm. But they vary in abundance from year to year, sometimes inexplicably and sometimes because of weather during migration times. People say that certain species, notably snow geese and shoveler ducks, have grown consistently less common than in the past. Not only the numbers but also the quality of waterfowl fluctuate—ducks are fat and excellent in some years, lean and poor in others. Elders also point out that as lakes become overgrown they are lost as summer and fall waterfowl habitat; but sometimes the resulting meadows attract geese in the early spring.

Small Mammals

Most small game and fur animals experience population changes that significantly affect the Koyukon economy. Of these, the snowshoe hare is probably most important, because it can be a vital food source during its periodic highs. I have seen such an abundance of hares that they pounded the snow hard in the willow thickets, and such scarcity that a track was rarely seen. Usually their numbers oscillate in a roughly ten-year cycle between consecutive highs or lows, but this can vary greatly. Predators, especially lynx and owls, fluctuate somewhat with the rhythm of hare populations.

The other small mammals important in the Koyukon diet—muskrat and beaver—also experience great increases and declines. Muskrats can almost vanish from a whole region, as they recently have along much of the Koyukuk River, then become abundant again five, ten, or even twenty years later. Beavers were apparently absent from much of the Koyukuk country until thirty or forty years ago, and men traveled to distant places to hunt them in spring and fall. But once they appeared they became prolific, so that even small lakes often had several beaver houses along their shores. In the past decade they have declined, however, apparently because of lowering water levels in the lakes.

Fur animals such as mink, marten, fox, and wolf vary considerably in numbers from year to year, and over longer periods as well. For example, the marten has spread onto the flats around Huslia since the early 1960s, having previously been common only in the surrounding hills. Wolves used to be so rare in the same area that people seldom trapped them. But when moose moved in during the 1940s, wolves came with them and eventually became common. Since then, they have fluctuated from year to year, most recently declining somewhat.

Large Mammals

Black bears are unique among the economically important animals because their population is said to be fairly stable. Some Koyukuk people say they are less common today than in the past; but others believe they must be increasing because they are less intensively hunted nowadays. In former times they were the only resident (nonmigratory) big-game animal, but this is no longer true. Brown bears were found only in the high country until recent decades, but now they have spread down into the Koyukuk valley itself.

Of all the animal resources used by Koyukon people today, none even approaches the moose in importance. Yet moose were absent from Koyukuk country until this century; and none reached the flats around Huslia until almost 1940. In the next twenty years they became increasingly common, reaching a peak in the late 1960s. Since that time they have declined, alarmingly in some areas and less so in others. Although the moose is a special case—a species expanding its range in many areas of the north—it epitomizes the dramatic inconsistency of boreal resources.

Not far behind moose is the caribou, whose capriciousness includes both population changes and the whim of a migratory nomad. In the past century, caribou in northwest Alaska underwent a severe decline, then experienced a long phase of increase and expansion that peaked about 1970, and most recently they have had another sudden decrease. The cause of this latest decline is unknown. Initially, subsistence hunting and wolf predation were blamed, but biologists later concluded that they had probably become significant factors only after some unknown agent such as disease or overgrazing had reduced the population. In any case, the Koyukon are only marginal users of the caribou herd in question.

Now, under strict hunting regulations, caribou seem to be on the increase again. During their low phases, they have sometimes abandoned the Koyukuk country for decades, while in periods of abundance they migrate into the region each winter. Yet even in the good times these wanderers are unpredictable; they can be prolific in a given area one winter and completely absent the next. It is an uncertain world.

Table 1
Population Variability in Boreal Forest Resources

Species	Pattern of Population Variability				
	Extreme	Moderate	Slight	Cyclic	Noncyclic
Caribou	X			X?	
Moose		X			X?
Black bear			X		
Wolf		X			X
Red fox		X			X
Marten		X			X
Mink		X			X
Lynx	X			X	
Beaver		X			X
Muskrat	X			X	
Porcupine		X			X?
Snowshoe hare	X			X	
Waterfowl			X		
Grouse	X			X	
Ptarmigan				X	
Salmon		X		X	
Whitefish		X			X?
Pike		X			X
Berries	X				X

Explaining Temporal Variation of Resources

Koyukon life is continually swayed one way and another by the instability of natural populations, and it is no surprise that such important events need explanation. This is done in part for the simple end of understanding, but there is a more practical goal as well. If the cause of an increase or decline can be found, perhaps it can be controlled in the future. Drawing from their cultural experience—their own perceptual world—the Koyukon explain natural population changes in two ways. The first of these is principally spiritual or nonecological; the second is empirical or ecological. I could see no priority of either perspective among my teachers, but I will begin with the spiritual explanations.

Koyukon people account for some declines in resource species by recalling past offenses against their protecting spirits. In these cases animals shun entire areas as retaliation against a grave affront, punishing everyone instead of just the person who mistreated them. For example, sheefish have declined considerably in the Koyukuk River near Hughes. Many villagers believe this was caused by fishery biologists who took live sheefish from the area and transplanted them somewhere else. Manipulating live animals this way is a serious insult to their protecting spirits. People say that similar decreases in marten and beaver populations have followed live trapping and tagging projects elsewhere in the Koyukuk country.

In former times, hundreds of pike would gather around a spring outlet in a lake called *Neenok'idilaah Da Kkokk'a,* and people went there to catch them with special hand snares. Today the spring remains but the pike are gone. Elders explain that a pubescent girl came into close contact with the place while fish were being caught, violating a strict taboo and alienating the pike. Since then the valuable resource has been gone.

Recently people have noticed a general decline in game populations throughout the wildland, and some feel that a growing neglect for taboos and other respectful gestures toward nature is at fault. As more and more rules are ignored, especially by the younger generation, many of the animals have been deeply offended. At an earlier time, Sullivan's Nulato instructors felt that a general scarcity in their region resulted from the disappearance of the shamans, who had always used medicine power to attract and hold the game (1942:121).

Koyukon people seem less concerned with the cycles of population increase, often leaving them unexplained. I only heard them account for the sudden dramatic growth of small animal numbers, which are so striking that they almost demand explanation. Snowshoe hares can sometimes increase so quickly that they seem to appear out of nowhere. According to Koyukon tradition, the hares come with a blizzard, falling from the sky with the heavy, windblown snow. Similarly, when muskrats have a population boom they are said to emerge in profusion from the mud.

At least as often as Koyukon people account for natural dynamics as spiritual events, they look instead to ecological processes for explanations. Although I have not emphasized it, Koyukon tradition contains an enormous wealth of empirical knowledge covering the entire spectrum of natural history. This includes a sophisticated understanding of interrelatedness among environmental phenomena, an ecological perspective essentially identical to that recently evolved in Western scientific thought. I will summarize the Koyukon empirical explanations for natural population changes, which encompass many of the biological interpretations set forth independently by biologists in my own culture.

Floods, which occur with some regularity, are regarded by the Koyukon as an essential force in creating ecological cycles, because they revitalize lake habitats in the river valleys. Lake fish populations are said to need periodic flooding from the river if they are to remain healthy. After several consecutive years without a flood, fish in some lakes will die off completely, to be replaced only when another surge of water occurs.

Sometimes a flood has the opposite effect, however. Many whitefish-producing lakes around Huslia, for example, have been ruined when an inundation brought pike into them. Pike soon exterminated the whitefish, which were a far more valuable resource. Two large lakes between Huslia and Hughes once had so many whitefish that people maintained large camps there to harvest them. But pike came in with a flood, and the fishing ended.

Over the past forty to forty-five years, lake levels in the Koyukuk country have fallen and floods have become less common. People say this has reduced the populations of animals like beaver and muskrat, which cannot live in lakes that now freeze to the bottom. They also assert that waterfowl numbers have declined in these areas; lake-dwelling fish are less abundant; and predators such as mink have dropped off as a result. And so each spring the villagers hope that floodwaters will spread over the lowlands and regenerate them once again.

Koyukon people are aware of numerous interdependencies between prey and predator species. They say, for example, that vole and lemming populations strongly influence the numbers of weasel, mink, marten, and red fox. When "mouse" tracks are abundant on the fall snow, trappers look forward to good catches of fur animals. Snowshoe hares are also considered a key species, controlling especially the number of lynx in an area. In the flats around Huslia, people blame successive floods of 1964, 1965, and 1966 for wiping out the hares, which have never really recovered. The corresponding scarcity of lynx has been an obvious lesson in the relationships between animal populations.

The Koyukon also understand certain ecological effects of wildfires, which are a powerful dynamic influence in the northern forest. They have seen the results of fires time and again, the destruction of mature timber stands, followed by emergence of forbs and brush thickets, giving way to deciduous trees, and finally the slow return of the forest. Their homeland is covered by vegetation in all stages of succession, and they know which animals are fostered by each one. Like Western ecologists, they recognize fire as an important factor in animal population dynamics.

Interestingly, the Koyukon do not consider fire a creative force, nor did they ever mention intentionally using it to enrich the environment. This contrasts with people farther east in the boreal forest, notably the Athapaskans (Beaver, Slavey, and Chipewyan) and Cree Algonkians of northern Alberta studied by Lewis (1977) and the Upper Tanana of eastern Alaska studied by Johnson (1981). These groups carried out controlled systematic burning of the vegetation to create or maintain open habitats and increase their faunal productivity. Similar practices were widespread among other native North American peoples (see Stewart 1971).

But the modern Koyukon apparently prefer to do without what they regard as fundamentally destructive. After all, the natural vegetation would be highly diversified without fire, because of differences in terrain and the constant reshaping of rivers. What the people fear most is the barren land that is left for some years after a wildfire (note that *controlled* fires like those mentioned above do not have this effect, but uncontrolled fires do). And they are especially concerned that fires be prevented or subdued anywhere near their villages.

The Koyukon people live in a land where change is the norm and where stability is almost unheard of. The old-timers have watched natural cycles undergo their countless repetitions as the years and decades and generations have passed. They have felt the weather "grow old," as winters lost their former intensity. They have seen the climate become drier, the waters diminish, the lakes become meadows, the meadows become thickets, and the thickets become forests. They have watched the river gnaw at its banks and carry timber stands away, while elsewhere it builds sandbars for new brush to clothe in abundance. And they have seen the animals vacillate between proliferation and scarcity, each in its turn, cycle after cycle. They have learned the variegated mosaic of the land, and they have seen it move, a kaleidoscope of time.

The old-timers' knowledge is extended farther into the past by teachings of the elders before them. Taken together, these accumulated observations yield a thorough and sophisticated portrayal of an environment and its dynamics. It is small wonder the Koyukon people perceive the interrelatedness of nature with such clarity, living as they do in a natural laboratory for the study of change.

Wait, I see something: The river is tearing away things about me.
Answer: An island; in the metaphorical language of the riddle, it becomes
*   smaller and smaller until it is gone.*
[Jetté 1913:647–48]

The Impact of Change

I have described the scattered and chronically unstable resources of the boreal wildland, and I have discussed some Koyukon explanations for these ecological patterns. Now I turn to their direct, practical consequences for the Koyukon people and for their indigenous economy. How stable or unstable is this economy? And for that matter, how certain is life itself in the sparse, inconstant subarctic world?

Abundance and Scarcity

At any given time, the array of potential subsistence resources in the Koyukon environment derives from a composite of cycles. Ordinarily, some species will be in phases of abundance, others will be scarce, and still others will be somewhere between. There are periods of years, however, when several important species will coincide at high population levels. This was true until a few years ago in the Koyukuk country, when moose and caribou were both at peak abundance and other resources like fish, bears, and beaver were at or above "normal" levels. At no time within memory had there been such natural wealth.

But, unfortunately, population cycles of the major food species can also reach simultaneous low levels, and the inevitable result is scarcity. From this the ominous possibility of temporary hardship or food shortage emerges; and in times past it could lead to eventual starvation.

> From childhood they have heard stories about families who perished from hunger in the cold winter, and perhaps they themselves felt its pinch when their supplies ran low before the spring-hunt was over. Persistent reminders of extreme want, even of famine, keep vividly before their consciousness the necessity of expending their full energies during the fishing season, and impel them to concentrate both their thoughts and their activities on the food quest. [Sullivan 1942:29]

During the summer or fall there is little or no danger that food will run short, even when resources are at a low ebb. And there is always a surplus to store in caches for winter use. But winter hunting, trapping, and fishing are often essential to make this cached food last through the season. If resources are scarce, winter harvesting may provide only scant returns, especially if long spells of intense, confining cold come after midwinter. Most animals "hole up" during these frigid spells, and those unable to do so (notably moose and caribou) are very hard to approach in the still, clear cold. And so weeks may pass when the grudging land yields little.

In earlier times, people sometimes exhausted the resources near their camps and villages by the end of February. This forced them to move in search of richer surroundings; but deep snow and bitter cold could make this very difficult. Luckily, they most often had enough stored food to get them through this lean season.

> *People used to really hope for a short winter and early breakup. They watched the days get longer and it just made them happy. If the winter was short, then they had a good chance to make it.*

Strangely enough, however, the most severe hardships frequently came later on, when spring had come upon the land. By this time stored supplies were probably gone, and people watched anxiously for the emergence and arrival of game. But if the thaw began and then a cold spell set in, real hardship could result. Open water froze over once more, sending the waterfowl southward again and locking the beavers and muskrats away beneath the ice. Hares were difficult to snare, because crusted snow freed them from their established trails. And if moose or caribou were around, they could easily hear a hunter approaching on the noisy crust. "Every day they would just pray," a woman told me. "It was just so hard for them to catch animals. They always showed respect for the animals, because that was all they had to live on."

People were sometimes reduced to searching the bare places beneath large spruce trees, where migratory songbirds fell when they froze to death. As recently as 1937 in the Huslia region, a family ate these birds to survive a spring cold spell. The small but abundant blackfish could also be netted through holes in the ice to provide another lifesaving food. Before this century, Koyukon people sometimes experienced such famine that women tried to sustain their husbands by breast-feeding them. Since men had to work harder, they were likely to die more quickly than women.

The late Chief Henry spoke often of the times when he had no food, when he made it from day to day on the animals he caught. "If one more day passed, then I would have to go to somebody's camp and ask for something to eat. But that day I got something—a rabbit and a marten—lots of grub then! So I stayed out on my trapline." After rifles came into the country, he said, people never died of starvation, but they still knew hungry times. Chief Henry himself had experienced extreme hunger and had become so weak that he could do nothing but lie down.

Koyukon adults have all been through times of shortage, and they know that the natural abundance of recent times is a transitory thing. It appears, of course, that "white man foods" would now be available to see them over the hard times, but they are not willing to take even this for granted. Memories of the difficult years remain deep inside them. Still, they are pleased that life seems less uncertain now, though only the young are free to accept it as assured and overlook the realities of the past.

*Some of these young kids, one time they asked Chief Henry if it
wouldn't be better if the white man never came around here in the first
place. He looked at them, and all he said was, "Did you ever have to
keep alive by eating ptarmigan droppings?"*

The Shifting Subsistence Base

During the modern era, Koyukon subsistence economies have centered
on big-game animals. This was not a matter of choice, though hunting large
animals is most efficient, is most personally gratifying, and provides the
most valued kinds of meat. It was nevertheless dictated by the environment
itself—caribou and moose were abundant and small game (except fish) was
fairly scarce.

Going back thirty years or so, the situation was exactly reversed. Koyukuk people subsisted primarily on snowshoe hare, grouse, ptarmigan, beaver, muskrat, and fish. The only large animals available were bears, which
were hunted extensively but could not be taken in large numbers. Although
it was diversified, this economy was fairly scant compared with the one that
evolved later. The older Koyukon usually emphasize their former dependence on snowshoe hares and ptarmigan through the winter months, and on
fish in the summer and fall. Of these, snowshoe hares are often singled out
as most important, because they happened to be plentiful during the years
after caribou had vanished and before moose had arrived here. A Huslia
man recalled his mother bringing in catches of forty hares from routine
checks of her snare line. "If it wasn't for rabbits," an elder once told me,
"we wouldn't be alive today."

The temporal variations in Koyukon economy are made more complex
by regional differences. Some of these are ephemeral—for example, when
an essential game species is common in one area and rare in another. Others
are more consistent. Most important in this regard is the heavy reliance of
Yukon River people on fish, probably because the Yukon is so rich in this resource. In Sullivan's time the summer diet was so dominated by fish that
people might taste no meat for a month or two. Koyukuk people also
emphasize their dependence on fish in summer, but they used much less of it
in the other seasons. By contrast, their Yukon River neighbors fished
throughout the winter, primarily with traps set beneath the ice in tributary
streams. This resource was considered far more reliable than hunting (Sullivan 1942:62–63, 66); and indeed the Yukon people are said to have measured
a good provider by his ability to make effective fish traps (Loyens 1966:69).

These regional differences were superseded by the widespread economic
shift from fish and small game to big game that happened throughout the
Koyukon homeland beginning in the 1940s. This trend continued for
decades, culminating by 1970, but since then a number of changes have occurred. Caribou declined and became scarce, the numbers of moose began
to fall slowly, in many areas small game remained at low population levels,

waterfowl appeared less numerous than in earlier years, and salmon were becoming less abundant owing to commercial exploitation elsewhere. Approaching the decade of the 1980s, Koyukon elders looked with uncertainty at the signs of natural change, wondering what turns lay beyond their vision.

This shifting subsistence economy seems to characterize not only the Koyukon, but boreal forest peoples generally. How, then, should their lifeway be described? Earlier in this century the Koyukon were fishermen and small-game hunters; more recently they would accurately be called big-game hunters. At various times their economy has focused on completely different species or groups of species. Over the long run, I would guess that the smaller animal species and fish have been more reliable and abundant than big game. But the most important resource is always determined by present circumstances, the coincidence of time and cycles.

This is why simple characterizations of Athapaskan economies can be misleading, or at least simplistic: "Most of the Northern Athapaskan people depended for food primarily on fish and secondarily on land mammals" (Osgood 1937:26). Or, "Salmon and caribou...either separately or together probably formed the basis of diet of all Alaskan Athapaskans" (Graburn and Strong 1973:77). Even more risky is dividing traditional economy by percentages—for example, a 10 percent dependence on gathering, 40 percent on hunting, and 50 percent on fishing for the Kutchin and other Athapaskans, calculated from ethnographic sources by Lee (1968:46, 48). Such summary statements overlook the complexity and instability of subarctic life, where the economy is a matter of the moment.

Husbanding the Resources

Confronted by such uncertainty and instability, the Koyukon people have made some very important adaptations. They have attempted to manage their harvest in several ways, to encourage the highest productivity in an admittedly frugal environment. This is much more than making the best of a tough situation, for the Koyukon have made an important intellectual crossing, from the impulse of the immediate to the ethic of the future. They have developed an ethic of conservation, manifested in concepts of territory and range, attitudes toward competitors for subsistence resources, methods of avoiding waste, and implementation of sustained yield practices. I now look at each.

Territory and Range

When the wildland provides abundantly, as it has in recent times, Koyukon subsistence ranges tend to shrink in size. Food and furs can be found at a minimal distance from the village or trapline camp, and so the total harvesting range becomes smaller. Areas of the homeland go unused and appear abandoned, though of course they are not. They are only fallow.

When the inevitable happens and resources become scarcer, people must use larger areas to harvest the same amount of food. Because specific resources are found in highly localized places that are scattered broadly across the land, Koyukon providers must range widely and have open access to all areas within their reach. Mobility is the essential tool; territorial freedom is the essential concept. In traditional times, the Koyukon homeland was divided among a number of bands living in their own expansive regions, and people apparently moved freely within and between them. Any limitation on mobility and access to given areas could ultimately be fatal. This is why the Koyukon almost certainly had no family or individual territories before contact with Europeans. Ownership of fishing sites was exclusive and private among the Yukon River people (Sullivan 1942:11–12; Loyens 1966: 57–68), but otherwise access to the total landscape was apparently not restricted.

That such territories did exist *after* European contact, among boreal forest peoples clear across the continent, has led to much discussion, explanation, and disagreement in the literature (for a start, see Leacock 1954; Knight 1965; Tanner 1973; Rogers 1963; Nelson 1973). Suffice it to say here that individually owned territories, in the form of traplines, emerged among the Koyukon after the fur trade began, apparently as a way of regulating competition and conflict over furbearing animals. Most important, however, rights to an individual territory allowed the Koyukon trapper to manage his or her take of furbearers, to establish harvest levels for a given area and its resource places with an eye to long-range productivity.

This concept of exclusive domain is fairly well limited to animals that are not vital to the human diet. And an important distinction is made between trapping (or snaring) animals and hunting them. People are free to hunt anywhere, regardless of whose trapline they may enter; and this includes furbearers that are sometimes shot. Muskrat and beaver, the most commonly hunted furbearers, are also the only furbearers of much consequence in the Koyukon diet. And so the Koyukon people have maintained their freedom to harvest food species anywhere (with the ongoing exception of fishing sites, which are never in short supply), while adopting a system of territoriality regulating access to nonfood species.

The imperatives of survival are served first, by allowing free access to food resources and encouraging wide dispersal of the harvest in times of scarcity. Then the potentially competitive quest for commercially valuable resources is effectively regulated by creating individual territories and thus reducing conflict over access to nonfood species. Finally, the trapline territories encourage management of resources for which an incentive exists to make unlimited or excessive harvests (because a trapper can sell as many furs as he or she takes). Being bound to a specific tract of land and excluded from others, the trapper is naturally inclined to nurture it carefully. I will return to this subject shortly, when I discuss other kinds of intentional limitation on harvests.

Competitors in Nature

Confronted by a difficult and capricious environment, the Koyukon might be expected to resent competition from other animals that also use essential resources. Certainly, Western traditions have institutionalized this attitude and have shown little inclination to share the world with competitors, especially the large predatory animals. Almost without exception, Western societies have tried to exterminate the most effective predators, as the scarcity or absence of such creatures in much of Europe and North America attests. This attitude has recently begun to change in some quarters; but conflicts over reduction or extermination of predators continue, especially in the northlands, where a few large species maintain their last strongholds.

How, then, do people like the Koyukon view competition by predatory animals? From the outsiders' perspective, they ought to fear it and take measures against it, given their dependence on wild resources. This should be true especially for wolves, because they feed on moose and caribou, vital elements in modern village economies. But the Koyukon do not attempt to manage their environment by eliminating these natural competitors. In fact, they are far more moderate in this regard than are many people from our own society, who hunt game primarily for recreation, if at all.

As anyone who has read the foregoing chapters will understand, the Koyukon people would not be inclined to kill off any animal species just to eliminate it from the wildland. This is especially true for a being like the wolf, which is possessed of great powers and could severely punish anyone who slaughtered it wastefully. But from an ecological perspective, the modern Koyukon hold mixed attitudes toward the wolf, attitudes that affect their efforts and motivations in harvesting the animal.

If wolves become so plentiful in an area that moose begin to decline or move elsewhere, people are likely to intensify their trapping in the affected region. They say that wolves need to be held in check by hunting and trapping, as a straightforward management practice. And the local abundance of wolves is an extremely valuable resource in itself, so the harvesters are doubly rewarded.

But villagers strongly oppose outside efforts to control wolves, such as hunting them from airplanes; and they are universally against eliminating wolves altogether. First of all, wolves are an important source of hides for personal use or sale; second, they are considered to have a proper role in the overall environmental scheme. Wolves are a part of the natural society of beings, ordained in the Distant Time, and it is not for humanity to overturn the basic design.

A Koyukon elder once explained to me that all animals can communicate with each other and that they treat one another properly. This is why animals do not kill each other senselessly or without purpose. Wolves hunt with care, he said, checking the animals "to see which one they want." If they leave a kill behind they usually come back to feed on it again and again, until nothing remains except the bones. But he added that wolf packs can become too large, and when this happens they will sometimes overkill. Then it is important that hunters and trappers "thin them out." In other words, wolves should be managed, based on practical, ecologically based considerations.

Koyukuk River people seem to have little fear that wolves will annihilate game stocks, perhaps because they have watched the moose population grow steadily despite constant predation. In fact, they often mention that before moose appeared in the country wolves were very scarce. Later, both of them increased together, and wolves have remained common in the wildland ever since. So it is clear to the Koyukon that wolves are not exterminating the game.

The only other competitors that affect game resources important to the Koyukon today are fellow humans. As Alaska's population has grown in recent years, "outside hunters" have come more and more into the Koyukon homeland, mostly to hunt moose. Reduction of game around Alaska's urban centers, coupled with natural declines elsewhere, has intensified the traffic of boats and float planes entering country that the Koyukon once had to themselves. Village people view these newcomers with anything but the equanimity with which they accept competition from wolves. Outside hunters are considered unwelcome intruders on a territory that the Koyukon have always reserved for themselves, in times past excluding even other Athapaskans.

Village people have no alternative to their staple subsistence foods. Unlike the outsiders who enter their lands, they do not have the option of hunting elsewhere or depending on purchased foods. So when animals are killed and removed by others, the Koyukon feel that it diminishes their opportunity to live from the land and to manage the harvest of a limited resource. The elders recall times when moose and caribou were unknown or absent in their region, and they fear the increasingly intense hunting that could lead toward such scarcity. They tell stories of hunting for weeks in distant places to find a single moose, and none wish to experience it again. Because of this, the growth of intrusive hunting pressure has caused deep concern among the villagers; indeed, no other issue in this time of change so dominates their minds.

When they talk of this problem, Koyukon people emphasize that their relationship with the land and its living resources gives them a special priority in its use. First, their entire culture, their lifeway and world view, is founded on harvesting from nature and sustaining the intimacy with the environment that this entails. Second, they feel a strong attachment to their established homeland and a favored right to its use and protection. Their ancestors hunted here, and it is their inheritance to continue living on this land as did those before them. And third, the land's resources are the basis of their economy and livelihood. They cannot afford, nor would they care, to replace them with store-bought foods. Reducing this matter to its most basic terms, a young Koyukon man once told me: "For us this land is the supermarket; for them it's the playground."

Avoidance of Waste

To this point I have discussed Koyukon resource management in terms of subsistence range, territorial regulation, and dealing with competitors. The rest of this chapter will focus on limiting the harvest in an effort to maintain environmental productivity—ethics and practices with the goal of conservation.

One of the pervasive themes in Koyukon ideology is a prohibition against wasting anything from nature. If someone kills an animal and then leaves it unused or neglects to return for its meat, bad luck or illness will come as punishment. Meat should be carefully butchered and cached where it will not spoil or be defiled by scavengers, and it should be used as fully as possible to avoid offending the animal's protective spirit. Even if a diseased or starving animal is killed for humane reasons, it is still butchered and cached. Thus, when a man killed a starving bear to end its suffering, he cut the animal up, covered the meat with brush, and told his son they would come back for it later. He did these things as symbolic gestures to appease the bear's powerful spirit, knowing quite well that the meat was not usable.

Koyukon hunters may go to great lengths to avoid losing wounded game, and they would be genuinely upset if they could not locate an animal. A man from Hughes once told me that he had just wounded a bull moose and could not find it, so he returned to the village to get help in searching for it and hauling its meat to the river. He could have shot another, but it was not what he chose to do.

Practically all animal species are considered potentially valuable sources of food, so they must be reserved as much as possible against the uncertain future. Although avoidance of waste is based first on spiritual sanctions, Koyukon people also believe it has practical significance in maintaining populations of resource species. They are always encouraged to harvest only what they can use, and to use everything they harvest. After explaining these things to me, a Huslia elder leaned across the table and concluded, "We don't kill something for fun."

Sustained Yield Practices

Avoidance of waste, so pervasive in Koyukon environmental ethics, is one dimension of the effort to conserve resources. The other is intentional limitation of resource harvests, which they feel will encourage the highest possible population levels. In wildlife ecology this concept is called sustained yield, and it is fundamental to modern resource management. The Koyukon have inherited it from their own intellectual tradition.

Sustained-yield considerations are important to the entire spectrum of hunting, trapping, fishing, and gathering activities. This empirically based approach to conservation of resources derives from the Koyukon people's practical understanding of ecological dynamics. People attempt to keep the resource populations healthy by regulating or manipulating their harvests —either they consciously avoid taking more plants or animals than could be replaced naturally, or they take special measures that they hope will enhance the productivity of a species. Some examples follow.

1. Koyukon people attempt to encourage the reproductive success of resource species. For example, like other Alaskan native peoples, they have always hunted waterfowl during the spring migration. Ducks and geese are in prime condition then, and sometimes they are the only source of meat available after the thaw. But near the end of the spring season Koyukon hunters avoid killing female waterfowl, because they are mating and preparing to nest. Some people take no waterfowl at this time if they have other food, assuming that it will encourage the highest possible reproduction.

2. The Koyukon also avoid using young animals or plants, explaining that they will become more valuable with age. When they cut wood, for instance, they select the largest trees and leave smaller ones for a future time. This is done partly to save labor, partly to nurture the forest, and partly to avoid what is considered wasteful cutting of young trees, a spiritual affront with potentially harmful consequences to the offender. Villagers who seine whitefish on the upper Koyukuk favor large-meshed nets that allow the smaller fish to escape. Much of the catch is used as dog food, for which small fish are as good as large ones; but people assert that the small ones should be allowed to reach full size before being used.

3. Trappers carefully watch the populations of furbearers in their traplines, then manage their take to bring the best long-term yields. They are especially cautious about the sedentary beavers, and they are proud of their ability to trap them over many years in the same area without depleting them. Newly made beaver houses or those with small feed piles (indicating few occupants) are usually left untrapped. Snare and trap sets are made to select for the larger, more valuable animals; and after two are caught the sets are generally taken out. This leaves a nucleus of young ones behind. A man from Hughes told me that he recently took only one beaver from each

house, because they seemed to have declined in his area. People consider it best, however, to take at least a few animals each year, because this appears to stimulate population growth.

4. Conservation practices like these are followed for other trapped animals as well. For example, a man criticized himself for taking too many otters from his trapline in one year, feeling that he had probably reduced the stock. Another said that after long experience in an area a trapper learns where most of the mink dens are, and then it would be easy to overharvest these animals. It is important to plan each year's take very carefully, to avoid "cleaning them out."

5. Koyukuk villagers are especially concerned nowadays with trying to manage big-game populations in their homeland. For example, black bears are fairly easy to take in the spring, and in earlier years they were often hunted at this season. But today other good sources of food are available during springtime, so bears are seldom taken before they reach their prime in the fall. "You know, we really like to hunt bears in the falltime," a Huslia man explained. "So we talked about it and decided to leave them alone in the spring." The same kind of self-limitation applies to moose hunting, though the methods are different. People are generally careful to regulate their harvest according to their needs, to spread it over a wide area to avoid excessive hunting in any one place, and to foster the birth and growth of calves.

In each of these examples, the Koyukon have used some intentional means to limit their harvest of a subsistence resource. Also in each case, people explained that the limitation was intended to sustain or enhance the population of a resource species. The logic of these measures is clear, they are explained in empirical terms, and it seems likely that Western ecologists would accept their reasoning.

I should point out, however, that we have no data to *prove* that intentional limitations of subsistence harvests by the Koyukon people actually achieve their conservation objectives. Only careful long-term quantitative study could establish this with certainty. The same qualifier applies to many of our own resource management policies, which are also intended to optimize sustained yield—they are based on sound logic and practical experience, but statistical data to prove their effectiveness are either unavailable or incomplete.

Some boreal forest species, like the snowshoe hare or the ruffed grouse, undergo large-scale population changes that are almost surely unaffected by subsistence harvests. Others, such as the sedentary beaver or the moose, are clearly susceptible to local or regional reduction by overharvesting. But for many of the remaining species it is difficult to establish for certain what effect limitation of subsistence use has on population levels. The Koyukon follow their presumption that it is significant and beneficial. Like Western ecologists, they generalize principles learned from the clear examples to those that are less sure.

Although the Koyukon people have no particular affection for game wardens or wildlife managers, whose presence they have felt for many years, they have little difficulty understanding their perspective on wildlife ecology. Intentional, empirically based attempts to manage resources, founded on principles identical to those of modern Western ecology, are well established in their own intellectual tradition.

Summing Up

In this chapter I have looked at another kind of interchange between the Koyukon people and their natural universe. The focus here has been on pragmatics rather than spirituality, but the goal has been to further elucidate Koyukon environmental perceptions in relationship to ethical principles. As a final comment, I suggest that Koyukon conservation practices and principles are a logical outgrowth of the environment I described earlier.

Boreal forest species tend to be fairly sedentary, concentrated in specific locales, subject to dramatic fluctuations in abundance. Because of this, the Koyukon people are constantly confronted by the *finite* dimensions of natural resources. During their lives, they have seen the full spectrum of animal population changes, and they have seen that overharvesting of sedentary, localized resources appears to reduce them to artificially low levels. In short, they inhabit an ecosystem that can be *comprehended* from their perspective. They can see the consequences of their harvesting activities, and once aware of these consequences they can attempt to adjust these activities in ways that serve their own future interests. Furthermore, the memory of severe shortages in the past gives them strong motivation to follow in practice what they know in principle.

Cultures within the Western sphere seem to be arriving at the same conceptual turning point that underlies Koyukon ecological thinking. They are gaining a comprehension of their total environment—in this case the entire earth—and of its ecological dynamics. Essential first steps in the management process are being taken: (1) understanding of absolute human dependence on the environment, (2) comprehension of its finite nature, and (3) recognition of the human capacity to overexploit the environment and damage its ability to sustain human life.

Based on this comprehension of the total environment, Western cultures are taking the same measures that the Koyukon have, though on a vastly different scale. They are developing principles by which to regulate and limit the use of natural resources, with the environment's future capacity to sustain human life as the primary consideration. The intellectual process, in our two entirely separate traditions, seems to be essentially identical (see

Nelson 1982 for more discussion of this issue). It remains to be seen whether the ethic that has sustained the Koyukon people and their environment over the course of centuries will be as successful for us.

Every time I have lived in an Athapaskan or Eskimo community, someone has eventually suggested the same idea to me. Usually it comes up when we are talking about snow machines, as it did today. The old man mused quietly, "Oh, I don't use my dogs hardly at all now, since I got a machine. But I always keep at least two dogs around anyway, just in case I need pups. We never know how long we'll have all this white man stuff, so we might need a dog team if there's no more machines."

The rest was left politely unsaid, because it wasn't just snow machines he was thinking about—it was their makers. The white man, like all else in the northern world, is destined to ebb and flow. [Huslia journal, May 1977]

12
Principles of Koyukon World View

This chapter is a summary statement about the Koyukon view of nature. It begins by setting down some general principles of Koyukon belief, drawn from the detailed ethnographic accounts in previous chapters. These rules and tenets are not explicitly stated by Koyukon people themselves; they emerge as a pattern in what may otherwise appear to the outsider as a rather fragmented and incohesive array of beliefs. After listing these basic beliefs, the chapter discusses the degree to which modern Koyukon people still adhere to them. Individualism, relativism, and culture change are important factors considered here.

The Watchful World

> *Each animal knows way more than you do. We always heard that from the old people when they told us never to bother anything unless we really needed it.*

For the Koyukon, the human and natural worlds are tightly interwoven by threads of spiritual power. The natural events that affect people's lives are often caused or influenced by human actions. Failing to behave correctly toward nature will bring harmful consequences, while acting properly helps to ensure good luck and health. The concept of random events has little relevance—things happen for a reason, often a spiritual one. If something becomes scarce, people either recognize a cause (such as disrespectful behavior toward it) or assume that there was one. If someone "runs out of luck" with a natural entity, that person's actions toward it are somehow at fault.

This perception of nature dramatically influences the Koyukon people's behavior toward their environment, binding them to a multitude of rules established by tradition. While this has a limiting effect on them, it also releases them from the caprices of an unconcerned and impersonal environment that affects people through its own random and unfathomable whims.

In return for myriad gestures of respect, the Koyukon are given special powers to enhance their chances for success and survival. And so the environment is like a second society in which people live, governed by elaborate rules of behavior and etiquette, capable of rewarding those who follow these rules and punishing those who do not.

These perceptions accentuate the intimacy between the Koyukon people and their surroundings. Underlying their closeness to nature is the need to subsist on resources that are often elusive and difficult to obtain. Thus, for the Koyukon, life has always been fraught with insecurity, in a land that can bless with abundance or curse with scarcity as the ebb and flow of nature dictates.

Confronted with these uncertainties, and depending so completely on the beneficence of the land, the Koyukon protect their livelihood by augmenting practical skills and knowledge with an understanding of the supernatural. They perceive the environment as a conscious, sensate, personified entity, suffused with spiritual powers, whose blessings are given only to the reverent.

Viewed from this perspective, Koyukon subsistence is more than just an economic pursuit—it is manifestly bound to religious ideology and ritual practice. In the traditional milieu, nature is approached as a sacred realm that provides tangible sustenance. This approach remains true for most adults in the Koyukuk River villages despite a century of change. Although expressed in varying manner and degree, it is a living reality. Any understanding of the way modern Koyukon people relate to their environment and use its resources must incorporate these concepts.

Tenets of Koyukon Ideology

At the most fundamental level, Koyukon beliefs about nature derive from a single basic assumption, and this encompasses three broad categories or precepts. Within each of these categories are a larger number of specific rules or principles.

Basic assumption: The natural and supernatural worlds are inseparable; each is intrinsically a part of the other.
Precept 1: Explanations for the origin, design, and functioning of

nature, and for proper human relationships to it, are found in stories of the Distant Time.

Precept 2: Natural entities are endowed with spirits and with spiritually based power.

Precept 3: Humans and natural entities are involved in a constant spiritual interchange that profoundly affects human behavior.

I will now detail the more specific principles of Koyukon world view, grouping them under the general categories above. There is nothing absolute in the way these principles are arranged, but I hope it will help bring out some of the order inherent in Koyukon belief and behavior.

The natural and supernatural worlds are inseparable. This is the most basic concept of Koyukon world view, one that embraces all the others. Everything in nature is conscious and imbued with what Western traditions consider extranormal powers. Because this concept is so inclusive, I have not listed any of the more specific beliefs under it, preferring to let it stand alone.

Explanations for the origin, design, and functioning of nature, and for proper human relationships to it, are found in stories of the Distant Time. Koyukon tradition includes a voluminous and instructive body of oral literature, called the Distant Time stories (*Kk'adonts'idnee*). My instructors often compared the significance of these stories to the significance the Bible has for orthodox Christians, and the analogy is appropriate.

The following specific principles of Koyukon belief derive from this body of oral literature.

1. *The world's creation and its transfiguration to modern form took place in the Distant Time.* Koyukon stories explain the world's origin and evolution, beginning in a time when animals and other natural entities were human, living in an essentially human society.

2. *Many natural entities acquired their physical, behavioral, and spiritual characteristics through transformations in the Distant Time.* Guided by the enigmatic genius of Raven, the Distant Time world went through a process of creation and re-creation. In this way many animals, plants, and elements of the physical environment attained their present form. For example, the lynx came to have a stubby, black-tipped tail because it was burned in the Distant Time. Or bones in the head of the sucker fish resemble the shape of objects it stole.

3. *Relatedness among animals is revealed by Distant Time stories, and by observable behavior patterns.* The Koyukon emphasize social and behavioral attributes as measures of relatedness, rather than morphological characteristics. Thus, Distant Time stories teach that the raven and the mink are related (uncle-nephew). A tendency to "get along" reveals that other animals are relatives, such as the black bear and the porcupine, who sometimes share a winter den. On the other hand, dogs and wolves do not get along, so they are unrelated although they look much alike. Some very similar creatures,

such as the brown bear and the black bear, are considered siblings (older and younger brother).

4. *The distinction between humans and animals is less sharply defined than in Western thought.* Based on Distant Time stories and their own interpretations of animal behavior, the Koyukon attribute many characteristics to animals that Western thought reserves for humans. For example, animals were human in the Distant Time, they still understand human speech, they have spirits, and they must be treated according to a code of moral and social etiquette. Thus the closeness between humans and animals is based more on animals' possessing human qualities than on humans' possessing animal qualities.

5. *Characteristics of natural entities during the Distant Time influence Koyukon attitudes and behavior toward them today.* This is especially true for animals, whose Distant Time personalities may be regarded as good or bad, pleasant or offensive, and whose status in the present world is affected accordingly. For example, people think badly of the sucker fish because he was a thief in the Distant Time, and of the rusty blackbird because he was born from an evil being in an unclean way. Both thievery and uncleanliness are considered bad human behavior by the Koyukon. On the other hand, they admire the sandhill crane because in the story times he was kind and helpful to people.

6. *Rules governing human behavior toward natural entities are revealed through stories of the Distant Time.* Koyukon stories provide a source and explanation for the multitude of rules for proper human behavior toward living and nonliving elements of the environment. There are hundreds of examples, ranging from specific acts like a prohibition on scraping hides at night to complex instructions like the ritual treatment of killed wolverines.

Natural entities are endowed with spirits and with spiritually based power. Spirituality is a pervasive dimension of natural existence as it is perceived by the Koyukon people. Knowledge of these spirits is considered essential for success in harvesting natural resources and living harmoniously within the environmental community. The general concept of spirituality is manifest in a number of specific Koyukon beliefs.

1. *All animals, some plants, and some elements of the physical environment possess spirits and spiritual power.* This rephrases the general precept above to indicate that, while most natural entities have spirits, some may not, especially those that have little direct significance for humans. I suspect that the Koyukon regard literally everything in nature as somehow spiritual, but I was never told this and cannot be absolutely sure it is true.

2. *Spirits of natural entities have different amounts of power.* There are apparently two main categories of spiritual power among natural entities—those with very potent spirits (*biyeega hoolaanh*) and those whose spirits are less powerful. Wide variation exists within each category, between the most potent entity and the least. Occupying the upper echelon of spiritual power

are eight animal species—wolverine, brown bear, black bear, wolf, lynx, otter, beaver, and marmot (in descending order of importance).

3. *Spiritual power does not necessarily correlate with importance in the Koyukon economy.* For example, despite its prominent role in Koyukon subsistence, the moose is not spiritually potent; and the marmot, which has very little economic significance, possesses a very powerful spirit. The measure of spiritual power attributed to each natural entity is known largely from Distant Time stories, and Koyukon people seek no further explanation for it.

4. *Spirits of natural entities appear to be vaguely conceptualized.* Koyukon people are somewhat obscure about spirits, especially the less powerful ones. This does not imply that they are unimportant, but it seems to indicate that precision is unnecessary. For example, there is no term in Koyukon for spirits in the less potent category—"the animal's name and its spirit are the same thing; if you name the animal you are naming its spirit." People also seem to vary in their ideas about the characteristics, power, and predispositions of different nature spirits. Vagueness and individualism pervade Koyukon belief.

5. *The source of preeminent spiritual power is the earth itself.* This was emphasized by some of my Koyukon teachers; but I should note that the earth's power (*sinh taala'*) seems less directly relevant to people today than most animal spirits are.

6. *Environmental events are often caused or influenced by spiritual forces; they apparently do not occur randomly but happen through design and consciousness.* Things that happen in nature often have an underlying cause in the spiritual realm, something that could not be explained in strictly empirical terms. Often these events are caused by some human action, especially a spiritual offense that alienates a part of the environment. This principle anticipates the next category of beliefs, in which humans enter the spiritual equation.

Humans and natural entities are involved in a constant spiritual interchange that profoundly affects human behavior. This is the crux of Koyukon world view, the meeting ground of humanity and nature. A large number of specific beliefs and principles come under this general category, and these are summarized below.

1. *Human behavior toward natural entities is governed by spiritually based rules.* Hundreds of such rules have been transmitted through Koyukon tradition, affecting the entire range of human interactions with nature. Their basic purpose is to show respect, or avoid disrespect, for all natural entities, in accordance with a code of etiquette and morality.

Koyukon rules of respect toward nature fall into the following general types, each with innumerable variants and specific applications, depending on the entity involved:

a) Respectful indirect address. Whenever people speak of animals, plants, or physical entities, they must be respectful and deferential. For example, bragging about hunting exploits or making uncomplimentary comments about animals is strictly tabooed.

b) Respectful direct address. In certain contexts, people should speak directly to natural entities (especially animals) in prescribed ways, as a gesture of deference and respect.

c) Respectful use of names. The names of some animal species should not be used by certain people (especially women) or in certain contexts, such as while the animals are being hunted. Circumlocutions are often used in these cases.

d) Avoidance of live capture and captivity. Trapping animals is not disrespectful in itself, but they should always be killed as quickly as possible and used. None should be released alive after being caught. There are a few exceptions—animals that can be kept as "pets," for the benefit of their contagious good qualities. But even this is done at some risk.

e) Humane treatment of living organisms. Killing should always be done as quickly and painlessly as possible within practical limitations. Wounded or infirm animals should be killed to end their suffering.

f) Avoidance of waste. Excessive harvesting or waste of any plant, animal, or other natural resource is disrespectful and prohibited.

g) Treatment of usable animal or plant remains. All usable parts of natural entities must be treated respectfully, according to rules pertaining to the species. This includes following prescribed butchering procedures, keeping carcasses away from offensive smells or noises, avoiding disrespectful contact with metal, protecting remains from contact with scavengers or other alienating species, and preventing disrespectful acts such as stepping across meat.

h) Treatment of unusable animal or plant remains. Unusable remains or uneaten portions must be disposed of in respectful ways, as prescribed for the species involved. This shows deference, avoids contact with alienating or contaminating influences, and encourages regeneration or reincarnation.

i) Respectful behavior toward the physical world. Many rules set forth proper behavior toward the physical environment and appropriate uses of its resources.

j) Total avoidance of use. Some animal and plant species cannot be killed or used, although people may interact with them in other ways. For example, a plant called *kk'an dikina* is completely avoided because of its evil spirit powers; and most Koyukon people would never kill a raven because doing so is disrespectful and dangerous.

2. *Powerful spirits tend to be highly sensitive, vindictive, and dangerous.* Animal species invested with powerful spirits (*biyeega hoolaanh*) should be treated with the utmost care and respect, because their retribution against offenders can be severe. There are some exceptions, such as the raven, whose spirit is

very potent but has a benevolent inclination toward humans. Each spirit possesses its own "personality," which affects how it should be treated and how it reacts.

Less powerful spirits (those not classed as *biyeega hoolaanh*) also demand respect and can punish transgressors, sometimes severely. But they are generally less demanding and dangerous. Again, spirits of the various species manifest themselves in different ways, depending on their character.

3. *The physical environment is spiritual, conscious, and subject to rules of respectful behavior.* Spirits of the physical world are similar to those of living entities; they must be treated with respect, and they are capable of punishing offenses against them. Physical entities invested with spirituality include the earth itself, certain landforms or places, water or ice, elements of the weather, and some features of the sky.

4. *Living organisms die slowly and/or their spiritual essence lingers after death.* Animals with powerful spirits are said to "live" or remain sensitive to certain kinds of treatment for several days to several years after they are killed. This is also true, though to a lesser degree, for animals and plants with less potent spirits. Meat, hides, and other organic remains should therefore be treated as spiritual and conscious substances for a period prescribed by tradition. The essence of luck does not vanish at the moment of death, a concept that strongly affects Koyukon behavior.

5. *Offensive behavior toward natural entities is punished by bad luck, illness, or death.* A transgression against a natural entity alienates its spirit, which then takes vengeance according to the gravity of the offense. Each animal or plant has its own spirit, but an affront to the individual can affect all members of its species. Thus, someone who mistreats a fox may be unable to catch any foxes for months or years afterward. Serious offenses may bring illness or death, either to the guilty person or to a near relative.

6. *Spirits of natural entities are affected differently by men and women.* The female menses has its own spiritual power, which can have an intense alienating effect on natural entities, especially certain spiritually potent animals such as the bear, wolf, and lynx. Because of this, women are subject to many more rules of respect toward nature than are men; they are also expected to adhere more strictly to such rules; and they are more likely to trigger severe retribution if they offend a natural entity.

7. *The interchange between natural spirits and people is affected by age.* A heightened spiritual sensitivity exists between young people and natural entities. This manifests itself in varying ways during childhood, puberty, and early adulthood (especially for females), when offenses against nature are most likely to cause severe punishment. Susceptibility to contagious effects (see rule 12 below) is also especially great in youth. Spiritual sensitivity decreases toward older adults, and those beyond reproductive age are completely released from many restrictions. Elders who no longer har-

vest resources are even more free, partly because they have no need for luck in subsistence pursuits, and partly because natural spirits are less sensitive to their behavior.

8. *Rules governing spiritual interchange are dynamic and respond to new contexts.* As time passes, new rules of respect toward nature emerge and old ones disappear. By accidentally or intentionally violating taboos and then watching for subsequent bad luck, people test the rules and may drop those that seem to have no effect. On the other hand, they sometimes relate new or unusual behavior to subsequent ill fortune, and in this way new rules emerge. Thus modern Koyukon people avoid using metal tools in certain contexts, because they can alienate natural spirits. For example, a bear killed in its den should not be pulled out with a chain or snow machine.

9. *Applicability of rules is contingent on belief.* People who do not believe in a rule, or set of rules, or the entire ideology may be exempted from punishment for violations against natural entities. This is an important contributor to the individuality or heterogeneity that characterizes belief and practice among the Koyukon.

10. *Devices used to catch and kill animals are involved in spiritual interchange.* Traps, snares, deadfalls, nets, guns (and perhaps other items such as snowshoes) are imbued with spirits much like natural entities. They must be shown proper respect; they can become offended and lose their effectiveness; and they can become polluted or offensive to the animals they are intended to catch.

11. *Luck is an essential element in the spiritual interchange between humans and natural spirits.* Success in all phases of subsistence, from harvest to preparation of hides, is heavily affected by luck. Individuals possess varying amounts of luck for each plant or animal species, and this luck can be retained, lost, recovered, or transferred to other people willfully or accidentally. For the most part, luck is kept by following rules of proper behavior toward nature, and it is lost by violating them and offending natural spirits.

Just as people are invested with luck, so is the equipment used for subsistence, such as guns, traps, snowshoes, and mittens. Luck is also bound to bodies of knowledge—for example, a man who teaches someone a trapping method may find that he has transferred his luck for that method along with his knowledge. When someone loses his or her luck it may take months or years to return, and there is apparently no way to hurry the process. All a person can do is avoid further offenses so that it will not take even longer. In a few cases people have willfully alienated animals to keep them away, such as the man who offended a wolverine to stop wolverines from raiding his trapline.

12. *Characteristics of natural entities are contagious.* This is a very important concept that strongly affects Koyukon uses of, and interactions with, natural entities. Certain behavioral or physical attributes of animal and plant species, most of them undesirable, can be acquired through their use or

proximity ("like produces like"). This is especially true for children, young adults, and women of childbearing age—contagious qualities are likely to affect them directly or to be acquired by their children.

Rules for dealing with contagious effects fall into several categories.

a) Taboos affecting physical agility or speed. Slowness and heaviness are highly contagious, so people (except older adults) should avoid using certain awkward or "dense" animals like grebes and loons or eating meat from slow-moving portions of animals, such as the upper neck of a moose.

b) Taboos affecting other physical attributes or well-being. For example, women should avoid eating cloudberries, because they rot quickly and would cause early aging. Boys should not eat muskrat tail, because it wiggles a great deal and would cause shaky marksmanship.

c) Taboos affecting behavior. Meat from animals that are wasteful, stingy, dirty, mean, mischievous, or dishonest should be avoided (especially by the young) because these undesirable traits are contagious.

d) Practices encouraging desirable qualities. Use of some foods can have positive contagious effects. For example, drinking water melted from fluffy snow encourages light-footedness; and young girls are likely to be beautiful if they eat soup made from the swallow.

e) Contagious effects of proximity. Nearness to certain animals can have good or bad effects, both on physical attributes and on behavior. Thus, sleeping on a pillow made of feathers from a clumsy bird species can cause slowness. If a boy raises a young fox he may become mischievous, but if he raises a hawk owl he may become an expert hunter.

13. *Foods are subject to contaminating influences.* Most important, the Koyukon must protect foods from the polluting and alienating nearness of scavengers. Ravens should not be allowed to defile meat by eating it or defecating on it, although unusable animal remains can be left for them. Dogs should not be given meat from certain spiritually powerful animals. For example, if they eat bear they will alienate the animal and acquire its contagious mean temper. Female taboos, especially those related to menstrual blood, are apparently also intended to prevent contamination or some alienating proximity of powerful spirits.

14. *Natural entities can forecast and foreordain events.* Signs can be given to people through many kinds of natural occurrences. They seem to both predict and compel, and they are usually (though not always) ominous. Thus, if a person can avoid seeing a sign, the bad luck it predicts may not come; and there are ways to negate signs, with the same effect.

Certain "normal" events are regarded as signs—for example, a hawk owl's flight over a hunter's trail can presage good or bad luck, depending on its direction. But the most powerful and ominous signs are rare or unusual events, such as a squirrel chattering at night or a bird being caught in a fishnet. These strange occurrences forecast illness or death, while the "normal" signs are more evenly divided between good and bad omens.

15. *Animal intrusions into the human domain may be dangerous.* Some animals, like songbirds, regularly enter Koyukon communities and are given no special notice. Others, like voles, are unwelcome and may give ominous signs by penetrating human space too deeply (nesting in someone's possessions). Still others—such as marten, moose, or red fox—are felt to "belong" in the wildland. When they enter a village they are considered a spiritual danger, usually an omen of bad luck. That these are rare events must be significant; but in former times such intruding animals were also considered emissaries of unfriendly shamans. This danger apparently no longer exists, yet people are still uneasy when they see animals of the wildland near their homes.

16. *Natural entities can be propitiated.* Koyukon people have ways of turning the spirit powers of nature to their own benefit. Usually this is done by asking an animal for help—for example, making a short prayer to a raven—or by using part of an animal as an amulet. Flicker and least weasel skins are the most potent amulets, kept as sources of good luck. Dried parts of fish are useful for warding off spiritual danger; and certain other items have specific beneficial functions.

17. *Shamanistic practice manipulates the spirit powers of natural entities.* This practice, once very important in Koyukon life, has largely or entirely vanished. Shamans harnessed natural spirits to cure people, bring luck in subsistence pursuits, enrich areas of land, or cause harm to their enemies. Many Koyukon people have experienced shamanism in the past, and it still affects the way they live and view the world. For example, they may observe individual taboos given them long ago after a shaman's cure; and they explain regional abundance of game as the result of former shamanistic activity.

18. *The spiritual interchange between humans and nature is dominated by hostile forces.* Proper human treatment of the natural world is enforced by the omnipresent threat of retribution by potent spiritual powers. This retribution can impair an offender's ability to harvest resources, or it can bring illness, and possibly death, to the offender or a near relative. Some other manifestations of natural spirits are also fearful—their ability to give ominous signs that seem to compel what they predict, and their ability to transmit undesirable qualities to humans by contagious effects.

The natural world does have a benevolent side, however. There are signs of good fortune, some contagious qualities are beneficial, humans can propitiate and manipulate natural spirits to their own advantage, and humans are able to foster a nurturing environment by adhering closely to traditional codes of behavior.

I will say more later about the positive significance of moral and ethical regulation of Koyukon behavior toward the natural world. But first I will discuss adherence to this entire system of belief today, in an era of change that is affecting all aspects of Koyukon life.

The Believers

Traditional ideology is a prominent and active element in Koyukon life today. This open adherence to customary belief and practice is sharply different from the situation among other native Alaskan peoples, who are extremely reluctant to discuss or reveal such things. Elsewhere, acceptance of Christianity has caused abandonment of the old religion or has driven it underground; but not so for the Koyukon, at least in the adult generation.

> *Christianity works for all people everywhere on earth, including us.*
> *But the Indian way works for us, too, so I've got to have both.*

Many Koyukon people are faithful Christians, but they are equally committed to their traditional religion. This is one expression of a general characteristic among Koyukon adults—they have attained a fairly high level of fluency in white culture without losing the vitality of their own Athapaskan lifeways. There is a native way and a white man's way, and the two can coexist comfortably. It is important to bear in mind, then, that the traditional beliefs and behavior toward nature described here are not merely the recollections of elders; they are a living part of the present-day Koyukon culture.

But it would be a mistake to assume that all Koyukon people approach religion or the natural world in the same way—far from it. They take a highly individualistic approach to all aspects of life, and religion (both traditional and Christian) is no exception. Most adults seem to follow a similar basic ideology and conceptualization of nature—the environment is sentient and filled with spirit powers that should be treated properly to avoid bringing misfortune.

Many taboos are widely observed as well, but there has always been considerable variation here. For example, a woman who follows them carefully said that her grandfather, a powerful shaman, was very lax and even allowed her to ignore the special rules for females. People who are equally strong believers may respect quite different sets of taboos or may differ greatly in how much they adhere to their own beliefs. Sinners, after all, are often still believers.

This pervasive individualism sometimes makes it difficult to characterize Koyukon belief and practice, especially to outsiders, who often expect much greater uniformity than actually exists. It is almost impossible to make a general statement about the way Koyukon people approach any aspect of their ideology without noting that many individuals do it differently. This is true not only of their beliefs but also of the full array of ritual practices and gestures of respect to natural entities.

Added to this heterogeneity is another strong pattern that I have already mentioned several times—the apparent inconsistency and amorphous nature of Koyukon ideology. This impression may result from translation problems, and fluency in the Koyukon language might clear away the haziness that seems to exist. Or perhaps Westerners are accustomed to a more rigid set of formulations. In any case, I was often baffled by what seemed to be inconsistent beliefs or obscure concepts. My inability to fully comprehend the nature of spirits, which are fundamental to the entire Koyukon world view, epitomizes this difficulty.

Koyukon people might find these problems immaterial. I suspect this because of their strong tendency to be relativists, who will say of another's belief or behavior, "That's just his way." What works or is meaningful for one person may not for another, and neither party seems troubled by it. With this in mind, individuals may test out beliefs or practices to see which ones they should follow. This is usually done only with the less spiritually powerful animals, however, or with rules of fairly minor consequence. A story I was told will illustrate:

> Six of us were hunting bear together, and we decided to see what would happen if we ate a certain part of a bear's stomach. Old people always used to tell us that if young guys ate this part their moccasins would just slip around under them when they walked around the woods looking for animals. So three of us ate that thing, and the other guys didn't.
> Next day we had a terrible time. We slid around and just kept falling down! And those other guys, they had no trouble. Nothing. So we found out right there. We knew better than to eat that part afterward.

There is a feeling among believers that faithful practice leads to a long and healthy life. To illustrate this, someone pointed out two very fit and active elderly women who had always strictly followed taboos, then compared them with several younger women who often ignored important taboos and who suffered declining health and vigor. Also, the children of frequent violators are likely to be shiftless, inept, and incapable of supporting a family.

In former times even the most orthodox people were sometimes forced to break taboos when food became scarce—they ate what they needed to survive, regardless of the strongest prohibitions. But desperation brought no reprieve from the spirits. One man who gave women and children parts of a bear that were forbidden to them saved his family from hunger, but for the rest of his life he never took another bear.

The younger generations of Koyukon people, especially those under age thirty, have moved strongly away from traditional beliefs. Young villagers seem to have limited understanding of the ideology and they often ignore their elders' teachings and ritual practices. Open violation of even the strictest taboos is common, and some youths who follow them are more concerned with placating their elders than placating natural spirits. The older faithful expect that nonbelievers will not be directly punished:

Everybody is different, you know. Some don't follow any taboos and they don't get bad luck from it. But like me, I always believe it, and if I don't treat animals right something bad will happen.

But while they express sentiments like this, Koyukon people are also acutely conscious of growing social problems in their villages, afflictions centered on the health and well-being of the young. Many of the elders wonder if the recent decline of traditional beliefs and morality might be at fault.

There is always some chance that younger Koyukon people will eventually acquire or resurrect the traditional ideology. As they reach adulthood, they may become more interested in their elders' ways and see more value in following them. A strengthening sense of native identity exists here, and it might lead to an interest in perpetuating customary religious beliefs. But so far this has not happened, and the older Koyukon grieve both for their beliefs and for their young.

Me, I got to live by these things. These kids nowadays, I don't know how it'll be for them. But I grew up with it and I just got to stick by what I know and the way I believe is right.

13

Nature and the Koyukon Tradition

I turn now to some broader considerations of Koyukon ideology and the natural environment. This concluding chapter will begin with a brief discussion of Koyukon world view as a way of conceptualizing reality, focused on the power that their perception of nature has for the Koyukon people. Then it will discuss the code of morality or ethics that governs interactions between Koyukon people and nature. Finally, it will look at this human cultural tradition as an integral element of the natural landscape.

The Natural Reality

As I was living among the Koyukon people, nothing struck me more forcefully than the fact that they *experience* a different reality in the natural world. This can be viewed as belief, of course, but it also goes firmly beyond belief. For the Koyukon, there is a different existence in the forest, something fully actualized within their physical and emotional senses, yet entirely beyond those of outsiders (Euro-Americans). But however different this reality might be, its impact on the Koyukon is equal in depth and power to the experiences of others elsewhere. Theirs is a pervasive, forceful, highly tangible view of the world, no less than our own.

Coming into Koyukon society from a very different background, I was suddenly confronted by the power of this reality. Although I had lived for several years among other native Alaskan peoples, I had never found access to this element of their lives. Among the Koyukon, my teachers clearly perceived in the fullest measure a different world than I did, or than people

238

from my culture could perceive. Each of them was also rational and intelligent by any measure, biculturally fluent, and acutely observant. The great difference in our points of view was something I had been prepared for intellectually; but I was entirely unprepared for it emotionally, unready for the impact of *living* it.

My clear and certain comprehension of the natural world was ended. Fundamental assumptions I had learned about the nature of nature were thrown into doubt. I must emphasize that I underwent no great conversion and emerged no less an agnostic than before. But now I had to face an elemental question, as an anthropologist of course, but even more so as someone who had always been deeply involved with nature: Is there not a single reality in the natural world, an absolute and universal reality? Apparently the answer to this question is no.

The issue that perplexed me is far from new in anthropology, though it was certainly new for me to deal with it as a direct personal experience. Anthropologists and linguists have written at great length about the different realities that humans perceive as members of different cultures and speakers of different languages. Early in this century, Edward Sapir and Benjamin Whorf began a whole school of thought on the ways that language structures reality (see the collections of essays, Whorf 1956 and Sapir 1949). The idea that cultural learning predisposes us to our own concepts of reality pervades modern anthropology, especially in ethnoscience, structural anthropology, and "meta-anthropology."

The basic premise underlying anthropological writings on this subject, as I understand it, is this: Reality is not the world as it is perceived directly by the senses; reality is the world as it is perceived by the *mind* through the medium of the senses. Thus reality in nature is not just what we see, but what we have *learned* to see. In other words, my Koyukon teachers had learned through their own traditions about dimensions in nature that I, as a Euro-American, had either not learned to perceive or had been explicitly taught do not exist.

Perhaps this question of reality seems rather abstract and esoteric, but in fact it has profound effects on people's individual and cultural lives. Each human society bases its interactions with the external world on the implicit assumption that its reality is absolute. Furthermore, each society sets forth its own regulations for dealing with the environment, and these regulations derive in large measure from the way natural reality is perceived. The interactions between Koyukon people and nature illustrate this clearly, for theirs is a world in which nature moves with power and humans are bound to a special system of environmental morality.

> *You know, we had a terrible thing happen to us last year. I went to look at our summer camp, get stuff ready. But when I got there I found something. A wolverine, it crawled in there and died. It went in the*

*smokehouse and it was dead right there. I just looked at it. It was a
terrible thing. It meant something bad for us . . . something might happen
to somebody in our family.*

*I took it away right then, put it way out there in the country, far from
any trails or anything. Don't want anybody to go near it, see; that's a
dangerous place once you put it there. I gave it food and burned everything there. Burned it good.*

*Afterward I went to some old people and told them the whole thing.
They told me what to do, get away from that camp and stay someplace
else that summer. We did that. We had a different camp. I felt so bad I
just stayed with my family all summer. I really wanted to get a job like I
always do, but I couldn't leave them after that happened. Oh, it just hurt
my feelings so bad! It really broke my heart.*

Nature and the Moral Code

The Koyukon people's traditional religious ideology is pervaded by elements of nature. Spiritual beings are predominantly associated with natural
entities. Creation was undertaken by a nature god (Raven) who brought
humans into existence as part of a primordial society of nature beings. The
creation was human-centered only insofar as animals, plants, and physical
elements possessed human qualities at their time of origin.

In the moral system that this ideology encompasses, the proper role of
humankind is to serve a dominant nature. The natural universe is nearly
omnipotent, and only through acts of respect and propitiation is the well-
being of humans ensured. Because spiritual power is everywhere in nature,
gestures of reverence are nearly constant as people interact with their environment, as they carry out the necessary activities of subsistence and
survival.

Thus, one of the principles emerging from the Koyukon ideology—
perhaps the basic principle—is that a moral system governs human behavior
toward nature. The proper forms of conduct are set forth in an elaborate
code of rules, brought down from the Distant Time. Through this code,
deference is shown for everything in the environment, partly through gestures of etiquette and partly through avoiding waste or excessive use.

In the Koyukon world, therefore, human existence depends on a morally
based relationship with the overarching powers of nature. Humanity acts at
the behest of the environment. The Koyukon must move *with* the forces of
their surroundings, not attempting to control, master, or fundamentally
alter them. They do not confront nature, they yield to it. At most they are
able to placate and coerce nature through its spiritual dimension.

In the Koyukon people's world view, the conceptual distance between
humanity and nature is narrow; furthermore, there is a coalescence of nature
and the supernatural. The Koyukon thus perceive a world in which humanity, nature, and the supernatural are not separated but are united within a

single cosmos. And binding this conceptual design is the moral code. Humanity, nature, and the supernatural are all joined within a single moral order.

The Koyukon people are not unique in conceptualizing the world this way. Similar systems of thought and perception are held among many non-Western peoples. The codes of morality associated with them are also broadly similar:

> The universe is morally significant. It cares. What man sees out there, that which is not himself and yet in which he somehow participates, is a drama of conduct. . . . The universe is spun of duty and ethical judgement. . . . The universe is not an indifferent system. It is a system of moral consequence. [Redfield 1957:106]

Today the Koyukon people are encountering an entirely different world view, one in which these moral restraints on behavior toward the environment do not apply. Occasionally they express concern about the well-being of their own lands, as Euro-American culture impinges steadily upon them. Their concerns are mainly practical, but they include some ideological considerations as well. For example, older people worry about the young, who have given up many traditional beliefs and frequently violate the customary moral code toward natural entities. They fear the long-term effects that this change may have on both their people and their surrounding environment.

Rarely, I heard Koyukon people mention the possibility of spiritual offenses against nature by outsiders. The most striking example of this occurred on the Yukon River some years ago, when the ice jammed during breakup, threatening to cause a flood. From a nearby military base, airplanes were sent to bomb the ice in an attempt to dislodge it. This violent effort to overwhelm nature was regarded as extremely disrespectful by traditional Koyukon people, who customarily pray to the river ice, asking it to flow away easily and cause no harm. Floods that submerged nearby villages in following years were seen as spiritual retribution for this offense. Nature is to be petitioned and pacified, not forcibly conquered, because nature holds the ultimate power.

> *The country knows. If you do wrong things to it, the whole country knows. It feels what's happening to it. I guess everything is connected together somehow, under the ground.*

Does this mean, then, that while Western cultures have dramatically altered their environments, the Koyukon have left theirs entirely unchanged? The answer, of course, is no. All human populations leave a perceptible impression on their environments, and the Koyukon are not an exception. For example, hunting and fishing have some effect on animal population levels, as well as on their age and sex ratios. And harvesting of plants, especially trees, is reflected in successional patterns. But these changes are not far different from the ones caused by other large omnivorous predators, and they may be less marked than natural changes such as population cycles, wildfires, and shifts in river courses. Overharvest is rare, and there have been no extinctions or imperiling reductions of resource species by Koyukon hunter-gatherers.

The Koyukon environment functions much as it would if no humans inhabited it. Evidence for this can be seen at the northern and eastern edges of Koyukon territory, where human activity of any kind is rare. The transition from utilized to unutilized environment is not perceivable.

But perhaps ideology cannot account for this; perhaps the Koyukon have simply not been technologically capable of altering their environment. This is to some extent true, because they have indeed lacked the capacity to deforest the landscape, divert waterways, reshape the terrain, or eliminate any living species. But their technology has undergone substantial changes, and of a sort that could allow severe overexploitation of some resources. Rifles, snow machines, chain saws, and motorized boats are notable among these. Yet ideological restraints are applied to the new technology, as to the old, and the integrity of the natural landscape remains.

A Human Imprint on the Land

Inhabitation of the Koyukon homeland over the long passage of millennia has had little visible impact on the natural environment. Despite continuous and intensive human activity, the country remains essentially pristine. The only tangible evidences of this lengthy occupation are scattered campsites, narrow trails through the thicket, the widely dispersed village clearings, and the overgrown remnants of abandoned camps or settlements. And even these are difficult to see amid the vastness of forest and muskeg.

But the Koyukon have created another kind of imprint, one that is known only through the mind, through traditions that unite the people with the environment that has sustained them. Direct and enduring dependency upon the environment has created a special kind of reciprocity encompassing the Koyukon and their natural surroundings. It has perpetuated the traditions that not only make the Koyukon who they are, but also make the land around them what it is. Although an outsider cannot immediately see or feel these dimensions in the environment, they are a fundamental part of its natural history. They can be known only through Koyukon tradition, through the Koyukon mind. They create in this forested wildland a nearly intangible human imprint.

This imprint can be illustrated by describing the cultural and personal meanings with which Koyukon people vest places on the landscape. Some of these are founded in the domain of recent human events; others are ancient and more spiritual than human. Traveling through the wildland, a Koyukon person constantly passes by these places, and the flow of land becomes also a flow of the mind. I will give some examples of the human imprint, beginning with the personal and historical, then moving to the more tradition-bound.

Once, in early summer, I went with an old woman to look at her fishing camp. After resting there for a while, she led us off into the woods. Before long she stopped and gestured toward a nondescript place in the brush—it was the old fish camp of the late Chief Henry and his wife Bessie, she said, abandoned some twenty years before and now isolated from the river by a growing sandbar. We explored the forest nearby, and she pointed out many birch trees with dark bands where the bark had been removed long before. Bessie often made birchbark baskets here, she recalled. Looking closely at the rotting stumps, we could see that ax cuts had felled the trees, perhaps because Chief Henry had not yet obtained a saw. Long vertical scars on a few birch trees showed where Chief Henry had cut strips of wood to test their grain for making sleds or snowshoes.

The woman became a little sad as she looked at these old signs, talking about Bessie at work here long ago in this place, now left to its silent wildness. But a stranger would almost certainly walk through this forest without taking the slightest notice that anyone had ever been here, much less made it a home every summer for many years. Almost nothing visible remained to associate it with humanity. Only the memory of people and events set this place apart from its surroundings and gave it special meaning for the Koyukon.

The Koyukon homeland is filled with places like this, places invested with significance in personal or family history. Drawing back to view the land-scape as a whole, we can see it completely interwoven with these meanings. Each living individual is bound into this pattern of land and people that extends throughout the terrain and far back across time.

Other places in the Koyukon homeland have both personal and supernat-ural meanings. This is especially true where people have died, because something spiritual remains there and imbues it with power. The old site of Cutoff is such a place, an abandoned village where many of Huslia's older residents once lived.

> We took a trip to Cutoff today with the dogs. The old village is almost unidentifiable now, except for a few fallen remnants of cabins. The place elicits thoughts of all that happened there, as related in stories so often told by Huslia people—the daily and yearly activities of village life, the excitement of holiday dances, courtships and marriages, seances by medicine people, and those lingering deaths from tuberculosis and other mysterious dis-eases that came after Europeans arrived.
>
> Cutoff is so alive in the minds of Huslia's people today, yet one

could easily pass it now without noticing those crumbled remains of cabins and caches. But it is more than just a memory place. It is still inhabited by the spirits of those who lived and died there. And for this reason it is a place of very real danger, where no one would think of camping or staying after darkness brought these spirits up from the silence of the day. [Huslia journal, December 1976]

These kinds of spiritual powers, and others as well, exist in a multitude of places, scattered everywhere across the terrain and amid the maze of waterways. For example, a slough downriver from Huslia (*Notol'o Dinh*) is haunted by a nebulous spirit form that causes strange noises or makes people "feel watched" in the night. Because of this, anyone who knows about it avoids camping there. A stretch of the Koyukuk River along *Dilbagga ts'oolnik nogga* ("ptarmigan sandbar") is cursed with power that caused the drowning of two boys long ago, "even though they were good swimmers." In the flats east of Huslia (near *Tsotlyeet*) is a lake made powerful when the bodies of two murdered Eskimo shamans were thrown into it. Even in deep winter cold this lake is said to have open holes, and people always avoid going near it. Similarly, people should not travel through the mouth of the *Dulbaatna* (Dulbi) River at night, because shamans battling one another long ago invested it with a "trap" of power. Spiritual places like these give the wildland invisible dimensions and fill it with meanings that can be known only through Koyukon tradition.

Koyukon people also identify the landscape with a profuse array of place names. Some of these names are used primarily for location, as outsiders use street signs. Others have special meanings that derive from personal or traditional history. Many examples have been mentioned in earlier chapters. Aside from these, there are hundreds of special places such as bear dens, many of which have their own names. Sometimes a bear den is named for the person who found it ("Sammy's den"), and he is given first chance to check it each fall. Or the name might simply describe something about it; for example, "moldy den." Some of these dens have been known for decades, even generations, and when hunters visit them they often recall the history of events there. In this way bear dens have become much more than just named places.

Known places on the landscape have a multitude of associations with hunting events or animal experiences. When Koyukon people traverse the country, their recollection of these events not only gives the land meaning but also perpetuates useful knowledge for locating resources and finding the way from place to place. Some important animal associations are extranormal as well, and because of these, people avoid certain areas or treat them with special respect. For instance, there are haunts of the woodsman, or of spiritually powerful creatures like the giant pike or the "muskrat mother."

Examples to illustrate the interchange of meanings between Koyukon people and the surrounding land could be multiplied almost inexhaustibly. The terrain is permeated with different levels of meaning—personal, historical, and spiritual. It is known in its finest details, each place unique, each endowed with that rich further dimension that emerges from the Koyukon mind. Yet, as real and alive as this dimension is, it cannot be known except through the people whose lives and culture derive from this landscape. I do not mean to imply that such associations are unique to the Koyukon; I mean that the Koyukon homeland itself is unique because of the particular human imprint that it has embodied over the centuries.

After a long evening spent poring over maps, recording the place names he knew, one of my Koyukon instructors told me how pleased he was to ensure in this way that they would be preserved. He and several others had talked of doing this before, he said, because they feared the names would otherwise be lost. "If I died," he mused, "then that country would die with me." The dimension beyond vision is an essential element of the Koyukon homeland, a human imprint that adds to its richness and meaning.

And even after death the Koyukon people remain tied to the homeland on which they lived. The wandering human spirit follows one of two trails. If the person has lived badly, it takes the poor trail, the trail of suffering. But if the person lived well, it moves along the easy trail, without suffering or hardship. Both the good and the bad will reach the same pleasant afterlife place, but one will make the trip easily and quickly, the other slowly and with much travail.

The trails to the afterlife follow the land, either upriver or downriver. The spirits of the dead remain for years near the places where they resided in life. This is why graveyards are always on high ground that protects the body and lingering spirits from being swept away in floods. These are hallowed places. Then, in the final afterlife, spirits of the dead range widely over the land, hunting as they did before. Fossils that wash from the riverbanks in summer are bones from the animals they have killed.

Here, then, is the final dimension of the Koyukon reality, the enduring nexus of nature and mind. It may be forgotten, yet it will always be there.

A Legacy of Land

> **wilderness** A tract of land or a region (as a forest or a wide barren plain) uncultivated or uninhabited by human beings; an empty or pathless area or region. [*Webster's Third New International Dictionary*, 1966]

To most outsiders, the vast expanses of forest, tundra, and mountains in the Koyukon homeland constitute a wilderness in the absolute sense of the word. For the Western mind, it is wilderness because it is essentially unaltered and lacks visible signs of human activity, and it must therefore be unutilized. But in fact the Koyukon homeland is not a wilderness, nor has it been for millennia.

This apparently untrodden forest and tundra country is thoroughly known by a people whose entire lives and cultural ancestry are inextricably associated with it. The lakes, hills, river bends, sloughs, and creeks are named and imbued with personal or cultural meanings. Indeed, to the Koyukon these lands are no more a wilderness than are farmlands to a farmer or streets to a city dweller. At best we can call them a wildland.

The fact that Westerners identify this remote country as wilderness reflects their inability to conceive of occupying and utilizing an environment without fundamentally altering its natural state. But the Koyukon people and their ancestors have done precisely this over a protracted span of time. From this standpoint, they have made a highly effective adjustment to living as members of an ecosystem, pursuing a form of adaptation that fosters the successful coexistence of humanity and nature within a single community.

But the Koyukon people have entered a new era of contact with other cultures and other perceptions of the world, and their relationship to nature appears destined to change. Before this happens, we might wish to look closely at their concepts of natural order and the proper role of humanity in the environment, not only to learn about them but perhaps to learn *from* them as well.

And we might also give thought to the legacy that they have created, by which the people continue to live today. What is this legacy? We often remember ancient or traditional cultures for the monuments they have left behind—the megaliths of Stonehenge, the temples of Bankok, the pyramids of Teotihuacán, the great ruins of Machu Picchu. People like the Koyukon have created no such monuments, but they have left something that may be unique—greater and more significant as a human achievement. This legacy is the vast land itself, enduring and essentially unchanged despite having supported human life for countless centuries. Koyukon people and their ancestors, bound to a strict code of morality governing their behavior toward nature, have been the land's stewards and caretakers. Only because they have nurtured it so well does this great legacy of land exist today. Here, perhaps, is the greatest wisdom in a world that Raven made.

> This evening I went to Chief Henry's house, where the long death watch continues. After listening to the men outside for an hour or two, I went in to warm up. Several women were there, talking softly in Koyukon. Chief Henry, looking small and frail now, was sleeping peacefully.
> Shortly the room fell silent, and then an old woman began softly singing. She sat in the amber twilight that entered through a

small window, her eyes downcast, her hands folded in the black satin of her old-fashioned dress. Her voice was exquisite, making even richer the slow, sweet phrases of her songs. Although I could not understand the words, they were filled with lamenting, and I was sure they were either songs for the dead or perhaps the loneliest of love songs.

I wondered if Chief Henry, now approaching death, could hear those lovely, sad songs. It would be good, I thought, if he could die with that sound in his ears, something that was purely Koyukon, born from the voices of birds and understood by the listening forest. Then I thought of the times that have passed irretrievably away, when people spent their entire lives in the forest and shared complete familiarity with its spirit. Chief Henry spoke of them so often with such eloquence.

I stared out the window, and while the woman's enchanting voice filled my ears I watched evening fade to deep orange and purple behind the distant timber. A clear image of the future entered my mind, an image of beautiful green forest, lush and alive with summer, in a time when Koyukon people were long vanished from this land. Drifting among the silent trees, along the overgrown trails and through the vanishing remnants of ancient camps, I could hear the beautiful phrases of that Koyukon song. [Huslia journal, July 1977]

Epilogue

I stood beneath the tall timber and watched a raven fly above me, vanishing and reappearing as it passed behind the treetops. And I wondered what, or who, it really was. Certainty is for those who have learned and believed only one truth. Where I came from, the raven is just a bird—an interesting and beautiful one perhaps, even an intelligent one—but it is a bird, and that is all. But where I am now, the raven is many other things first, its form and existence as a bird almost the least significant of its qualities. It is a person and a power, God in a clown's suit, incarnation of a once-omnipotent spirit. The raven sees, hears, understands, reveals . . . determines.

What is the raven? Bird-watchers and biologists know. Koyukon elders and their children who listen know. But those like me, who have heard and accepted them both, are left to watch and wonder. The raven tucked a wing and went topsy-turvy in the sky, then flew away toward the river, its resonating croaks pouring down into the forest. I turned awkwardly away, almost fearing a question: Was it laughing?

Appendix 1
The Study

In April 1975 I set out with three companions and two dog teams for an overland trip to the village of Huslia. Our point of departure was Shungnak, an Eskimo community on the Kobuk River. The trip was not a long one, something over a hundred miles, but soft spring snow forced us to walk a good part of the distance. Our trail took us past Angutigruaq Mountain, through the low peaks of the Zane Hills, and into the notorious wind funnel of Dakli Pass. There we detoured into a sheltered valley and joined some Eskimo and Koyukon people for a soak in the hot springs called *Uunaqtuq*. We had an easy ride down rolling tundra out of the pass, followed by many hours of winding through timber along the Koyukuk River. After three days' travel, the trail suddenly opened into Huslia, and a chaos of barking dogs greeted us.

We had spent the previous winter living in Kobuk Eskimo villages, studying subsistence activities in the area of the Kobuk Valley National Monument. Our work there was nearing completion, and in a few months we hoped to begin a similar project among the Koyukuk River people. This study would focus on the Gates of the Arctic National Monument proposal, on lands traditionally used by the Koyukon and neighboring Eskimos. We had come to ask the Huslia people if they would participate in the research; when they agreed, we arranged to leave our dogs in someone's care until our return at summer's end.

The project was also discussed with people in villages farther up the Koyukuk—Hughes, Allakaket, Alatna, and Bettles—and with the Eskimos of Anaktuvuk Pass. Another anthropologist would work there, while I would focus on Huslia and to some extent Hughes. The overall goal was to study all dimensions of land use by people from these communities—where it took place, what resources were harvested, how they were taken, how they were used, their economic importance, and the integration of subsistence into Koyukon intellectual culture.

I had chosen the last topic as my special focus, and I knew beforehand that Huslia and Hughes were ideal places for such a study. I had stayed in both villages several times before and had visited all the Koyukuk communities as well as several on the Yukon. My earlier trips were extended visits with friends who had lived in Huslia and Hughes for some years, and through their help I had become fairly well acquainted with the people and their environment. I always had a special liking for Koyukuk people, and for years I had wanted to work with them to record at least some of their traditional knowledge. When the chance came as part of the National Park Service's subsistence research, I was excited and eager to begin.

Some special qualities of the Huslia and Hughes people heightened my enthusiasm for the project. Most important, they have always been extremely friendly, helpful, and kind. They also communicate well, and one of their greatest sources of pleasure is visiting, a real help to someone who wishes to learn from them. In addition, they have a strong interest in their cultural traditions, which they love to discuss among themselves or teach to others who are willing to listen. These advantages were intensified at the time by the presence of some very knowledgeable older people, most of whom I knew before the project began.

Finally, the Koyukuk villages are especially well suited for the particular kind of study I had planned. Traditional subsistence activities are very much a part of modern life here, despite the changes that have taken place. And besides maintaining the practical elements of these activities, the Koyukon still follow the associated ancestral ideology and world view. This strong and open commitment to customary beliefs may be unique among native Alaskans today, and so I felt compelled to focus my work on the subject.

Familiarity with the people, plus the earlier arrangements we had made, allowed us to settle in very quickly. We moved into a tiny log cabin next door to Steven and Catherine Attla, who were to become my principal teachers in Huslia. I went to work immediately, not only on my instruction, but also on necessary tasks such as cutting wood, building a cache, maintaining the dog team, and hunting and fishing (which supplied our staple foods throughout the year of the project). I had previously spent a year in a Kutchin Athapaskan village, six months with the Kobuk Eskimos, and a year with Eskimos on the Arctic coast. This spared me having to learn from scratch the practical skills of living in the north and allowed the luxury of self-sufficiency.

But these jobs did consume a great amount of time. The year in Huslia was perhaps the busiest of my life, and there were periods when the high level of activity was very hard to sustain. Fortunately, these jobs were as much pleasure as work. And once the year's supply of firewood was in, I could take daily trips with the dog team for recreation and relaxation. These trips were often short, but they gave me a chance to escape the village and enjoy the wilderness and beauty of the surrounding country.

> Temperature −40°. Earlier today I took the dogs for a trip, despite the cold and soft trails. Along Racetrack Slough we left a cloud of fog that spread out over the snow and gradually contorted itself into misty peaks and spirals, probably caused by the gentle current of our passing. Looking behind, I saw this fog hang iridescent in the orange light of sunset. Clear back along the slough, for a mile at least, it glowed brightly in the sun's oblique rays, with flaming sky and silhouetted timber for a backdrop. It is hard to imagine a more profound peace than I experienced there. [Huslia journal, February 1976]

The dog team was also important for longer trips, including an extended working visit to Hughes and several excursions to remote camps. During the winter, spring, and summer I had chances to stay with people in their camps, joining in their activities and studying with uninterrupted intensity. Most of these outings were with Steven and Catherine Attla, although I visited, traveled, and worked with other people as well.

I was sometimes troubled by the dilemma of spreading my time among many people versus getting to know a few very well. It seemed both personally and professionally best to do the latter, while still visiting as widely as possible and reciprocating the friendliness that was so freely given. But more than any "fieldwork" experience I have had, this one focused on a small number of teachers. Of these, two were by far the most important. and because they shaped my knowledge so strongly I will describe them briefly.

At the time of this study Steven and Catherine Attla were both about fifty, which is rather young for an anthropologist's principal instructors. But both of them are steeped in their traditional culture, have phenomenal memories, and are uncommonly intelligent. Catherine is a deep thinker, an analyst of her culture, and probably a genius by any measure. She was raised by her grandparents, and her grandfather was said to be the last powerful shaman in this region. Until age fourteen she knew no English, but she taught herself to speak fluently; she learned to write by copying the words on food cans. She has given much thought to the question of two cultures coexisting in one person, and without diminishing her thoroughly Koyukon identity she has achieved true biculturality.

Steven had also acquired an impressive mastery of both cultures, in his case without Catherine's analytical introspection. As a teacher, he illustrates or epitomizes his culture, while Catherine can temporarily assume an outsider's perspective and describe it. Steven spent twenty summers as a river-boat pilot on the Yukon, but he comes from a very traditional background. He is one of Huslia's most skilled hunters and has devoted most of the winters in his life to trapping. Like Catherine, he is both a Christian and a devout follower of Koyukon religious belief and practice. His knowledge complements Catherine's, having a somewhat different focus and perspective. For this reason I always tried to work with both of them together.

Aside from all this, Steven and Catherine Attla are two of the finest people I have ever known—they literally took us in, and I often wondered how we could have been so lucky. But there were other special teachers as well, who added important dimensions to the study. Lavine Williams, an older man from Hughes, had a great feeling for animals and a gift for eloquent expression. He was especially attuned to the aesthetic qualities and personality of each species, and I spent many hours listening in fascination as he spoke. And there were several others—an old woman who told stories more beautifully than anyone else, an elderly man who had amazing knowledge of animal behavior and ecology, and another man near eighty who once said to me: "I understand what you're interested in, because for my whole life I been studying the white people!"

The year of this study in Huslia and Hughes was not without difficulty and frustration. Often there was too much work to be done, there was some hostility from younger people, the winter was very long and cold, and at times I longed for the familiarity of my own culture. But the positive experiences reduced these problems to insignificance—the rewards of living in this wild forested northland, the growth of mind and person that comes from being within another culture, the expansion of perspective in learning a different view of the world, and the fulfillment of developing friendships that transcend cultural differences.

Almost every day had moments and experiences that seemed profound to me. One of the most powerful happened near the end of my year in Huslia, on a trip I took with two elder women and two little children.

> By the time we started for home the sun was blazing low on the horizon, and the water was glassy calm. Lydia sat ahead of me in the boat, holding her tired little granddaughter on her lap. Behind her, I saw looming black clouds and dark timbered hillsides that dropped to meet their reflection on the mirror of Hunggadinh Slough.
>
> After a time, the old woman began to rock back and forth, and in a deep, quietly powerful voice she sang Koyukon songs. The child, now half-asleep, rested peacefully against her grandmother's shoulder. Lydia turned so her lips almost touched the girl's soft, warm cheek. As she sang, her usual ruggedness faded away; then tears welled up and streamed slowly down her face.
>
> I was transfixed, and for those moments there was no world

beyond what I saw. My senses could scarcely contain the beauty around me. Sometimes I am overwhelmed by my feelings for this place and people, and I wish for a way to possess them in words or pictures. But neither will do, and the most I can hope for is a memory that is burned forever into the core of my mind. [Huslia journal, June 1977]

Appendix 2
The Boreal Environment

The subarctic environment of the Koyukon is part of the great North American timberland called boreal forest or taiga, known more popularly as the north woods. Many of us have direct experience with boreal forest landscapes, which cover a vast stretch of the continent including much of Canada and the uppermost parts of some northern states (for example, Maine and Minnesota). This appendix will describe some important features of the subarctic forest environment, including its climate, landforms, plants, and animals.

The Boreal Forest

The subarctic forests where the Koyukon live are very near the poleward margin of human habitation. Here the earth's surface is tilted so it receives only a quarter of the solar energy absorbed by tropical regions. This limited energy intake means austerity for all living things, including humans; and for a large part of the year it means *cold*. Winter holds absolute sway in Koyukon territory for about seven months of the year, with temperatures dropping as low as −50°, −60°, even −70° (F). To one who has not experienced it, this cold is beyond imagining; but to the Koyukon it is an ordinary aspect of the world that must be met through adaptation and understanding.

However severe this environment may be, life has shown itself tenacious enough to flourish here. A few hundred species of plants and animals (compared with many thousands in the tropics) are arranged in a dynamic living community. Drawn thinly over the shallow soil and often permanently frozen substratum is an array of forest, muskeg, marshland, and tundra habitats, each with its particular complement of land and water animals. Some of these animals live here year-round, others come north only for the brief flourish of summer. In any case, there is enough life in this environment to sustain a people and to powerfully influence the design of their culture and lifeway.

Climate

All the Koyukuk River villages are in the great interior land mass of Alaska, very near the Arctic Circle. The climate is subarctic continental, strongly reflecting this far north and inland situation. If any feature of the total environment is paramount, it is surely temperature. The range of extremes is among the greatest on earth—in summer it is likely to reach 90° F, and each winter it falls at least to −55°, if not considerably lower.

Almost as remarkable as the intensity of winter cold is its duration. At Allakaket, about 125 air miles northeast of Huslia, the mean temperature remains below freezing for seven months of the year, from October through April. And for five of these months (November through March) the mean is below zero (°F). During the normal course of winter there are spells of −40° to −50° or colder, lasting from one to several weeks. Needless to say, thaws are extremely rare during the five midwinter months.

Table 2 summarizes temperature and other climatic data for Allakaket and Galena (the latter should closely resemble Huslia, for which information is not available).

Table 2
Climatic Data for Two Koyukon Villages

	Allakaket (66°33′N)	Galena (64°45′N)
January		
Mean maximum temperature	−7 (°F)	−2 (°F)
Mean minimum temperature	−29	−18
Overall mean temperature	−17	−10
July		
Mean maximum temperature	71	68
Mean minimum temperature	45	52
Overall mean temperature	58	60
Annual mean temperature	21	24
Highest recorded temperature	92	89
Lowest recorded temperature	−70	−65
Annual total precipitation	13.8″	13.7″
Annual total snowfall	75.9″	56.4″

Source: United States Department of Commerce 1959, 1963.

Winter activities in a Koyukon village are strongly influenced by the weather. When temperatures reach −30° or colder, people are reluctant to take long trips for hunting or trapping. Traveling is not only uncomfortable but also dangerous, for even the smallest accident can be deadly in the hard cold. For example, an Indian teacher used to warn me against felling trees alone in such weather, because if I was knocked unconscious I might freeze to death before anyone came to look for me. On the other hand, woodcutting near the village is one of the few activities that goes on during cold snaps, aside from occasional short hunting or trapping excursions.

Seasonal transitions in the boreal forest come abruptly, making for a brief spring and fall. At Huslia the thaw begins in late April, and under bright sunshine the snow melts within two weeks or so. By mid-May the river ice breaks up and drifts away, marking the beginning of summer. What summer lacks in duration it makes up in intensity of warmth and long days that allow continuous activity for animals and people. From May to September the average daily high at Allakaket is above 50°. But freezing temperatures return by late September, and ice will cover the river again in early October.

Interior Alaska's climate is surprisingly dry, with total precipitation averaging only 6 to 15 inches. Very low evaporation prevents the country from becoming arid, and poor drainage creates standing water everywhere on the flatlands. Heaviest precipitation comes in the summer, both as showers and as prolonged soaking storms. In the winter precipitation falls as powdery snow, and the absence of thaw allows deep accumulations; it is not unusual to step off a packed trail and find yourself waist-deep. Winter survival in the boreal forest is almost impossible without snowshoes.

Wind is generally light, although breezes are common in summer and storm winds occur in all seasons. Winter snows ordinarily come with storms that rush inland from the Bering Sea, accompanied by powerful north or west winds. Local topography has considerable effect on the wind, and consequently on other elements of the climate. Allakaket, for example, is in a pocket of calm and extremely cold winter weather. Huslia, being exposed to more wind and somewhat nearer to the coast, has less intense winter cold but is perhaps a bit cooler in summer.

At these northern latitudes, the length of day and night changes dramatically over the course of the year. Midwinter is dominated by darkness. The sun rises for only an hour in late December, but twilight extends the day to six or seven hours, and moonlight or aurora can diminish the totality of night. Spring and fall bring very rapid changes in the light cycle, as the sun remains above the horizon six or seven minutes longer each day. From mid-April until mid-August the sun never sinks far enough beneath the horizon to cause darkness.

Landscape

The traditional domain of the Koyukuk people includes a diversified landscape of river valleys, flatlands, foothills, and rugged mountains. The largest single feature is a broad flat some one hundred miles long and wide, surrounding the lower and middle course of the Koyukuk River. Huslia is isolated and virtually hidden amid this flatland. From atop the village's low ridge the nearest mountains are visible twenty-five miles to the north and east, beyond the edge of the shimmering flats.

Moving upriver, the lowlands give way to hills and mountains that impinge closely on the Koyukuk, creating a steep-sided valley. The village of Hughes is near midpoint in this valley, in a setting of exceptional peace and beauty. The nearby terrain includes high and low mountains, gentle ridges, small flats, and narrow floodplains. Just east of Hughes, the lower slopes of four-thousand-foot Indian Mountain afford a clear view of the Brooks Range, which lies about fifty miles north. The wall of distant snowcapped peaks stretches east and west, dissolving into the haze.

People from Huslia and Hughes travel widely across the high and low terrain that surrounds them, and they know its every feature in minute detail. The most important element of this terrain is not land but water, and above all else the people are tied to the Koyukuk River and the environment it creates. The major Koyukuk headwaters are in the Brooks Range, and the river flows swift and clear until it enters the flat below Hughes. There it becomes sluggish and brown with silt, and so it remains all the way to its confluence with the Yukon.

The Koyukuk twists and meanders widely across the great flat surrounding Huslia. Tracings of its geologic history are revealed by innumerable sloughs, oxbow lakes, meadows, timbered ridges, and meander scars scattered everywhere along its flanks. The riverbed is continually shifting today, creating a rich, diversified, and dynamic environment along its course.

Besides the river itself, there are innumerable tributaries, ranging from major watercourses more than a hundred miles long to insignificant creeks that trickle down over the banks. The flats are a scramble of streams wandering sinuously through a landscape of swamps, muskegs, ponds, and lakes of every size and shape. In some areas there is more water than land, and when the river floods there may be no land at all.

The river, streams, and lakes are key elements of the Koyukon environment. From the water itself come fish, waterfowl, and mammals that depend on aquatic habitats. The shifting of watercourses creates an endless process of plant succession, which helps support game such as moose, black bear, and snowshoe hare. And the water is an important medium for both summer and winter travel. It is small wonder the Koyukon people identify themselves with reference to the river drainages that delineate their individual or group territories.

Flora

We often think of the north woods as a vast, uninterrupted expanse of timber; but no such homogeneity exists here. Instead, boreal forest wildlands are covered by diverse plant communities, patterned according to elevation, local climate, soil type, drainage, and fire history. In the low country, closed forests, muskegs (open forests), bogs, and shrub thickets intermingle in a complex pattern. Mountain slopes and valleys create another mosaic, this one of forest and thicket on the lower slopes, fingering into moist tundra higher up, and finally alpine tundra above three thousand feet or so.

Despite its apparent disarray, this complexity sorts itself into a few identifiable plant communities. First among these is the closed forest of white spruce, paper birch, and quaking aspen (for a listing of English, Koyukon, and scientific names, see Appendix 3). Beneath the forest is an assortment of shrubs (such as willows and heaths) growing from a thick carpet of moss. Fires are a common natural event, and where they have occurred forests of aspen or birch predominate, with an understory of shrubs and young spruce. Along the rivers, stands of large balsam poplars are common. Forests growing beside the Koyukuk River frequently contain very large spruce and birch trees, the best available sources of building materials and firewood.

In cool, wet, or high-altitude areas (especially away from the river) muskeg often dominates the terrain. This is an open forest of black spruce, with a ground cover of thick sphagnum, sedges, grasses, and heath shrubs. In extremely wet situations, muskegs are replaced by soggy, treeless bogs. Muskegs and bogs provide fall harvests of blueberries and cranberries, but otherwise they are relatively poor in plant and animal resources.

Along the margins of wetlands, lakes, and river courses are shrub thickets dominated by willow and alder. These thickets grow especially tall and dense near the river, on newly formed land where the soil is frequently enriched by floods. Elsewhere, on the flats and mountain slopes, there are thickets of scrubby willow, alder, and resin birch. Shrub communities are widespread in Koyukuk country, and they are the richest habitat for game animals.

On the high mountain slopes, tundra vegetation hugs the windswept terrain, a dense mat of lichens, forbs, grasses and prostrate shrubs. In many areas, patches of bare ground disrupt the continuity of living cover. The tundra provides habitat for caribou and brown bear and allows easy, open traveling for hunters on sleds or afoot.

Fauna

Most of us have an image of the northern forest as a rich land that fosters a great abundance of wildlife; but it is actually among the poorest of natural environments. We perceive it as rich only because we have so impoverished the rest of the continent. Boreal forest animals are elusive, thinly dispersed, and only periodically abundant. They are also sensitive to overexploitation, and their persistence into the present era reflects the moderation with which they have been used. Plenitude is an illusion in the subarctic, as the old Koyukon people can attest in their tales of shortage and near starvation.

About 120 species of fish, birds, and mammals are named and accorded some cultural significance by the Koyukon (see Appendix 3 for a listing of animal names). Of these, approximately 70 are used today, although a much smaller number form the basis of modern village economies. Animals are important to the Koyukon not only as food and objectives of the subsistence quest, but also as personages and powers who share the world in which humans live.

Of all the animals, moose are by far the most important to the present economy and lifeway of Koyukuk villagers. They are found throughout the low forested country, especially where extensive willow thickets line the meandering river courses. Moose are said to have entered the Koyukuk region only in this century; other species dominated the economy in times past.

Caribou is the tundra counterpart of moose. This smaller ungulate migrates south from the arctic each winter, often entering the Koyukuk lowlands and the surrounding mountains. The size and abundance of herds vary considerably over the run of years, and so caribou are an unpredictable resource for the Koyukon. The only other large animals found here are black and brown bears. Both are accorded great importance, for cultural as well as economic reasons. They are nearly ubiquitous, although brown bears prefer tundra country and black bears are animals of the forest.

Smaller mammals include an assortment of northern species, nearly all sought by the Koyukon for meat, fur, or both. Snowshoe hare, beaver, and muskrat have at times been principal food sources, and their hides have also been used extensively, but at present big-game animals are much more important. Other small mammals commonly found here include porcupine, red squirrel, arctic ground squirrel, and marmot. Trapping furbearers is an important winter activity—the animals taken include wolf, red fox, wolverine, otter, marten, mink, least and short-tailed weasel, and lynx.

Birds are also an essential element of the natural world surrounding the Koyukon. About 125 species have been recorded in this region, and all the culturally or economically significant ones are named in Koyukon taxonomy. Most important are the 17 species of ducks and geese that contribute substantially to the diet, but others such as grouse and ptarmigan are economically significant as well. The power and personality of certain birds elevate them to great importance for Koyukon people, quite apart from their role in the diet.

Finally there are fish, found abundantly in boreal forest rivers, creeks, and lakes. Along the major rivers, fish may be the most stable and productive resource over the long run. The people of Huslia and Hughes have access to excellent fishing, although they say that Yukon River fish are far more abundant and of better quality. Chum salmon, often called dog salmon in recognition of its principal use, is the most important single species. Some king and silver salmon are also caught in Koyukuk fishnets. Several species of whitefish provide an often-abundant harvest, and there are good numbers of sheefish, grayling, pike, burbot, and sucker.

Compared with boreal forest regions elsewhere, the Koyukuk country seems favored with abundance. The trees are large for so far north, thickets are dense and widespread, and in recent times game has been plentiful. A hunter or a watcher here is likely to be well rewarded, if not with animals themselves, then at least with the signs of their passage. At times, in spite of the encompassing silence, there is a sense of living and moving things everywhere in the forest.

Appendix 3
Koyukon Terms for Natural Entities

This tabulation includes the basic terms for elements of the physical and biological environment, but it is far from a complete dictionary. Most of the terms are either from my own research or from Jones (1978), and the majority have been checked for accuracy by Eliza Jones of the Alaska Native Language Center.

Astronomical Terms

Sky: *yo*
Sun: *so, gha'olee*
Sunshine: *hak'idee'onh*
Sundog: *didziy no'un hudaatłkk'onh*
Moon: *dołt'olee*
Moonlight: *k'idołt'oł*
Darkness of no moon: *hał k'ideełłlah*
New moon: *nok'ideelt'onh*
Half moon: *k'akk'ał anok'iłilaat*
Full moon: *kk'aanok'inaalyonh*
Lunar eclipse: *yo t'ik'idagheełt'onh*
Moondog: *dołt'olee nton nok'adałnok'anadlik'at*
Star: *łoon'*
Twinkling stars: *łoon' na'ałts'eeyh liyaah*
Big Dipper (constellation): *nosikghaltaalee, nosikghaltaala*
Meteor: *łoon' tsona*

Meteor that breaks up in flight: *nokk'un' dagheeghal*
Aurora borealis: *yoyakkoyh*

Weather Phenomena

Bad weather: *ts'ohudeetłaagga*
Good weather: *hudeezonh*
Cold: *adzoo hoolaanh*
Cold spell: *haaneełkk'otł*
Intense winter cold: *k'ak'utł danaał*
Hot weather: *ło'ts'i haak'inee'onh*
Warm weather: *hunlik'uh*
Wind: *ałts'eeyh*
Whirlwind: *ałts'eebaaya*
North wind: *yoonłits'in'*
South wind: *yoodots'in', soł kkayahts'in'*
East wind: *yooneets'in'*
West wind: *yoonhłinhts'in'*
Storm: *taałts'iyh*
Cloudy: *dzaatsin'*
Cumulus clouds (fair weather type): *yokk'ut*
Humid: *hul'aakk*
Fog: *okk*
Misty rain: *okk kona'*
Rain: *konh*
Pouring rain: *nokonh dila*
Hail: *k'inloo*
Thunderstorm: *yok'i dok'idaadli tl'ee*
Heat before thunderstorms: *k'inoh kkona*
Thunder: *niłtina*
Thunderclap: *hunk'iltuytł*
Rolling thunder: *k'idilghus*
Lightning: *huditiltłik*
Rainbow: *naaggadla dik'inaaltł'oonh, niłtin ggaabeela*
Snow: *tseetł, noodaagha*
Deep snow: *tseetł nikoh*
Falling snow: *ałyot*
Blowing snow: *yoł yił taalts'iyh*
Snow on the ground: *noodaagha*
Granular snow beneath surface: *łiyh*
Hard drifted snow: *tseeytłtł'ina'*
Snow thawed previously and then frozen: *naahoołtinh*
Earliest crusted snow in spring: *hoołtinh*

Thinly crusted snow: *hogadokilggał*
Snow drifted over a steep bank, making it steeper: *daalts'iyh*
Snow cornice on a mountain: *tseetł dokk'aats'in'*
Heavy drifting snow: *ałtseeyh dona*
Slushy snow on the ground: *noodzaah*
Snow caught on tree branches: *duhnooyh*
Fluffy or powder snow: *tseeł koodla*
Thawing weather: *nohulgheeh*

Land and Water

World: *nin'kkokk'a huyeet*
Land: *nin'*
Hill: *tiyh*
Mountain: *dlił*
Mountain range: *dagheeloyee*
Valley: *deeneetł'o*
Canyon: *dinyeet*
Cliff: *tłaakin*
Cutbank: *deekk'aatł'ona*
Island: *toneedzidonoo*
Peninsula: *nooyeets*
Rock: *la'ona*
Sand: *łaats*
Mud: *k'iditł'is*
Earthquake: *nin'ghono*
Water: *too*
River: *hana*
River mouth: *hudokkaakk'at*
Slough: *nughutła, kk'ałna*
Slough behind an island: *noonagga*
Stream: *kk'ałna*
Current (swift): *hulinh*
Slack water (no current): *hoołdlinaa*
Flood: *eelbinh*
Shallow: *toonigudza*
Sandbar: *daas*
Shore: *tobaana*
Lake: *binkk'a hukuh*
Pond: *todaal-onh dinh*
Meadow ("grass lake"): *tł'uh yee, tł'uh kkokk'a*
Wave: *tot*
Ice (pieces): *łoo*

Lake or river ice: *tinh*
Rough ice: *łootsin*
Rotten (spring) ice: *taatinhdaaneekk'onh*
Honeycombed spring ice: *tinh azoos*
Crack in ice: *tinh naadlituł*
Glacier (frozen overflow in stream): *dilggeetł*
Icicle: *na'onłooghanaadlitinh*

Times of Day and Night

Earliest morning twilight: *yoonoogh hoyołkkoł*
Just before the sun peeks up: *yołkoł*
Sun just peeking up: *hok'o'oł*
Sunrise: *hok'aghee'onh*
Early morning: *kk'odohun' dona*
Morning daylight: *yeetłkkonh*
Day: *dzaanh*
Midday (noon): *dzaaneets*
Afternoon: *dzaaneets daa'ana*
Evening: *hałts'in'*
Sun going down: *nok'o'oł*
Sunset (after sundown): *nok'aghee'onh*
Night (darkness): *tłidaał hoolaanh*
Before midnight: *k'iłeeł neets do'ots'in'*
Midnight: *k'iłeeł neets*
After midnight: *k'iłeeł neets daa'ana*

Season and Calendar

Winter: *huy*
Midwinter: *huyneets*
Late winter (about March): *yoo-an yaats'ina*
Early spring (snow begins melting, about early April): *sonot*
Spring (time when people travel on crusted snow): *hotinh kkokk'a*
Breakup time (early May): *hulookk'ut*
Summer: *saanh*
Midsummer: *saaneets*
Late summer: (August): *saan tł'oghots'in'*
Fall (freeze–up time): *huyts'in*
January: *Bininh neełkk'aa dzaanh dilaayee* ("Month when days are becoming longer")
February: *Tilil zo'o* ("Bald eagle month")
March: *Kk'oolkk'ey zo'* ("Marsh hawk month")

April: *Bininh huditeey* ("Month when snow is crusted")
May: *Bininh tots'eeyh liyaaye* ("Month when boats are put in the river")
June: *Bininh tok'aggoyhk'uhudilaayee* ("Month when ducklings are put in the water")
July: *Ggaał nogha'* ("King salmon month")
August: *Saanlaagha nogha'* ("Summer silver salmon month")
September: *Nołdlaagha nogha'* ("Fall silver salmon month")
October: *Huyts'in' łookk'a nogha'* ("Fall fish month")
November: *Sooga zo'* ("Marten month")
December: *Ba'ooz kkalyee* ("No name")

Plants

Plant: *midinołyaal*
Vegetation: *hunyaah*
Forest: *teek'ot*
Tundra: *kin kkokk'a*
Brush: *ts'itł*
Caribou lichen (Cladonia): *bidziyh dona'*
Mushroom: *deeltsaa' baaba, nin' dzagha'*
Puffball: *dotson' nołkitł'a*
Shaggy mane: *dotson' kkuskkoya'*
Birch fungus (grows on live birch): *k'ididziyh*
Birch fungus (*Polyporus betulinum*): *adzibaangit*
Birch fungus (*P. aplanatum*): *kk'eyh anee'ona*
Sphagnum moss: *tł'otł*
Lake bottom moss: *taah naana'*
Floating water moss or algae: *dlot*
Goosegrass: *hunyaah, dits'in' baaba*
Horsetail rush: *tłaatługha*
Grass (general term): *k'itsaan'*
Wide grass or sedge: *tł'uh*
Hummock of grass: *nokinyaał*
Water lily: *taah dilodzeeda'*
Wild rhubarb (*Polygonum alaskanum*): *ggooł*
Prickly rose (*Rosa acicularis*): *hus dikina'*
Cloudberry (*Rubus chamaemorus*): *kkotł*
American red raspberry (*R. idaeus*): *dits'in tł'aakk*
Nagoonberry (*R. arcticus*): *noghuy tł'aakk*
American red currant (*Ribes triste*): *nots'ahtł'oona*
Black currant (*R. hudsonianum*): *dotson' geega*
Crowberry (*Empetrum nigrum*): *deenaatł'aas*
Kinnikinnik (*Arctostaphylos uva-ursi*): *diniyh*

Alpine bearberry (*A. alpina*): *geez nogha*
Highbush cranberry (*Viburnum edule*): *donaaldloya*
Bog cranberry (*Oxycoccus microcarpus*): *daałnodoodla'*
Lowbush cranberry (*Vaccinium vitis*): *dinaałkk'aza*
Bog blueberry (*V. uliginosum*): *geega*
Bunchberry (*Cornus canadensis*): *sis geega*
Red osier dogwood (*C. stolonifera*): *nik'inla'een geega*
Labrador tea (*Ledum decumbens*): *k'ilaakk'uyh*
Paper birch (*Betula papyrifera*): *kk'eeyh*
American green alder (*Alnus crispa*): *kk'as*
Quaking aspen (*Populus trichocarpa*): *t'aghał kk'ooga*
Balsam poplar (*P. balsamifera*): *t'aghał*
Willow (general term): *kk'uyh*
Littletree willow (*Salix arbusculoides*): *kk'uyloo*
Diamondleaf willow (*S. planifolia*): *kk'uydlits'eela*
Bebb willow (*S. bebbiana*): *kk'uydleeyh*
Pussy willow buds: *kk'ololeega'*
Small willow shoots: *kk'olgees*
Young willows: *kk'oontseeyh*
Willow sap: *kk'aghoz*
Leaf (any species): *k'it'on'*
Black spruce (*Picea mariana*): *ts'ibaa t'ał*
White spruce (*P. glauca*): *ts'ibaa*
Spruce sapling: *ts'ibaa t'aadla*
Spruce needles: *ałbagga*
Spruce bough: *ał*
Spruce cone: *dilodzoyh*
Top of spruce: *ts'ibaa tłee*
Dry branches near bottom of spruce: *k'itłoo'*
Ball of branches in spruce: *doht'oh*
Bark: *k'ilot'oodza*
Rough outer part of bark: *ts'ibaalot'oodza*
Whole bark of spruce, when removed in sections: *ts'ibaalotłaakk*
Girdled tree: *doltsidzee*
Sap, pitch: *dzaah*
Knot in wood: *tłookin*
Spruce with wood inside full of knots, but few branches on the outside:
  biyee k'itłoo ghee-oy
Straight-grained tree or wood: *tł'eel-o*
Twisted grain: *taałtutł*
Straight tree trunk: *tł'eedaal'o*
Crooked trunk: *kidaatłgits*
Straight tree with few branches: *taat'aghał*

Trunk, stump: *k'ikina'*
Burl: *ts'ibaa anee-onee*
Standing dry (dead) tree without limbs or bark: *huldaggola'*
Standing dry tree: *hulda*
Fallen dead tree: *k'itodeetło, daaleegida'*
Wood: *kkun'*
Dry wood: *doditsits*
Half-dry wood: *dil'aakk*
Green (freshly cut) wood: *łaan, kkun' diltł'is*
Hard wood inside spruce or birch tree: *gguyh*
Heart wood: *k'iyeetsidza*
Spongy dry wood inside rotten tree: *nodughoyee tsona*
Stick, log: *dikinh*
Driftwood: *todidla*
Large roots: *kaggadla'*
Small roots: *huyh*
Small top section of tree (left after cutting): *bidilo'*

Invertebrates

Insect (general term): *nin'ggoogha', ggooh*
Ant: *nołdiyhtł*
Bumblebee: *k'inodzeedza*
Mosquito: *tł'eeyh*
Gnat: *k'inodaguyhdla'*
Dung fly: *tson' dibiyh*
Bluebottle fly: *dun'*
Horsefly: *k'inot'odla'*
Maggot, worm: *gheeno'u*
Warble fly: *bidziyh ggoo'*
Louse: *yo'*
Flea: *geeł*
Snow flea: *yił kkutłiga*
Carpenter ant, wood worm: *dikinhghułga*
Spider: *taahoodzoya*
Staghorn beetle: *bidziyh yeega'*
Water beetle: *taagidzee'an*
Crane fly: *tł'eeyhbaanh*
Clothing moth: *k'ik'il ahona*
Butterfly: *nidinlibidza*
Yellow swallowtail: *naggaałk'idinlibidza*
Caterpillar: *k'eent'oogga, diyoodza*
Dragonfly: *tł'eeyh ahona*
Clam: *noghuy lootł'ok, hułtł'ołga'*

Fish and Amphibians

Fish (general term): *łookk'a*
Chum or dog salmon (*Onchorhynchus keta*): *noolaagha*
King or Chinook salmon (*O. tshawytscha*): *ggaał*
Silver or coho salmon (*O. kisutch*): *saan laagha, nołdlaagha*
Broad whitefish (*Coregonus nasus*): *taasiza'*
Least cisco (*C. sardinella*): *tsaabaaya*
Alaska whitefish (*C. nelsonii*): *holahga*
Round whitefish (*Prosopium cylandraceum*): *hułtin'*
Sheefish (*Stenodus leucichthys*): *nidlaagha*
Grayling (*Thymallus arcticus*): *daghalbaaya*
Dolly Varden (*Salvelinus malma*, uncertain identification): *ggaał yeega', siłyee lookk'a*
Northern pike (*Esox luscius*): *k'oolkkoya*
Blackfish (*Dallia pectoralis*): *oonyeeyh, dzonhyee, dagheets'eelee, gidzeełbaanh*
Burbot (*Lota lota*): *dł'aghas*
Longnose sucker (*Catostomus catostomus*): *toonts'oda*
Slimy sculpin (*Cottus cognatus*, uncertain identification): *nitsoodee'*
Fish gills: *k'akk'usga'*
Fins: *baghoga'*
Air bladder: *k'ilusga*
Scales: *k'aggoołga*
Slime: *k'idł'isga'*
Tail: *bikaala'*
Pyloric ceca: *k'itseeda'*
Viscera: *k'its'eega'*
Fish eggs: *kk'oon'*
Wood frog (*Rana sylvatica*): *noghuya*
Freshwater clam (unidentified species): *hułdł'ołga', noghuy lootł'ok*

Birds

Common loon (*Gavia immer*): *dodzina*
Yellow-billed loon (*G. adamsii*): *dodibeeya*
Arctic loon (*G. arctica*): *dł'idlibaa*
Red-throated loon (*G. stellata*): *tokootsaagha*
Horned grebe (*Podiceps auritus*): *dzeeyaakk*
Red-necked grebe (*P. grisegena*): *tokkaa'a*
Whistling swan (*Olor columbianus*): *tobaa*
Goose (general term): *dits'ina*
White-fronted goose (*Anser albifrons*): *k'idot'aagga'*
Canada goose (*Branta canadensis*): *bileelzina*
Black brant (*B. nigricans*): *kideeł'gho nodaala*

Snow goose (*Chen hyperboreus*): *hugguh*
Duck (general term): *nindaala*
American widgeon (*Mareca americana*): *siseeya*
Shoveler (*Spatula clypeata*): *dilolagga*
Pintail (*Anas acuta*): *k'idzonula*
Mallard (*A. platyrhynchos*): *tlitlkkughuyh*
Green-winged teal (*A. carolinensis*): *k'itsutl, tobaa ha'alghalee*
Greater scaup (*Aythya marila*): *tontseedla*
Lesser scaup (*A. affinis*): *tontseedla*
Bufflehead (*Bucephala albeola*): *toodakk'ona*
Common goldeneye (*B. clangula*): *dikeenoya*
Barrow's goldeneye (*B. islandica*): *dikeenoya*
Old-squaw (*Clangula hyemalis*): *aahaaga, aanhaaga, nodabaaghayee*
Harlequin duck (*Histrionicus histrionicus*): *taasa hut'aana*
White-winged scoter (*Melanitta deglandi*): *ts'inh daadlagguya*
Surf scoter (*M. perspicillata*): *dotson'alaayh, yoolyeesga*
Red-breasted merganser (*Mergus serrator*): *tsaghul*
Ruffed grouse (*Bonasa umbellus*): *tsongguda*
Spruce grouse (*Canachites canadensis*): *diyh, al ahona*
Sharp-tailed grouse (*Pedioecetes phasianellus*): *k'iltulga*
Willow ptarmigan (*Lagopus lagopus*): *dilbagga*
Herring gull (*Larus argentatus*): *baats*
Mew gull (*L. canus*): *baats*
Bonaparte's gull (*L. philadelphia*): *tleelzina*
Long-tailed jaeger (*Stercorarius longicaudus*): *dzonh*
Arctic tern (*Sterna paradisaea*): *k'idaggaas*
Lesser yellowlegs (*Totanus flavipes*): *dzolnolga*
Common snipe (*Capella gallinago*): *yoleel*
Semipalmated plover (*Charadrius semipalmatus*): *bilaanh nok'idaalk'idee*
?Whimbrel (*Numenius phaeopus*): *bidilts'idla'*
American golden plover (*Pluvialis dominica*): *bibidisis*
Northern phalarope (*Lobipes lobatus*): *tolyidla, tiyee*
Black turnstone (*Arenaria melanocephala*): *bitleenik'idaa'onee*
Spotted sandpiper (*Actitus macularia*): *dilbeedza*
?Long-billed dowicher (*Limnodromus scolopaceus*): *tl'eeyh ts'ineega'*
Sandhill crane (*Grus canadensis*): *dildoola*
Goshawk (*Accipiter gentilis*): *yoda, nik'eedoya*
Kestrel (*A. sparverius*): *hukeenoya*
?Swainson's hawk (*Buteo swainsoni*) or red-tailed hawk (*B. jamaicensis*): *ts'ibaak'itlaa*
?Rough-legged hawk (*B. lagopus*): *kk'olkk'eya*
Marsh hawk (*Circus cyaneus*): *bakkant'ogga'*
Osprey (*Pandion haliaetus*): *taagidzee'aana*
Golden eagle (*Aquila chrysaëtos*): *tilila, k'iyona'*

Bald eagle (*Haliaeetus leucocephalus*): *tilila, k'iyona'*
Great horned owl (*Bubo virginianus*): *nigoodzagha, nodneeya*
Great gray owl (*Strix nebulosa*): *nołduł*
Hawk owl (*Surnia ulula*): *k'iłeedzodza, noo ghanonodint'ugha*
Short-eared owl (*Asio flammeus*): *kk'oondzaah, hunlik*
Snowy owl (*Nyctea scandiaca*): *yiłbaa, nokinbaa*
Boreal owl (*Ageolis funereus*): *ałkeeh doldoya*
Raven (*Corvus corax*): *dotson'*
Gray jay (*Perisoreus canadensis*): *zuhga*
Belted kingfisher (*Megaceryle alcyon*): *dikiłł'aasga*
"Fish mother" (unidentified): *łookk'a baanh*
Northern shrike (*Lanius excubitor*): *ts'inok'iłk'oodla*
Yellow-shafted flicker (*Colaptes auratus*): *tsinił*
Downy woodpecker (*Dendrocopus pubescens*): *dikiłłaala*
Hairy woodpecker (*D. villosus*): *dikiłłaala*
Northern three-toed woodpecker (*Picoides tridactylus*): *dikiłłaala*
Olive-sided flycatcher (*Nuttalornis borealis*): *duhtseeneeya*
Bank swallow (*Riparia riparia*): *bił'on hoodloyee, kaałnooya*
Violet-green swallow (*Tachycineta thalassina*): *łaats anogha*
Cliff swallow (*Petrochelidon pyrrhonota*): *łaa'ak'iługha, kaaltsaa'a*
Boreal chickadee (*Parus hudsonicus*): *k'its'ahultoona*
Black-capped chickadee (*P. atricapillus*): *k'its'ahultoona*
Gray-cheeked thrush (*Hylocichla minima*): *gguzaakk*
Swainson's thrush (*H. ustulata*): *gguzaakk*
Hermit thrush (*H. guttata*): *gguzaakk*
Robin (*Turdus migratorius*): *dilk'ahoo*
Varied thrush (*Ixoreus naevius*): *diłł'eeza*
Bohemian waxwing (*Bombycilla garrula*): *diltsooga*
Rusty blackbird (*Euphagus carolinus*): *ts'uhułts'eegga, bikeehułgit*
Horned lark (*Eremophila alpestris*): *dlił łeekk'a bahoolaanee*
Dipper (*Cinclus mexicanus*): *nitsoo taaneelot*
Yellow warbler (*Dendroica petechia*): *diłtsits*
Yellow-rumped warbler (*D. coronata*): *łatsontłida*
?Orange-crowned warbler (*Vermivora celata*) or Wilson's warbler (*Wilsonia pusilla*): *tsoł ghu doghon' neeł'oya*
?Blackpoll warbler (*Dendroica striata*): *k'oot'anh*
Ruby-crowned kinglet (*Regulus calendula*): *tahoodzee neeyee, taahoodzoya*
Pine grosbeak (*Pinicola enucleator*): *kaayooda, t'aghał daloggudla' ahonee, kk'ogholdaala*
White-winged crossbill (*Loxia leucoptera*): *saak'idaatłggatł, saadok'idaatłggadla*
Common redpoll (*Acanthus flammea*): *k'ilodabeeza, dilogha hutaadilghuzee*
Hoary redpoll (*A. hornemanni*): *k'ilodabeeza, dilogha hutaadilghuzee*
Slate-colored junco (*Junco hyemalis*): *k'it'otłt'ahga*
Snow bunting (*Plectrophenax nivalis*): *hugguh yoza, k'akk'utł ggaagga*

Fox sparrow (*Passerella iliaca*): *tsook'aał*
Savanna sparrow (*Passercula sandwichensis*): *kitsaan' loy doldoya*
White-crowned sparrow (*Zonotrichia leucophrys*): *k'itł'in ts'ahut'aana*

Mammals

Boreal redback vole (*Clethrionomys gapperi*): *deeltsa'a*
Tundra redback vole (*C. rutilus*): *deeltsa'a*
Meadow vole (*Microtus pennsylvanicus*): *deeltsa'a*
Northern bog lemming (*Synaptomys borealis*): *binobintł'ogga,*
   kk'uyhk'ideeltsa'a
Brown lemming (*Lemmus sibiricus*): *binobintł'ogga, kk'uyhk'ideeltsa'a*
Tundra shrew (*Sorex tundrensis*): *łoodolts'iyhdla, toodohuggo*
Masked shrew (*S. cinereus*): *łoodolts'iyhdla, toodohuggo*
Dusky shrew (*S. obscurus*): *łoodolts'iyhdla, toodohuggo*
Snowshoe hare (*Lepus americanus*): *gguh, saanh zooga'*
Red squirrel (*Tamiasciurus hudsonicus*): *tsaghaldaala, tłiga*
Flying squirrel (*Glaucomys sabrinus*): *nindibidza, ts'ikinleeda'*
Arctic ground squirrel (*Spermophilus undulatus*): *hundaggaza*
Hoary marmot (*Marmota marmota*): *tłaa ggaagga*
Porcupine (*Erethizon dorsatum*): *dikahona, ligidza*
Muskrat (*Ondatra zibethicus*): *bikinaala*
Beaver (*Castor canadensis*): *noya'a, ggaagga*
Short-tailed weasel (*Mustela erminea*): *kaaghozina*
Least weasel (*M. rixosa*): *kusga*
Mink (*M. vison*): *taahgoodza*
Marten (*Martes americana*): *sooga*
Otter (*Lutra canadensis*): *bilaazona*
Wolverine (*Gulo luscus*): *niłtseeł, doyonh*
Lynx (*Lynx canadensis*): *kaazina*
Red fox (*Vulpes fulva*): *nohbaaya, naaggadla*
   red phase: *diltługha*
   cross phase: *daałt'ogga*
   silver phase: *dilzina*
Wolf (*Canis lupus*): *teekkona*
Dog (*C. familiaris*): *łeek*
Black bear (*Ursus americanus*): *sis*
Brown bear (*U. arctos*): *ghonoya, ghonoy tłaaga*
Caribou (*Rangifer tarandus*): *bidziyh*
Dall sheep (*Ovis dalli*): *dibee*
Moose (*Alces alces*): *dineega*
Human (*Homo sapiens*): *dinaa*
Woodsman (*Homo sapiens*): *nik'inla'eena, nuhu'anh*

Note: Anatomical terms for large mammals are listed in Appendix 4.

Appendix 4
Uses for Selected Major Species

This tabulation is intended to show the thoroughness with which some species are used by the Koyukon, as a supplement to discussions in the text. The anatomical terms are a basic list; many more exist for other species and for parts of the human body.

Moose and Caribou

Head (*bitłee'*): The head is one of the best parts of a moose. Nearly all its tissues and meat are eaten, except for the glands (*kkotł*), which are not used from any animal. Head meat is very rich and is usually cut from the skull for cooking "moosehead soup" or "head cheese." Sometimes an entire head is suspended over a campfire and roasted—this is a great delicacy.

Nose (*bintsiyh*): This is boiled, roasted in a campfire, or dried and then soaked and boiled for eating.

Eyes (*binogha'*): Eyeballs are not eaten, but surrounding tissues and fat are boiled and eaten. Fat is also dried or eaten raw.

Ears (*bidzagha'*): Cartilage at the base of the ears is boiled or roasted for eating.

Tongue (*bitłoola'*): This is eaten after boiling, roasting, or drying.

Lower jaw (*biyaatł'ina'*): The entire jaw is boiled, then the meat and tissues are eaten. Marrow from inside the jawbone is also eaten. The lower jaw is tabooed for all except old men.

Lips and mouth tissues (lips = *bidobaana'*): These are cooked and eaten, but the lower lip is tabooed for all except old men. Tabooed parts are not included in dishes such as moosehead soup.

Head muscles (face muscles = *binaakoodla'*): These are cooked and eaten.

Brain (*bitleetaaggadla'*): This is used in preparing "head cheese" and in tanning hides.

Neck (*bakk'ul*): All meat from the neck is eaten, except that from the first joint (*bits'anotleek'itnol-olee*), which is permitted only to old people beyond childbearing age. Like most taboos on food, this one is imposed to prevent undesirable characteristics in the user or the user's children. Often (as in this case) the penalty for eating tabooed foods is slowness or clumsiness.

Shoulder blade (*baggokina'*): The shoulder meat is cooked or dried, and the moose's scapula can be dried and used for a moose call.

Foreleg (*bitl'eela'*): The upper leg muscles (*bitl'eela'*) and lower leg muscles (*k'itl'eellookk'a'*) are cooked or dried. The marrow (*biyagha'*) is eaten raw or cooked. Joints of the leg bones may be pulverized and boiled to obtain grease. The lower foreleg bone (*bidzotina'*) is fashioned into a scraper for removing fat from animal skins.

Foot (*bakkaa'*): Forefeet and hind feet are boiled and the tissues are eaten. This food is tabooed for all except old people.

Hoof (*bakkaalagguna'*): The hooves and dewclaws (*bakkatutl*) are not used today.

Backbone: The meat (*tlaahnilaana'*) is cooked or dried and is considered very high in quality. This is especially true for the anterior meat (*baghona'*) along the high shoulder vertebrae. The bones (*binina'*) are not used, but the spinal cord (*bininyhaagha'*) is removed from the cooked vertebrae and eaten. The sinew (*tlaah*) is removed, dried, and used for sewing. Back sinew is considered the best for sewing and (formerly) making snares.

Pelvis (bone with meat = *bok'oya;* bone alone = *bok'oyhtl'ina'*): The meat is highly esteemed and is prepared by cooking or drying.

Tail (*bikaalts'ila'*): This is cooked and eaten but is tabooed for all except old people.

Hind leg (*bilidla'*): The upper leg muscles (*boggul*) are extremely valuable as food; the lower leg muscles (*badolookk'a*) are less preferred because they are too sinewy. The hind-leg sinew (*k'ik'altlaagha*) can be used for sewing, but this is not often done. The bones may be pulverized and boiled for grease, and the marrow is removed and eaten.

Ribs (bones and meat = *bikoga;* meat outside ribs = *bikoktlin*): This is one of the best parts of moose or caribou. All rib meat is either dried or cooked, often for special occasions.

Brisket (*bitseeyeetlina'*): This is excellent meat, prepared by boiling.

Belly meat (*bitsokklit*): Dried, or boiled for a long period before eating. Considered very good meat.

Lungs (*bidzaadeela'*): Sometimes cut into thin strips and boiled with meat;

but primarily used for (cooked) dog food. The trachea (*biloot*) is only given to dogs.

Liver (*bikol-ona*): Cooked and eaten.

Omasum (*k'idee-ona'*): This organ, often called the "Bible," is boiled and eaten.

Large stomach (*bibit*): This is not eaten but may be filled with blood from the kill, frozen, then chopped up for dog food.

Intestines (*bits'eega'*): The upper (large) intestine is used only for dog food. When the lower intestine has much fat, it may be turned inside out and boiled with the fat inside, then eaten like sausage. The fat is also eaten raw or used in cooking.

Kidneys (*baggoldzeeda*): These are fried or roasted and eaten (except those from a rutting bull).

Heart (*bidzaaya'*): The heart is cooked or dried but is tabooed for children or young people. The membrane surrounding the heart (*k'idzonotł*) is dried, then used for an all-purpose bag to store things in.

Blood (*bilkkona*): This was formerly cooked and eaten or boiled with meat, but it is used for dog food today.

Udder (*bidooga'*): Milk from the udder was formerly used as food.

Fat: Body fat (*bakk'oh*) and mesentary fat (*binooł*) are highly prized, eaten dried or cooked, usually with meat. Grease (*bagga'*) is rendered from fat by frying or boiling and is eaten with meat. The cooked fat that remains is also eaten. "Indian ice cream" is a great delicacy prepared from moose grease and other ingredients.

Antlers (*bida'*): These are made into awls, platters, spoons, knife handles, other tool handles, and a variety of miscellaneous objects.

Hide (*bilił*): Moosehide is almost as important as the meat. Koyukon women continue to tan the hides themselves and use them for sewing a multitude of items. Moose skin with the fur intact is used for mattresses, the hair is mixed with waterfowl feathers for mattress stuffing, and rawhide from moose skin is used for sled and snowshoe lashings. Meat sliced from the hide when it is cleaned for tanning (*kkaggootł*) is cooked and eaten.

Caribou hide is a very important clothing material. The leg skins are especially important today, for making warm winter footgear. Entire hides are used for camp mattresses. Caribou rawhide is used for fine snowshoe lashings and other general purposes. Warble fly larvae from caribou skins were formerly eaten.

Black and Brown Bear

Basic anatomical terms are the same for all animals, and so only a few specialized terms are listed below. Uses of black and brown bears are essentially identical, except that brown bear meat is completely tabooed for women.

Head: Roasted on a stick or boiled, always in the woods to avoid tabooed contact with women. After cooking, the face muscles, cartilage at the base of the ears, and fat behind the eyeballs are eaten. The lower jaw and tongue are tabooed for all except old men. The brain is tabooed completely, and the teeth are not used.

Neck: The meat is a delicacy, reserved for use at "bear parties." Neck meat is tabooed for women, and meat from the first joint behind the head is completely tabooed.

Foreleg and shoulder: All meat is eaten but tabooed for women. This and other bear meat is prepared by drying, roasting, or boiling.

Bones: Bear bones are not used, and the marrow is not eaten.

Feet: These are esteemed as food, often roasted over a fire at the men's bear parties. Forepaws are tabooed for eating by women who are not elderly; and hind paws are also tabooed for young men. The claws (binlogguna) are usually discarded to insure against their being dropped "just anywhere" and offending the animal's spirit.

Backbone: The meat is always reserved for bear parties and is tabooed for women. Sinew from the bear's back and legs is not used.

Pelvis and hind legs: All meat is eaten, and the highly esteemed pelvis meat is usually saved for distribution at potlatches.

Tail: This is eaten only by old women.

Ribs: The first three ribs are reserved for men at the bear parties, except that old people can eat them at home. The rest theoretically are eaten only by men, but today most women eat them too. Rib meat is a delicacy, often saved for potlatches. The brisket is also eaten, as is the belly meat; but the diaphragm is considered inedible.

Small organs: The lungs, windpipe, and liver are considered inedible. Kidneys are eaten only by women, and the heart is eaten by any adult (but tabooed for young people). Bear blood is not used. The bitaala' (a foot-long organ between the stomach and the liver) is eaten, but only by older people.

Stomach: Bear stomach is turned inside out, then filled with fat-laced mesentary (bikooya'); the openings are tied shut, and the entire thing is roasted over a fire. The resultant "sausage" is eaten only by older men and women.

Small stomach (dikadlo lodzida): This is a small, fatty "bag" situated like the omasum of a moose. Only old men are allowed to eat it, after it is boiled or roasted.

Intestines: The first three or four feet are discarded, and the rest is turned inside out so the fat is inside, then placed on a fire to roast. The result is a sausagelike delicacy. Only hibernating bears are used this way, because their intestines are empty.

Fat: Back, body, organ, and mesentary fat are highly valued. They are rendered in a big pot to make grease, which solidifies and is eaten with meat. Bear grease was formerly burned in a shallow bowl to provide light.

Hide: Formerly used, by men only, for mattresses, mittens, parka ruffs, and dog harnesses. Seldom brought home today, owing to the danger of offensive contact with young women who might disregard the avoidance taboo.

White Spruce

Wood: Dry spruce wood, half-dry wood, and live "green wood" are the principal firewood in most Koyukuk village households.

White spruce logs are also the major material for most homes in this region. Lumber from split or ripsawed spruce is used in making houses, boats, sleds, canoes, caches, tent frames, and countless other items. Rotten spruce wood is pulverized and mixed with rotten willow for smoking hides.

Boughs: These are used for covering tent floors in camps and for insulative bedding for dogs. Dried, needleless boughs (k'itloo') are excellent tinder for starting campfires.

Spruce tops: These are cut from small trees and carried for spiritual protection in certain places. Formerly used in shamanistic activities.

Needles: Spruce needles are boiled in water, and the resulting infusion is drunk to cure kidney problems or to obtain spirit power from the spruce. This may also be applied to heal dry skin or sores.

Bark: Bark is peeled from green trees to make camp floors, roofs, and tops for fish-cutting tables.

Roots: Small, supple roots are used for lashing birchbark baskets; large, woody roots are carved into spoons and bowls.

Pitch: Soft, clear sap is put on sores as a disinfectant. Hard, yellowish pitch is chewed like gum. Both types can be used for waterproofing boat seams or mixed with fat to make "varnish." Pitch was formerly burned in shamanistic curing sessions, yielding spiritual power from the spruce.

Bibliography

Allen, H. T. 1887. *Report of an expedition to the Copper, Tanana, and Koyukuk Rivers, in the Territory of Alaska in the year 1885.* Washington, D.C.: U.S. Government Printing Office.

Anderson, Douglas D., et al. 1977. *Kuuvangmiit subsistence: Traditional Eskimo life in the latter twentieth century.* Washington, D.C.: U.S. Government Printing Office.

Armstrong, Robert H. 1980. *A guide to the birds of Alaska.* Anchorage: Alaska Northwest Publishing Company.

Attla, Catherine. 1971. How to tan your moose hide. *Alaska Magazine* 36 (10): 12–13, 54.

Carlo, Poldine. 1978. *Nulato: An Indian life on the Yukon.* Fairbanks: Poldine Carlo.

Clark, Annette McF. 1970. Koyukon Athapaskan ceremonialism. *Western Canadian Journal of Anthropology* 2 (1): 80–88.

———. 1974. *Koyukuk River culture.* Mercury Series, paper no. 88. Ottawa: Canadian Ethnology Service.

———. 1975. Upper Koyukuk River Koyukon Athapaskan culture: An overview. In *Proceedings: Northern Athapaskan Conference,* 1:146–80. Ottawa: National Museum of Man.

Cooperative Extension Service. 1974. *Alaska's game is good food.* Publication no. 126. Fairbanks: Cooperative Extension Service, University of Alaska.

De Laguna, Frederika. 1969–70. The Atna of the Copper River, Alaska: The world of men and animals. *Folk* 11–12:17–26.

Elton, Charles. 1942. *Mice, voles, and lemmings.* Oxford: Clarendon Press.

Feit, Harvey A. 1973. The ethno-ecology of the Waswanipi Cree; or, How hunters can manage their resources. In *Cultural ecology: Readings on the Canadian Indians and Eskimos,* ed. Bruce Cox. Toronto: McClelland and Stewart.

Graburn, Nelson, and Strong, B. Steven. 1973. *Circumpolar peoples: An anthropological perspective.* Pacific Palisades, Calif.: Goodyear.

Hallowell, A. I. 1955. *Culture and experience.* Philadelphia: University of Pennsylvania Press.

Heller, Christine A. 1966. *Wild edible and poisonous plants of Alaska.* Bulletin F-50. Fairbanks: University of Alaska Extension.

Helm, June. 1976. *The Indians of the subarctic: A critical bibliography.* Bloomington: Indiana University Press for the Newberry Library.

Hemming, James A. 1971. *The distribution and movement patterns of caribou in Alaska.* Wildlife Technical Bulletin no. 1. Juneau: Alaska Department of Fish and Game.

Henry, David, and Henry, Kay. 1969. Koyukon locationals. *Anthropological Linguistics* 11:136–42.

Hippler, Arthur, and Wood, John. 1974. *The subarctic Athapaskans: A selected annotated bibliography.* Fairbanks: Institute of Social, Economic, and Government Research, University of Alaska.

Huntington, James. 1966. *On the edge of nowhere.* New York: Crown.

Irving, Lawrence. 1958. Naming of birds as part of the intellectual culture of Indians at Old Crow, Yukon Territory. *Arctic* 11 (2): 117–22.

Jetté, Julius. 1907. On the medicine men of the Ten'a. *Journal of the Royal Anthropological Institute* 37:157–88.

―――. 1908–9. On Ten'a folklore. *Journal of the Royal Anthropological Institute* 38:298–367; 39:460–505.

―――. 1911. On the superstitions of the Ten'a Indians. *Anthropos* 6:95–108, 241–59, 602–15, 699–723.

―――. 1913. Riddles of the Ten'a Indians. *Anthropos* 8:181–201, 630–51.

―――. n.d.*a.* Koyukon dictionary (untitled). Unpublished manuscript provided by Gonzaga University.

―――. n.d.*b.* On the geographical names of the Ten'a. Unpublished manuscript provided by Gonzaga University.

―――. n.d.*c.* On the time reckoning of the Ten'a. Unpublished manuscript provided by the Oregon Provincial Archives of the Society of Jesus, Crosby Library, Gonzaga University.

Johnson, Roy D. 1981. Upper Tanana Athapaskan fire ecology. Paper presented to the Eighth Annual Conference of the Alaskan Anthropological Association.

Jones, Eliza. 1978. *Junior dictionary for central Koyukon Athapaskan.* Anchorage: National Bilingual Materials Development Center.

―――. 1979. *The stories Chief Henry told.* Fairbanks: Alaska Native Language Center, University of Alaska (also an earlier draft, cited as n.d. in text).

Jones, Eliza, and Chief Henry. 1976. *K'ooltsaah Ts'in'* [Koyukon riddles]. Fairbanks: Alaska Native Language Center, University of Alaska.

Keith, Lloyd B. 1963. *Wildlife's ten year cycle.* Madison: University of Wisconsin Press.

Kennicott, Robert. 1869. *Biography of Robert Kennicott and extracts from his journal.* Transactions, vol. 1. Chicago: Chicago Academy of Sciences.

Knight, Rolf. 1965. A Re-examination of hunting, trapping, and territoriality among the northeastern Algonkian Indians. In *Man, culture and animals,* ed. Leeds and Vayda. Washington, D.C.: American Association for the Advancement of Science.

Krause, Michael E. 1974. *Native peoples and cultures of Alaska* (map). Fairbanks: Alaska Native Language Center, University of Alaska.

———. 1980. *Alaska native languages: Past, present, and future.* Alaska Native Language Center Research Papers, no. 4. Fairbanks: University of Alaska.

Leacock, Eleanor B. 1954. *The Montagnais "hunting territory" and the fur trade.* Memoir 78. Washington, D.C.: American Anthropological Association.

Lee, Richard B. 1968. What hunters do for a living; or, How to make out on scarce resources. In *Man the hunter,* ed. R. Lee and I. DeVore. Chicago: Aldine.

Lewis, Henry T. 1973. *Patterns of Indian burning in California.* Ramona, Calif.: Ballena Press.

———. 1977. Maskuta: The ecology of Indian fires in northern Alberta. *Western Canadian Journal of Anthropology,* vol. 8, no. 1.

———. 1978. Traditional uses of fire by Indians in northern Alberta. *Current Anthropology* 7 (1): 15–22.

———. 1982. Fire technology and resource management in aboriginal North America and Australia. In *Resource managers: North American and Australian hunter-gatherers,* ed. Nancy N. Williams and Eugene S. Hunn. Washington, D.C.: American Association for the Advancement of Science.

Loyens, William J. 1964. The Koyukon feast for the dead. *Arctic Anthropology* 2 (2): 133–48.

———. 1966. *The changing culture of the Nulato Koyukon Indians.* Ph.D. diss., University of Wisconsin. Ann Arbor: University Microfilms.

McClellan, Catherine. 1975. *My old people say: An ethnographic survey of southern Yukon Territory.* Ethnological Publications, no. 6. Ottawa: National Museum of Man.

McKennan, Robert A. 1959. *The Upper Tanana Indians.* Yale University Publications in Anthropology, no. 55. New Haven: Yale University.

————. 1965. *The Chandalar Kutchin.* Technical Paper no. 17. Montreal: Arctic Institute of North America.

Martin, Calvin. 1978. *Keepers of the game.* Berkeley: University of California Press.

Michael, Henry N., ed. 1967. *Lieutenant Zagoskin's travels in Russian America.* Arctic Institute of North America, Anthropology of the North: Translations from Russian Sources, no. 7. Toronto: University of Toronto Press.

Nelson, Richard K. 1973. *Hunters of the northern forest.* Chicago: University of Chicago Press.

————. 1980. Athapaskan subsistence adaptations in Alaska. In *Alaska native history and culture.* Senri Ethnological Studies. Osaka, Japan: National Museum of Ethnology.

————. 1982. A conservation ethic and environment: The Koyukon of Alaska. In *Resource managers: North American and Australian hunter-gatherers,* ed. Nancy N. Williams and Eugene S. Hunn. Washington, D.C.: American Association for the Advancement of Science.

Nelson, Richard K.; Mautner, K.; and Bane, R. 1978. *Tracks in the wildland: A portrayal of Koyukon and Nunamiut subsistence.* Occasional Paper no. 9. Fairbanks: Cooperative Park Studies Unit, University of Alaska.

Osgood, Cornelius. 1937. *Ethnography of the Tanaina.* Yale University Publications in Anthropology, no. 16. New Haven: Yale University.

————. 1940. *Ingalik material culture.* Yale University Publications in Anthropology, no. 22. New Haven: Yale University.

————. 1959. *Ingalik mental culture.* Yale University Publications in Anthropology, no. 56. New Haven: Yale University.

Pruitt, William O. 1967. *Animals of the north.* New York: Harper and Row.

————. 1978. *Boreal ecology.* London: Edward Arnold.

Redfield, Robert. 1957. *The primitive world and its transformations.* Ithaca: Cornell University Press.

Rogers, Edward S. 1963. *The hunting group–hunting territory complex among the Mistassini Indians.* Bulletin 195. Ottawa: National Museum of Canada.

Rooth, Anna B. 1976. *The importance of storytelling.* Stockholm: Almquist and Wiksell.

Sapir, Edward. 1949. *Culture, language, and personality: Selected essays,* ed. David Mandelbaum. Berkeley: University of California Press.

Speck, Frank G. 1935. *Naskapi.* Norman: University of Oklahoma Press.

Stewart, Omar C. 1971. Fire as the first great force employed by man. In *Man's role in changing the face of the earth,* ed. W. L. Thomas. Chicago: University of Chicago Press.

Stuck, Hudson. 1915. *Ten thousand miles with a dog sled.* New York: Charles Scribner's Sons.

Sullivan, Robert J. 1942a. Temporal concepts of the Ten'a. *Primitive Man* 15:57–65.

——. 1942b. *The Ten'a food quest.* Washington, D.C.: Catholic University of America Press.

Tanner, Adrian. 1973. The significance of hunting territories today. In *Cultural ecology: Readings on Canadian Indians and Eskimos,* ed. Bruce Cox. Toronto: McClelland and Stewart.

——. 1979. *Bringing home animals: Religious ideology and mode of production of the Mistassini Cree hunters.* Social and Economic Studies, no. 23. St. John's, Newfoundland: Institute of Social and Economic Research, Memorial University of Newfoundland.

Tedlock, Dennis, and Tedlock, Barbara, eds. 1975. *Teachings from the American earth.* New York: Liveright.

United States Department of Commerce, Weather Bureau. 1959. *Climates of the states: Alaska.* Washington, D.C.: U.S. Government Printing Office.

——. 1963. *Climatic summary of Alaska: Supplement for 1922 through 1952.* Washington, D.C.: U.S. Government Printing Office.

VanStone, James W. 1974. *Athapaskan adaptations: Hunters and fishermen of the subarctic forests.* Chicago: Aldine.

Viereck, Leslie A. 1973. Wildfire in the taiga of Alaska. *Journal of Quaternary Research,* vol. 3, no. 3.

Viereck, Leslie A., and Little, Elbert L. 1972. *Alaska trees and shrubs.* Agriculture Handbook no. 410. Washington, D.C.: U.S. Department of Agriculture, Forest Service.

Whorf, Benjamin. 1956. *Language, thought, and reality: Selected writings,* ed. John B. Carroll. Cambridge: Massachusetts Institute of Technology.

Yukon-Koyukuk School District. 1979. *Moses Henzie: A biography.* Vancouver: Hancock House.

——. 1980a. *Henry Beatus, Sr.: A biography.* Vancouver: Hancock House.

——. 1980b. *Joe Beetus: A biography.* Vancouver: Hancock House.

Index

283